THE
DOCTOR
WHO
WOULD
BE
KING

A THEORY IN FORMS BOOK
Series editors Nancy Rose Hunt and Achille Mbembe

THE DOCTOR WHO WOULD BE KING

Guillaume Lachenal

Translated by Cheryl Smeall

DUKE UNIVERSITY PRESS
Durham and London
2022

Library of Congress Cataloging-in-Publication Data
Names: Lachenal, Guillaume, [date] author. | Smeall, Cheryl Lynn,
[date] translator.
Title: The doctor who would be king / Guillaume Lachenal; translated
by Cheryl Smeall.
Other titles: Médecin qui voulut être roi. English | Theory in forms.
Description: Durham : Duke University Press, 2022. | Series: Theory in
forms | Includes bibliographical references and index.
Identifiers: LCCN 2021032234 (print)
LCCN 2021032235 (ebook)
ISBN 9781478015246 (hardcover)
ISBN 9781478017868 (paperback)
ISBN 9781478022480 (ebook)
Subjects: LCSH: David, Jean Joseph. | Medicine—France—Colonies—
History—20th century. | Medicine—Cameroon—History—
20th century. | Medical ethics—France—Colonies—History—
20th century. | Medical ethics—Cameroon—History—20th century.
| Physicians—France—Biography. | Physicians—Cameroon—
Biography. | Colonial administrators—France—Biography. | Colonial
administrators—Cameroon—Biography. | Cameroon—History—To
1960. | France—Colonies—Administration—History—20th century. |
BISAC: HISTORY / Africa / Central | POLITICAL SCIENCE /
Colonialism & Post-Colonialism
Classification: LCC R506.C65 L3313 2022 (print) | LCC R506.C65 (ebook)
| DDC 610.96711—dc23/eng/20211001
LC record available at https://lccn.loc.gov/2021032234
LC ebook record available at https://lccn.loc.gov/2021032235

Duke University Press gratefully acknowledges the laboratory
SPHERE, UMR CNRS 7219, Université de Paris, which provided funds
toward the publication of this book.

Utopia, the show which always closed on opening night.

—JONATHAN LETHEM, *The Fortress of Solitude*, 2003

During the Second World War, one doctor was responsible for governing an entire region of Cameroon. He was trying to bring about a utopia: a place where medicine would guide all politics and where politics would be the medicine of society. He was called the Emperor of Haut-Nyong.

In the 1930s, one doctor was responsible for governing the island of Wallis in the Pacific. He was called King David.

Dr. Jean Joseph David was an officer in the French Colonial Army.

THIS BOOK IS ABOUT THE TRACES HE LEFT BEHIND.

CONTENTS

On October 25, 1939, after three weeks of travel, Dr. David disembarked in Douala, in the mandated territory of Cameroon. He was about to begin an assignment of a few years' duration with the Health Service. There were several hundred colonial doctors across the empire just like him, practicing in bush clinics and major hospitals in capital cities. They were members of the French Colonial Army, but the bulk of their activities were centered on the health of local populations. They led the battle against the tropical diseases that were hindering the development of the colonies.

Major-Doctor David's mission was a very special one. Assisted by five other doctors, he was preparing to take command of an entire region. The doctor would be granted the highest power, greater than that of any administrative or military authority. Not only would he be responsible for maternity wards and vaccinations, but he would also take charge of all governmental activities, which from then on would be entirely subject to the humanistic and scientific principles of medicine. His role would extend beyond the realm of public health: David would undertake a real-life experiment in an attempt to revitalize a region depopulated by epidemics. From family nutrition to school programs, from gymnastics to improving sheep breeds, the doctors were required, in their own words, to "teach" the locals "how to live" and reorganize their world according to rational terms; in short, to reinvent a new society based on healthy foundations. In early November 1939, Dr. David took up his post in Abong-Mbang, the administrative center of the Haut-Nyong Medical Region, an isolated area in the heart of the eastern forests of the colony, situated several days' travel from the capital at Yaoundé.

This book takes this utopian project, sometimes referred to as the Haut-Nyong experiment, as its starting point. It is a minor story, almost an anecdote, but in a way, it summarizes the entire history of European colonialism, or at least its most fundamental principle. This principle was laid out by Joseph

Conrad in his 1899 novel, *The Heart of Darkness*, in a few short lines that remain well known:

> The conquest of the earth, which mostly means the taking it away from those who have a different complexion or slightly flatter noses than ourselves, is not a pretty thing when you look into it too much. What redeems it is the idea only. An idea at the back of it; not a sentimental pretence but an idea; and an unselfish belief in the idea—something you can set up, and bow down before, and offer a sacrifice to.[1]

This idea, powerful and yet contradictory in its very terms, was the one behind the emancipatory mission of the colonial enterprise. Liberating the native from misery, ignorance, and sickness; liberating the native by fair means or foul: colonial policies were based on a messianic, authoritarian, utopian fantasy that the story of Dr. David illustrates in its purest form. This book is a study of the sometimes-disastrous material effects of this political dream, of the affective misunderstandings it gave rise to, and of the bizarre mix of megalomania and desire for failure that fueled it.

At the same time, the Haut-Nyong experiment was also the realization of a dream of the European medical profession, that of making the imperatives of public health the driving force behind a complete reform of the laws, government, and economy, giving doctors the role of policy guides. This oft-repeated and always thwarted dream is woven through the medical literature from the beginning of the nineteenth century, when the doctor and deputy Pierre Thouvenel stated, "it is important for the happiness of all that man be placed under the sacred power of the physician [. . .] that he be brought up, nourished, clothed after his counsel and that the systems according to which he should be governed, educated, punished, etc., be designed by him,"[2] until 1935, when the eugenicist and Nobel laureate Alexis Carrel envisioned a Supreme Court of doctors overseeing the higher good of the "race." The story of Dr. David illustrates how entrepreneurs in hygiene and modern public health saw the colonial world as an opportunity, an exceptional space where it was possible to break free from the constraints and intrigues of normal political life. Lands of epidemics and death, the colonies also became perfect places, so-called laboratories where modern medicine could demonstrate its capacity to transform society and cultivate life. With France at war, the colonial doctors of Haut-Nyong could envision this dream coming true. They were enthusiastic and resourceful. They wanted to cure society.

Asphalt only made its first appearance in Abong-Mbang in 2012, after years of roadwork financed by Kuwait. The city is only a few hours away from Yaoundé, but time seems to have stood still there. The course of the Nyong River, once navigable, is overgrown with grasses and water hyacinths. The new road crosses it and heads toward the north and the east of the country, and then on to the Central African Republic and Chad. Enormous trucks, tractor trailers and logging trucks, circulate on it day and night, sometimes stopping for gas. At night, you can have a beer on the terrace above the service station and watch the headlights come and go in the dark. There is no electricity, most of the time.

Leaving the N10, one enters the city, passing by the large brick market warehouses that were built by the Germans at the beginning of the twentieth century, just like the small fort that is now used as a prison. The dirt roads are wide and straight, blocked by mud puddles; beautiful colonial houses with tile roofs, large lawns, and old trees bear witness to the former grandeur of the city in the time of the coffee plantations. A little farther along, a monumental building with a colonnade bears the inscription "Regional School 1942" in the elegant typography of the era. The educational complex spans hundreds of meters. Everything is green, red, and calm. Students in uniforms play under a tree. A rim from a car, hanging from a pole, is used as the bell to sound recess. Right next to the school is an old brick house, doubtless one of the oldest in the city. Sitting on the veranda was an elderly man in a wheelchair, spending his day watching the street.

It was the sub-prefect who suggested we go see this "old man" as soon as possible and hope that he would be in a good mood. Valentin Angoni, the driver who worked with me on this investigation, parked the pickup. We approached cautiously. Valentin was wearing dark sunglasses and an American football jersey with shoulder pads, which gave him a look somewhere between that of Jay-Z and a plainclothes police officer. I adopted a more discreet style: jeans, a button-up shirt, and leather shoes. In general, we made a good team. I asked the questions and Valentin took photos and smoothed things over with jokes and small bills. Speaking loudly and slowly, I explained to the elderly man that we were working on a history of Abong-Mbang and had been told that he was the great historian of the city, the elder to whom we had to speak at all costs, or something similarly vague and flattering. One of his sons, who was around our age, brought us chairs and leaned on the railing to listen. I took out my business card and my digital recorder.

GUILLAUME LACHENAL: You say you're ninety-one years old?

JEAN-MARIE MEVAA EVINA: Yes. Or I will be, next June 23.

GUILLAUME: And your name?

JEAN-MARIE: Evina, Mevaa with two *a*'s, Jean-Marie.

GUILLAUME: Okay. And so, you were born here in Abong-Mbang?

JEAN-MARIE: In Abong-Mbang, on June 23, 1925.

GUILLAUME: And then you went to school here?

He pointed to the school just next to us. "I did my fourth grade there. In 1941." He was in the first graduating class. A motorbike passed by.
I continued, being careful not to say his name, not to say "Dr. David."

GUILLAUME: So, what I'm particularly interested in is the history of the doctors here . . .

JEAN-MARIE: The what?

GUILLAUME: The doctors.

JEAN-MARIE: Yes. I know all about that.

GUILLAUME: Ah! Okay. Which doctors did you know?

JEAN-MARIE: There were several of them here. When the war broke out, I was in Obala [in the center of Cameroon], but my father made me come back here. It was a military government: everything was run by the military. The district commander, or the prefect: in the military; the paymaster: in the military; even health workers were in the military; everything, everything was run by the military. They sent us a colonel-doctor named Jean David. An Israeli. He's the one who brought light to Abong-Mbang. Colonel Jean David. I can tell you about him.

Evina then told us how David, "a guy who worked hard," ordered that the cornerstones of the different hospitals in the Abong-Mbang region be laid at the same time, on the same day, in Doumé, Messamena, and Lomié, which were all built according to the same blueprint. "He's the one who brought us light": I repeated this sentence at the end of our interview and everyone smiled indulgently when I asked whether this meant that he brought electricity to the city. The expression is a metaphor, apparently common in Cameroon, for "evolution," "modernity," or "development."

"David is a man who did a little bit of everything. He shook things up." Evina spoke quickly, with a somewhat hoarse but joyful voice. He seemed somewhat amused to be telling us all of this. With his wife, there were four of us listening to him on the veranda.

Mr. David! He wanted everything to be moving. Sports: that's what he wanted, he said. He had a sports [field] built there [. . .]; it was the first stadium in Cameroon, the first, it beat the Yaoundé Hippodrome. [. . .] He created a team, Étoile d'Abong-Mbang [The Star of Abong-Mbang], they were hot. They were hot! They were a threat to all teams, except maybe the team from Douala, and Yaoundé.

I had spent several years trying to find traces of Dr. David. His family in France was polite but not very talkative, and apart from two official reports, I found almost no archival material about his time in Cameroon. Old Evina was like a gift from above.

GUILLAUME: I'm pleased to hear that, because I had seen "Dr. David, Dr. David, Dr. David" in the archives in France, but I've never met anyone who's seen him.

JEAN-MARIE: Jean David, a strong guy! Strength: he had that, and everything. Blunt! [*Laughs*] You wouldn't mess around with him or he'd punch you in the face. [*Imitating his voice*] "Let's go! Put him in the box!" He'd throw you in the slammer!

GUILLAUME: He could put people in prison?

JEAN-MARIE: [*Laughs*] And how! He's the one who made Abong-Mbang the way it is. Without him, we wouldn't grow coffee, cocoa, nothing.

Listening to it, I realized that this story would be complicated to tell, that there would not be just one way to write about this burly "Israeli" doctor, hospital builder, and soccer coach, without whom "Abong-Mbang would not be Abong-Mbang," but who was born in Normandy into a Catholic family, who complained about the locals throughout his reports, who beat them up and threw them in prison. I also realized that it was going to be a pleasure. Although the sub-prefect had described him to us as a tough old man, Evina spent the interview laughing, especially when he imitated David getting angry, and so did we. A laugh can say a thousand things. Did Evina also laugh in 1942, at the age of seventeen, when he watched the young doctor get angry? Was he laughing because there was something comical about it? Was it a laugh of fear or admiration? Distressed laughter? Mocking? Dumbfounded?

The story is not really funny, but one must be faithful to that laugh in telling it. First, one must give an account of the unprovable, ambivalent, bizarre, even indescribable, part of this story as it was experienced. Then, one must give an account of David's presence in the present: the burst of laughter is not really, or not only, a punctuation, a modulation of the narrative, a tone of memory; it is also, simply, something from the past that returns and "replays," as geologists say, an emotional, embodied, shared, and material presence from the past. For these reasons, I wanted to play with this story of medical utopia, to try to tell it several times, in different ways, by untangling the threads that lead to it and connect us to it; to tell it as it came to me, first in Cameroon and then in the middle of the Pacific, with its jumps in time and space, its disorder, its repetitions, its surprises. The challenge is not to reconstruct a slice of the colonial past, or even less so, to deliver a calm truth. Rather, it is to make it a playful visit, starting from the rust and mud of Abong-Mbang, with an old man who looked at his fourth-grade school and laughed while imitating the colonel. More than a narrative contained within the confined time of history, what I propose is a stroll through a past that takes place only in the present, in bricks, ruins, jokes, gestures, documents that are crumbling away. This book is a journey into the traces of Dr. David, but also a work on traces themselves. It is the affective geography of a colonial moment, the archaeology of a utopia, the ethnography of what remains and what returns in the present of an investigation.

Wang Sonné

The rediscovery of the episode of the Haut-Nyong Medical Region was made by a Cameroonian historian, Wang Sonné. He wrote an article on the subject, which he presented in 1996 in Italy at a conference on ethnopharmacology.[3] Wang Sonné was, as the expression goes, the kind of historian they don't make anymore, trained at a time when budget cuts had not yet decimated African universities, and his work on the history of health in Cameroon remains an important reference. He specialized in the study of the history of sleeping sickness, a parasitic disease also known as trypanosomiasis, which at the beginning of the twentieth century was responsible for an epidemic that ravaged all of Central Africa and was therefore the main health priority of the colonial powers.

I met him in 2002. I was a student, coming to Yaoundé for the first time, and I wanted advice for my MPhil on the history of medical research in Cameroon. I was late for our appointment and he gave me a cold welcome, ending the interview quite quickly after giving me a list of archives to consult and people to interview. He had an office at the Organization for the Coordination of the Fight against Endemic Diseases in Central Africa (OCEAC), a health organization inherited from French colonial medicine, located in a somewhat empty 1970s building where some army doctors and French foreign aid workers were still working. The Cameroonian historian was part of a team of biologists specializing in sleeping sickness, most of them expatriates. As a "local executive," he probably earned five or ten times less than his French colleagues, but at least he had a computer, electricity, and paper, all of which were almost impossible to get at the university; French cooperation had made this mixture of humiliation and benevolence its operating principle. Wang Sonné did not hesitate to speak out against it. I saw him do so during a conference in Paris. His comments were received with shoulder shrugs.

Wang Sonné died of a stroke a few days after our conversation, in May 2002. He was conducting field research in Bipindi, in southern Cameroon, where he was tracing the history of one of the last outbreaks of sleeping sickness in the country. He left behind a widow and three children.

Ten years later, I visited them in their house in Biyem-Assi, a neighborhood in the south of Yaoundé, in the company of Jean Lucien Ewangue, a historian close to the family. Once the introductions were taken care of, I jokingly told his wife Elise and son Daniel that I remembered Wang Sonné well, that he had "told me off" the only time he had seen me. Apparently, this did not come as a surprise to anyone. The family had emptied his office at the OCEAC and had kept his archives in large plastic bags: dozens of cassettes, envelopes of photos, stacks of photocopies, files, rough drafts of articles, student theses, and, with the archives, the suitcase and pair of shoes he had with him the day he died. "I didn't touch anything, I left everything as it was," Elise told me. While going through his papers, I found the files containing the work he had done on Haut-Nyong.

In a way, it is "his" history that I have written here. This is something that historians are not supposed to do, and I am not sure he would have liked it. I started my work after he died, he was never able to read what I wrote, and we had never discussed Haut-Nyong, but I followed in his footsteps in search of Dr. David, and I will never have his help. A year ago, with the money from the project that financed my trips in Cameroon, I bought cardboard boxes, iron cases, a scanner, and a laptop computer to protect and digitize his archives, in part as a means of settling my debt to him, even if I do not really know precisely what it is.

Wang Sonné worked with a Bic pen, on small sheets of paper, half pages, sometimes cut from university administrative forms. To research his article on the Haut-Nyong Medical Region, he had taken copious notes at the National Archives in Yaoundé. He made himself reminders, noting chronologies, important figures, and definitions of syphilis and gonorrhea from medical textbooks. He had searched the *Journal officiel* (Official journal) of Cameroon to track the appointments and movements of doctors. He had also copied the speech in which the governor-general of Cameroon, Richard Brunot, announced the launch of the experiment in a 1940 issue of the *Journal officiel* that I was never able to find in France, probably because the war had interrupted shipments to Paris. He had underlined the last sentence of the speech twice: "I thought it important to clarify my thinking," said the governor after presenting the principle of experiment, "because this initiative has caused some surprise."[4]

Since the early 1980s, Wang Sonné had often returned to the region, to Abong-Mbang, Messamena, and Lomié, to interview elderly people who had lived during the time of the Medical Region. I think Dr. David fascinated him a little, that he felt that there was something more to this story of the Medical Region than a history of epidemic and public health, something else, something a little surprising, in this group of young doctors who had taken over the governing of an entire society during a war. His file includes several transcripts of interviews. The one with Joseph Dobo, a retired teacher who was eighty-one years old in 1992, is sixty pages long:

WANG SONNÉ: In Yaoundé, I was told that you are a mine of information, a living library, and that I should do everything possible to meet you. [. . .] Since I'm a historian of health, what we will focus on most during this interview is the Medical Region, the famous Medical Region, Koch, Soubde, Raymond, Colonel David, Major Pape. [. . .]

JOSEPH DOBO: '39. It was the Second World War. General mobilization. The country was empty. The epidemics were there too. Yeah! It was at that time that Colonel David, district commander, was sent to Abong-Mbang, Major Pape to Doumé, Koch to Messamena, to manage them. [. . .]

WANG SONNÉ: What about Major David or Colonel David? What was his personality like?

JOSEPH DOBO: The colonel!

WANG SONNÉ: What was his personality like?

JOSEPH DOBO: A very authoritarian gentleman! We called him "Emperor!" "Emperor of Haut-Nyong." Very authoritarian with everyone, with blacks, whites, civil servants, administrators.[5]

It was this mention of "emperor" that piqued my curiosity.

Major-Doctor David is appointed district commander of the region of Haut-Nyong to replace Mr. Seyert, deputy administrator of the colonies.

Decision No. 2852
The High Commission of the French Republic to Cameroon

Art. 1.
Major-Doctor David, district commander of the region of Haut-Nyong, is authorized to exercise on the territory of this region the disciplinary powers provided for by the decree of August 8, 1924.

Art. 2.
Captain-Doctor Pape, commander of the subdivision of Abong-Mbang
Captain-Doctor Gailhbaud, commander of the subdivision of Doumé
Lieutenant-Doctor Koch, commander of the subdivision of Messamena are entitled to exercise on the territory of their respective subdivisions the disciplinary powers provided for in the decree of August 8, 1924

Yaoundé, November 17, 1939

Signed RICHARD BRUNOT

PART I.
THE MANDATED TERRITORY OF CAMEROON

1939–1944

Die Medicin ist eine sociale Wissenschaft,
und die Politik ist weiter nichts als Medicin im Grossen.

Medicine is a social science, and politics is
nothing more than medicine on a grand scale.

RUDOLF VIRCHOW, 1848

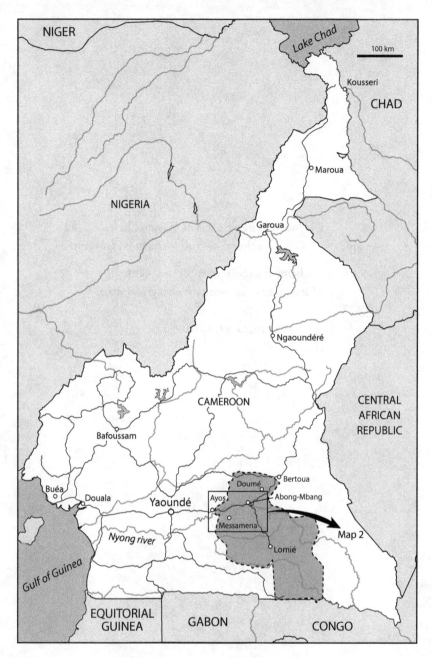

MAP 1. Cameroon and the Haut-Nyong region (dotted line). © d-maps.com. https://d-maps
.com/carte.php?num_car=4582.

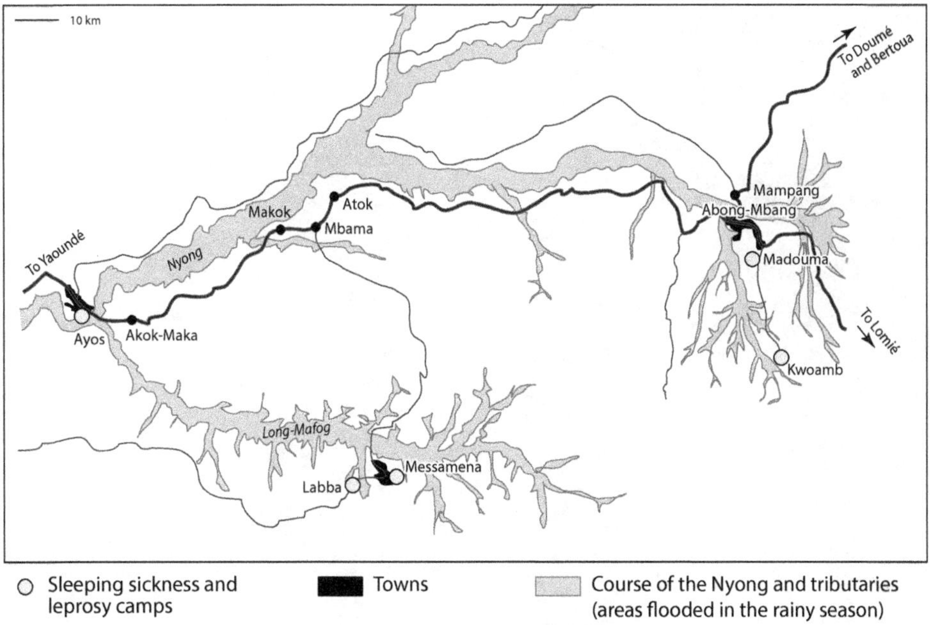
10 km
To Doumé and Bertoua
Mampang
Abong-Mbang
Madouma
To Lomié
Kwoamb
Atok
Makok
Mbama
Nyong
To Yaoundé
Ayos
Akok-Maka
Long-Mafog
Messamena
Labba
Sleeping sickness and leprosy camps
Towns
Course of the Nyong and tributaries (areas flooded in the rainy season)

MAP 2. Haut-Nyong region (detail). Source: Guillaume Lachenal.

1. A Showcase for Colonial Humanism

In atlases of the French Empire, the word *rubber* is written across the Abong-Mbang region. When Major-Doctor David arrived in November 1939, Haut-Nyong was no longer really a useful region, but it bore the marks of its brutal integration into the world economy at the very beginning of the twentieth century. The military conquest of the upper reaches of the Nyong River between 1905 and 1910 had coincided with the boom in rubber, the main export of the German colony of Kamerun. The world needed tires, and rumors were spreading about the region's swamp forests, which were said to have the richest rubber in all of Africa. As in the Congo or the Amazon rain forest, the latex rush, during which rubber was harvested directly from the forest by tapping different species of vines and wild trees, had been synonymous with forced labor and unspeakable violence. It caused a great deal of tension in an area that was simultaneously being devastated by fierce repression by the German army.[1] In this context, the Nyong was a strategic axis: navigable over a 250-kilometer stretch to Mbalmayo, where the road and then the railway led to the port of Douala, the river allowed latex to be drained from the forests in the eastern part of the German colony, which porters then transported to Abong-Mbang where the river route began. At the time, the region experienced a brief period of growth, with a sudden influx of money and goods, which was halted by the collapse of world rubber prices in 1913 and the First World War.

The Rubber Age was one of a terrible epidemic of sleeping sickness, which had spread throughout the entire region in just a few years. Doctors were quick to make the connection: latex harvesting in the forest, caravans of porters, war violence, and river transport provided an ideal environment for the epidemic. Both the Nyong River and rubber cakes caused the disease to spread. Tsetse flies, which transmit trypanosomes, the parasites responsible for the disease, abounded along the river and its tributaries, infecting paddlers of pirogues, as well as porters, soldiers, and laborers.

Crossed by a river that is both providential and cursed, the region where David arrived was marked by a history of illness and death, "ghost villages," and abandoned fields. However, Dr. David also inherited a more glorious past. Since German times, Haut-Nyong had been a showcase territory for colonial medicine, a land of epidemics and saviors, scrutinized by imperial propaganda, where a story of redemption through medicine had been written. The launching of the Haut-Nyong experiment was simply an extension of this, one which would hopefully bring the story to a successful conclusion. Even though he had never set foot there before, the colonial army doctor arrived in familiar territory.

Haut-Nyong was a prime location for colonial medicine, conducive to health utopias. Having become a French territory under the mandate of the League of Nations after the First World War, Cameroon was a distinct colony where the French were under international supervision. The mandate system, established by the Treaty of Versailles in 1919, entrusted the victors of the conflict with the former German and Ottoman colonies with a "sacred mission": to ensure the "well-being and development" of peoples considered, in the words of the treaty, to be "not yet able to stand by themselves under the strenuous conditions of the modern world."[2] The mandate system thus legitimized the idea of colonial humanism, making Europe's "civilizing mission" an obvious principle of international politics.[3]

Although the League of Nations had no real influence on the racist, violent, and extractive nature of colonial policies in the mandated African territories (which also included Togo, Ruanda-Urundi, and Tanganyika), it was a game changer in terms of health, which was subject to unprecedented constraint of publicity. The health effort, an area of intervention that was both consensual and quantifiable, became in a way the benchmark of colonial benevolence, the subject of evaluation and comparison through questionnaires, statistics, visits by experts, and conferences. The chapter on health in Cameroon's annual report to the League of Nations was thus examined each year at the Permanent Mandates Commission, where German and British delegates liked to interrogate the governor of Cameroon regarding tropical medicine. During the interwar period, the health services of mandated territories were largely privileged in comparison with those in other colonies of the various empires, as the need for visibility determined, through a game of anticipation and self-control, the priorities and nature of the imperial powers' health programs. "Representing the 'civilizing mission'" became a crucial issue,[4] not only after the fact, when the reports were being drafted, but also beforehand, as medical action had to be financed, conceived, and practiced as a spectacle. The League of Nations brought international public health into an era of glossy paper and press conferences. Starting in the 1920s, Cameroon got a preview of this new reality.[5]

The German shadow, in a colony that had been considered the jewel of the Reich's African possessions, added an additional dramatic element. The game was simple: on the German side, where a virulent colonial lobby had been organized, French inaction in health matters seemed to be an irrefutable argument for demanding the return of the colony, in the name of the humanitarian principles required by the League of Nations; on the French side, the Germans' colonial experience in the medical field was both ignored and used to demand greater financial support from the French state. "Cameroon, which had become almost entirely French since the war, was for the Germans an admirable field for colonial experimentation [. . .] . It would be disastrous, for our national self-esteem and for the prestige of the 'great civilizing nation,' if the prosperity of this rich domain did not increase rapidly in our hands,"[6] wrote Albert Calmette, deputy director of the Pasteur Institute in Paris, in 1923.

The comparison with Germany served as a point of reference for French physicians. Upon arriving in the territory escorted by Allied troops, they discovered the devastation caused by the sleeping sickness epidemic, and the vestiges of the German system set up to control it. The verdict was both admiring and critical: "Our predecessors in Cameroon made enough mistakes from the point of view of colonization that we can do them justice with regard to their medical organization in this colony,"[7] acknowledged Gustave Martin, a Pasteurian doctor whose book on public health in Cameroon, published in 1923, included over one hundred pages of translations of German documents.[8] Relying on the infrastructure, archives, and Cameroonian nurses left behind by the Germans, the French launched their own program to combat sleeping sickness focused on the main area of the epidemic identified by the Germans: the administrative subdivisions of Akonolinga, Abong-Mbang, and Doumé, which formed the "Haut-Nyong Sleeping Sickness Prophylaxis Sector" from 1921 onward.[9] Inherited from German plans, which had envisaged the division of Kamerun into numbered "action clusters" corresponding to the main centers of the epidemic,

Haut-Nyong began its existence as an epidemiological and health territory, even before becoming an administrative entity.[10]

I IMAGINE THAT DAVID knew the rest of the story by heart. Having graduated in 1929 from the Pharo School in Marseille, the school where future colonial doctors undertook their specialization internships and learned the bush stories of their elders, he was part of a generation that pursued their studies at the time when, on the banks of the Nyong River, the "Jamot mission" was at its height. Dr. Jamot's campaigns to combat sleeping sickness were attracting journalists, politicians, writers, and photographers, and his doctors had access to resources unparalleled throughout the empire. David, who graduated near the bottom of his class, had surely not ranked high enough to join them.[11]

Dr. Eugène Jamot, a doctor with the Colonial Army, had been assigned to the area in 1922. His stay there would have a profound impact on the region. The main difficulty I faced during my time in Haut-Nyong was to explain that I was *not* working on Jamot, while politely listening to people recite his biography and tell me where to find traces of his time there. Given that most of the health facilities built in Haut-Nyong in the first half of the twentieth century were named after him, "Jamot" has become the generic name for colonial medicine.

Building on Belgian and German experiments in the domain, Jamot had developed a systematic approach to fighting sleeping sickness, based on the screening of trypanosome carriers in their villages by mobile teams, followed by the treatment of those infected with the disease with injections of Atoxyl, an arsenic derivative developed in Germany. The epidemic was catastrophic, exacerbated by the violence and destruction of the war. Along the Nyong River, villages had up to an 80 percent infection rate; more than fourteen thousand people in total faced death without treatment.[12] The epidemic originating on the Nyong decreased in severity the farther away from the river one got but seemed to be spreading, following the newly built roads, throughout central and southern parts of the country, including the area around the capital, Yaoundé.[13]

The Jamot mission, launched in 1926, is a well-known chapter in the history of modern humanitarianism.[14] Its creation owes much to Jamot's entrepreneurial talent: he knew how to use the media to forge an alliance between the medical profession, the Pasteur Institute, the French state, the Parisian colonial lobby, and the pharmaceutical company Rhône-Poulenc. While a press campaign denouncing the current health crisis in Cameroon was raging across the Rhine, Jamot increased his public presence in Paris. He played a clever and risky game, which manipulated the German specter to construct the crisis he was offering to resolve. His catastrophic accounts of the sleeping sickness epidemic were widely reported, even in the newspaper *L'Illustration* (Illustration), and within a few weeks convinced the Ministry of the Colonies to finance a "permanent mission of sleeping sickness prophylaxis in Cameroon" with the aim of fighting the epidemic to the point of "extinction."[15] The announcement was timely: a few weeks later, the Permanent Mandates Commission examined the case of French Cameroon.[16] Summoned to explain the decrease in the number of doctors and to respond to the accusations of German publications,[17] the governor of Cameroon was able to announce the organization of the Permanent Sleeping Sickness Mission in the French mandate and receive congratulations from the commission.[18]

The Jamot mission had marked a change of scale: for the first time in history, Paris was directly financing colonial health action. A therapeutic and administrative machine, which included hundreds of Cameroonian nurses and laborers, was set in motion throughout the country. Jamot and his teams became figures of imperial propaganda, photographed and filmed at work, and the Nyong River, the subject of international politics. Reports to the League of Nations now included an illustrated supplement, with graphs and images of Jamot. The mission's figures provided strong arguments to French diplomats, who were ritually heckled by German members of the Permanent Mandates Commission on the subject of sleeping sickness. Therapeutic injections numbered in the millions, and press clippings on the subject of the mission piled up on desks at the Ministry of the Colonies. In 1931, at the Colonial Exhibition in Vincennes, visitors were able to see the doctor's good-natured face in a film produced by Spécia, the branch of Rhône-Poulenc that sold the leading medications used for trypanosomiasis. Just before the word "Fin" (End), with violin strings sounding in the background, a voice comments on images of the Nyong Valley: "It can be estimated that 100,000 Cameroonians escaped certain death thanks to the intervention of his teams. Three years after the beginning of the prophylactic operations, Jamot was able to announce [. . .] the success of the mission he had led. Life had returned, the rivers had resumed their quiet courses, and Cameroon, reawakened, could once again safely set off toward its new destiny."[19]

I do not know whether David saw the movie.

2. An Archipelago of Camps

It must be repeated once more, the country is made up of sick people:
trypanosomiasis, leprosy, syphilis, gonorrhea. Out of 80,000 inhabitants,
a general census would indicate the presence of 6,000 leprosy patients.
JEAN JOSEPH DAVID, Haut-Nyong, 1939

I also do not know whether David arrived from Yaoundé by the river or by the
road, but most likely by the new road, built by the French, which serves the
regional capital Abong-Mbang, running parallel along the left bank to the old
German trail that ran along the other side of the Nyong. However, the geography of the area remains strangely insular. The Nyong and its main tributaries remain a major transportation route; they make up a sprawling network
of marshy plains, entirely flooded in the wet season, which complicates land
travel, requiring the construction of dikes and permanent brush cutting to
make navigation possible. But no matter how David arrived, he would have
passed through Ayos along the way.

During the interwar period, the Ayos camp was the African capital of colonial medicine, a photogenic locale that served as a backdrop for propaganda
related to the Jamot mission. Halfway along the waterway between Mbalmayo
and Abong-Mbang, on a cleared hill overlooking the river, the site offered

magnificent views and a pleasant breeze for settlers on vacation. In a way, it was the monumental gateway to Haut-Nyong.

Ayos was conceived as a camp, in the strongest sense of the word: a place of segregation, incarceration, experimentation, and care; a "biopolitical" device par excellence, the function of which was to affect, by isolating a group of sick people, the life and death of a population considered to be a biological entity. The site was chosen in 1912 by the colony's chief physician, Dr. Philalethes Kuhn (1870–1937), to segregate trypanosomiasis patients, following the approach recommended by the bacteriologist Robert Koch, who had designed the first *Konzentrationlager* for trypanosomiasis patients during his research mission in Uganda.[1] The term is borrowed from the internment camps used during the German colonial wars, including in Haut-Nyong during the repression of the Makaa in 1910.[2] Architecturally, it was a mix of prison and hospital. The buildings, restored by the French in 1919, were built following a grid plan, the entire camp was fenced in and guarded, and the doctors' houses were the most dominant constructions. The buildings, which multiplied during the height of the Jamot mission, formed a complete complex with brickworks, laboratory, dispensary, pavilion for the mentally ill, post office, orchards, water pump, electricity generator, tennis court, swimming pool, regulation-size soccer stadium, and a cemetery for the "Europeans" and a mass grave for the others. The camp was the nerve center for the fight against sleeping sickness throughout the territory. It was there that new treatments were tested; standard doses were developed; the writing of files, reports, and circulars was centralized; and new doctors arriving in the area came to get experience. In 1932, Ayos became a "medical training center" that would train generations of Cameroonian and African nurses from all over the empire; a "medical city," as it was reported in the French press, where laborers, guards, nurses, and their families settled.

Starting in the German period, the *Schlafkrankheitlager* in Ayos was connected to a network of camps in the region that brought together thousands of patients believed to be incurable. The segregation of those afflicted with sleeping sickness in Ayos quickly ceased to have a crucial epidemiological function, however, as the Jamot mission's itinerant screening and treatment work had led to a dramatic collapse of the epidemic from 1927 onward. The epidemic really persisted only along the upper part of the Nyong, upstream from Ayos. The territory's largest *hypnoseries*, as the French called them, were those in Messamena, Doumé, and especially Madouma, the "native" neighborhood of Abong-Mbang, separated from the colonial city by an arm of the Nyong. In 1936, the government of Cameroon built several brick buildings there, intended to accommodate five hundred people afflicted with the disease.

The segregation infrastructure for people infected with sleeping sickness doubled as a network of leprosy camps, known as leprosaria. Haut-Nyong saw some of the highest prevalence rates for leprosy in Africa, with several thousand people affected. The disease was not a priority for the administration because the available treatments were not effective, because little was understood about how it was transmitted, and because it was "delegated," by tacit agreement, to the missionaries. Leprosaria—"agricultural colonies for leprosy patients," in other words, camps of huts that occasionally had a nurse or nun living on site—remained in the 1930s neglected places that attracted no visitors or photographers. The largest leprosy camps in Cameroon were those in Haut-Nyong: in 1938, the one in Madouma housed 683 leprosy patients, the one in Messamena, 512, and the one in Doumé, 156.[3] Reports also counted "escapees" (over three hundred per year) and deaths (about a hundred), but these figures were not often discussed in Parisian newspapers.

In 1939, David found himself at the head of an archipelago region where the experience of medicine was linked to encampment. He inherited a territory identified with the outbreak of an epidemic, where "prophylactic operation," as it was called, also depended on the confinement of an entire portion of the population. In addition to the number of lives saved, there was another number that was calculated but less talked about, that of incurable interned patients. During the worst years of the epidemic, Jamot's teams brought all the inhabitants of the villages near Ayos, infected or not, to the *hypnoserie* for a few weeks of injections and free food. In the Abong-Mbang subdivision, Ledentu, one of Jamot's assistants, administered Atoxyl to everyone. "He felt that the outbreak was so virulent that all the inhabitants were carriers of germs,"[4] wrote his successor in 1936. A sick country: a country where everyone was sick.

THE NYONG CAMPS PRODUCED an ambiguous imagery, where utopia, the perfect world of the heroes of colonial humanism, seemed to merge with dystopia, the horror of death on a massive scale. This ambiguity will hang over the rest of the story.

In 1931, an emaciated young child, held upright by a nurse from Ayos, was on the cover of the chapter on health in the annual report to the League of Nations.[5] I do not know whether the image was meant to be horrifying or moving or both, or if the emotions were in any case filtered by the double distance of racial difference and medical objectivity, but it seems to signify both one thing—health, Cameroon free of disease—and its opposite. I also do not know what the ballet of the gray skeleton men wandering in a line between brick buildings evoked at the time. I do not know what people found desirable or beautiful in these images, but they were used to make large-format prints, with Art Deco typography, to decorate the Cameroon pavilion at the Colonial Exhibition.

They inspired commentators:

Ayos! Ayos! A place of misery and death, but also of refuge and the promise of life. Have I seen any of these poor, poor human beings whose skimpy, ash-gray skin stretches over their extremely visible skeleton and whose two eyes, sometimes lit with a diabolical fire, sometimes extinguished, make them so pathetic? Ayos! [. . .] Ah! I won't forget it anytime soon, this "walk of the dead bodies" that I attended on my first afternoon. Patients, already dead, stretched out, warming up in the sun. Time to go home. Gently, they are made to get up. Following jerky efforts, there they were, almost all of them, standing. Hands out in front of them, like blind people, feeling around in the void, less to feel it and guide themselves than to lean on it and support themselves, painfully, skeletons that still have their skin, their eyes, move forward . . . , move forward . . . They reach you, hold out a hand to you that you shake, with such emotion! Weakly, they say "bezour" and continue on . . . Ayos! Place of misery, locality of death, but also *center for the regeneration of lives*.[6]

One is tempted to smile at the fanfare, the nasal voices of the 1930s, Jamot, "savior of the Black race." There are reasons to be skeptical and to believe that Haut-Nyong was not, on the eve of the war, as devastated as the propaganda indicated. The numbers of the epidemic may have been exaggerated, and decades of research suggest that infection by trypanosome may not have been as deadly as colonial heroes said. In other words, it may be that the priority given by the administration to sleeping sickness was not self-evident in terms of pure public health rationality, and that the colonial powers had above all chosen a target that was conducive to stories of redemption and healing and could be managed with the few antimicrobial drugs available at the time. But, in the end, I do not really know. With a team of researchers, I interviewed an elderly woman in Ayos in 2012 who had memories of the time of the epidemic. I could not understand what she said in Yebekolo to my Cameroonian colleague, but one French word kept coming up over and over again: "carnage."

3. Madame Ateba

Madame Ateba is the guardian of the East. This is what she often tells visitors, half jokingly, when she welcomes them in her living room under the portrait of the "former president," as they say in Cameroon to avoid speaking his name (Ahmadou Ahidjo). Hers is the first cement house on the side of the road in the village of Akok-Maka once you have crossed the Nyong, coming from Ayos. In a way, it is the first house in the eastern region when you arrive from Yaoundé. It's a veritable guard post: one can keep an eye out for cars and trucks from the veranda, and the grounds go down to the banks of the river. Madame Ateba is a powerful woman, to use a word that has a thousand meanings in Cameroon. She is the widow of a somewhat mythical nurse from Ayos hospital, André Ateba Mvondo. The intensive care unit of that hospital, housed in a pavilion inherited from the sleeping sickness camp, was named the Ateba Ward in his honor. He was later named mayor of Abong-Mbang in 1967. Until his retirement in 1985, in addition to being mayor, he held the position of general supervisor of the Abong-Mbang hospital; medicine and politics inextricably linked, as the local tradition requires. The Atebas were part of the first generation of elites in the region and were integrated into the single-party system in the years following independence, he as mayor, she as president of the departmental section of the Women's Organization of the single party (first the Union Nationale Camerounaise [UNC], then the Rassemblement Démocratique du

Peuple Camerounais [RDPC]), a function which is more strategic than it may appear.[1] They were both loyal to the first president, enough to give them an ambiguous air in the present regime (the current president has been in power since 1982), in which nostalgia for Ahidjo may seem like a veiled political criticism. I had met Madame Ateba while researching the history of Ayos. We went to visit her husband, who was bedridden in their house in Abong-Mbang.

Both of them had experienced the era of the *trypano*, she as a child (she was born in 1939), he as a nurse. Their villages, Akok-Maka and Makok, were right in the middle of the epidemic zone, among the most affected and most visited by the mobile teams. She remembered it with a laugh. She enjoyed imitating the "general visit," when the nurses would arrive in the village and palpate everyone's necks to detect swollen lymph nodes. If the nurse found one, he would shout, "Minenga bele mban!" ("The woman has a nodule in her neck!") in Ewondo, the working language of the nurses and that of the clerks and catechists of Yaoundé. Another would reply, "Owé! Mawok! Azak!" ("Yes! Okay! Tell her to come!"). In this way, the visit was like a call-and-response song, like those sung while working in the fields, a strange choreography—the "therapeutic machine" so often filmed and photographed that it had a soundtrack. Everyone doubled over with laughter when Madame Ateba imitated what followed: the nurse who had just called the suspected sick woman over would prick her lymph node, collect some fluid (the "juice"), and examine the fluid under the microscope for trypanosomes. "He tells you to stop moving, he asks you to sit behind that chair [the one occupied by the person using the microscope] where we can see your blood or this juice. You're already sick." The nurse would examine the slide while keeping an eye on the patient ("he watched you with the eyes in the back of his head") so that she would not run away. Madame Ateba imitated the nurse, who would keep turning around. "You start shaking . . . Trypanosomiasis! No, it's not something you should think about, because it hurts." With lime, they would paint the plus sign on her forehead to indicate that she had tested positive for trypanosomiasis. "[Afterward] they would take you to another room where they would take water from your spine [she imitated a lumbar puncture, leaning forward, shaking her arms], they would draw the liquid from here. You were beside yourself, just starting to fall asleep, and shaking like this. Oh no, that disease traumatized people. It was mostly in this area, all the way to our place there. I saw it with my own eyes. They transported them once, to cram them in here in Ayos." They transported them *once*; they did not come back.

"It's like a disease you have cast upon you," Madame Ateba often says when she explains sleeping sickness: like a spell being cast. The metaphor is not a simple analogy, but an allusion to the fact that medicine, especially campaigns against sleeping sickness, was experienced and practiced (i.e., not only *interpreted*) as a form of witchcraft; Wang Sonné had extraordinary accounts on this theme in his thesis.[2] The "positives," sent to the camp and to their deaths, were sent because someone had wanted it to happen, out of revenge, jealousy, or greed, and the nurses who made the diagnosis were the lead suspects, as were the chiefs with whom they ate and drank in the evening. As a result, some nurses were feared throughout South Cameroon because they sent or cast the disease, choosing their targets and sowing death through their injections and punctures. The name Abessolo still inspires fear from Obala to Doumé today. Nurses always came from elsewhere, by definition, since the colonial health service deliberately appointed nurses to posts far away from the places they came from, far from their loved ones, so that they would have, as Madame Ateba says, "the courage to be mean." The people of Madouma, where the large Abong-Mbang sleeping sickness camp was set up in the 1930s, said even more simply that it was Jamot, the so-called savior, who had brought the disease to Haut-Nyong. It was he who was responsible for the mass mortality he had come to fight (and from which he drew professional success and an obvious portliness); he who emptied the villages, according to a logic that only he understood, by drawing white crosses on the sick with lime (as can be seen in the propaganda films); he who had created an immense place of death on their lands. An elderly man from Madouma told Wang Sonné that they killed his father by telling him, "You are also sick." The chief had let it happen: "He was also afraid that the nurses would call him, test him like a sick person and inject him with large doses. And they would kill him!"[3] I stress this point, well known in other African contexts.[4] For the people of eastern Cameroon, colonial medicine was a fundamentally ambivalent experience and practice, in which care was aggression, in which diagnosis was performative, in which words could both comfort and kill.[5] Medicine was a "dark" art. The fight against disease was a zero-sum game in which the heroes' dedication was not the solution to but the cause of the epidemic, causing the decline of some to feed the development of others, in a way that is not inappropriate to identify as cannibalistic.[6] The nurses had to say, "No, we're not here to give you the disease, we're here to cure you, we're here to save you."[7] In Madouma, it was said that it was the fight against the disease that brought death to the area,[8] a belief that was not at all irrational: the campaigns were dotted with accidents, and the treatments were generally ineffective at the individual level. Colonial medicine thus found itself integrated with the vernacular forms, both therapeutic and malicious, of the manipulation of invisible forces. Madame Ateba never told me this directly, of course, but her stories hinted at it, as is always the case with discussions relating to the occult. I imagine that her husband also had to deal with the mixture of admiration and suspicion that he undoubtedly aroused, with his miraculous therapies, his "voice that healed,"[9] his political power, his cocoa plantations, and his cement house, one of the first to be built in the region in the 1950s. Doctors like David were also no exception to these Cameroonian diagnoses of the sources of charisma, of the success of some and the misfortunes of others.

In this atmosphere that sometimes smelled of death and violence, Madame Ateba, who as a little girl was called Emilienne Ngono, had her own tricks, a "little business" with her friends, a cunning stratagem. When she was required to line up in front of the nurse, who would examine her neck from her jaw to her shoulders to determine whether her lymph nodes were swollen and had to be punctured, she put small, very round white stones in her mouth. When the nurse arrived, she would gulp, but without swallowing the stones, which she would squeeze to the back of her throat. Tightening her throat in this way would hold her lymph nodes in, making it impossible for the nurse to feel if they were swollen.

Madame Ateba, Valentin, and I got along immediately. Madame Ateba is funny, full of tales that are stories within stories, with the piercing eyes of a "little girl who's too curious," as she herself says, who learned a lot by spying on adults. I quite liked her house in Abong-Mbang, with its old photos hanging on the wall, its flowered courtyard, its basketball net, and its little *boukarou* (round hut). I promised her I would come back, so that we could work together in the city on the story of Dr. David. She knew his name, as did her husband, who had spent time with David during the war. She became my "key informant," as the saying goes. She knew exactly what I needed to see, starting with the "Jamot stuff," and in particular the remains of the Madouma *hypnoserie*, located two kilometers from the center of Abong-Mbang. We went there several times. "The graves were there, everywhere," villagers told us, and also on the other side of the road, where the high school was later built. The village chief of Madouma described to me the "pits" where they "dumped all the bodies, four or five a day." "People died in a brutal way, like the Seleka in Bangui, like in Libya,"[10] Madame Ateba told me once as we walked past the school in December 2013, at the time when, just at the end of the road that leads east, the Central African Republic was descending into civil war.

She was an extraordinary informant, perhaps too extraordinary, a leading figure in the city that the police let pass through the roadblocks while looking the other way. Madame Ateba was more well known than I thought, because of her political career and that of her husband, but also because her first daughter (she had eleven children), Anne Marthe Mvoto, was for a long time the anchor on the CRTV (state television) news program. To take a point of comparison, it is a little as if my guide in this investigation were Claire Chazal's mother.[11]

4. Advocating for a Regime of Exception

> Paperwork is more and more of a plague.
> PROFESSOR LOUIS PASTEUR-VALLERY RADOT, also known as PVR, 1939

When David visited Ayos at the end of 1939, at the top of the hill, next to the tennis court, he would have found a white pyramidal monument bearing this inscription:

IN

MEMORY OF

DR. JAMOT

WHO VANQUISHED

SLEEPING SICKNESS

HIS FRIENDS

HIS STUDENTS

Jamot's career had come to an eventful end: arrested in 1931 when he returned from the Colonial Exhibition, he was blamed for a therapeutic mishap caused by one of his assistants in Bafia, in the Mbam region. The Jamot mission as such had been dissolved and transformed into a "Sleeping Sickness Prophylaxis Service" with reduced powers and budgets once the epidemic seemed under control. Jamot had briefly resumed service in French West Africa, charged with setting up a system based on the Cameroonian model, before returning to his native Creuse, where he would die in April 1937.[1]

Two years later, the commemoration of Jamot was already a well-established ritual. A flood of obituaries appeared upon his death, taking up the plot of the glorious accounts written about him during his life. In Ayos, the flag at half-mast, a solemn ceremony was held just after the news arrived on June 5, 1937; the white monument was unveiled in November with the governor in attendance.[2] At that time, another monument was under construction in the court-yard of the Yaoundé hospital, which was to be inaugurated with great pomp and ceremony before the propaganda cameras in January 1939.[3]

Jamot the figure played several roles at once. One was that of the "savior of the Black race" to whom the "natives" owed their "existence," the head physician explained to the nurses of Ayos who had gathered in June 1937, because without him, "Cameroon would be a vast cemetery and the regions of Abong-Mbang [and] Akonolinga would be deserted."[4] Jamot also played the role of the "great Frenchman," a symbol of the generosity and friendship of colonial tutelage, which Cameroonian schoolchildren would remember for a long time to come through snippets of dictations and nursery rhymes. Finally, Jamot also played the role of the bushman, the man of action, whom nothing could stop, and who could be driven to despair by administrative delays. It was this Jamot who, on the eve of the war, became the hero of an entire professional body, embodying its style and physical ethos, its love of Africa and bawdy songs, its taste for soccer and rugby, its joking and outbursts, and most of all, its hatred of the "lice" of the administration. Among colonial doctors, the commemoration of Jamot carried a private message: they must remember that Jamot had been forgotten, that he embodied both victory and defeat, that they were both heroic and unlucky, and that their mission was constantly being impeded. Jamot definitively eradicated an epidemic that was once again becoming a threat along the Nyong River in the late 1930s. However, there was no contradiction inherent in this: "they" made him fail; "they," the administration, traders, plantation owners, jealous people, who conspired to have him fired and dissolve his autonomous mission. His failure was therefore the colonial doctors' success; it proved the pertinence of their cries of alarm, their methods, their mission. In 1939, it was this that David and his colleagues repeated to themselves and each other at aperitif time on the verandas of Yaoundé or Ayos.

Among doctors in Haut-Nyong, complaining about the administration (and dreaming of doing away with it) was a tradition as old as the fight against sleeping sickness. Already in 1912, the German Philalethes Kuhn hoped to "subordinate the administration of areas of high incidence to the doctor" in his plan to combat sleeping sickness.[5] In 1925, while he was in Paris negotiating the establishment of his mission, Jamot famously said the following words at a conference at the Society for Exotic Pathology:

> In my opinion, the screening, treatment, and monitoring of trypanoso-miasis patients are the three necessary but sufficient conditions for medical prevention. In the environment in which we operate, this will not be feasible as long as issues of pure administration dominate questions of health, and as long as the physician does not have, in contaminated areas, the authority that the surgeon has in the operating room.
>
> Gentlemen, it is up to those who preside over the destiny of this country to decide whether the thousands of human lives that sleeping sickness takes every year that could be saved are not worth the sacrifice of a few accepted principles and whether, ultimately, it is not appropriate to give the doctors who dedicate themselves to this work of salvation there the authority that is indispensable to them in order to carry out their task.[6]

The tensions to which Jamot alluded were public knowledge. The collective logic of the campaigns—testing and treating parasite carriers to reduce the virus reservoir and protect the healthy population—required that populations present themselves in their entirety during visits by the mobile team, which depended on the proper functioning of the entire chain of command, from the administrator to village chiefs. In practice, the equation was often impossible to solve. The population was suspicious of screening, already being familiar with the side effects of treatment, deportations to camps, sanctions for absenteeism, and abuse by nurses. Doctors were calling for action; administrators were reluctant to increase pressure on village chiefs, who were already being asked to collect taxes and recruit laborers for forced labor; and local chiefs (a function invented by colonial authorities in the Abong-Mbang region) had to juggle to keep a handle on things, retain their positions, avoid sanctions, and spare villagers who had been subjected to severe hardship for several decades. On a larger scale, doctors were aware of the role of the movement of laborers, carrier caravans, roadwork sites, and river traffic in the spread of the epidemic, and called for drastic measures to control movement or even "close" entire regions. Here again, the colonial administrations hesitated and tried to protect the economic interests of plantation owners and traders, relying when they could on internal rivalries within the Health Service, where Jamot's standardized approach met the resistance of managers and clinicians.[7] The disputes were systematic, even if they were limited to local dramas, resolved by the transfer of a doctor who was too enthusiastic or an administrator who was too particular.

Throughout the interwar period, colonial doctors therefore vacillated between patient lobbying and more energetic campaigns to demand a state of emergency. In 1931, for example, the Pasteurian Albert Calmette spoke at the Academy of Medicine in Paris to demand that "true administration of a government or a *cercle* [district]" be given to "doctor-administrators" in the colonies, starting with the areas of Cameroon and French Equatorial Africa most affected by sleeping sickness.[8] The result was an undeniable success: Cameroon had a particularly extensive legislative arsenal at the end of the 1930s. The Code de l'indigénat (Native Code), the legislative framework that applied to the Cameroonian population, included several ad hoc offenses on the list of thirty-four "special offenses" defined in 1924, including "failure to comply with the hygiene and prophylaxis measures prescribed by the administration," "simulation and aggravation of natural injuries," "use of medication not under the control of the administration," "wandering by individuals inflicted with insanity, epidemic or contagious diseases, sleeping sickness, or leprosy," and "abandonment of individuals suffering from contagious disease,"[9] all punishable, at the discretion of the administrators, by lashes of the sjambok, fines, or imprisonment. The Ayos camp had even been granted by decree the status of extraterritoriality, becoming in 1924 an "independent administrative post, reporting directly to the Commissioner of the Republic," where the head physician was "empowered to inflict corporal punishment on the natives."[10] The Jamot mission allowed a new stage to be reached in this health utopianism: its head had the rank of inspector of administrative affairs, reporting directly to the high commissioner; the mission directly managed the registration of patients and villages, the health passport and individual card systems previously delegated, in theory, to the administrative authorities; and Jamot had long hoped to obtain for the doctors in his service the "disciplinary powers" (the right to punish) reserved for the administrators of the colonies.[11]

The international attention paid to the fight against sleeping sickness did nothing to stop this escalation. French, British, Belgian, and German doctors who were specialists in the epidemic agreed on this point and placed the question of "the conferment of police powers on medical officers" on the agendas of the meetings they held under the framework of the League of Nations.[12] In 1938, as part of an increasing involvement by the administration to regulate labor recruitment, a decree was issued that strengthened control over the movements of "former sufferers of sleeping sickness" and forbade any importation of laborers into "endemoepidemic regions," the list of which was established by decree.[13] The "health policy" chapter of Cameroonian legislation was particularly thick. Its special decrees dealt, for example, with racial segregation in urban centers, the compulsory isolation of leprosy patients, and exceptional measures provided for under the regime of "epidemic and imminent danger to public health." Compared with the rest of the empire, Cameroon resembled something of a doctor's paradise.

This was, in a way, what was commemorated through Jamot. In his 1937 Society for Exotic Pathology tribute, a Pasteurian doctor recalled that Jamot understood "the importance of administrative measures to improve the well-being of the Natives" and that "he would have gladly subordinated the powers of the administration to those of the doctor."[14] The reminder was welcome, as the figures backed this up: throughout the 1930s, sleeping sickness persisted in Abong-Mbang, Doumé, and Messamena, with prevalence rates even rising in 1937. "The last traces of the disease are found in the immediate vicinity of the marshy banks of the Nyong River,"[15] reported a brief in the *Annales coloniales* (Colonial annals) on January 10, 1938. In Akok-Maka, the village opposite Ayos on the road to Abong-Mbang, the epidemic was on the rise again, as though it were a provocation.[16] In the annual report of the Health Service written in early 1939, there was impatience: in areas where the disease persisted, doctors had been ordering the displacement of entire villages and prohibitions on movements in or out of the area for years, but the directives were not being applied. Medical action had to be taken "despite the indifference shown by the region's administrative authorities."[17] The report further noted: "Unfortunately, the considerable effort made in Abong-Mbang remains the sole responsibility of the Health Service. Certainly, there is no shortage of written directives that prohibit anyone afflicted with trypanosomiasis from leaving their village, prohibit access to dangerous roads, and order the destruction of plantations located in highly contaminated areas. It is frustrating to be able to confirm without risk of exaggeration that administrative measures limited to the drafting of these texts do not take into account their application."[18]

Jamot's name was like a sigh: just leave the task of administration to the doctors.

5. A French Dream

The creation of the Medical Region at the end of 1939 was marked by a climate of anxiety. The threat of the Germans returning to their former colony became an obsessive theme, as well as an increasingly credible possibility from 1936, when the Nazi regime intensified its colonial propaganda.[1] A security apparatus was set up to monitor German nationals and Cameroonian "Germanophiles," and a counterpropaganda campaign was rolled out in the French colonial press, where statements about the "Francophilia" of Cameroonians and the greatness of the work accomplished by the French regime competed for space.

At the beginning of 1939, a rising star in the Parisian medical world, Louis Pasteur-Vallery Radot, known as "PVR," professor at the Faculty and member of the Academy of Medicine, was sent on a mission by the Ministry of the Colonies "to examine the functioning of medical assistance to natives in French Equatorial Africa and Cameroon."[2] PVR, grandson of Pasteur on his mother's side and son of René Vallery-Radot, who chaired the board of directors of the Pasteur Institute until his death in 1933, had just been appointed general delegate to the overseas network of Pasteur Institutes, an important position that aimed to make the Pasteur Institute a central player in colonial scientific and health policy.[3] During his trip, he visited Ayos and inaugurated the Jamot monument at the Yaoundé hospital on January 17, 1939. "[Jamot] was both a great idealist and a great man of action,"[4] he recalled in his speech, before handing things over to Governor-General Richard Brunot, who had governed Cameroon since November 1938. The people of Yaoundé paraded in honor of the occasion, "brandishing banners: 'We want to remain French,' 'France is our mother.'"[5]

The resonance given to the inauguration of the monument and the mobilization of a figure of Parisian medical high society for the occasion testify to Cameroon's importance in French colonial strategy, the fears generated by German claims, and medical intervention's flag-bearing role. Back in France, PVR presented his conclusions in a thick report in which he congratulated himself for the "loyalty" of the Cameroonians. On February 24, he gave a lecture, later published in the *Revue des deux mondes* (Review of the two worlds),[6] titled "Pourquoi le Cameroun doit rester français" (Why Cameroon must remain French):

> For twenty years now, the French have demonstrated initiative, energy and faith in this country. Their efforts have been entirely successful. There can be no question of giving up Cameroon, to the organization of which our administrators have brought the best of the French spirit. It would be an unjustifiable abdication. There are not two Frances, one metropolitan and intangible, the other overseas and dissolvable at will. [. . .]
>
> For all those who have seen the work accomplished by France, the abandonment of this African land, where our people have shown so much initiative and tenacity and where they have brought about the birth of a new life, would be deplorable. It would not simply be a territory that we would hand over to Germany, it would be French energies of twenty years that would be sacrificed. A wave of discouragement would wash over our empire. What is the point of so much effort if one day everything is delivered into foreign hands?[7]

On March 15, PVR celebrated the fiftieth anniversary of the Pasteur Institute in Paris. He announced the imminent establishment of a Pasteur Institute in Yaoundé "to develop the magnificent effort of the Health Service in this Mandated Territory." Established throughout the empire since the end of the nineteenth century, the overseas network of Pasteur Institutes was the jewel in the crown of French colonial medicine. The Yaoundé Institute would be "the testament of France's permanence in Cameroon."[8]

The Pasteurians had grandiose plans. Lieutenant Colonel Marcel Vaucel, head of the Health Service in Guinea, was dispatched to Cameroon in March to be the emissary of the Pasteur Institute and to negotiate the establishment of the Yaoundé branch. Vaucel was a prominent colonial physician who had once headed the Pasteur Institutes in Brazzaville (1929–32) and Hanoi (1933–38). He was the "man for the job,"[9] his Parisian colleagues congratulated him. In three months, he obtained from Governor Brunot ("a charming man, extremely well placed for us,"[10] advised Pasteur-Vallery Radot, who knew his way around society) assurances concerning the budget, organization, and plan for the institute, which would be the capstone of the pyramid of the Cameroon Health Service on the organization charts. Beautiful watercolors depicted the institute on the hospital hill, a stone's throw from the Jamot monument.[11]

However, over the course of the summer, clouds began to appear on the horizon: the situation was uncertain and exceptional military spending was expected. Cameroon had to prepare to defend itself. On September 7, 1939, four days after the declaration of war, Marcel Vaucel wrote to Pasteur-Vallery Radot: "Governor-General Brunot informed me of his decision to abandon, for the duration of the hostilities, the project of establishing a Pasteur Institute in Cameroon."[12] Vaucel considered his mission "terminated" and once again made himself available to the Ministry of the Colonies. A few days later, the governor appointed him director of the Cameroon Health Service.

The Haut-Nyong Medical Region was born of this setback. In the absence of a Pasteur Institute, Marcel Vaucel and Governor Brunot implemented a project that was less costly but also worthy of a colony where doctors were "great idealists and great men of action": to make Haut-Nyong a sheltered enclave, subject to an unprecedented regime of medical administration.

In his first report, submitted in early 1940, Marcel Vaucel presented the initiative. "The physiognomy of the Haut-Nyong Region," where the sleeping sickness epidemic was resisting all efforts to curtail it,

> legitimizes the new administrative formula devised by Governor-General Brunot perfectly: since December 1939, the command of the region has been entrusted to a major-doctor assisted, for administrative functions, by three doctors from the Colonial Army and a colonial official. Two other doctors act as treating physicians, bringing the total medical staff to six doctors for the region.
>
> Thus will end the gnawing conflict that had been going on for several years between administrators and doctors in the Haut-Nyong region: administrative officials applying a regulation that they claimed was incompatible with the life of the country a little loosely, doctors convinced of the futility of their purely technical efforts and demanding compliance with the regulations. [. . .]

Haut-Nyong, which has been criss-crossed for years by field doctors familiar with all its hidden corners, was already a *region of medicine*. Thanks to Governor-General Brunot, it is now a *medical region* where everything will now be done with the health of the natives in mind. The doctors set to work with enthusiasm but without ignoring the difficulties. The certainty that they will receive a great deal of assistance from the governor is a valuable help to them.[13]

6. Haut-Nyong Must Be Saved

"I would like to remind you that I have handed the Haut-Nyong region over entirely to the medical authorities." On January 17, 1940, the governor-general of Cameroon, Richard Brunot, explained his approach to the territory's administrative council:

> As you know, this region was once one of the most active hotbeds of trypanosomiasis. Sudden resurgences of the epidemic vanquished by Dr. Jamot have been occurring there, however. Other lamentable diseases—leprosy, yaws, and syphilis—have found a fertile breeding ground there. The contrast between the dazzling richness of the soil and the physiological poverty of its inhabitants is stark. In giving the management of this region over to these doctors, I wanted to signal my determination to grant in all matters an absolute priority to all that is human. Before developing the land, it is necessary to produce men; and to achieve this, what better method than to entrust the task to health technicians? Their policy will mainly center on the thriving of bodies and the development of families. In a word, they will carry out medical administration. To plan, raise, feed, heal, this will be their role.[1]

Brunot concluded by evoking the astonishment his announcement had caused, but his presentation was a condensed version of the common ground of colonial policy in the interwar period.

"To produce men": since the early 1920s, the demographic issue was the declared priority of colonial intervention in Africa and the main motivation for investment in health infrastructure. Africa's depopulation was an obsession of the Ministry of the Colonies. Indeed, it was considered the first obstacle to the "*mise en valeur* [improvement] of the colonies," the economic and social doctrine laid out in 1921 by Albert Sarraut, which served as a road map for Oudinot Street.[2] Africa lacked the labor force needed for the major infrastructure projects and agricultural cultivation that would enable its economic takeoff. In this context, the improvement of the living conditions of the colonized people, starting with their health and nutrition, was a primary and rational objective, particularly in a context in which economic crisis was making Paris feel its "need for Africa." The "conservation of the race" was "our most immediate and practical interest." It was necessary "to preserve and increase human capital in order to make financial capital work and grow,"[3] explained the Sarraut Plan; it was necessary to "produce some Blacks," declared the governor of French West Africa, Jules Carde, in the late 1920s.[4] Colonial doctors were able to throw themselves into the political space now opened to them, obtaining the establishment of a rural health system, Assistance médicale indigène (Native Medical Assistance), throughout French Africa, and financing for exceptional operations such as the Jamot mission in Cameroon. In return, doctors applied themselves to demographics—they conducted the first estimates of infant mortality indicators, for example—and above all viewed their activities as medicine of the masses, or of the "race," practiced and thought about according to the objective of demographic increase.[5] Areas with outbreaks of sleeping sickness thus became pilot project territories, where census-taking and individual registration efforts made it possible to carry out demographic monitoring that was impossible elsewhere in the colonial space. Jamot, for example, kept a close eye from Ayos on the balance of deaths and births in the sectors for which his teams were responsible and was able to announce his victory in 1930 with the return of population growth.[6] In 1939, at the time of the general mobilization, the commotion of combat gave the language of numbers an obvious military significance. France, "whose birth rate is in deficit," needed "to have in its colonies able-bodied men capable, if need be, of making good infantrymen,"[7] General-Doctor Blanchard explained to the Ministry of the Colonies in September 1939. Incidentally, the importance of African infantrymen in the First World War was behind the origin of the Sarraut Plan. At the same meeting, Gaston Muraz, who succeeded

Jamot as the person in charge of the fight against trypanosomiasis, summarized the problem when negotiating budget extensions for his department. As simple as cross-multiplication:

> All that is necessary is to present it to them in the form of an American calculation and tell them: "You want to save this many people. Well, that will be this much." [. . .] There are two "master arguments" to be made:
>
> 1 You need people to be infantrymen
> 2 You want to save this many people, that will be this much.[8]

After two decades of major announcements, however, the "population policy" was still in its infancy across the empire. Paradoxically, the demographic obsession of colonial governments did not require figures, owing to the lack of an effective system for gathering statistics.[9] In Haut-Nyong, Richard Brunot wanted to give doctors the means to acquire knowledge.

The other principle invoked—concern for the "human"—is also not surprising. The humanitarian reference is omnipresent in the colonial writings of the time. The population-based arguments of the administrators and technocrats coexisted with the celebration of a selfless medical action, justified by moral and emotional principles: healing out of duty and love for the native. The humanitarian argument was not reserved for missionaries like Dr. Albert Schweitzer, who at the same time made "reverence for life" the meaning of his medical-evangelical action. Army doctors like Jamot moved from one register to another, alternating between emotional calls to "save the Black race," including at the cost of sacrifice, and patient analyses of demographic data.[10]

The governor of Cameroon, who quoted Jean Jaurès when paying tribute to Jamot in 1939, was in any case an old hand at declarations of humanism.[11] He was one of the few high-ranking administrators who had long since been recruited into the socialist ranks of the French Section of the Workers' International (SFIO). His appointment to the mandated territory of Cameroon at the end of 1938 extended the timid reformist experiment of the Popular Front, which, in Cameroon, had resulted in attempts to control labor recruitment and promote the agricultural activity of small farmers.[12] Brunot's social policy, like that of his predecessor Pierre Boisson, limited its ambitions to the areas of charity and health. In the opinion of even the most virulent settlers, Brunot was indeed a "good craftsman of the greatness of the empire," who knew how to refrain from any "excesses of false humanitarianism"[13]—a way of saying that he knew how to protect the interests of plantation owners and traders without calling into question any of the foundations of the colonial economy. The work of doctors, which the Jamot commemorations already spoke of in the past tense, was a consensual domain in Cameroon. Since the early 1930s, the construction of new health infrastructure such as the Madouma *hypnoserie* had continued despite budgetary constraints, thanks to a policy of special loans. Operating budgets devoted to health were constantly increasing (they doubled between 1936 and 1939), enabling Cameroon to become the African colony that was the best equipped with doctors and medications. The Haut-Nyong experience was the little fantasy of a reasonable governor.

IT IS DIFFICULT TO trace the origins of the project in a more precise manner. Wang Sonné had his own theory, which was based on his interview with Joseph Dobo. In 1938, he had just moved to Messamena, after having left the education department to take up the position of chief created by the Germans for his father:

> JOSEPH DOBO: So, in '38, there was a doctor passing through. His name was Dr. Weber. He took me aside, he said to me: come with me on my tour. I helped him with secretarial work. [. . .] I traveled all over the country with him. However, this gentleman was already preparing his report. Now, I followed him well. What we prepared, he would pass it on to the typist, and so on; he would follow the nurses' work while I stayed with the typist. I did the whole tour, the whole country. After, he said to me: Well, the country is really dead. This country, if France does not act otherwise, is really a country that will be erased from the map. So, he told me [. . .] I'm preparing a report. I'm asking that the doctors be given command.

> WANG SONNÉ: After having done the whole Haut-Nyong area?

> JOSEPH DOBO: The whole area, I tell you. The whole Haut-Nyong area. I was here, in the Messamena subdivision, I didn't go to Abong-Mbang. It was catastrophic. So, he prepared this report. And he sent it to overseas France, to Paris.

> WANG SONNÉ: It was 1938.

> JOSEPH DOBO: 1938. Exactly '38. It was in 1938 that Dr. Weber requested that the region be handed over to the doctors and that the civilians, that the administrators withdraw.[14]

Wang Sonné underlined this three times. In the margin, he wrote in pencil: "It looks like a scoop. It's an exclusive." He was probably as happy as I was to have a lead. "In '39 the report goes to France. Overseas France accepts."[15] Dobo's story was very precise, but Wang Sonné made him repeat himself. Was Weber a civilian doctor? "Military doctor," replied Joseph Dobo. "I will go on and say that in '38, there was no Medical Region but there was demand. Weber had asked that this region be entrusted to doctors in 1938 and it came into effect in '39."[16]

I have never seen any reference to an investigation by a Dr. Weber in the Health Service reports. The doctor in question was the "field doctor" in charge of the fight against sleeping sickness in Haut-Nyong. His conclusions undoubtedly inspired the alarming diagnoses contained in the 1938 and 1939 annual reports. The only trace I have of him is a letter sent to the Catholic mission in Messamena in 1939 with the letterhead "R. A. Weber—Doctor—Yaoundé."[17] At this time, the Catholic missionaries noted that he had come to do his "prospecting" as he did every year, and that he was so kind that one could "forget that he is a Protestant."[18] It is possible that he was assigned a fact-finding mission in 1938, at a time when the Popular Front was sending the questionnaires of the Guernut Commission of Inquiry "on the legitimate needs and aspirations of the populations living in the colonies" throughout the empire, but there is little trace of him in the archives. During the war, an R. A. Weber appeared several times as a doctor specializing in trypanosomiasis, apparently based in Bobo-Dioulasso. During this time, he wrote for the journal *Médecine tropicale* (Tropical medicine), the organ of the Colonial Army's Health Service, but he disappeared from the radar after the war.[19] He may have written a report somewhere, but I have not seen it.

7. Lessons in Medical Administration

> We do not omit any measure that can interest the natives and encourage
> them to improve their own well-being in spite of themselves.
> DOCTOR JEAN JOSEPH DAVID, Haut-Nyong, 1942

The time for utopia had arrived. Appointed district commander, Jean Joseph
David settled in Abong-Mbang in a residence that looked like a castle, which
had been built by one of his predecessors in 1927. Five other doctors, all under
forty years of age, were there to assist him. Henri Koch, the youngest at age
twenty-eight, had just left the Pharo. He inherited the post of Messamena, a
few hours by pirogue from Ayos, where he would be "subdivision commander."
Eugène Pape, a Breton who had just completed an assignment in New Hebrides, would be commander of the Abong-Mbang subdivision. Two "Cameroonians" who had been assigned to the region for several years completed
the team: Fernand Gailhbaud, who was appointed subdivision commander at
Doumé, an old German military post built on top of a hill, and Sylvain Lagarde, who would simply have the role of "assistant" doctor, just like the sixth
member of the team, Captain Giraud.[1] Only Lomié, the most remote center,
which was practically cut off from the rest of the region, was entrusted to a
civil servant. The region assigned to David was vast, even immense—as large as

Switzerland or the Rhône-Alpes region—and the roads linking the main towns were barely passable. A telegraph line linked Abong-Mbang to the rest of the world, but internal communications were carried out by post.

I do not know what David and his supervisor, Marcel Vaucel, said to each other in Yaoundé, but one can imagine that the doctor had carte blanche. There was not much to lose, in any case, in a region where everything always seemed to fail. Before his brutal demise the administrator Barbarin, one of David's predecessors in Abong-Mbang, in 1938 had drafted a grand plan to regain control of the country by strictly regulating how the villagers made use of their time.[2] David spent his first few months coming up with an action plan, submitted to the authorities in Yaoundé and Paris in February 1940 and approved immediately. I have never been able to locate it in the archives, but it is referenced in David's first progress report, kept at the National Archives in Yaoundé.

The report, dated October 23, 1942, is entitled "Cameroun français—Région médicale du Haut-Nyong—Rapport de Gestion—1941" (French Cameroon—Haut-Nyong Medical Region—Management Report—1941) and is surrounded by small plus signs that form a frame (I can just imagine the finesse required to adorn the document in this way with a typewriter). The accompanying letter, sent to Brazzaville and Yaoundé, bears the motto of Free French Africa, "Honor and Homeland." Cameroon and the territories of French Equatorial Africa rallied behind Charles de Gaulle at the end of August 1940, giving Free France a considerable territorial, military, and economic base. The Gaullists tried their hand at colonial government, in a strange empire without a metropolis where the motto "Liberty, Equality, Fraternity" had been abolished. The upheaval did not appear to weaken the Medical Region. It must be said that colonial doctors were well placed: Jean Mauzé, the director of the Institute of Hygiene in Douala, and Vaucel, the head of Cameroon's Health Service, had distinguished themselves by rallying to de Gaulle's cause at the end of August 1940, joining the side of Free France.[3] In 1941, de Gaulle, who had made Cameroon the site of his first parade as head of state wearing a colonial helmet, appointed Adolphe Sicé, a colonial doctor whose convictions were not strictly republican, high commissioner of Free French Africa, making him the highest military authority in the empire. Former "Scout leader of French Equatorial Africa," the colonel was in favor of the move toward hygiene and a return to moral order.[4] The time of doctors governing had arrived; and incidentally, this was a long-standing tradition in the empire.[5]

It was a political kind of medicine that the district commander was trying to design, not just a simple public health program; a "social enterprise with resolutely demographic aims."[6] "Medical administration" did not simply aim to make doctors' work easier by giving them free rein to organize public health campaign. The aim was to give them the widest possible scope for intervention, including social and political organization. When David warned, in his first report, that "no demographic adjustment should be envisaged without the introduction of profound reforms in native society,"[7] he did not intend to list targets that were beyond his reach but rather to enumerate the priorities of his "direct medical administration": "It would be vain to think that isolated medical action would suffice to restore demographic balance if it is not complemented by major projects in hygiene, culture, and economic infrastructure. The sanitation of the country, the construction of model villages, the development of individual resources, in a word, the improvement of the native's social situation are ultimately the most effective weapons. It is this, the administrative task that falls to the Medical Region."[8]

He began like this, with "child welfare": "Vital in combating the decline in birthrate and in forming a physically and morally healthy generation, this protection must be flexible and varied for the different ages of childhood. The development of maternity wards, nurseries, and schools, the institution of home health visits for infants, and the organization of sporting associations, which would put all native youth under medical supervision, are the fundamental principles."[9]

The first chapter, maternity care, was the first to be applied. Beginning in March 1940, the women of the Abong-Mbang subdivision were subjected to a new "health discipline."[10] This was applied to the remainder of the region in the months that followed. The principle was to systematically screen pregnant women in their villages during the doctor's rounds. Each pregnant woman was examined on site, registered, and asked to present herself at the "birthing center" one month before her due date. Thirty-six new buildings were built to set up maternity camps in the administrative center of each subdivision. Women were meant to be hospitalized for forty-five days so that they could "[escape] customary labor obligations and [receive] advice on the elementary principles of hygiene for newborns."[11] Their food intake during this period "when all they are doing is eating and resting" was established,[12] to the nearest gram of salt, by a regional memorandum. At birth, each mother received a boubou, a block of soap, and a blanket "to enable them to comply [. . .] with the principles of hygiene instilled during hospitalization."[13] More than one thousand women in the region followed this regimen in 1940. The figure reached nearly two thousand in 1942, which amounted to more than 80 percent of births registered in the civil registry. One must reread these lines and think about what it meant for two thousand pregnant women to be hospitalized and fed for more than a month.

Educational policy was the second area in need of work. Dr. David envisaged a complete reorganization of education so that it would meet "its true purpose, which is to shape adolescents and, above all, to teach them how to live."[14] "To achieve this humanitarian goal,"[15] the program included weekly conferences on hygiene led by the doctor or one of his assistants; monthly screening visits; the keeping of individual health records; "courses in the domestic arts and childcare reserved for girls and young women"; work in the fields, the workshop ("carpentry—forge—basketry"), and the brickworks; eating in cafeterias, where schoolchildren would "learn to eat in a sanitary and healthy way";[16] and shower rooms. It ultimately aimed to take "the native child at the age when he is most receptive" and, David imagined, to create "for the future a class of small farmers and modest village craftsmen, open to our ideas and trusting of our methods."[17]

Work did not begin until 1941, once the "maternal and child care assistance service [had been] developed."[18] The region's schools were completely overhauled, and a "beautiful school village" was built of temporary material in the Doumé subdivision. A new regional school was established in "a beautiful building" in the regional capital Abong-Mbang,[19] on a large plateau of two and a half hectares, with dormitories, workshops, a kitchen, toilets, and showers. More than a thousand students aged seven to fifteen were enrolled; those from Abong-Mbang were clothed in shorts and shirts made of khaki canvas. David noted that "nudity, rags, and uncleanliness are disappearing."[20] In 1942, the inspection report of the head of the territory's Education Service was full of praise: "The Haut-Nyong School District is on its way to becoming the one that will showcase the best educational achievements."[21]

The teaching focused on agriculture. The school's fields, the purpose of which was to "popularize the use of green manures and crop rotation," were well used by students, "despite the slight distaste [. . .] for performing a task that the oldest customs of their race have always reserved for women."[22] In terms of raising livestock, it was a question of "teaching the art of selecting, caring for, and even feeding small livestock, all of which is totally ignored by the native."[23] In Abong-Mbang, David reserved seven sheep, eleven goats, ten pigs, seven rabbits, eleven hens, five ducks, and twenty-one pigeons for the school farm.

Sports rounded out the program; after all, they do constitute a form of "health discipline." While the idea was not exceptional at the time, particularly in the colonial context,[24] the Haut-Nyong experiment stood out in its ambition to "[put] all native youth under medical control."[25] It was announced in the 1940 action plan: "The number of pupils being limited, many young people run the risk of not escaping their isolation. Sporting associations seem to us the organization best suited for keeping them under our medical and administrative supervision."[26] Every morning, between seven thirty and eight, a physical fitness lesson was held in all centers of the medical region; according to David, one thousand young people were thus assembled every day. Twenty-six soccer teams, equipped with jerseys, shorts, and balls, competed against each other in a regional championship. The practicing of sports was compulsory in schools.[27] Each year, the memorandum stated, was to be punctuated by events leading up to the championship. At the end of the semester, all students were to compete in each subdivision's administrative center, classified in one of two categories, one for the younger children and the other, for the older. These "playoffs" were to be carried out in the presence of David himself, who was to supervise a long series of events, from the hundred-meter dash to "assegai throwing." At graduation time, the best players were brought together in Abong-Mbang, where a large stadium was built, for the annual final. The initiative was a success, noted David in 1942: "The native youth truly appreciate the games at the stadium: through them, they gain the health and spirit of discipline lacking to them."[28]

The second part of the action plan focused on "adult welfare." The aim was to "one day provide the fertile lands of Haut-Nyong with the strong arms they require." The program, developed in 1940, consisted of "a range of administrative and health measures inextricably linked with one another,"[29] most of which were implemented before the end of 1942. This aspect of the plan was based on the results of a preliminary socioeconomic study of the farmers in the region that had been conducted by the doctors. The study's conclusion was that "the balance sheet is terrible." The average per capita income, evaluated using three pages of calculations, "does not even come close to covering the amounts required for taxes, as far as the maintenance of old people and children is concerned, nor does it cover the purchase of the extremely necessary machete, blanket, and bag of salt, there is no question about it."[30]

Taking as a model the Bulu area in southern Cameroon, which was considered a success story for "improvement," David proposed to enrich the region by developing intensive cocoa cultivation, with the planting of five hundred feet per taxable man. To improve the local diet, soybean seeds were purchased and distributed. In 1941, the subdivision commanders were ordered to produce a special report on the raising of livestock. The doctors did a census of the entire livestock population and bought hundreds of sheep which were given to "nonowners." The sheep and their owners were then listed on a control registry. David drew up a plan for improving the breed through the selection of rams. It included "castration of defective animals" and the annual rotation of studs to avoid inbreeding.

"Community hygiene" came next. This aspect of the plan focused on re-thinking housing, reorganizing communities, and redesigning space. The ideal village was defined, with its model huts, sports field, bathhouse, and cesspits.[31] Twenty-five model villages were planned, with brick and cinder block houses. Major road works were launched: approximately thirty kilometers of road were opened in 1942 to make Messamena accessible via "an impeccable route that highlights the endurance and initiative of Dr. Koch, the young subdivision commander."[32] On the agenda for the future, spread over several years to "save the workforce," were the ninety-four kilometers of the Ayos–Abong-Mbang road, countless sections of which were in need of repair.

The question of work was also in need of thorough review, in order to put an end to poverty and free up the workers for development. Starting at the beginning of 1940, Dr. David went on the offensive by imposing a series of amendments on European plantation owners in the region: mandatory sign-ing of long-term employment contracts for natives who so wished; raising the minimum wage to two francs per day for adults and 1.50 francs for children; travel allowances; strict rules regarding workers' housing; the keeping of infir-mary records; and, for the largest plantations, the creation of "social projects of interest to children." In return, the doctors were to strive to "achieve satisfac-tory diligence and productivity."[33]

The doctor had one last idea to accelerate the demographic recovery of the region: the "repatriation of emigrants and the forced return of vagrants to their places of origin." With a statistical study to back them up, the doctor-administrators wanted to put an end to emigration, responsible for "continu-ous losses affecting a population already so greatly reduced by major endemics." David called for the repatriation of at least two thousand people to Haut-Nyong from other parts of Cameroon, beginning with plantation workers who would find "similar employment at home."[34] David listed a few shocking mea-sures: it would be necessary to prohibit "the export and hiring of workers from the Medical Region"; to undertake, "without prior detention," the "forced re-turn of vagrants to their places of origin"; and to send emigrants back "after examining their situation."

Finally, David requested the return of prisoners serving their sentences elsewhere. "We are only reclaiming our citizens," David concluded. "In short, there is nothing strange about all the people from Haut-Nyong cooperating in its rebuilding rather than going to neighboring regions to fill jobs which would be returned without inconvenience to the inhabitants of these lands!"[35]

Within the framework of this comprehensive conception of a population policy, medical intervention itself was almost secondary. Since everything had been transformed into medicine, medicine itself was only one tool among many. The fight against sleeping sickness was of course continued as it had been "for many long years."[36] The main new issue was syphilis, "one of the most probable factors in depopulation."[37] A systematic prevention program was put in place, the approach of which was "based on the sleeping sickness model," with mobile screening of all populations and treatment of the "virus reservoir." Several thousand people infected with syphilis were identified, treated, monitored, and studied. The prevalence of leprosy, which affected nearly 10 percent of the population according to the first estimates carried out in 1940, justified the construction of a huge leprosy camp near Abong-Mbang, a veritable utopia within the utopia, expected to bring together in a location fifteen kilometers from any inhabited area two thousand leprosy patients segregated in different "villages" according to their tribe. It was to include a dispensary, a maternity ward, a court, a prison, a shopping center, and cultural buildings.[38]

8. Paradise

The car radio was playing Congolese rumba, which made Madame Ateba nostalgic. It made her recall her years as a young bride. She was sitting in the front of the pickup truck, I was in the back with her daughter Gisèle Rouly, and Valentin was at the wheel. It was a kind of guided tour, with mandatory stops, as if the itinerary were self-evident. I had already taken this tour without Madame Ateba, in 2012, on the advice of the sub-prefect: the regional school, the residence of the district commanders, the hospital, the Kwoamb leprosy camp, and the ruins of the Madouma *hypnoserie*. This last site is listed somewhere in an inventory of tourist attractions: a "white man" had come to visit, notebook in hand, and had never returned. Wang Sonné had done the same tour twenty or thirty years ago and had snapped the same photos as I had.

The most impressive site was the immense leprosy camp created by David in the middle of the forest, in the place known as Kwoamb (which apparently means "bush" in Makaa). Arriving at this site is always spectacular: after a short hour of travel, twenty kilometers in a tunnel of vegetation, a large clearing suddenly appears and a monumental clinic, a cloister with a roof made of small tiles, two old mango trees, two large villas, a school, a small soccer field, and a church with a collapsed roof appear, along with houses lined up on perfectly straight streets, much like workers' housing at mines or on large plantations, except that they are surrounded only by swampy forests and Baka people who sometimes pass through to sell freshwater shrimp and honey. A kind of island at the end of the world, where the trail ends. The clinic is half-operational, with 1960s medications in the cupboards and paper with "French Cameroon" letterhead on the lab benches, as though the settlers had just stepped out to take a nap. There are still leprosy patients living there with their families, some of whom have been there since the 1940s, with the support of Fairmed, a Swiss NGO that installed solar panels that make the people of Madouma a little jealous. Along with John Manton, an Irish historian specializing in leprosy, I interviewed, in 2012, an elderly man called Biak, who had lost all his fingers and gone blind. As I told John when we got back into the car, I felt like Lady Di when I shook his hand, because the "visit to the leprosy patients" is such a cliché scene: "demonstrations of an ethical order, which receive their ultimate value from the publicity they are given,"[1] as Roland Barthes wrote in "Bichon among the Blacks," mocking the ridiculous and obscene courage, the "heroism without an object" as stupid as mountain climbing, of humanitarian tourism in Africa.[2] In any case, Biak was born in 1946. He arrived as a leprosy patient in Kwoamb when he was a child, but he did not remember David, just the engineer who built everything. John and I exchanged glances when he told us that the engineer's name was Marlo, like Marlow, the narrator of *Heart of Darkness*.[3] He told us a strange story, the founding myth of the leprosy camp. The authorities at the time had decided that "to eradicate leprosy, the leprosy patients must be burned" and had gathered them in a building that they had intended to burn down, when a "white woman," the wife of the subdivision commander, intervened, saving them and bringing them here. Thereafter, the leprosy camp became a "place without borders," as Biak put it, suspended outside the rest of the world and Cameroon, without a land registry, with a vague leader; a place that brought together Baka people and people from all over the country, from Douala, the West, the South, and Yaoundé; people who remained there, regardless of whether they were ill, to farm their fields; a sort of Zone to Defend.[4] In the 1970s, there was an airfield just outside Kwoamb, used for presidential visits and aerial spraying of pesticides on coffee plantations; today, it has been completely reclaimed by the forest.

The leprosy camp had its greatest moments in the 1950s, when a Spiritan, Father Delhemmes, settled there full time with some nursing nuns, attracting official visits, photographers, and journalists who would turn him into a minor celebrity in France, the "Father of the Pygmies." His logbooks, kept in school notebooks, are in the archives of the mother house in Chevilly-Larue;[5] they begin with a "history," which traces how David had had the road built and the site cleared by able-bodied leprosy patients from Messamena, Doumé, and especially Madouma, where they had been placed in the sleeping sickness camp. Madame Ateba remembered when the regional leprosy camp was ready. At that time, hundreds of leprosy patients traveled under escort to Kwoamb from other camps in the region. Those from Ayos passed her house on the way, insulting the villagers who were reluctant to assist them. A 1952 article in *Le Figaro* stated that the leprosy patients of Kwoamb, of whom there were a good thousand at the time, divided by ethnic groups in mini-villages, called the camp "Paradise."[6]

The other mandatory stop is the *hypnoserie* in Madouma, which is on the way to the leprosy camp. The two sites in fact belong to the same complex, forming a huge and somewhat cursed space of care, exclusion, and death that begins at the main road. A Spiritan father recorded in his diary that a 1950s high commissioner who visited Kwoamb would compulsively wipe his feet when he got back in his car. The old buildings have since been torn apart by trees and have the inscriptions "December 1935" and "February 1936," and large windows surrounded by bricks, like the schools of the Third Republic. Inside, "I love Samir Nasri," "Beyoncé the star," and other declarations of love have been graffitied in charcoal. On the facades are the remnants of an electrical system with blue glass insulators that are no longer connected to anything. People have stolen the bricks, breaking up the paving on the ground. The disused clinic was used successively as a pigsty and chicken farm, and the homes of Baptist doctors, as orphanages and restaurants. Gisèle remembered the atmosphere. Likely to make me happy, Madame Ateba explained to me that the most beautiful villa was Jamot's house; the villagers who had gathered around us agreed.

All around the buildings, there remains the same kind of tree, which is said to have been planted by Jamot (or sometimes David), like the eucalyptus trees that line the city's main streets. I am not very knowledgeable when it comes to tropical botany, so I did not recognize it, with its locust leaves, its clusters of small white flowers, and its garlic scent. In retrospect, it seems to me that it was a neem, an empire tree par excellence, native to India and planted in all European colonies in Africa. What is special about it is that it "stinks," as its name in Makaa patois (*ebobok*) indicates, and that it repels tsetse flies and even sleeping sickness itself. Its powers are ambivalent, as always: the tree killed the flies that smelled its odor and finally allowed the country to "heal," but I was also told that Jamot had been driven out of Abong-Mbang because of this tree, which becomes hollow as it ages and attracts evil spirits. In short, these trees from the past are much talked about. They are the trace of sleeping sickness. In 2012, Dr. Amougou insisted on making the detour to Madouma to try to find seeds; we photographed machete marks on a trunk, which showed that someone had removed some bark. As we left, Madame Ateba broke off a branch to replant in the village. Valentin and I also took one, to show to botanists in Yaoundé.

The other stops on our tour took less time. The prefect was not at his residence to welcome us, but while waiting on his veranda, we were able to get a closer look at the house: strange architecture, modernist concrete fortress style, with "1927" on the facade, at the end of a monumental alley about a hundred meters long. Gisèle talked about the games she played with the children of the prefects of her time, the balls that were held in the past, to which she would go to spy on her father, who did not really know how to dance. I still wonder what the interior looks like. The residence was built by a French citizen who eclipses David in most of the stories that are told, a district commander named Henri Joseph Armand Chefdrue.[7] Of West Indian origin, Chefdrue married a local woman, Madame Bilounga, Madame Ateba's paternal aunt, who managed, by "using her charms" (or so the story goes), to convince him to relocate the regional capital, which had been Lomié since German times, to Abong-Mbang. Through Chefdrue, people remember that Haut-Nyong was, in a way, founded by a mysterious and powerful woman. We also walked around the immense school complex, filled with students playing volleyball. "Diamonds" by Rihanna was playing on the car radio.

We made a brief stop at the stadium, parking our big Toyota with the Research Institute for Development logo right in the middle of the field. We arrived at the end of the training session, and Valentin took one of our packages of bottled water to distribute to the players, who were asking for beer. I explained my project to anyone who would listen; we stood around chatting, drawing on the red clay with our feet. They were preparing for a big game in Yaoundé, to play for entry into the higher-ranked D2 league, and finished off with a prayer. I took photos of the old colonial-era bleachers. There were still a few rows of red plastic seats; the others are scattered throughout the city's bars and backyards. Five minutes later, the police arrived. They had seen me photograph the police station (right behind the bleachers). "There are things going on here that we don't know about," they began, in a vaguely threatening tone, trying to make us nervous. Ten minutes later, warned by someone or other, the sports delegate arrived and said, "I thought they might be benefactors." Valentin explained to me that they wanted "their share." We managed to walk away. For the rest of the day, a police pickup truck circled around us. The atmosphere got a little heavier.

The last "must-see" site was the hospital, which is on the hill of the colonial city. It was disappointing on first viewing: it had just been renovated—that is, largely destroyed and then rebuilt—as was the case just about everywhere in Cameroon during the humanitarian real estate boom of the 2010s. This disheartened Madame Ateba, who missed the old brick buildings, and me as well. Madame Ateba managed to get the head doctor to see us, Dr. Denis Nsame, a young English-speaking Cameroonian who looks as though he works very hard. He had us sit in his office while he consulted the patients in line, then dealt with Madame Ateba while I flipped through a hospital activity report. I learned that the main cause of death here is HIV, as is the case elsewhere in Cameroon, but the figures here are particularly alarming: in 2007, of two hundred pregnant women tested at the hospital, seventy-six were carriers of the virus (38 percent), and of four hundred hepatitis C tests carried out, 190 were positive. The two epidemics are hitting the eastern region hard, something that is met largely with general indifference. The situation is supposed to be under control in Cameroon, where HIV treatment is free, and until very recently, those working in the field reserved catastrophist rhetoric for southern Africa;[8] shiny UNAIDS reports never talk about power cuts or roads full of potholes. The doctor then gave us a brief overview of the renovations at the hospital (he has a whole photo album, with "before and after" photos) and apologized for the archives, all of which disappeared during the work on the building. Development agency "projects" tend to devour the traces of the past even more thoroughly than termites. We went out for a walk with Madame Ateba, my digital recorder in hand, looking for the pavilions where Dr. David's pregnant women had lived—Dr. David, "the one who picked up women in the villages," as Madame Ateba always says when she speaks his name, as if to remember.

We strolled around, a little overwhelmed by the sun hitting the laterite (the land surrounding the new hospital has no trees or grass). As Madame Ateba walked, her memories came back to her. For once, she no longer spoke vaguely of Jamot but pointed out buildings, trucks fit for the scrap heap, and empty spaces, saying, "It was there." Walking is a mnemonic device.[9] Everything was "switched around" after the renovation: the director met with us in the former delivery room, where there were two beds where the desk had been; the new maternity ward, renovated thanks to the charitable work of the first lady, Chantal Biya,[10] is where the former hospital used to be, on the other side of the central aisle, and vice versa. "The hospitalization of the women who were taken here from the villages to give birth" had occupied a good half of the site, with pavilions spread over a hundred meters, all now razed. At the very end, behind the fence were "the warehouses where food was stored in Colonel David's time." Every day at 3 p.m., a few honks of a horn would announce that food was being distributed. Every woman, explained Madame Ateba, "would go out with her small dish for oil, and the other one for the meat, and the small basket for plantains. And salt, eh! Or even laundry soap." Her memories are mainly about food, the "ration," as she calls it. Doctors did not buy from the market but went to the villages to get the plantains and palm oil that made up the dietary regimen. There were no funds earmarked for this, so the doctors sent trucks, the same ones they used to transport the women, to collect the plantains, taro, and manioc gathered by the village chiefs. The superior chiefs and the administration organized all of this, decreeing which village was to provide what. The same principle was used to supply the prison with food: "It was received by the subdivision commanders who at that time were called Colonel David, Colonel Koch, Colonel and so on." Only beef was provided directly by the government: "We did the slaughtering and shared the small pieces. People lived, they were all right. They were well fed." Colonel David had established a nutritional relationship between the villages and the women, confiscating food and workers from the former, and offering the latter three months away from the men and the fields, among women, with salt and soap. This relationship seems to have been switched around today: one must pay for everything at the hospital, vehicles rust the tires flat, and generators remain silent owing to a lack of fuel. Progress is a memory in the maternity ward of Abong-Mbang.

The trucks came and went, full of plantains and women with their luggage. Hospital staff went to "do tests" in the villages, find pregnant women, and keep records. "They counted them to send them here." The women would stay in rooms with rows of beds, with a small shelf for their belongings; they would bring "their second-last," their other young children, with them. Perhaps this is why Madame Ateba knows the place so well: she was there, at five or six years old, with her mother, who was expecting another child. She can even remember which house they were in, though it is no longer there. "And when a woman finished giving birth, she had to wait another two months at the hospital before being dropped off at home. She had to rest and she was always monitored by the health service here. I saw that when I was little." The babies who returned to the village were the first to have birth certificates.

9. A Real-Life Experiment

> The inhabitants of this country present themselves
> to us, still imbued with their barbaric customs of times past, as a
> magnificent field of wonderful and humane experiments.
> DOCTOR HENRI KOCH, Messamena, 1943

Dr. David's program was characterized by its experimental vocation. A dual objective, both political and cognitive, ran through the project: to rebuild the population, on the one hand, but also to describe this rebuilding in detail and thereby test the value of "administration" as a public health method on the other. The medical region was therefore an attempt at scientific government, not only in the sense that enlightened technicians were to be in charge but also in the sense that government itself was an experiment.[1] This experimental approach justified the effort made in assigning a large number of qualified personnel to the task. It was at this cost that "the Haut-Nyong region will pursue its destiny favorably; it is also at this cost that a possibly unique collection of documentation will be assembled," explained David. Without the means to give the project a scientific dimension, he warned, "this experiment loses most of its interest and its true meaning."[2] Significantly, reports concerning the Haut-Nyong were not only transmitted within the local administrative hierarchy but also sent to specialized circles in Paris. The Sleeping Sickness Committee, which brought together colonial doctors and the leading figures of Parisian parasitology in Paris, welcomed the initiative in 1941 as "an indication of all the interest taken by the administration in the greater well-being of the native population." Experts pointed out that this was only a test: "The creation of medical regions should multiply on a large scale."[3] The results were published as research papers. A journal established in Brazzaville, which bore the Cross of Lorraine on its cover,[4] the *Revue des sciences médicales, pharmaceutiques et vétérinaires de l'Afrique française libre* (Free French Africa review of medical, pharmaceutical, and veterinary sciences), offered a forum for doctors from the Haut-Nyong, who would also publish in the *Bulletin de la Société d'études camerounaises* (Bulletin of the Society of Cameroonian Studies), which was published in Yaoundé beginning in 1935.[5]

The administrative exercise was transformed: in addition to the usual annual report, hundreds of pages of studies on birth rates, customs, and agriculture were written. The demographic question dominated all the work carried out, summarized in David's "Étude sur l'administration médicale directe d'une région démographique [*sic*] éprouvée" (Study on the direct medical administration of an afflicted demographic region),[6] which serves as the experiment's final report. Added to the political reporting exercise were doctors' medico-sociological diagnoses and reflexive feedback on their program, the performance of which was quantified and discussed. "Medical administration" was a documentary enterprise: individual health records were systematized, and the "prospecting tour," a medico-administrative technique par excellence, went beyond vaccinations and the fight against sleeping sickness to identify and monitor pregnant women, syphilitics, infants, the crossbreeding of sheep, and cocoa plantations. From 1940 onward, the reference to the Haut-Nyong Medical Region as an "experiment" or "experimentation" was therefore not only metaphorical. It informed action and gave materiality (on paper, at first) to a utopia.

Experimental ambition permeated all aspects of the program, from the treatment of leprosy patients to soya cultivation. The medicalization of motherhood, a classic objective of public health programs in colonial Africa,[7] was characterized by the meticulous and repeated monitoring of mothers and children. In early 1940, Marcel Vaucel expected "substantial results from the new organization in Haut-Nyong with regard to the education of native women, prenatal consultations, and childcare." For Vaucel, the head of the colony's Health Service, Haut-Nyong would have demonstration value: "Interesting conclusions will certainly be drawn from the behaviour of the natives and will be very useful for our propaganda in the rest of the territory."[8]

The success of the camp for pregnant women, according to David, was due to the fact that "the influx of women and children has made it possible to gather information."[9] In addition to the recording of pregnancies, an "individual file" was opened for each infant and added to during "home visits" and during precisely planned monthly monitoring rounds. The system made it possible to monitor the survival and growth of children, as well as their progressive infection with helminths and malaria. Infant mortality was therefore monitored with an accuracy rarely achieved in Africa at the time.[10] Average weight curves were established for each administrative subdivision and compared with European data. Better still, the effect of the program itself was quantified in that the doctors assessed the impact of maternal hospitalization time on infant birth weight.

Once the Medical Region was established, Cameroon's Health Service planned to concentrate all its experimental work there. In a memorandum to standardize leprosy treatment throughout the country, Vaucel specified in November 1939 that "all new trials will be entrusted to the teams of the Haut-Nyong region and facilitated by the new formula of the general administration of this region (doctors as district and subdivision Commanders)."[11] In August 1940, he sent David a detailed experimental protocol, to be implemented at the leprosy camp in Doumé, to test the importance of "nutrition in the evolution of leprosy." Twenty patients were to be chosen; they were not to receive any medical treatment but were to be "fed an abundant diet," with fresh fruit every day, supplemented by mineral salts, meat, and oil, taking care that "the provisions supplied are not used to feed other members of the patient's family."[12] These patients were to be compared with twenty others, subjected to the same diet and treated with the usual medication (methylene blue and chaulmoogra oil, therapies that would fall into disuse in the 1950s). All of these patients were to undergo a careful follow-up every six months, with a "special file" for each leprosy patient. The program set up to combat syphilis, with mandatory screening and registration, standardized treatment protocol, and internment of those infected, was also an unprecedented experiment. Finally, the doctors were also able to undertake projects of their own initiative. For instance, Koch embarked on a vast anthropological study of his Messamena subdivision, corresponding with Dr. Chabœuf, posted in Ayos, for advice on how to measure facial angles and corpulence.[13]

However, the main medical objective of the experiment had to do with sleeping sickness. It was to understand how, after twenty years of what was doubtless an unparalleled effort in Africa, doctors had not managed to "eradicate sleeping sickness,"[14] wrote Vaucel at the beginning of the undertaking:

It is evident that something is missing that completes or even stabilizes our efforts. One could not hope for better screening and treatment of patients. Should administrative measures be reinforced or even applied? [. . .]

We will soon see what can be expected from these measures in the Haut-Nyong region, where Governor-General Brunot has just invested doctors with the functions of district and subdivision commanders. But is the full implementation of the prescriptions of various orders compatible with improving or maintaining economic life? Will we perhaps be limited in our effort?[15]

Behind the Haut-Nyong experiment was a desire to know, a scientific curiosity that drove the project as much as the demographic emergency and humanist dreams. This was largely owing to the status of sleeping sickness: at the end of the 1930s, sleeping sickness remained a major scientific issue, of interest to biologists and hygienists well beyond colonial circles. The largest pharmaceutical companies and the best European medical research institutions were in a race to discover new molecules, and the public health services of all the colonies from Tanganyika to Senegal were trying to out-invent each other in implementing massive programs to fight the illness. The League of Nations Health Organization served as a sounding board for the debates. In 1938–39, the field was in turmoil when Nazi propaganda developed a film, *Germanin*, about the miracle molecule that would alone, according to the Germans, justify the restitution of the Reich's African territories, and this as the British Medical Research Council launched tests on a new family of compounds, diamidines.[16] In northern Nigeria, the Sleeping Sickness Service embarked in 1938 on a major population displacement program, the British specialty for trypanosomiasis control, developed in East Africa. This became the Anchau Experiment, which involved transferring dozens of villages and the entire city of Anchau to healthy areas where tsetse flies had been eradicated, and taking advantage of this opportunity to create model villages and an ideal city, New Anchau, or Takalafiya (the "path to health," in Hausa), with a school, a dispensary, latrines, a police station, and tree-lined streets laid out on a grid pattern.[17] "A successful and interesting experiment," the English wrote in 1940 to caption the propaganda photographs, which, once completed, "will provide a pattern for rural development in Africa."[18]

As the war had suspended international trade, the launch of the Haut-Nyong experiment came at a bad time. However, it likely raised real hope in French circles, in which the Jamot method was considered a national triumph. For the first time, it was the "policy" factor that could be varied in a controlled experiment. Vaucel, who in 1939 was a rising star of French tropical medicine, had great expectations regarding the model villages and major projects: "A new experiment will be attempted in the Haut-Nyong region to regroup away from the breeding sites of the Glossina [tsetse flies] in towns that are more comfortable and better protected [from] the dust of small villages where the endemic persists and thwarts our chemoprophylaxis. It is to be expected that there will be many difficulties: traditions, native habits, the establishment of new communication channels, and insufficient funds allocated."[19]

Vaucel would publish these words, with a few variations, in three different articles: in 1942 in Brazzaville, in the *Revue des sciences médicales, pharmaceutiques et vétérinaires de l'Afrique française libre*; in Paris, at the end of 1941, in the *Annales de l'Institut Pasteur* (Annals of the Pasteur Institute); and, also in Paris, in *La Presse médicale* (The medical press).[20] The reach of the last two journals extended beyond the small colonial world.

10. The Invisible Men

The doctors' thirst for knowledge, which presupposed a strict control of the population in order to make them "legible,"[1] rested in practice on local actors: nurses, teachers, and administrative heads, of course, but also agricultural monitors, "police," houseboys, orderlies, interpreters, and secretaries. One must read between the lines of the reports to find the traces of these intermediaries, who were responsible for the majority of the work of health surveillance, information collection, and hygiene education. The only explicit mention of them is about the training of "matrons" for maternity wards.[2] This is a recurrent paradox in the history of science and medicine in the colonial context (and even in colonial government in general): the production of knowledge and the exercise of power are based on the mediation of local actors, whose contribution was both crucial and invisible, and undoubtedly all the more invisible because it was crucial.[3] The "isolation" of the colonial agents is of course a romantic projection. The doctor-administrators of Haut-Nyong did not carry out their duties alone but operated as part of a group and were always flanked by assistants of all kinds, such as cleaning women, servants, translators, and typists.

The experimental ambition required the growing involvement of subordinate agents to repeatedly carry out prospecting, surveying, and agricultural monitoring rounds. First, there were the Cameroonian nurses and health assistants.

There doubtless were more than a dozen of them working in the region, many of whom were exclusively involved in the screening and treatment of trypanosomiasis. All trained in Ayos, they were part of a prestigious professional body, and their postings were published in the *Journal officiel*. Wang Sonné, who wrote his doctoral thesis on the history of this profession,[4] had attempted to draw up a list of those who were there during the time of the Medical Region. Their names were N'Geme Tchamanga Laurent, Mbarga Pierre, Etoundi Edmond, Onana Ambroise, Fouda Stanislas, and Nkoa François. They came from all over Cameroon and continued their careers elsewhere, but I know nothing else about them. The most notable absence in the sources (he is not mentioned anywhere in the reports) is Bernard Meke, an "African doctor," as Cameroonians who were trained in medicine at the Dakar School of Medicine after studying in Ayos were known.[5] He practiced in Lomié throughout the experiment, where he was the only doctor. Following the war, he was awarded a medal for having "impeccably ensured the functioning of the prophylaxis and maternal and child protection services."[6] He may have had fellow Cameroonian doctors elsewhere in the Medical Region, but if so, they were even more invisible than he was.

The agricultural dimension of the program involved a new category of go-betweens: "monitors" recruited by the regional Société indigène de prévoyance (Native Welfare Society). Created in 1937 as part of a colonial initiative of the Popular Front in Cameroon, these cooperatives aimed to improve farmers' equipment and methods, under the control and supervision of the administration. The Abong-Mbang Native Welfare Society, which until this time had been limited to the few Cameroonian coffee farmers, acted as representatives for doctors in Haut-Nyong, who broadened the group's focus by reorienting it toward the management of village cocoa plantations.[7] Dozens of "monitors" or "supervisory assistants" were recruited for this task. They worked all year long supervising agricultural work in a given sector, overseeing land clearing, sowing, and harvesting according to a schedule set by the doctors; the to-do list for one January was four pages long.[8] They were also in charge of livestock and crop censuses (the reliability of which was checked by regular surveys carried out by the doctors) and the monitoring of the Welfare Society's sheep, as part of the "methodical development of sheep farming in the region" as defined by a long memorandum issued by Dr. David in 1941.[9] According to a principle that was both productive and didactic, each ewe was placed under the care of a family, which became the owner of the lambs born of the ewe, before passing the ewe on to the next family, all of which requires supervision and coordination. But the monitors' role was in fact much broader:

for the use of N.W.S. monitors.

TO BE READ AND EXPLAINED TO THE INHABITANTS
of the villages upon each of your visits

I—medical section—

1—Syphilis—

Anyone who contracts syphilis must come to the dispensary in Messamena immediately for treatment.

Those who are syphilitic must not sleep with those who are not syphilitic.

2—Pregnant women—

Pregnant women must declare their pregnancy from the very beginning.

If a woman who has had syphilis becomes pregnant, she must come to Messamena for treatment for the duration of her pregnancy.

Pregnant women must give birth at the Maternity Ward in Messamena. They must arrive on the date indicated on their ticket.

3—Child care—

Mothers must take special care of their children, feed them well, keep them clean, and ensure they are not cold.

Children must be dressed. Parents must buy clothes and soap for their children. In order to do this, they are to prepare palm kernels, or palm oil, or husked rice, which will be purchased from them at two francs per kilogram.

Children should not have chewing tobacco. Orphans as well as others. Mothers who do not care for their children will be punished. Parents with children who attend school must dress them.

4—Adult care—

The village chiefs must bring people who are ill to Messamena.

Porters designated by the chief will be paid at the Special Agency.

II—administrative section—

1—vagrancy—

It is forbidden to leave the village without the permission of the village chief. If a native leaves the village without permission, the chief must send a capita [assistant to the chief, a henchman given customary police powers] to follow him, catch him, and bring him to Messamena where he will be punished. The chief must also dispatch one of his inhabitants to notify the subdivision commander as soon as possible.

It is prohibited to leave the subdivision without a pass.

All those who apply for a pass must be in possession of a written authorization from their village chief.

Soccer players must work on Mondays, Tuesdays, Wednesdays, and Thursdays. The days reserved for training are Friday, Saturday, and Sunday.

The monitors' handbook contained four more pages in the same vein on livestock and agriculture, written by Dr. Koch in 1942.[10]

The experiment put increased pressure on "native command," as chiefs had not only to guarantee access to the pregnant women, syphilitics, sheep, and plantations of their villages but also, once the experiment began, to carry out labor recruitment, start new crops, renovate huts, and clear their section of the road. It seems rather obvious, but a "real-life" experiment places the burden of proof on those who are the subjects of it, before making them disappear in a table of figures.

The conferring of medals on the most deserving chiefs provides some clues. In 1943, Chief Bangda André of Doumé, superior chief of the Bakoum, received the medal of Native Merit, second class: he "has always shown himself to be an understanding and attentive collaborator in the medico-social intervention pursued in the region." In 1944, a "Belinga woman" received the medal of Native Merit, third class: "An exemplary mother of eleven living children who are a model of good behavior and cleanliness." Chief Dang Nguele, superior chief of the Mvang, "made a great effort in 1942–1943 to restore his villages. Personally owns a herd of sheep in perfect condition and which is constantly growing." Mvomo Joseph, superior chief of the Bikélé in Messamena, "performs his duties in an effective and very active way [. . .], [he] has intensified cocoa and peanut cultivation in his chiefdom." Atangana Mpene, chief of the Njem of Mindourou, "is completely satisfactory although he has long been infected with, and is still being treated for, trypanosomiasis." The chief of the village of Madouma, near Abong-Mbang, was "very devoted and deserving"; he "established important food plantations for the supply of Abong-Mbang." Nicolas Abada, "notable man and court assessor [. . .] of Abong-Mbang has a plantation of five thousand cocoa trees and one thousand coffee bushes."[11] Although it was a ritual in the colonial administration to reward "devoted" chiefs who brought in taxes and appeased the "palavers," it was the adherence to the developmental project of the French doctors that was highlighted in Haut-Nyong, all the more so in that it was demonstrative and quantifiable, as though experimental logic were at the heart of the patron-client relations that formed the basis of colonial peace in Cameroon.

The "chiefs" were recent inventions in eastern Cameroon, dating back to the time when the French occupier demanded that people scattered in the forest settle in resettlement villages along the roads, where they could be monitored, treated, imposed on, and rounded up for forced labor. In this way, the colonial authorities established a hierarchical political structure (as well as a new mode of housing) in societies that had until then been without a "central authority" or "segmentary"—that is, without a formal hierarchy beyond the level of the "household" (composed of an elder and his descendants).[12] Village chiefs, canton chiefs, and finally superior chiefs (ten in Haut-Nyong, each in charge of a canton corresponding to an ethnic entity, itself delimited and fixed by this process) were thus appointed, remunerated, rewarded (and eventually dismissed) by the administration. In the context of the widespread coercion that had marked the region since German times, the chiefs (who had very little that was "customary" about them) often distinguished themselves by their violence, acting as administrative intermediaries for the forced recruitment of laborers and porters.

Several of the superior chiefs in place during the time of the Medical Region were chosen for their education and cordial relations with the French: Joseph Dobo, superior chief of the Bajoué in Messamena, was a schoolteacher who had served as David's secretary before being appointed superior chief in Dr. Koch's subdivision;[13] Effoudou, the superior chief of the Makaa on the left bank of the Nyong (alongside the road between Ayos and Abong-Mbang) had been trained as a "boy-interpreter" in Abong-Mbang.[14] These and other chiefs were the right-hand men of the doctors of Haut-Nyong, with whom they established mutually dependent relationships, which were a mixture of friendship and underhandedness, punishment and reward, and surveillance and dissimulation. When interviewed by Wang Sonné, this is how "Effoudou Rodolphe de Marqueyssac" (named after Jamot's main assistant in Ayos, Henri de Marqueissac), the son of Superior Chief Effoudou, remembered Dr. David, who slept and ate at their home when he came to inspect the area:

WANG SONNÉ: And Colonel David has never had any quarrels with Dad [Chief Effoudou]? Because they say he was very strict.

EFFOUDOU: Very strict! No, he never had any quarrels with Dad. He loved sports. So, when a chief gave him a lot of gifts, through the people, the women who give birth to many children, he gave them a lot of gifts, sheep, shovels, machetes, hoes and all that. He made these tours himself.

WANG SONNÉ: Oh, yeah? Himself!

EFFOUDOU: Himself! Colonel David at the same time as Dad! He went from village to village. He gave gifts to women like that, to men who worked hard at growing crops for market and for local consumption. A woman who gave birth to five children had two or three goats, shovels, machetes.[15]

In Haut-Nyong, the smooth running of the experiment rested on these impulses of generosity. Demonstrations of affection were part of the experimental protocol. For the results, come back after the war.

11. Social Medicine, French Style

The 1930s were the golden age of social medicine experiments. The Haut-Nyong experiment was therefore part of a much broader movement, even though it did not refer to it explicitly. "Social medicine" was a nebulous set of approaches that, to put it briefly, share the conviction that improving the health of populations can be achieved only by changing living conditions, starting with nutrition, work, and housing—what would later be known as the social determinants of health.[1] The idea was somewhat akin to that of the hygienists of the early nineteenth century, who saw almost "no social institution where the intervention of medical understanding is not necessary,"[2] and to those of reformist figures such as the German biologist and doctor Rudolf Virchow, who had given a considerable echo to the ambition of social medicine acting on the primary cause of pathologies, poverty, as opposed to more reductive approaches acting on microbes or the physical environment. "Medicine is a social science," Virchow wrote in one of his most famous aphorisms, "and politics is nothing more than medicine on a grand scale."[3] It should also be noted that this approach corresponds quite well to the vernacular conceptions of "medicine" in nineteenth- and twentieth-century African societies, where therapy was thought to concern the community, the environment, and the body, to the point that it often merged with politics itself.[4]

With such broad aims, social medicine was both everywhere and nowhere, invoked by movements as diverse as socialist medicine, eugenics, and American philanthropy. However, the creation in 1921 of the League of Nations Health Organization was an opportunity for an unprecedented convergence. Social medicine was established as a discipline, promoted internationally by a group of experts who traveled between Europe, the United States, the Soviet Union, China, and the colonial empires of Africa and Asia.[5] Under the leadership of its director, the Polish doctor Ludwig Rachman, the Health Organization was in an "activist mood,"[6] as the historian Sunil Amrith put it, and advocated, in cooperation with the International Labour Office, an aggressive vision of health intervention directly linked to the socioeconomic causes of diseases. The repercussions of the Great Depression reinforced this orientation. The links between poverty, nutrition, education, work, and health became an international field of research and measurement, which was reflected in the development of indicators and the systematic collection of statistics. For the experts associated with the League of Nations, including, in France, Dr. Louis-Ferdinand Destouches, also known as Céline,[7] medicine was a form of applied sociology whose field of intervention must be as broad as possible.

In practice, these realizations applied primarily to rural areas. This marked a turning point, as the urban environment, in the context of cholera epidemics and the fight against tuberculosis, had previously been the natural matrix of public health in Europe and the United States. Doctors and politicians were rediscovering with concern the countryside impoverished by the 1929 crisis, the misery of which could be the source of political unrest, particularly communist unrest. While the emergence of knowledge on nutrition made it possible to establish a chain of causal links between health, food, and agriculture, "rural health" was at the center of discussions and was the subject of several conferences organized in the 1930s by the League of Nations that examined the issue continent by continent.[8]

Pilot projects multiplied from Eastern Europe to China, where interventions based on health education, the establishment of a "health center" offering basic care accessible to farmers, and careful attempts at land reform were being tested. They were the subject of veritable pilgrimages of experts, under the aegis of the League of Nations Heath Organization and the Rockefeller Foundation. The latter, created in 1913 by the American industrialist and oil executive John D. Rockefeller, transposed its almost evangelical approach to hygiene, which had been tested in the Deep South of the United States, by launching health propaganda campaigns in "backward" regions of Europe, beginning with France during the First World War. The Rockefeller Foundation's intervention was not limited to this form of public health campaign, with mobile cinemas and traveling conferences.[9] In Yugoslavia, it participated in the implementation of an ambitious program, led by Dr. Andrija Štampar, which combined educational efforts, networks of health centers, and agricultural co-operatives. Mraclin, near Zagreb, served as a model village (and the setting for propaganda films), where residents recited and applied their lessons on temperance, the cleanliness of streets and homes, water supply, agricultural techniques, and medical examinations. American experts affectionately referred to it as "Dr. Štampar's realm."[10]

An experimental approach was necessary, particularly under the influence of American philanthropic foundations. These foundations exported the model of demonstrations, which were experiments conducted at the neighborhood or rural district level in the United States, where the creation of health centers and education efforts were used both to produce scientific evidence of the effectiveness of the intervention and to publicly convince people, starting with the target populations, of the ability of modern hygiene to create enlightened citizens, prosperous households, and future consumers. The models circulated and spread. Among the health and experimental utopias that were emerging, one of the largest and most influential was the Tsing Hien experiment, conducted by the Chinese government with the support of the Rockefeller Foundation and the Millbank Memorial Fund. The experiment was carried out in a model district of 500,000 inhabitants a few hours by train from Beijing, where a rural reconstruction program combined political reforms, agricultural cooperatives, mass literacy, and the training of village health workers, all under the supervision of administrators and experts from all disciplines.[11] "There is no need to repeat," wrote the Chinese doctor C. C. Chen in one of the reports on the experiment to the League of Nations, "that health is a sign of civilization; the progress of rural hygiene depends as much on masters, engineers, economists, and politicians as it does on doctors. But it is the duty of the latter to expand their horizons and work to improve the health of the human community as a whole."[12]

The European colonial empires took part in this experimental and rural turn in social medicine. The resettlement schemes for trypanosomiasis control in the British colonies did not refer to the ideals of the new rural hygiene, but, as in the Anchau experiment, they used forced population displacement as an opportunity to teach literacy, educate, change agricultural practices, or even reform the organization of societies, and the doctors who oversaw these programs stated this loud and clear.[13] More directly, in the late 1930s, experiments in China and England (including the famous Peckham experiment, in which a team of doctors and social workers literally observed hundreds of families from a southeast London neighborhood in a health center made entirely of transparent glass) inspired programs for Black populations in southern Rhodesia (Zimbabwe) and South Africa.[14] In Natal, from 1940 onward, a charismatic physician couple, Sidney and Emily Kark, led the Pholela experiment, in which a health center offered Zulu populations "community" medicine (the term, very commonly used today, was coined on this occasion) combining education, prevention, care, and training of local health assistants.[15]

Belgian and French achievements in Africa were less avant-garde and rarely claimed to be social medicine as such—figures like Jamot preferred to defend a militarized and purely Pasteurian medicine, targeting a single pathogen—but their scale was almost excessive. The Office du Niger (Nigeria Office), a vast irrigation program created in 1932 in French Sudan, inaugurated the era of white elephants for development and combined agriculture and "homoculture" (sic) with standard housing, care for workers, and demographic monitoring.[16] In the Belgian Congo a private foundation, the Foreami, took charge of the medical system of vast areas chosen to avoid the scattering of resources and test a rapid method of health intervention that the government could then extend to the rest of the territory.[17]

However, the most significant achievement came from Java. Starting in 1933, John L. Hydrick, an American doctor sent by the Rockefeller Foundation, organized a "Demonstration Regency Unit" in the Purwokerto Regency to serve as a test bench and showcase for the Dutch colony's health service. In a context of budgetary austerity, Hydrick insisted on a preventive approach to medicine, based on health education—lessons, films, posters—and, more originally, on the training of local health workers, the *mantris*, whose main function was to relay information from the doctors through home visits. For Hydrick, adaptation to local culture was one of the key points of the new rural hygiene, the only way to ensure the active participation of the population in the behavioral transformation process.[18]

The visit to the model villages of Purwokerto was one of the highlights of the Intergovernmental Conference of Far-Eastern Countries on Rural Hygiene, organized in Bandung by the League of Nations in 1937.[19] The conference brought together experts from all the colonies in the region, as well as from China and Japan. It both revealed and cemented a long series of exchanges between French, British, American, and Dutch colonial physicians from Indochina, Ceylon, Malaysia, Burma, the Philippines, and the Dutch East Indies. As was the case in the fight against sleeping sickness in Africa, the social medicine initiatives of the League of Nations in the Far East were an opportunity for a game of comparison, collaboration, and competition between empires. Intervention paradigms—in this case, that of "rural recovery" through hygiene and peasant agriculture—and shared challenges, such as ignorance to be overcome, lifestyles to be reinvented, and the need to encourage the consent of the people, were exchanged and reinforced. Among the French colonial physicians present at the conference was Pierre Dorolle, a colonial doctor who completed his training at the Pharo in 1925 and spent his entire career in Indochina.[20] He played the role of a broker of ideas in the interimperial medical world and published in 1938 his French translation of John Hydrick's monumental report on "intensive hygiene" in Java. In a long introductory commentary, he saluted the "experimental and realistic spirit" of the program: "Everything is subject to the strict control of experimentation. In terms of hygiene and public education, preconceived notions and a priori theories are not appropriate. It can never be said in advance that a particular method will succeed; it must be tested through experimentation, applying the most vigorous critical spirit to this experimentation. [. . .] [Let us note] immediately the good faith, the truly scientific spirit with which errors are recognized and corrected. It is in this way that some methods, while attractive in some respects, have been completely or partially abandoned."[21]

Experimentation is of course a powerful metaphor, one of the favorite images of colonial administrators when it came to thinking "like an empire,"[22] especially in Africa, a continent that "presents itself as a *living laboratory*, in which the reward of study may prove to be not merely the satisfaction of an intellectual impulse, but by an addition to the welfare of a people,"[23] as Lord Hailey, former governor of Punjab, wrote in 1938. Referring to the colonies as a laboratory was also a means of placing them at the heart of scientific debates in Paris. During the 1930s, Louis Tanon, professor at the Faculty of Medicine, promoted colonial medicine in Paris as an avant-garde science: "Nowhere will [doctors] find a more interesting and newer field of experimentation; nowhere will they be able to appreciate the immediate results of well-understood prophylaxis, nor better understand the efforts that are needed to achieve it. The hygiene of our countries, like pathology, has every interest in drawing inspiration from the experiments carried out in these vast territories, where relatively primitive races live which European civilization has not yet transformed."[24]

But for Dorolle, who was deputy director-general of the World Health Organization (WHO) for nearly twenty-five years, and for other figures who moved through the world of international public health in the 1930s, the reference to experimentation was not only rhetorical. It informed material practices and formed the basis for the international circulation of interventions;

it guaranteed both comparability and adaptation to the "local," which was the mantra of the time.[25]

This leads to a somewhat disappointing conclusion: the Haut-Nyong experiment was not very original, neither in substance nor in form. Almost by definition, most of the utopias inventoried here were led by a charismatic, isolated, and misunderstood expert. The watchwords of the Haut-Nyong doctors were thus not *colonial* in themselves but part of a more general project, as international as it was imperial, in which a very modern definition of development was formulated, conceived of as a real-life experiment.[26]

I am not sure, however, that David and his assistants had read the voluminous scientific output of the late 1930s on "rural recovery." Indeed, they made no reference to it, even though it was precisely what they were trying to do. One of the sponsors of the experiment, Marcel Vaucel, was stationed in Indochina between 1933 and 1938. He was an associate of Dorolle's and may have been welcomed in Hanoi, where he headed the Pasteur Institute, the delegates of the League of Nations who visited Indochina in 1936 to prepare the Bandung Conference. In short, he was certainly familiar with the vocabulary and reveries of rural hygiene, even if it was not his cup of tea. He may have read Hydrick's report on Java, which recommended that colonial health services establish "Demonstration Regency Units" to have "a place somewhere within [their] territory where new materials and new methods can be studied and tested."[27] But whatever its direct or indirect influences, the Haut-Nyong project adhered to a rather rudimentary, though radical, version of the rural hygiene of its time, a variant that was provincial and military, authoritarian and emotional, cobbled together and grandiose. At the League of Nations, they would say, "French style."

12. Life Has Returned

On April 2, 1943, General de Gaulle promoted Dr. David to the rank of lieutenant-colonel-doctor by Decree No. 871.[1] Henceforth, he would be known as "Colonel."

His marks were particularly complimentary. He had demonstrated "intelligence, moderation, ease of adaptation," noted his superior in 1940. "The first results obtained by Major-Doctor David confirm his activeness, his tenacity, and promise a brilliant result." One year later, the director of the Health Service of French Cameroon confirmed these impressions: "The year 1941 was an excellent one in the Haut-Nyong region. [. . .] Major-Doctor David has succeeded, despite many pitfalls, in accomplishing things that are admired by all, even the most biased and malicious. The Health Service of the Colonial Army can only be grateful to him for this, and the interesting information collected will certainly have great scientific value."[2]

The results were "unforeseen," wrote his supervisor in his record book in 1943, exceeding the best expectations. "His fruitful work makes it possible to gather first-rate scientific information and improves the material situation of the Native."[3] Dr. David "truly brought a dying population back to life."[4]

The apotheosis took place one day in September 1943. A large official delegation came from Yaoundé for the inauguration of the Chefdrue stadium, right next to the Residency, which included, among other personalities, the governor of Cameroon, the director of the Health Service, the director of Public Works, the district commander of the neighboring region of Nyong et Sanaga, and their wives. The colonial newspaper *Le Cameroun libre* (Free Cameroon) devoted a long article to this "grandiose sporting event," which was rather unusual as its pages were largely dedicated to the news from the front. They were all seated in the grandstand, decorated in blue, white, and red, discovering "a magnificent stadium surrounded by a running track." They were surrounded by "natives," who had "come in droves." On the program was a huge gymnastics show, performed in front of the grandstand for forty-five minutes by "a thousand children gathered in impeccable order," followed by individual events, "races, jumps, shot put, and javelin throwing," then a parade in song "to the wild rhythm of a drum kit composed of a snare drum and a bass drum." In the afternoon were soccer matches, refereed "in an impeccable manner by Captain-Doctor Koch." Three teams, among the best in the country, came from Yaoundé and Douala. The newspaper commented at length on the matches and supported the Abong-Mbang team, with its players in their yellow star jerseys and black shorts. The team was defeated, though honorably, because it was weakened by a sick player. "Small setbacks at the beginning must be profitable lessons and not causes for despondency." One interlude that was particularly amusing was a match between "miniature" teams, children under twelve lost on the large field, who still managed to score a goal, to the applause of the crowd. The day was a great success, ending with a reception at Dr. David's home. He had never been in such good company: "This inaugural celebration was in every respect and in every detail managed in an absolutely impeccable manner. The players from outside the region found beds and food waiting for them upon their arrival and all felt an atmosphere of friendly cordiality, which is desirable in every sporting event. Unreserved congratulations must be given to the district commander and all his collaborators for general organization, the stadium work, and the 'taming' of some one thousand children."[5]

The people of Haut-Nyong remember other visits, in particular, that of the American Colonel Harry Cunningham, who came in 1941 with General-Doctor Adolphe Sicé on a French Forces inspection mission.[6] The boys did not appreciate being called "boy" by the American until the misunderstanding was explained to them.[7] The children of the region also traveled around the country to demonstrate their talents and those of their "tamer." During the Red Cross celebration in Yaoundé in December 1943, the Têtards d'Abong-Mbang (Abong-Mbang Tadpoles) presented their "group exercises" as a show opener for the soccer game.[8] I imagine David beaming in the grandstand.

The experiment was a success, and the account of its success was ratified less than three years after its launch. While in London in September 1942, Sicé was invited to give a lecture at the International Institute of African Languages and Cultures, a sort of think tank chaired by Lord Lugard, one of the great theorists of British colonialism, who at the time sought to promote international discussions on "the progress and development of the African people" and on "the many problems awaiting . . . postwar Africa."[9] After presenting the experiments on the preventive hospitalization of pregnant women, which allowed children to gain "5 to 600 grams" of birth weight, Sicé was able to indulge himself before the audience:

> We attempted another experiment. It was carried out in a region that had been particularly affected by sleeping sickness and malaria, Haut-Nyong. The demographic situation was so serious that the economic output of the area had lost all value. It was decided to entrust its management and administration to doctors of the Colonial Health Service. The results seem to have exceeded all expectations. Death has stopped decimating villages, the treatment of sleeping sickness and malaria has put an end to the infertility of households, and mother and child welfare measures have, in many villages, led to a sharp increase in the population. Freed from obsession with death, [the population] has regained its self-confidence, regained its liveliness and cheerfulness. In this region, life has triumphed, prosperity has reappeared, man has defeated the forces of destruction.[10]

This satisfied account is the main thing that remains of the Haut-Nyong experiment. David's final report is quite brief, ten pages in total, and I know of only one copy. Dated January 18, 1944, it ends with a summary sheet listing the achievements of the Medical Region, including the 45 maternity buildings built, the 20,000 annual visits to children in their villages, the construction of the leprosy camp, the 1,630 syphilitics identified and treated, the 5 million cocoa trees planted, and the 60 kilometers of roadways suitable for use by motor vehicles built.[11] David does not mention the Star of Abong-Mbang, whose progress was sluggish (I found the trace of a victory against Yaoundé in May 1943, before a "crushing" 7–0 defeat in the rematch in August), but the young soccer players of Haut-Nyong regularly distinguished themselves, even earning the top places in a competition of centers, shoots, and corners held in Douala in 1943.[12]

The brevity of the results seems to have mattered little, as though success was self-evident, or rather as though the main result of the experiment was its very existence, the fact that it had been possible. From early 1944, the experiment thus served as a reference, an example to be reproduced. The circulation of the account created its success, with an obvious though not embarrassing circularity. The Medical Region has proven itself; the proof is that it was used as an example. *Quod erat demonstrandum.*

Colonel David finished his report at the same time that Marcel Vaucel, who became director of the Health Service at the Commission for the Colonies in Algiers, was finalizing the "Plan d'hygiène sociale et d'assistance sanitaire" (Social hygiene and sanitation assistance plan) that he would present at the French Africa Conference in Brazzaville in early February; the two documents are now in the same archive box. Vaucel, promoted to general-doctor after his service in the Free French forces from Cameroon, had become the patron saint of colonial medicine. An accomplished scientist and now a statesman, he was planning the reorganization of health intervention in the French colonies at the end of the war. For the colonial technocrats in Algiers, the postwar period began at the end of 1943, at which time they already had David's report in hand.

On January 30, 1944, General de Gaulle declared the Brazzaville Conference open. The conference brought together colonial administrators and officials of the French Committee of National Liberation to debate the future of the African colonies and the political, economic, and social reforms to be implemented to ensure their "development" (it was at this time that the term began to replace "improvement"). Health was on the agenda, the sixth of twelve points. The ad hoc committee included two doctors.[13] Vaucel, arriving from Algiers with his family, was housed in the premises of the Inspection générale du Service de santé (Inspectorate General of the Health Service); the other doctor, sometimes mistakenly mentioned as the "Director of Cameroon's Health Service," was housed at the hospital. It was Jean Joseph David.

The Brazzaville Conference in 1944 has become a classic in history textbooks. Beyond the somewhat Franco-centric myth of a conference that would have planned the peaceful decolonization of Africa (there should be quotation marks everywhere), the Brazzaville debates in fact imagined the future of the African colonies in the form of a bucolic and reactionary utopia, where reforms would certainly ease some political tensions but above all accelerate the emergence of a prosperous and docile peasant society—and prevent the effects of poorly controlled modernization, where "detribalized" Africans would help the large cities expand.[14] Health intervention played an important role in these projections, both as an allegory of French humanism and as a prerequisite for any social and economic progress. The Brazzaville Conference reaffirmed the primacy of medicine in the colonies geared toward "the development of the race."[15] The conference unambiguously recommended the implementation of "a medical system that preserves and treats not individuals, but the masses."[16]

Vaucel was the inspiration behind this population-based approach, which echoed the discussions on the demographic issue then underway in Algiers in the French Committee of National Liberation among medical experts such as Robert Debré.[17] In this way, the plan presented by Vaucel to the conference, while taking up the postulates of colonialism in the interwar period, provides a snapshot of a moment in French hygiene when it was invigorated by the extraordinary technical innovations developed by the Allied armies, such as off-road vehicles, mass blood transfusion, synthetic antimalarial drugs, DDT (a new insecticide of unprecedented efficacy), and penicillin, the prowess of which was being discovered at the very time of the conference. Algiers, as has often been written, was a "[site] of experimentation for modernity" for the Gaullist state.[18] René Pleven, commissioner for the colonies in the French Committee of National Liberation, put it this way upon his return from Brazzaville: "There is no fundamental difference between the social problems facing Africa and those that will attract Europe's attention in the future. On both continents, it is a question of liberating man from poverty, disease, and ignorance."[19]

Point four of the Brazzaville Declaration of February 5, 1944, is perhaps the best tribute to the posterity of the Haut-Nyong experiment: "For regions exceptionally affected by a social scourge, the temporary use of the formula of the Haut-Nyong Medical Region, which has proved capable of remedying a disastrous situation by giving the chief medical officer the necessary administrative powers, is recommended."[20] During the discussions, Vaucel provided details on the experiment, stating that "if the Haut-Nyong Medical Region has been so successful, it is because Cameroon has spared no expense on the allocation of financial and material resources."[21] On a more technical level, the commission's attention to syphilis, confirmed as in Europe in its status as demographic enemy number one, was based on the "surveys conducted in the Haut-Nyong Medical Region of Cameroon, where all deliveries [were] monitored,"[22] which allowed the weight of "hereditary syphilis" to be demonstrated. The proposed "control of syphilitics modeled on that of trypanosomiasis," with mandatory treatment, systematic record keeping, and "sanctioning of recalcitrants," was also an innovation that had been tested in the Medical Region. The importance given to "medical command" in the report presented at the conference also recalls Dr. David's measures: it was imperative that "doctors [obtain] the necessary authority to summon natives and punish [those who fail to appear]"; at the state level, the authority of a "director-general of public health with broad powers" must be strengthened. The recommendations of the Brazzaville health component were implemented in the following months by a cascade of decrees and memorandums sent from Algiers, notably creating a futuristic mass medical system, the Service d'hygiène mobile et de prophylaxie (Mobile Hygiene and Prophylaxis Service), which generalized the formula of mobile teams experienced in combating sleeping sickness. In more ways than one, Haut-Nyong had been a school of immoderation.[23]

David did not return to Abong-Mbang after the conference. He crossed the Congo River and on February 14 boarded a Sabena flight to Douala. He left Douala a few weeks later for Algiers, where he was seconded to the Political Affairs Service for a few months.[24]

The experiment was replicated starting in 1944 in Oubangui-Chari, where the Haute-Sangha region was entrusted to Dr. Roland Choumara. The formula even attracted a South African doctor from Cape Town, Professor John Fleming Brock, who made a three-month study trip throughout Central Africa at the end of 1944. He saw this as an effective way to ensure that the administration's "red tape" did not hinder efforts to combat sleeping sickness.[25] There are references to the Medical Region, described as a "human reserve,"[26] in the accounts on Free French Africa that appeared after the war; Vaucel and Sicé each wrote one.[27] The success of Haut-Nyong heralded further victories, as an anonymous report on "the achievements of the health service during the war" summarized: "medical regions" could be set up in the last "stains" of sleeping sickness that were still resisting.[28] In January 1945, the Ministry of Information in Paris published a study, "Les réalisations de la France combattante au Cameroun sous mandat français" (The achievements of France at war in the mandated territory of Cameroon), to celebrate the colony's war effort and to affirm that Cameroon "is an integral part of the lands of France." "The Abong-Mbang Medical Region," which was "entirely entrusted, in December 1939, to the administration of doctors," occupies a large part of the chapter on public health. The report includes David's figures—the 60 kilometers of roads, the 5 million cocoa trees, the 9,504 sheep—which proves that his report did make it to Paris. "The trials in the Abong M'bang [sic] medical region are remarkable, from both an administrative and a medical point of view,"[29] according to the summary published by La Documentation française. References to Haut-Nyong were even included in textbooks on tropical medicine: "In areas particularly affected by endemic diseases, the 'medical region' formula, which confers administrative power upon the health service is particularly recommended as achieving the goal of medico-administrative unity to the maximum degree," according to the chapter on sleeping sickness in the 1950s reference manual, published by Flammarion and written by none other than Vaucel.[30]

That's about it. The experiment did not benefit from any real publicity effort, unlike Anchau, where the British experiment being conducted at exactly the same time would become the subject of a film, photographs, and articles published in the *Lancet* and *National Geographic*.[31] The most substantive accounts were, in the end, those of Henri Koch, Messamena's doctor-administrator, who remained in office until December 1945. He wrote several articles, a thick report on agriculture and livestock, and, most important, an "absolutely remarkable" demographic study on his subdivision: 161 pages of statistics and comments that were medical, ethnological, and political all at the same time, "a powerful work that does as much credit to the heart of its author as to his intelligence,"[32] it was said in high places. Koch's studies impressed his superiors, who clearly saw him as an extraordinary young doctor. Captain-Doctor Koch has made "his subdivision into a model subdivision," they said; "a true apostle of the medical faith," he could "be considered an elite colonial doctor."[33] These remarks earned him an official commendation from the high commissioner and a recommendation for the Legion of Honor, but the reports were never published.

In the postwar years, Haut-Nyong was still used as an experimental platform, doubtless because of the quality of the medical and demographic monitoring of its populations. The Messamena subdivision was chosen to test drugs developed during the war by the French firm Spécia (Rhône-Poulenc), which heralded a revolution based on the "chemical prevention" of tropical endemics. In 1947, the district commander organized a "wonderful experiment,"[34] one of the very first trials in Africa of the "premalinization" of children to prevent malaria through the twice-monthly distribution of premaline. In another trial, conducted in February 1948, the inhabitants of Messamena were summoned and separated into two groups, one of which was designated "controls," to test "lomidinization," the administration of a preventive injection of Lomidine against sleeping sickness.[35]

But the Medical Region, still in force according to the documentation and successively directed by Dr. Jean Pape and Dr. Jean Raymond, gradually became normalized while funding decreased. Colonial army doctors were scarce because of the mobilization on the Indochinese front, and the miracle cure of "chemoprophylaxis" seemed to deliver what it promised, rendering the old social medicine obsolete through its effectiveness. In October 1947, the French high commissioner to Cameroon wrote to Vaucel asking him for permission to stop the experiment. The general-doctor did not see a problem with that. He suggested that an "official tribute" be paid to the doctors' work and archived the correspondence with David's final report in box 115.[36]

Major David was appointed district commander. He set to work, reviewed the population and its resources, identified the healthy elements, regulated work, and developed the food supply system. In the most affected areas, he established permanent or periodic consultation centers and, remarkably, he established maternity wards; women agreed to take prenatal rest there, and the newborn child had his identity recorded on a special card, with summary but clear indications, outlining his physical state at birth, weight, height, etc. Hundreds of black infants were registered in this way, allowing them to be seen and followed after their return to the village; they ceased to be strangers whose disappearance was not reported, whose causes of death remained forever unknown. [. . .] David accomplished, in four years, a feat that must henceforth serve as a model for monitoring a black population, studying its evolution, the causes of its failures. Death has stopped decimating the villages of Haut-Nyong, the treatment of sterilizing infections—malaria, trypanosomiasis, syphilis—has put an end to miscarriages and household poverty; the well-considered protection of motherhood and childhood has served mother and child, so that, in many villages, it has finally been possible to note a significant increase in population. Freed from the obsession that is death, it regained its self-confidence, regained, along with its cheerfulness, its taste for work, because David did not hesitate to set up, and even to multiply, work sites.

ADOLPHE SICÉ, "Le rôle social du médecin colonial," *Médecine tropicale*, 1944

13. Colonel David Will Become a General

André Ateba had a lot to tell us. We went to see him one morning in March 2012 at his house, a stone's throw from the prefect's residence, the German prison, and the hospital. There were six of us at his bedside: his wife; Valentin; me; Joseph Owona Ntsama and John Manton, the two historians with whom I was working on the history of Ayos; and the director of the Ayos hospital, Dr. Amougou. Monsieur Ateba was very tired and had been an invalid for several years. He spoke to us lying down, in a deep voice and with long pauses, but his mind was as sharp as ever. For three quarters of an hour he told us about his career, his childhood in Akok-Maka, his nursing studies in Ayos, and his medical and then political careers. Taking the dates into account, I realized that he would have crossed paths with David in Abong-Mbang.

> GUILLAUME LACHENAL: Well, I still have some historical questions to ask. As you are the children of Haut-Nyong, do you remember, in the 1940s, around '43, Dr. David and the Medical Region? Do you remember all that?
>
> ANDRÉ ATEBA: A Dr. David who was here? I was in school, grades 4 and 5, he was a doctor, he even took a man from my village . . .

". . . To be his cook." It was Madame Ateba who finished his sentence for him. Then she began to speak: "I remember, I know I was a little girl, he used to have women taken from the villages to go wait to give birth at the hospital." She went on to talk about the plantain and meat rations that were given to women, and about one of her maternal aunts who often said, "Dr. David, Dr. David." Even though it was just bits and pieces, this was in fact the first time I heard someone recall Dr. David. Then I asked whether "David was loved for that, for this project." Everyone answered, in unison: "Yes, he was good! He did too much!" "He worked hard," Emilienne said, "he was loved for that, yes. Every time they even arrested the lazy chiefs who did nothing, he would come to calm them down and always gave advice. He didn't want Blacks to be bullied. We used to call this 'Black,' you know? We were 'Black' there." Everyone around the bed smiled, nodding their heads. "He was good. There was no nastiness in his leadership. No, no." "He was good," her husband confirmed.

Then he embarked on a rather tortuous story: just out of school, Ateba had been "wanted" in the region when he received results for the competitive nursing exam he had taken because he was absent from his official address at an uncle's house in Doumé—the kind of "vagrancy" that exasperated doctors, reason for immediate punishment. He had to return to Abong-Mbang from Lomié, where he was at the time, to present himself to the administration, exonerate his uncle who was accused of "hiding" him, and obtain his exam results. When he arrived at the district commander's house, the duty officer had warned him: "The commander was nasty this morning."

David, who apparently had his moods, had mornings when one should not go see him. He "scolded Ateba," then softened when Ateba explained to him that he was not "wandering" but rather coming to get his results from the nursing exam; incidentally, he was the only one who was accepted. Ateba continued: "Since whites are meticulous, he pulled [the results] of this competition from his shirt. Just my name. He starts congratulating me, he says: 'How you saved the honor of the region, the Haut-Nyong region! So, you're going to do six months in Ayos and then you can continue on.' He called the duty officer to pick me up and take me to the sub-prefecture for my assignment."

"And the people here remember Dr. David, the people of Abong-Mbang?"

"Yes! Oooh! He's not a person you forget; like me, I'm telling you about him."

Madame Ateba had one more anecdote from when she was a child, the story of a Bulu woman (the ethnic group of South Cameroon) who was looking for her husband, who had been sent on a mission by David to inspect the telegraph line. She could not find him and got angry and was swearing in Bulu, which made the little girls nearby laugh: "'Say, this Colonel David who sent my husband! It was Colonel David who sent my husband to work here, there! You don't want him to work [at home], why?! Where is my husband? Where is . . .' We came only to look at her, to hear 'Colonel David!' 'Colonel David!' Eehh."

And then her husband added: "We even had a song, a song in which we asked that 'Colonel David become a general,' when we did the torchlight processions." At that point, the story became downright mysterious, even though Dr. Amougou immediately explained to me that torchlight processions are a tradition in Cameroon: on the eve of holidays, young people, schoolchildren, and scouts march while singing, torches in hand. I saw one recently in Yaoundé, on the eve of May 20, the national holiday: excited schoolchildren singing in the night with torches, blocking traffic, surrounded by honking horns. Madame Ateba continued: "We took the papayas, put the palm oil in them and the cotton wick. And you would come to the sub-prefecture to get that! The barrel of oil to be shared among the students was at the sub-prefecture. We lit them, everyone had one, we walked in rows with them."

"Were the students the ones who made up the song?"

"Yes, yes! That was us!" There was a long silence. Then, Madame Ateba asked me, "Are you a member of his family?"

That was about it. Before leaving, we removed everything from the living room walls to photograph it, handsome portraits of the young nurse, framed diplomas, and photos of his official ceremonies with red, yellow, and green sashes. There were three of us historians, bent over the table, shooting everything. When the whole team came back a year later, André Ateba had passed away. He had gone back to live his last days at home in Akok-Maka. When he felt his time was coming, he asked to be taken to the hospital in Ayos across the river to the Ateba Ward, "to end it where it all began." Everyone was there, all the students from the nursing and nursing assistant schools, to look after him like a "hero of the hospital."

It was meeting Ateba that made me want to come back to Abong-Mbang to look for the traces of Dr. David, that made me want to write this book, in fact. So, I already had some ideas in mind in 2015, when I went with Valentin to visit Monsieur Evina, who must have met him at school, to hear about his adventurous life. After finishing grade five at the regional school, he went to "find himself," as we say here, in Gabon and Congo, from whence he brought back a perfect Lingala and old rumba records that he listens to on his record player. Evina had a lot of stories about David: he remembered that he loved athletes, that he taught courses at the school at night because there were not enough teachers, that he "wanted everything to move," an expression he repeated to me several times. He had his version of the internment of pregnant women: if, during an inspection in a village, David found your wife in the advanced stages of pregnancy, "you were thrown in prison and your wife was taken to the maternity ward," where she was housed, fed, and visited every day by the doctor.

Evina had a good time thinking back. David was "brutal," "categorical," and ruled by the sjambok and the prison—"without this, he wouldn't succeed in his mission." The men did not like him and were afraid of him, but he found favor in the eyes of students and women. The stories of his conflicts with the whites were colorful: he threatened traders and forced them to build permanent warehouses or risk being excluded from the region. It was much the same story where agriculture was concerned. One day, David went to the Compagnie Française Sangha Oubangi (CFSO) plantation in Mampang, opposite the city on the other side of the Nyong, to warn that he would be back the next day to do an inspection. "Be ready with your record books," he told the plantation owner. David went back, took the record book, and did a roll call of the laborers. He asked each one, "What race are you?" He put the Makaa on one side, the Bakoum on the other, and so on. "He sorted [them]." Then he said to the plantation owner, "Pay me for the Makaa, right now!" He had two trucks take them all to prison to be registered. From there, he organized "convoys" to send them back to their birth villages, with a "recommendation" (Evina insisted on the word) to create a five-hundred-foot cocoa farm, which would allow them to earn as much as working at the plantation. "You're strong guys like that, and you can't create for yourselves?" David said as he sent them away. "He was imposing. Those who didn't do what they were told: to the slammer. And he registered everyone. And he inspected; even if the field was three kilometers into the bush, he would walk there." Liberation, in David's time, was via the jail square.

This style, Evina explained to me, was the result of his "Israeli" side, a race of "hard workers," of "commanders." The village chief of Madouma, Nkoé Valère, whom I interviewed just after Evina, confirmed this: David was "Hebrew, not very French, but he worked for France."[1] He had frightened everyone in Madouma by demanding that new fields be cleared to plant cocoa trees. "What is this? Torture? He came to bully us, he came to make us suffer," people told themselves. They had no choice, in any case; it was "by choice or by force." It was after his departure that people understood, when "other whites" came to buy cocoa and money started coming into the village. When I asked him if David had a "good image," Nkoé Valère answered in his calm, controlled voice: "A very good image. He did a lot of work here. All the old people here know his name. When that white man was here, people ran off into the bush. Because as soon as he arrived, he said that this or that must be done in the village." David would point: 'Him, him, him, go on, take them!'" People were taken without being asked their opinion and would sometimes disappear for several weeks, if the work was far away, on the road. "People thought he was doing harm when really it was for their own good," concluded the chief of Madouma. Little children were named after him who have since grown old, as is often the case when "famous people, Ahmadou Ahidjo, Paul Biya, Colonel David" pass through one's village at the time of one's birth.

"The bad white man became the good white man." Sitting on a bench outside the chief's house, watching children trying to knock mangoes off a tree by throwing sticks, I was thinking back to what Evina had told me that very morning, a kind of summary of the story that had made Valentin laugh quite a bit: "At first, we thought he was an enemy. . . . But when he started to command . . . shit. And when he left, we were crying: Waah, our good white man! Waah."

Looking out over the road in front of his house, with its potholes as big as swimming pools, Evina also thought back to David's time, when the road was wide, one way, with sidewalks that were well maintained. "Those who stayed neglected [things]." The other district commanders "came here to sleep, that's it." When I spoke to him again about the pregnant women, about what he thought of this story, he came to the same conclusion: "Now there's nothing left."

It is never easy to listen to nostalgic stories from colonial times, even if neither Evina nor Nkoé ever used the word *nostalgia*. I am not sure what to do with them. Certainly, they did not seem to miss the authority or the brutality and did not avoid talking about the fear or the "resistance" of the Cameroonians, who ran off at the first opportunity. David, who is said not to even have been French, as though to detach him from colonization as such, had come "for development," the chief of Madouma told me. The word is important, because that is undoubtedly what has been lost: not the colonial order as such, but the possibilities that opened up during the time of the experiment, such as the beginning of the cocoa era, and the first signs of the region's economic takeoff, which would be borne out by small farmers and civil servants until the early 1980s. This trajectory has been interrupted. David's plantations have been reclaimed by wild vegetation, just like the presidential airfield; the price of cocoa has long since collapsed; the maternity ward no longer feeds anyone; and the diplomas obtained in his regional school are no longer worth much.

This observation is widely shared in Cameroon. Nostalgia is first and foremost a criticism of the present, even if it is not limited to it. For example, "This Cameroon is rotting," diagnosed Koppo (a Yaoundé rapper with a Doc Gynéco sound that we listened to on Valentin's USB key) before concluding:

"Back, guys, that's the only future."[2] It is the very possibility of projecting one-self into the future that has been lost along the way: "The police, the military are the new model, and not the doctors; so the kids want to be bandits, otherwise they'll end up selling beans or skewers."[3] Seen from Abong-Mbang, David's time is not a paradise lost, a golden age; what they miss is not a state but rather a movement, a moment of progress, reform, and transformation, in which "everything was moving," as opposed to a present that lasts forever, motionless like the trucks in the hospital garage, impermeable to time like the president (Paul Biya, since 1982). The nostalgia that comes across in stories about David is a nostalgia for the future, for moving forward, for simply being included in the story.

It was almost disappointing not to hear an outright denunciation of the doctors' methods, their records, their convoys, their police, their prison. I would have to come back for a "totalitarian" interpretation of the "exceptional measure that is the Medical Region,"[4] as David put it. It is tempting to describe the experience as a pure form of disciplinary power, somewhat worrying in this respect, based on a total supervision of populations, in the same way that Michel Foucault found in the plague-stricken town of the eighteenth century the "utopia of the perfectly governed city."[5] Such a "Foucauldian" reading causes a little shiver. It would have allowed me to paraphrase for entire pages the great scientific-colonial "grid" that enclosed leprosy patients, sleeping sickness patients, women, and workers and to make a rather easy criticism of medicine as a tool of social control.[6] Seen from this angle, the story of Haut-Nyong would have been fascinating, but it would have also been almost unintelligible to those who lived it.

Wang Sonné had likely not read Foucault or was unaware of how essential and "fashionable" the author was to historians of health in America and Europe. His interpretation of David's time in Haut-Nyong does not evoke any tropical gulag but rather directly echoes the nostalgia of the people he had interviewed, a nostalgia for this form of bio-political "top-down" government that seems so undesirable to us. Perhaps he was talking about himself, about what he was going through: the collapse of the state being caused by "structural adjustment," the lost generation of students in the 1990s, the devaluation of the CFA franc, the tenfold reduction of teachers' salaries, the "situation" that was battering his country. He presented his work on June 1, 1996, at the convention center in Genoa, during a session on "socio-cultural approaches to disease." I imagine he was a little lost among the presentations on health and family in Uzbekistan, Soviet neurosurgery, geniuses in Laos, and the "post-modern body."[7] He published his results in the conference proceedings afterward, a sort of unfindable potpourri in which researchers like Wang Sonné and me publish most of our work: "Looking very closely, the Medical Region created a strong dynamic [. . .] . All the people of Haut-Nyong were able to regain their health. [. . .] And the results recorded in less than a decade in terms of livestock, subsistence crops, and cash crops were promising."[8] After having completed an impressive amount of research, Wang Sonné had a progressive interpretation of the experiment, which he viewed as the starting point of a development trajectory which has since been interrupted; as evidence that a "vast spatial planning operation" had been possible; as evidence that "any reductive approach to health problems seems doomed to failure" and that only a comprehensive, ecological, or social approach could succeed.[9]

For my part, I preferred not to have an opinion at this stage, not to risk a diagnosis of failure or success. First, because I believed that the experiment resembled neither a colonial version of Foucault's *Discipline and Punish* nor a successful development project, but something more banal, mediocre, less coherent and less reasonable at the same time, in which powerlessness, spite, and even delirium had their place. And second, because the question I had been asking myself since the beginning, as historians often do, was more a question of form:[10] how should this story be told? Which tense should be used? What plot should be followed? Which unifying themes should be employed? And, at this point, I wanted to tell the story without imposing a structure, to be faithful to the mixture of wonder and fascination that the figure evoked, and which is in fact a recurrent tone in African memories of colonial violence.[11]

I had insisted that Evina tell me if, by chance, there was not something special that people did regarding David, an alias or nickname they gave him, a gesture of his that they mimicked, a song, maybe? I knew the answer, and so did Valentin, so we insisted.

After a silence, he replied: "We, the students, had a song when we were going to soccer. Every Sunday, we had to travel to play Doumé, Messamena, all that." Evina sang on key, to the tune of a military march that hits the high notes:

Colonel David will become a general
Colonel David will become a general
Colonel David will become a general
All the honors to him!

We all applauded. While singing, the verses came back to him, to the tune of "L'Alphabet scout" ("The Scouts' Alphabet"), which starts "One day the troop set up camp, amp, amp, amp":

Abong-Mbang, Mbang, Mbang, Mbang,
We're always happy, py, py, py,
[Down with?] the lazy, zy, zy
We're always happy, always happy.

He then got confused, but the next verse talks about government, vagrants, and idlers. "When David heard that, he was happy. We said, Colonel David, you're going to be a general. Because he came here as a major and he left as a colonel."

I asked: "And do people know what happened to him?"

"That, we don't know."

14. The Missionaries' Nightmare

"Major David [. . .] has gone completely mad."[1] By the end of 1941, the fathers of the Catholic missions in Haut-Nyong had had enough. "The district commander, David, [. . .] is certainly the most false and unbelieving man we have had in Abong-Mbang. [. . .] What a sad situation, and a dangerous one at the same time."[2] For the missionaries, the health utopia was turning into a nightmare. This was in part because Dr. David was of "vile character,"[3] but above all because his experimental policy was in direct competition with the very heart of the missionary enterprise: the daily management of bodies and souls.

In Lomié, the fathers lamented: when he was not summoning people on the Feast of the Ascension, David "purposely chooses Sundays to come and see six hundred people [for a medical visit]: pregnant women, syphilitic patients, and others. Obviously, this prevents all Christian or catechumen personnel from coming to Mass."[4] And when he came back in September 1942 to carry out his inspections, "it is always on Sunday!"[5] In Messamena, the subdivision commander, Dr. Koch, was not liked any better. He rounded up the students from the mission's schools to fill his own classes and make them work in the fields.[6] He even incarcerated two of the mission's teachers who were touring around, accusing them of "leaving their village."[7] One did not mess around with vagrancy in the Medical Region.

The surveillance and internment of pregnant or syphilitic women competed with the *sixa* of the missions. The *sixa* (a pidgin English deformation of "sister") were disciplinary institutions, somewhere between boarding schools and labor camps, where Christian women (so-called fiancées) spent many long months before their marriage. The "palavers" multiplied, with doctors accusing the *sixa* of, for example, sheltering women infected with sleeping sickness, who would normally be placed under house arrest in their village.[8] The Pétainist sympathies of some missionaries did not help. One of them despaired, "When will the reign of the Freemasons be swept away?"[9] This was a recurrent concern among missionaries.[10] They got annoyed with the health assistant Poinsignon (a "little white boy" whose medical training occurred on the job), who was in charge of searching for cases of sleeping sickness. He was "driven against the mission by Mr. David." Who did he think he was, this "slave to an emperor"?[11] The bishop of Yaoundé, Monsignor Graffin, was called on to help. He recommended moderation: "We do not have to enter the private lives of administrators, as long as there is no rape or other violence committed against our Christians."[12]

In the eyes of Catholic fathers, Haut-Nyong was a peripheral territory. Their main competitor in the area was the American Presbyterian Mission. In the early 1930s, this mission set up a hospital in Nkol-Mvolan, a hill a few kilometers from Abong-Mbang, which apparently enjoyed an unparalleled reputation in the region. Incidentally, the reports of the doctor-administrators were written as though this hospital did not exist. Haut-Nyong remained on the fringes of the missionary miracle that took place between the two wars in the central part of the country, around Yaoundé: more than 200,000 baptisms on Beti lands, which had been completely converted to Catholicism in two decades.[13] The region had a bad reputation—sleeping sickness, anthropophagy, and witchcraft—and the language barrier discouraged Cameroonian catechists from the Catholic bastions of central and southern Cameroon (Ewondo, the lingua franca of Mass and the nurses of the Jamot mission, was poorly understood in Haut-Nyong). It was not until 1930 that the Catholic missionaries—that is to say, the Spiritan fathers of the Congregation of the Holy Spirit—established their base in Doumé, the former German stronghold, from whence they intended to spread throughout the eastern part of the country. This was a means of playing cat and mouse with the administration, which had transferred the regional capital of Lomié (the other major center in the German period) to Abong-Mbang in 1927. There were only a handful of Spiritans and their presence remained discreet. In Abong-Mbang, Masses were celebrated only on major feast days and the Messamena mission was not created until 1937 in Labba, a peninsula separated from the administrative post by a large swamp.[14] Conflicts with the administration were by definition systematic as the missions in the region had developed by offering (relative) protection to converts living in the "Christian villages" around the station. These converts could thereby hope to escape "administrative service," the euphemism for forced labor, in exchange for participation (not always remunerated, however) in the mission's work. The *sixa* posed the same problem: the "fiancée schools" served both as a refuge and a coveted labor pool (in 1939, Doumé's had 184 women, who, for example, collected clay for the brickworks).[15] The doctors viewed this as a competition in terms of hygiene education, a hazardous intervention in terms of its demographic consequences, and inappropriate interference with health monitoring.

In such a context, the skirmishes between missions and colonial doctors had nothing exceptional about them.[16] The Cameroonian writer Mongo Beti would give a parodic account of the raid carried out by the service responsible for the fight against sexually transmitted infections on the *sixa* of a Catholic mission in his novel *Le Pauvre Christ de Bomba* (The Poor Christ of Bomba; 1959).[17] Dr. Koch's raid on the *sixa* in Messamena does not seem to have been too sad an affair either, according to the memories of a former seminarian interviewed by Wang Sonné: "Sometimes [Dr. Koch] would even arrest the women of the *sixa*—'women who did nothing, lazy women.' [. . .] Oh yes, they came to have the *sixa* arrested, all those women there: 'What are these women doing here? Missionaries are not allowed to have prisons! What are they doing here?' Things like that!"[18]

The "affairs" were never-ending and were inflamed by Koch's "police," locally recruited guards who zealously applied themselves to maintaining order. Father Stintzi, during his Sunday walk on the new road, found in February 1943 "ten schoolchildren tied up like common criminals, [whose] crime consisted only in attending the school of the Catholic mission."[19] Other quarrels concerned a dead goat (one did not mess around with goats in the Medical Region), incarcerations without reason, the presence of leprosy patients at Mass, and, always and again, women "refugees" (the word is revealing) at the mission, whose return was demanded by fathers, uncles, husbands, and doctors.[20]

15. The Dark Waters of the Haut-Nyong

Leafing through the missionaries' letters, one gets the sense that this was something more than mere squabbling, that something was not right in Haut-Nyong, that the utopia was not turning out as intended, that the doctors were losing their way. One gets the sense that there is another side to this story, a dystopic one this time.

Hints of trouble appeared even in the doctors' reports. Barely two years after his arrival, David seemed to be worried. "The reduction of European administrators has reached its limit," he wrote, and risked "the definitive failure of the 'Haut-Nyong experiment.'"[1] Of the six doctors present at the beginning of the experiment, only three remained in 1943: David, Koch, and Pape, who took over the Doumé subdivision.[2] The others had left the experiment. Dr. Lagarde is buried in Ayos, where he died in March 1941 of an intestinal obstruction. His tomb, adorned with the Lorraine cross, is next to Jamot's stela. A main wing of Yaoundé's central hospital, still standing today, would later be named for him. The final notes about him in his personnel file did not foretell such a fate: what had struck his superior about him was "his total absence of personality, his nonchalant appearance, his lack of authority, and his apathy."[3] Captain-Doctor Gailhbaud volunteered "to campaign" in 1941, in all likelihood to leave an assignment to which he had not, wrote Marcel Vaucel in his personnel file, "imparted [. . .] the new direction it should already have taken on the social level," allowing whatever was "easy" to happen, owing to his lack of "drive and enthusiasm."[4] David made his name disappear from the reports. Other doctors briefly passed through the region before being posted elsewhere or leaving for the front, in a game of musical chairs. Personnel records tell us that Jean Joseph David would remarry, choosing the wife of one of these doctors, Captain-Doctor Perves, as his bride, something the priests must not have appreciated. For the three doctor-administrators, the colonial assignment dragged on with no replacement in sight.[5]

Medications were lacking, including the arsenicals required to treat syphilis. Forced to economize, the doctors had to dust off the "old" mercury and bismuth treatments, which were more toxic and less effective. Budget cuts led to difficult decisions. For example, David's plan called for the compulsory internment, for one month of treatment, of all syphilitic patients living more than one day's walk from a dispensary. How could such a measure be applied, which was strict (there were disciplinary measures for the recalcitrant) but above all costly, since hundreds of patients had to be housed and fed? Dr. David proposed a radical solution to his assistants: turning the dispensary into a work camp: "In order for you to be able to continue in your task despite the present difficulties, you may exceptionally engage as administrative laborers the syphilitic men undergoing treatment. The statutory deduction from their wages will enable you to feed them. As for the question of housing, it can easily be solved by the quick construction of a few additional huts made of mats and bamboo."[6]

Putting patients to work became a widespread practice. People suffering from sleeping sickness and leprosy became laborers and were mobilized to clear the brush surrounding water sources ("agronomic prophylaxis" to eliminate tsetse flies) and to clear the site of the future regional leprosy camp. The "big kids" were mobilized for coffee plantations, to allow the women to devote themselves to domestic tasks and subsistence farming.

In fact, the doctors faced an old and unsolvable problem, which was the reason for their role as administrators of the region, and which they helped make even more explosive: the problem of labor, or, as the Germans had said, "die Arbeiterfrage."[7] A little recap is in order.[8] The lack of men had been endemic since German times. In addition to the effects of violence, the rubber boom, and sleeping sickness, hundreds of men were taken to serve as porters, and hundreds more were deported to serve in the plantations in southwest Kamerun. When taking power in a ravaged region, where fleeing into the forest or flooded areas was a survival tactic, the French administration immediately faced a lack of available workers. The villages were empty, taxes or benefits in kind were delivered only at the cost of constant police pressure, money was not circulating, and the region seemed definitively resistant to all economic life, something the administrators attributed to the laziness and apathy of the local ethnic groups. The French colonial government nevertheless dreamed of rubber and continued to impose quotas on the population, even though the rubber was literally worthless following the development of rubber plantations in Southeast Asia. In 1927, the General Agency for the Colonies congratulated itself on deliveries from the Mbalmayo railway and the Lomié and Doumé roads, making Abong-Mbang the hub of the "rubber region,"[9] which from this point forward would be directly linked to the world by the Nyong. However, the economic situation, further aggravated by the general collapse of prices following the 1929 crisis, remained at a standstill until the mid-1930s. Coffee cultivation, after several attempts supervised by the colony's agricultural service, changed the situation, generating enthusiasm among villagers, European traders, and especially the Compagnie forestière Sangha-Oubangui (Sangha-Oubangui Forestry Company) (CFSO), one of the major concessionary companies in French Congo, which had extended its activities centered on the rubber trade to eastern Cameroon in the 1920s.[10] The CFSO owned a former German rubber plantation directly on the Nyong River in Atok, between Ayos and Abong-Mbang, which would produce dozens of tons of coffee as early as 1934. The CFSO acquired another coffee plantation in Mampang, on the shore immediately opposite Abong-Mbang, and other European plantation owners, "private individuals," followed suit and cleared thousands of hectares to plant coffee trees throughout the region, expropriating entire villages as they went along, ordering the inhabitants to move into "native reserves" created in 1935.[11] Initially enthusiastic (favoring the European plantation owners over the villagers, who were also attracted by the economic profitability of coffee), the administration quickly realized that the expansion of plantations further complicated the issue of labor. At harvest time, the situation literally turned into a manhunt.

From 1937 onward, the situation became quite critical, to the point of causing concern in Yaoundé and Paris, where Marius Moutet was the minister of colonies of the Popular Front.[12] The solution found was essentially to tighten controls by instituting the "requisition" of populations in berry-picking season to prevent the berries from rotting on the bush and increased repression of "vagrancy" (i.e., attempts to flee the roundups).[13] However, a series of decrees issued in 1937 marked an attempt at reform or appeasement,[14] which implicitly revealed the dramatic nature of the problem. These included issuing a moratorium on new concessions; creating a Regional Labor Office, intended to centralize plantation owners' requests and distribute the people rounded up under mandatory recruitments to chiefs; establishing native welfare societies to help small farmers; banning the movement of workers into and out of Haut-Nyong; and, of course, reaffirming support for the intervention of doctors, the only people capable of really solving the underlying "human problem." In short, the long-awaited "improvement" turned into an open confrontation. At a time when France had just ratified the International Labour Office's Forced Labour Convention, the administration was forced to make impossible decisions to protect workers from exploitation by plantation owners and affirm the "freedom" of labor, all while reinventing its own system of mandatory "service" to pursue its goals.[15]

Dr. David thus found himself in command of a territory where tensions were high, which disarmed colonial power at the very time that something was finally happening, "a subdivision decimated by sleeping sickness, bled dry by exodus and the growing demands of European plantation owners,"[16] David wrote in one of his first accounts at the end of 1939. The emergence of spatially fixed, productive, taxable, and controllable village communities remained the objective to which all the doctors and administrators aspired, but the rise of large coffee plantations, which provoked the comings and goings of "miserable and capricious" workers, manipulated by "merciless recruiters and continually evading their obligations," was leading to the precise opposite, wrote David upon arriving: a country of "pitiful"[17] labor camps and "ghost villages [. . .] overgrown with brush."[18]

The question of labor was like a red cape being waved at the doctors, who continued to level accusations without fully understanding that they were facing something stronger than themselves, that they were choreographing their own failure. David attacked the European plantation owners in the region, who were accused of exploiting the population, promoting the emergence of a local proletariat, and flouting the authority of doctors.[19] As soon as he took up his duties, he worked, by repeatedly sending letters, to obtain from two settlers the back pay they owed to their laborers. In May 1940, he summoned the fourteen plantation owners in the region to Abong-Mbang for a meeting on the labor issue, but only seven of them made the trip. Resolutions adopted purely for the sake of form still provoked "a most strongly supported opposition."[20] In 1942, several plantation owners, including the president of the Regional Union, still did not bother with a minimum wage or an employment contract, and doctors' directives on housing, social work, and medical care for workers evidently went unheeded. The flames continued to be fanned. During a dinner, Dr. Koch caused a stir by calling plantation owners and mine operators "gangsters,"[21] which led to the governor conducting a discreet investigation.

Because the labor shortage was widespread, subsistence crops were neglected and the doctors had great difficulty finding able-bodied men to carry out their "administrative work," as they preferred to work for the plantation owners. The cause of the problem was an unfortunate decree issued in 1937 that stated, "In Cameroon, labor is free."[22] For David, this "declaration in accordance with our principles [. . .] nevertheless constitutes the gravest of errors as, in Haut-Nyong, where manpower is scarce, the interpretation of it has caused confusion and disorder."[23] David argued that it was therefore necessary to put an end to the "flawed principle of freedom of labor" and give the administration complete control over the recruitment and movement of laborers.[24] An order was issued on November 23, 1941, requiring all hiring to be approved by the district commander, and doctors redoubled their efforts to control movement and require everyone to remain where they lived, including through incarceration.[25] Similar measures were taken in other regions of Free French Africa in the name of the war effort, but Haut-Nyong took an original approach to this by transforming it into an emancipatory principle.[26] Forced labor appeared to be the last resort for colonial humanism. Undoubtedly, even if it was above all a question of getting one's hands on the few workers available, for whom "free" hiring by plantation owners was the only way to escape compulsory service, from the workers' point of view, there was never any question, even in the time of the Popular Front, of being free to *refuse* work.

So much for utopia, which had become a succession of bloody conflicts and realizations of powerlessness. It is not even possible to know whether the efforts of the doctors bore fruit in terms of demographics. The statistics seemed to be a source of embarrassment for them. After 1942, they disappeared from the reports. Infant mortality rates fell in the first year but were no longer calculated thereafter. The demographic assessment was postponed. To see a real "rise in the social level of the locals," it would be necessary, said the first report, to wait "a certain time." The evolution of the total population is not known, but there were fears that 1942 would see a "poor demographic balance."[27] Data tabulated after the experiment ended would in fact suggest a continuous decline in population.[28] The doctor-administrators counted the deaths that occurred on the roadwork sites they managed themselves. Epidemics of pneumococcal disease, a disease that had never been a target of colonial medicine, devastated entire villages.[29] One in two child deaths was caused by "illnesses of the lung," a broad category that eluded the medicine of the time.[30] At the end of 1942, model villages still did not exist "anywhere."[31] The construction of the leprosy camp only began in 1944. The Haut-Nyong experiment did not take place.

16. Rubber for the Emperor

Beginning in 1940, a dark shadow gradually spread over the forests of eastern Cameroon: that of the world conflict, which devastated Central Africa in its entirety. The establishment of the Medical Region coincided with the transition to the war economy.

The harvesting of latex resumed, after having been largely abandoned since 1915. World rubber prices, at their lowest during the interwar period owing to the development of rubber plantations in Southeast Asia, exploded with the loss of Malaysia, the Dutch East Indies, and French Indochina. Faced with an impending shortage, the Allies stockpiled strategically, intensifying research on synthetic rubbers and lowering speed limits on American roads to limit tire wear.[1] African rubber, which was extracted in forests from different species of vines and shrubs by itinerant harvesters, became essential despite its mediocre quality; in it, Free France and the Belgian Congo discovered an unexpected economic and strategic resource.[2] The forests of eastern Cameroon, where *Funtumia elastica* were numerous, were put to use.

The doctor-administrators had an ambivalent view of this new economic situation. In going from one franc per kilo before the war to twelve francs in 1944,[3] rubber was a real windfall, one which the local populations knew how to take advantage of. It should be recalled that the history of rubber in Africa since the nineteenth century, apart from the terrible "Red Rubber" episodes in the regions managed by concessionary companies, also testifies to the pragmatic adaptation of African harvesters and traders to the evolution of world prices, and thus to an integration into the international economy that the colonial powers simply "parasitized" by taxing it through levies and pure and simple predation.[4] The doctors in Haut-Nyong, whose economic policy aimed to accelerate the influx of cash, understood that the harvesting of rubber, along with that of palm oil—the prices of which were booming at a comparable rate—was the only means by which Cameroonians would be able to pay taxes while waiting for cocoa production to bear fruit. Faithful to their interventionist ambitions, the doctors therefore organized the harvest by entrusting it to specific ethnic groups,[5] and devoting the entire Lomié subdivision, the most "remote" area of the region and one in which the population had been masters of latex harvesting and preparation techniques since German times,[6] to it. Their official objective was to limit the impact of this godsend, which would "not withstand the end of hostilities,"[7] on the economic organization of the region. The demand for rubber, explained Dr. David, "dangerously revives the native's taste for long walks in the forest."[8] The harvesting of wild latex required long journeys, sometimes experienced as moments of freedom outside of colonial space-time.[9] The settlers described these movements of the harvesters as "wandering,"[10] and the term was in fact a fairly accurate description. The botanical knowledge and technical expertise required to harvest latex largely escaped the colonial experts. It was truly a way of life, in exact opposition to the wise peasantry that doctors dreamed of seeing develop in model villages. David feared a "general return to nature."[11] The missionaries, for their part, were worried about the money that was pouring in, which was "leading our people to their downfall." "What a fortune this rubber is leaving in the region and [it must be said] that it will be put to such bad use," wrote one father in Lomié.[12]

Even though it attempted above all to direct local initiatives, the compromise chosen by the administration in having a few tribes specialize in harvesting was not without brutality. Increasing quantities were required starting in 1942, at the express request of the governor,[13] and the use of coercion was becoming more systematic; incidentally, this was the case in the entirety of Gaullist Africa, as the Canadian historian Eric Jennings described in an edifying book.[14] The missionaries of Lomié denounced this in their diaries: "Very little assistance at the offices because the subdivision commander sends everyone out to [harvest] the rubber."[15] In 1943, "all the men are in the forest [. . .], sixty-two tons [of rubber] at the market on January 30. No one at Mass."[16] In 1944, the subdivision commander in Lomié cracked down after a poor harvest: "Everyone is out [harvesting] rubber because [the subdivision commander] used strong-arm tactics: all the [canton and village] chiefs in prison, the others are afraid."[17]

The doctors and missionaries were well placed to see the first effects of the region's economic development. "The other event," added a Lomié missionary in his 1943 chronicle, "is the ravages of sleeping sickness. Many cases are detected by health workers. In Pohendoum alone, more than a dozen have been discovered."[18] The doctors confirmed this in their health report for that year: an outbreak has just begun in Pohendoum, the village that "gives asylum to forest rubber harvesters."[19] The link between the harvesting of rubber and sleeping sickness had been known since the beginning of the century. It is present in African accounts of the disease and had posed unsolvable dilemmas for colonial administrations.[20] Latex-producing trees grow mainly along rivers and swamps, which are the primary habitat of tsetse flies; the permanent search for new harvesting sites and the provision of food to harvesters by women required crossing infested areas; and the convergence of people during tax collections or major market sales facilitated transmission. Everyone was warned: the "rubber harvest was, as we know, one of the biggest factors in the spread of trypanosomiasis," wrote Colonel Millous in 1937 after his stay in Ayos. "Rubber destroyed the populations it once enriched."[21]

Colonial doctors were confronted with the most painful of paradoxes, even if it was never explicitly formulated: the sleeping sickness epidemic, whose control was the raison d'être and the founding myth of the Medical Region, marked the failure of the project. And even worse, its resurgence was caused in part by the doctors' own actions. Sleeping sickness figures, however, had shown a region-wide decline since at least 1935. Between 1937 and 1939, before the "medical command" was instituted, the incidence of the disease (the number of new patients per year in relation to the total population) had fallen by almost 50 percent each year. The decline had continued, slowing, between 1940 and 1942. However, in 1943, the incidence rebounded from 0.17 percent to 0.29 percent, then to 0.34 percent in 1944, 1.29 percent in 1945, and finally to 4 percent in 1946, a figure rarely recorded even at the height of the epidemics of the 1920s.[22] Meanwhile, the harvesting of rubber in the Medical Region increased tenfold between 1940 and 1943, reaching over 400 tons and likely increasing further in 1944 and 1945,[23] at a time when American imports of African rubber amounted to 35,700 tons, compared with 7,300 tons in 1940.[24]

To the painful effects of the rubber boom were added the consequences of soaring world ore prices, which revived mining exploration and exploitation in Cameroon (and throughout Central Africa).[25] The Medical Region was involved in this, since it was discovered that the alluvial sands of the Nyong

River contained rutile, a titanium oxide used as a white pigment for paints and to produce metallic titanium, which is used as an alloy in special steels. Its extraction was traditional, slow, and difficult: it consisted of digging, rinsing, crushing, and sifting gravel.[26] The rutile rush disheartened Dr. David, who saw his few remaining workers leave for the mining sites scattered along the river, an area notorious for its tsetse flies. Dr. Koch, who we can imagine was appalled, wondered by what miracle the discovery of rutile had caused the "acute manpower problem" to disappear, so numerous were the miners.[27] Two thousand tons of rutile were produced in 1944,[28] making Cameroon the third-largest producer of ore in the world, after the United States and Australia. According to my calculations, the rutile of the Nyong accounted for 10 percent of global production at the time.[29] The irony of the story is that the discovery of this deposit would be celebrated as one of the Colonial Medical Corps' contributions to the "improvement" of Cameroon, as it had been two colonial pharmacists, Le Floch and Dufour, who had identified it during the war.[30]

The "awakening" of sleeping sickness, only two years after the entry into force of the emergency regime, was aggravated by the doctors' own major projects. It was in the vicinity of one of the last known outbreaks of sleeping sickness at the time, in the forest behind Madouma, that David chose in 1942 to build the future regional leprosy camp. From 1943 onward, "laborers" were sent to the construction site, where they contracted the disease. Because of the labor shortage, all the laborers were in fact leprosy patients themselves, brought in from other leprosy camps in the region. When they returned to their original camps in 1945, the leprosy patient laborers caused the "appearance of a new and significant outbreak [of sleeping sickness] at the Messamena leprosarium," which spread to the neighboring village, the administrative center, and the Catholic mission. What followed was even more terrible. When the famous Madouma regional leprosy camp (in Kwoamb) finally opened its doors in 1946, it was decided that all leprosy patients in the region would be transferred there, definitively this time. But, as the Health Service report stated, "many lepers who had become aware of the previous year's contamination in Madouma fled; the Messamena outbreak spread further and new small outbreaks were spread everywhere at random wherever these lepers with sleeping sickness stopped while on the run,"[31] which demonstrates, incidentally, a lucid resistance on the part of the leprosy patients to the generous intentions of the doctors. The story would be extraordinary if it did not explain the appearance in Messamena of one of the most severe epidemics in Cameroon's history.[32]

As for the final outcome of the medical administration experiment, it can undoubtedly be said that it was a failure, all the more painful because it left doctors powerless. As Vaucel wrote in 1940, the Medical Region was supposed to put an end to the latent conflict between the Health Service and the colonial administration. However, by entrusting the Health Service with the command of the region, the formula deprived doctors of their main resource to explain their difficulties, and of the historical basis of their professional ethos: the criticism of the "lice" of the administration.[33]

To hell with those who see in these doctors only midwives, pediatricians and syphilologists, and in these administrators only incompetent usurpers.

Doctors, they are judges, builders, surveyors, breeders, farmers; they become these things in spite of themselves, since in the current poverty of our time, the qualified personnel and equipment essential to their action cannot be made available to them.

CAPTAIN-DOCTOR KOCH, "Poste médical de Messamena: Enquête démographique," March 1945

17. "Here We Are the Masters"

There was something desperate in the Haut-Nyong utopia. There was, of course, a layer of sadness, a war machine devouring men and rubber that descended on the region as it did in the rest of Gaullist Africa, to which the African populations would "pay a heavy price," an inoffensive euphemism that has nevertheless been forgotten by the official histories of Free France.[1] But there was also a more specific and personal feeling, which can be read in the colonial doctors' own writings, a feeling of being torn between denial, bitterness, and rage.

"For many years, I have not signed a labor request without feeling a real physical embarrassment, without having the impression I was making a mistake," said Captain-Doctor Koch before leaving his post in Messamena in 1945. Koch knew his way around road construction sites: "one cannot," even if one was in perfect compliance with the regulations, "avoid overworking the workforce." The practice of making laborers "walk around under the sun for eight hours a day with a basket of soil on their heads" should be stopped. A schedule of "one morning of work per day" should be imposed. It should be decreed that "the native will be given rest." In this way, "a few human lives" could be gained, concluded Koch at the end of his demographic study on the subdivision of Messamena,[2] because the project he led, which was one of the most tangible achievements of the Medical Region and which earned him a medal and promotion, had cost a great many. He provided the estimate himself at the beginning of his report: some two hundred more deaths in 1942 due to pneumococcal epidemics during the construction of the road and especially the dike on the Log Mafog, the tributary of the Nyong: "50,000 cubic meters of embankment," said Koch, without converting it into baskets of earth. Since 1933, the year in which he began collecting data, the mortality rate had never been so high in Messamena as it was in 1942. The unique scale of his study (five years of demographic monitoring, more than six thousand women examined and interviewed, with the bonus of a superb economic and ethnographic monograph) would delight the medical-military hierarchy. However, its content remains unclear: the doctor himself was aware of his own contribution to the mortality rate, without anyone really understanding whether he was pleased with his diagnosis, mourned the dead, or both.

The entire history of public health, as the anthropologist Didier Fassin has pointed out, is a meditation on failure.[3] The real-life experiments of social medicine never work, and this is not news to anyone. The most comprehensive study on the history of public health in France is subtitled *L'utopie contrariée* (Utopia thwarted). This is not by chance: lamentation is the literary genre par excellence of nineteenth- and twentieth-century public health entrepreneurs.[4] The work of the historian is not, therefore, to identify the gap between the great ambitions, the beautiful images, and the desire for order and reason and the necessarily thwarted, imperfect, even detestable "reality." It is rather to determine how the acknowledgment of failure founded practices, criticisms, emotions, subjectivities; to consider the positivity of failure—that is, what it produces in the situations in which it is named.

Doctors are very good at admitting their helplessness. In fact, it is even one of the specialties of their profession, although historical or philosophical studies of medicine prefer to emphasize the ethical dilemmas associated with their "power of life and death," as though doctors were able to do something about this, as though this power were self-evident. The theoretical trajectory of Louis-Ferdinand Destouches, alias Céline, is a good example. After having embarked with the League of Nations and the Rockefeller Foundation on the adventure of social medicine in the 1920s, he returned from the United States with stars in his eyes, dreaming of "standardized medicine" and modern hygiene. After a few years of practicing in his suburban clinic, study trips to the colonies, and aborted projects, he darkened, hardened, and finally adopted a nihilistic position: the idea, rooted in the history of medical thought, that medicine is fundamentally a "natural science," that it must be satisfied with a powerless description of social pathology, that the arsenal of pharmacists is not worth much and that there is, in fact, nothing that can be done about it.

Nothing, in any case, besides purifying society through eugenics and the elimination of the Jews, concluded Céline in his anti-Semitic pamphlets.[5] His path was certainly extreme, but it is neither accidental nor exceptional. Rather, it reveals a fundamental interaction between hygienist (then eugenic) hubris and the desperate or raging nihilism of the doctor, one of which causes the other, in a cyclical and sometimes delirious sequence.

Another example from the 1930s, in which hygiene and anti-Semitism also intersect, is the famous model colony of Fordlandia, in Brazil, a pastoral and agro-industrial fantasy created by Henry Ford to produce rubber for his Michigan tire factories. Carried out in the middle of the Amazon, the project was a succession of failures as well as a financial disaster, but this did not deter American officials from doing ever more to bring about the advent of model families and punctual, clean workers who would make the plantation prosper. "Failure only made Ford and his emissaries more certain," wrote Greg Grandin in his study on this story. "The more Ford's errand to grow rubber, as originally stated, proved impossible, the more [he] revised their warrant, justifying their Brazilian mission in ever more idealistic terms."[6] It is this interaction between utopia and failure that interests me, because I believe it also runs through the history of colonial medicine—and the Haut-Nyong utopia.

The greatness of the heroes of colonial medicine is largely due to their failures. The biographies of Eugène Jamot and Gaston Muraz, whose achievement had been to "eradicate" sleeping sickness during the 1920s and 1930s (although the disease was rarely as much of a danger as it was after the Second World War), can be summed up in their thundering announcements and successive firings.[7] Inspired by these beloved and unhappy heroes, and thus traversed by an ambivalent "desire for failure," the ethics and aesthetics of the colonial doctor conceal a nihilistic possibility, which the literature on the subject, from Céline to Graham Greene, via Jean-Paul Sartre and Paule Constant, has reflected perfectly.[8] The doctors knew that they were exposing themselves to disillusionment. The historian discovers nothing new by bringing these disillusionments to light; however, in them, they seem to find the meaning of their actions. The difficulties the doctors faced—indifferent or hostile natives, fearful administrations—are the very proof of the greatness of their mission. The less well it worked, the more beautiful it was. They were reassuring failures.

The Haut-Nyong experiment gave the genre a new dimension. The rare texts written during the episode were even moving, as they appeared to say two things at the same time: utopia and dystopia, dreams and disaster, success and failure, without giving up on either. The doctors finally had power and yet they had never been so powerless. In a long and beautiful meditation on his work in Messamena, Koch compared himself to Parisian hygienists and their "protean activity." They too, he explained, were interested in everything, "in nutrition, drinking water, waste materials, and smoke from factories"; they too were deeply involved in efforts "to regulate women's work and build sun-filled buildings." And, in France as in Haut-Nyong, if "everything that concerns human beings cannot and must not escape their vigilant solicitude," it was "because they hope to stabilize, for the greater good of our country's future, a demographic situation that is becoming more alarming every day." It was in vain, of course, but "at least they have the excuse of not being able to get to the heart of the problem, because the very form of our society keeps them removed from it." All that remained for doctors in Paris was to petition patiently, backed up by figures, to try to convince politicians to act. "The problem facing the colony is just as serious, but with this difference in its favor, that here, we are the masters."[9] Here, we are the masters, we can change every aspect of society, even the Africans themselves, and yet we fail, continued Koch in the remainder of his text, which consists of three pages of anaphora.

HAD COLONEL DAVID "gone mad," as the missionaries suggested? I do not think so, but I do not know. What is certain is that he left Haut-Nyong on a stretcher, struck down in November 1943 by an unspecified "affliction," and was evacuated first to Yaoundé and then to Brazzaville, where he spent several weeks in the hospital and where he participated, perhaps by chance in the end, in the February 1944 conference before obtaining three months' convalescent leave in Algiers.[10] The causes of serious illness were not lacking, and Haut-Nyong's reputation in this regard was well established: malaria, filariasis, and amebiasis were frequent enough to cause severe fatigue or even death, as was the case for one of David's predecessors, District Commander Barbarin, who died suddenly in Abong-Mbang on August 15, 1938.[11] One may of course be tempted to refer to the voluminous medical literature of the time on colonial "diseases of the nerves"—psychiatric disorders, we would call them today—which were attributed at the time to isolation, climate, and lifestyle, and which spared neither administrators nor doctors. These included so-called Congolitis, tropical neurasthenia, nostalgia, and attacks of other forms of neurasthenia and delusions of grandeur.[12] However, I have not seen anything to suggest that this was the case with David. All that is known is that he was called the Emperor of the East and that he was perhaps at the end of his rope.

His deputy, Dr. Koch, stayed two more long years in Messamena. His return to France was full of promise. He worked with Marcel Vaucel as a technical assistant at the Ministry of the Colonies and he took the opportunity to follow a training course in ethnology at the Musée de l'Homme (Museum of Mankind), in which he made use of the extraordinary materials he had collected on "his" tribes, the Badwe'e and the Bikélé of Messamena. He was then appointed to the headquarters of the General Mobile Hygiene and Prophylaxis Service in Bobo-Dioulasso in Haute-Volta, where he developed his research in demography, a science still in its infancy in the colonial domain.[13] He ran for the National Assembly in 1948 with the Gaullist Rally of the French People party but withdrew right before the election. History records that he received "zero votes."[14] The notes in his personnel file, previously brilliant, began to lose a little of their sparkle. It was said that he had "let himself go" and that he would have to maintain the "right balance" in the future. A superior noted that his character was "shady."[15] He continued his career in the military hospitals of Indochina, in the middle of the war, and was repatriated in 1953 after contracting tuberculosis.[16] In Paris, he published an excellent ethnological study based on his experience in Messamena, *Magie et chasse dans la forêt camerounaise* (Magic and hunting in the Cameroonian forest), which is still cited today.[17] In 1967, two years before his death, he published another book, *La Médecine de l'espérance* (The medicine of hope) with the publisher Maloine. This work, intended "uniquely and exclusively for doctors," always leaves me daydreaming. There are indeed some allusions to Africa and sleeping sickness, but it is for the most part a product of automatic writing: a long, esoteric meditation on medicine, biology, art, matter, language, healing, beautiful in its phrasing, but in fact completely hermetic. When I tell this story, I like to end it with a sentence from a chapter entitled "La guérison de l'incendie" (The healing of fire). This sentence sets the tone for the book and perhaps helps the reader to imagine what medical rationality in power looked like during the long years of war and rubber: "No patient and no doctor, no individual or society, can ever deny that the dolmen of the druid is alone in the place it occupies in reason on this Earth."[18]

18. Koch! Koch!

The Land Cruiser had no problem getting us to Messamena. Thirty-eight kilometers in two hours, on a dirt road soaked by the morning's rain; it is the fastest way to reach the sub-prefecture from the national road. A few motorcycle taxis that serve the villages made the journey at a walking pace, with their feet on the ground to avoid falling into the mud. Valentin prefers this type of road to the main highways. One has to manage slides and choose whether to drive in the middle, right through a puddle, or go along the shoulder. We made the trip without Madame Ateba, whom we dropped off at her home in Akok-Maka. Tatiana, the Polish nun who welcomed us when we stayed the night at the Ayos mission, had warned us before we left that the road was difficult. When we got back, she laughed at us: after fourteen years of traveling this road, it rarely takes her more than an hour, because she knows every hole.

Along the road, a few electrical poles that were lying on the ground reminded us that there was once electricity here. People came out of their houses to watch us pass by in the cool morning air. Along the roadside are the "insignia" that drivers know how to interpret: a bowl indicates that you can stop to eat game; a yellow flower, that there is luggage to transport. Stalls sell bottles of gas for motorcycles for a few hundred francs. As we drove along, I explained to Valentin that we had come all this way to look for traces of a Dr. Koch, David's assistant. It would not be an easy task, as I had no contacts there, except for the phone number of the district's chief medical officer, a Dr. Prince.

Messamena appeared as a long straight line, on a dike that crosses a flooded forest, with a bridge in the middle that crosses the Log Mafog, a tributary of the blackwater Nyong. We passed old brick shops, vestiges of the time when Messamena was an important port, in the years 1910-30, when pirogues transported rubber to Mbalmayo, via Ayos. The houses are prettier, with flowers and cypress hedges growing around them. The children waved at us, shouting "Ntang!" when they saw the white man. A boy in a Bayern Munich jersey shouted something as the car passed by.

I did not catch it, but Valentin did: "Did you hear that he said Koch?" I found that hard to believe. He slammed on the brakes and put it in reverse to go back to the boy. "What did you say there?" The boy spoke in a quiet voice, eyes downcast. "No, sir, nothing, I was calling my little brother." "You didn't say anything there?" "No, I was just calling my little brother." Valentin laughed as we went on our way. "He was scared." It seemed a little far-fetched to me, but Valentin was sure that the boy shouted, "Koch! Koch!" (It is plausible, however: children are often heard crying, "Dr. Jamot!" in the regions of Cameroon where he had been.) A little farther on, we stopped on the side of the road. Valentin got out, called out to an old lady, and asked her if she had heard of Dr. Koch. She laughed and waved her sister over in patois, saying "coche" every second word. She said several times that he wrote a book, that someone here has that book. She asked, "Are you part of his family?"

The road, lined by a row of monumental palm trees, goes straight up the hill. In the distance, the sub-prefecture is in full view. On the left, there was a field of grass with a few buffalo and the new town hall building: the Henri Koch Stadium. Just behind that is the hospital with a beautiful building bearing the inscription, "Maternity 1940." The administrative city occupies the entire plateau, with a few old colonial houses, some of them in ruins. It emerges as an island above the swampy forest, where a light breeze blows. It took a lot of effort in Abong-Mbang to find people to whom the name David meant something; everyone always responded by mentioning Jamot, even Madame Ateba. For Koch in Messamena, it was the opposite: one does not even have to ask.

You always have to do things in the right order in Cameroon, to show your credentials, especially when, like us, you do not know anyone, so we parked at the sub-prefecture. It was a short journey back in time: we waited for the sub-prefect to the sound of the secretary using a typewriter, typing quietly with two fingers while looking at us over her glasses before going to sweep the office carpet. Outside, there was almost no one around, except for a sleeping dog and workers mowing a lawn with machetes. Every ten minutes, a motor-cycle passed by. Apart from that, there was silence. The sub-prefect, Abena Mvilongo Désiré, gave us a warm welcome—we had done things right, with our stamped mission orders and my business card. He allowed us to take pictures, recommended one or two "patriarchs," apologized for the archives "he did not inherit," and showed me a small bound report, in which I could find "all the elements regarding the climate, topography, and protected areas" of his subdivision. He told us about Messamena, somewhat melancholically. The administrative center is older than Abong-Mbang; he had a document somewhere with the date it was established . . . 1909; it was once "navigable to Mbalmayo," but today there is no road or electricity; "all that left with the departure of the expatriates." Above him was the "chart of sub-prefects who have led Messamena," with, on the sixth line, "Koch Henri, captain-doctor, 15/12/1939–14/12/1945." The last French citizen was called Delage, but the date has been erased by water leaking from the roof.

We then headed to the hospital, where Dr. Prince (that is his real name), young, bearded, cool, a little golden cross around his neck, was in the middle of a meeting with health workers for training in the distribution of Mectizan, the drug used to treat onchocerciasis, which is endemic in the region. As the generator was running, there were several power bars in the corridor, one plugged into the next, with about ten phones charging, as though the phones were having a meeting of their own at the same time. He put us in the care of someone called Serge, who got in the car with us to guide us. Where? No one knew, as he himself was not from the area and was in the middle of a conversation on the phone. Just after leaving the hospital, Valentin waved to a lady who was returning from the market. She knew Koch, of course, the man who had built everything here; people were still named after him. She knew all this from her mother, who lived five kilometers away, just after Labba. She obviously wanted to talk. She got in, Serge got out, and I plugged in my Dictaphone.

It was a little like pressing a button. As we drove along, Milong Zoa spoke non-stop; she spoke loudly whenever she said "Koch," making us finish her sentences with that intonation that pastors use in church. She showed us the prison where Koch kept his goats, the sub-prefecture where he meted out justice, the old market where he controlled the cocoa. Once we arrived in the village, we sat outside with her mother, Madame Zoa Tamare, "who was already born" when Koch had been there. Her listening audience quickly turned into a small group, the girls with babies in their arms, four generations together. I enjoyed every second of the discussion, a true researcher's emotion. I do not know what was most surprising, the content of the stories, or the fact that they were so present, so vivid, that the whole family came to laugh at the jokes, give their opinion on Koch, and sing choruses. Milong Zoa was supposed to translate, but instead she retold the stories her own way, adding elements; her mother simply helped her remember. First came the most eagerly awaited story: "We called him Captain Koch, Dr. Koch, Mr. Koch, he had all these names." He was "sub-prefect, doctor, farmer, agricultural supervisor, building engineer." He fed pregnant women in the maternity ward, fetching food from the villages himself, giving clothes to those who had nothing and medals to those who had more than ten children. He had launched the cocoa farms and asked people to get together to cultivate large collective fields, which were easier to protect from wild animals than small plantations. It was also he who had asked that the villages be settled along the road, and not scattered in the forest, because of "lions and panthers."

And then there were more surprising stories, stories of love and curiosity. First, he spoke the "patois" of Messamena, the Bikélé, and the Badwe'e, perfectly. He wanted people to explain everything to him. When the villagers managed to trap a panther, he came to see the carcass: "'Who did this? How did you do it?' They went to show him, and he wrote and wrote." One day he killed a "lion" by setting the trap himself,[1] using the technique he had been taught, without a gun or cable, with strings made from the palms growing in the swamps. He would come to the parties in the evening, when people lit large torches with moabi oil, and watch the dances all night long. He knew how to joke around. He had a favorite dish, eggplant tea and wild yams. His nickname was (I am writing it phonetically) *noum kaaa atwolo*, "mouth like a sparrow," apparently in reference to the fact that, when he was angry, he would open his mouth wide. "He captured live snakes. You can see he was something else," that there was no one like him. "When you knew something, you would go tell him, he would take it from there." We talked about his book again, which Milong Zoa's uncle owns a copy of. "He took everything from the life of the Bikélés and made a book."

I did not tell them that I have the book, that it's an unequaled study, although a bit dry, of forest hunting techniques, complete with drawings of traps, and that I have seen his photos of initiation rituals, tall trees, and dead panthers. I did not want to interrupt them. This time, I did not have to ask: "We sang songs with his name in them when he was leaving. Mother knows," said Milong, translating. The mother started on her own; the tune was soft, a little sad, with calls and answers. In the second verse, several of the women sang the second voice spontaneously. It was in Bikélé, so I understood only "Captain Koch-ééh," but it was beautiful. Milong translated:

Are you leaving?

You're really leaving, you're abandoning me, will we meet again . . .
where?

Yes, there will be plenty of opportunities to meet again.

Are you really leaving, abandoning me?

"This was the song that the Bikélé and Badwe'e sang when he left. People cried. It was a loss." The mourning period never really ended, in a sense. Milong's son, who is a little younger than I am, punctuated the interview: "Since then, not much has happened." Koch's departure marked an interruption, a suspension: "Messamena is the same age as Bafoussam [the large city in western Cameroon, known for its economic dynamism], you see what Bafoussam has become." The fact that Messamena is an ancient city adds to the pain. Everything that he did "was in the direction of development. If he had still been here, since that time, Messamena would not be what it is today. If he could still rise from where he lies and come back here." Talking about Koch evokes an alternative history, which is told in the present. We thought about how the city looked before. "If you film yourself, you think you are in France, all the roads with palm trees." We thought about the orchards, about the mandarins, the mangoes, the oranges. "It has only gotten older." We imagined another future, which was in the process of unfolding. "On the development side, he did everything he could to put Messamena-iais [here, everyone laughed, the neologism seemed improvised] on the road to development." Milong was trying to find the words to say something a little solemn:

> It is he who . . . it is he who, I don't know what word I can use, [did everything] to give Messamena a direction, the direction of a normal life for a human being. When he arrived, he had ideas, he created many things. He treated. When a patient arrived, he dropped [what he was doing], he was up to speed, he operated. So, his memory will never fade. What the mother there tells us, we will tell our children too. Here is my son who comes after us, he will also tell it to . . . He is a figure like Mandela today in Africa, Koch in Messamena. It's the truth.

Milong took the opportunity to inform everyone that Mandela had just died. Certainly, there is a "bias" in this type of interview, where one tries to tell the interviewer what they think he wants to hear. The song, for example, likely makes use of the generic framework of a song of mourning or farewell to someone going abroad (in passing, nobody at the Zoas' knew David, and Jamot was taken care of in one sentence, which somewhat invalidates the hypothesis of a "recited" story—everyone was both delighted and surprised to talk about Koch). There was something poignant in what Madame Zoa said about this doctor who will never be forgotten because he showed everyone that the people of Messamena could live the "normal life of a human being." I like this expression. It expresses what the anthropologist James Ferguson has identified in nostalgic speeches or nonprofessional writings by Africans young and old about colonialism or Europe: not a desire for Mbeng (the West) that would be a "false awareness," a misplaced desire, a masochistic attachment to colonial domination, but a demand for belonging and equality, based on the historical experience of an unfulfilled promise of "modernization" and inclusion in the "normal" world, a world where life is a little less absurd than it is here.

Once we were back on the road, bringing Milong back to the city, the tone changed a little. We passed by some old cocoa trees and got out to touch the trunks and the ripe pods and take some pictures. Other stories came back to her, of Koch getting angry with cocoa traders who tried to cheat people. He would come along and "whack!" he would slap them. She repeated the gesture several times, Koch's slap in the face, with his unique style: she started out like she was going to deliver a punch and, at the last moment, he would open his hand, to deliver only a slap. Whack! Koch is a gesture.

Pointing to the bushes, Milong explained that there were houses everywhere before, all along the road. "Too many people died." It was sleeping sickness. Her mother had just told us how, to get along with the chiefs, the nurses infected people with it out of jealousy, especially "young men and young women," by injecting them with contaminated blood. "It was the most beautiful neighborhood in Messamena," separated from the city by a dike, and there is almost no one left today because "hatred" has destroyed everything.[2] She thought about the dike on the other side of the city, at the beginning of the road to Mbama and Ayos, which Dr. Koch had built, and which earned him a medal and congratulations. Over there, "the people are dead! The people are dead! Because they dug with their hands, dug out the rocks. As they dug, those in the front, if the rock slid, it crushed everyone. They just went around, they kept going." Understand: they were buried on the spot, and the road passed over the bodies. She slapped her hands together. "It was forced labor." Everyone was involved except pregnant women and small children. "We're enjoying [the results] today, aren't we?" In December 1992, Wang Sonné interviewed someone named Mbouk Mvom Marc Claude, who said just about the same thing. "Koch did a lot of work here. At that time, there were the police, when the bridge was being built [over the Log Mafog]. People were dying too. It was our brothers who beat people up. These were Mr. Koch's police. A lot of people died. Here in Mbama, it was terrible."[3] Wang Sonné had noted at the beginning: "Frenzy: people never died like that before."

As we left the city, leaving in the light of late afternoon to travel the thirty-eight kilometers back to Mbama and Ayos, Valentin and I thought about the bodies buried under the road to development.

WHEN KOCH LEFT, Zoa the mother told us, they gave him "drums, tam-tams, balafons." She wondered if I would be able to find them "somewhere." I met Henri Koch's daughter in France. She told me that she had given things to the Musée de l'Homme in Paris, including poisoned arrows, keeping just a little African art and a few books from his large library. Her features include her father's face, his olive complexion, his black hair and eyes, his eyelashes that made his eyes stand out as makeup would. She told me that her grandfather, Dr. Koch's father, was the son of a French man who had married an Indo-Mauritian woman in Mauritius before leaving for New Caledonia at the end of the nineteenth century. Wang Sonné asked people if Koch was "Black," but apparently, this had not made an impression on anyone in Cameroon. People simply described him to me as "less giant than me," so less than 1.80 meters tall. She has archives at her home, a large pile of yellowed documents. I read them over several afternoons. They include his certificate of studies, his diplomas, the anthropology courses he took once he returned to Paris, and some documents that were not written in his hand, texts on customs and justice that were to serve as a reference for his judgments, gathered in a notebook that he must have assembled alone in Messamena, covered with part of the *Courrier austral* (Southern courier) newspaper, on which one can read summaries of Radio London programs. Most important, there is a series of precious documents from his work in Messamena: huge census tables, folded in eight, covering his entire subdivision, village by village, family by family, a thick folder full of anthropometric tables written in violet ink, one line per individual, about thirty columns with all kinds of measurements. There are also collections of Badwe'e and Bikélé proverbs and stories, Pygmy mythologies, drawings of knots and bows, lists of trees and plants, and his two reports, one on demography, the other on agriculture, perhaps five hundred pages in length between them, with whole pages of statistics, graphs, censuses of goats and coffee plants, and beautiful maps drawn in ink.

It is the archive of an ethnologist-administrator who wanted to know everything, doubtless not the only one,[4] but he had six years and unique means to try, backed by the emergency regime of a state at war. It is the archive of the

Haut-Nyong experiment in terms of the greatest accomplishments it produced, with each inhabitant of the subdivision leaving their trace, at the cost of a scientific and administrative effort that must have been immense. In leafing through the immense tables, the censuses, the thousands of skull measurements today, one notes that the archive has also recorded the delirious, mad, and vain aspects of the experiment. It is the archive of the experiment overextending itself, by fantasy or poetry, songs, shared hunts, and drunkenness on palm wine, the archive of the bit of folly nested in the scientific project itself, of its affective history. As I read through it, I thought of the analyses of Johannes Fabian, who diagnosed a constitutive madness in the enterprise of exploring and classifying the African continent through colonial ethnology. For Fabian, this madness was not only a sign of the folly of colonialism itself but also a mode of knowledge, from which anthropology has inherited the idea that ecstasy, that being "out of one's mind," is a necessary condition for anthropological knowledge.[5]

In his demographic study, Koch had taken an interest in the "desires" of young people and had also wanted to know "what plans they had for the future."[6] Of the fifty-seven schoolchildren interviewed, most wanted to become "functionaries," wrote Koch, with distress, so they could "sit in the shade"; "chauffeur" was the most frequent answer, just ahead of "nurse." One gets the feeling from the pile of papers that a crack had opened up, likely to close again immediately; the utopia of a common, friendly space, of a possible meeting, lasting the duration of a party or a football match, a utopia always postponed or contradicted.

I enjoyed spending time with these documents, while exchanging a few words with Madame Koch. Her father lacked almost nothing needed to formulate the drama of which he was one of the protagonists, when he wrote, in his fiery and poetic style, that everything about colonialism needed to be changed, that everything needed to be "nationalized," as was being done by the National Council of the Resistance in Paris, that the exploitation of the native must be stopped. He was not a Marxist, and his metaphors were instead taken from Cameroonian interpretations of the accumulation of wealth and the proletarianization of the Black peasant: "His sweat, his blood, and his life flowed like torrents [. . .] for the enrichment of a few Europeans,"[7] he wrote in a long indictment written in March 1945, when he was packing his trunks for France. Koch confusedly perceived that he was facing forces more powerful than himself, a world of dollars, rutile, and latex, which was crushing those he was trying to protect, which made him a "servant in practice if not in principle" of exploiters and which transformed "into helpless and desolate resignation [. . .] enthusiasm and faith."[8]

A missionary from Abong-Mbang once gave me a good quote from a nun who was there during the colonial era: "There were three types of administrators sent to Haut-Nyong: disciplinary transfers, the superambitious, and Professor Calculus types."[9] David the Emperor was doubtless in the second category, Koch the dreamer in the last. In Indochina, Koch had become so passionate about Chinese medicine that he practiced acupuncture when he returned to France. He consulted in the evening in Cholon, the Chinese district of Saigon, and was slapped on the wrist for it, receiving a disciplinary transfer to serve in Tonkin, in the combat zone. He did not really fit in, as he had a taste for the Other. Of the two, he is my favorite.

I also leafed through several curious manuscripts, novels in varying degrees of completion, with varying degrees of esotericism. Writing, as Koch seemed to have understood, is a form of knowledge as powerful as statistics. I spent a lot of time on "Les Serpents" (The snakes), a short story of about thirty pages. Koch did not say he had written the story, but he often talked about his experiences with snakes in Cameroon. The story begins with the arrival of a young doctor in Messamena, with the fear that overcomes him when he arrives at the end of the path with nothing but his luggage, then evokes his six years as a doctor-administrator, his incessant tours, the thousand babies he delivers, the friendships he forms with "a population of learned people and artists" that he hosts at the residence. The doctor's evenings were "magical," remembers the narrator; his house "no longer belonged to him," it had become a "caravanserai" where he provided "shelter and food" to "witch doctors, trappers, historians, healers, dancers, musicians" who stayed for several months.[10] He tells of his initiation by a "Snake Man," Baya; the snake breeding that he undertakes with Baya's advice to try to produce serums and antivenom vaccines; and then, finally, a bite, a moment of inattention or a broken spell, followed by a slow exit out of his body, toward death or the afterlife, and the text ends there.

PART II.
THE FRENCH PROTECTORATE OF WALLIS AND FUTUNA

1933–1938

The king is an outsider, often an immigrant warrior prince whose father is a god or a king in his native land. But, exiled by his own love of power or banished for a murder, the hero is unable to succeed there. Instead, he takes power in another place, and *through a woman*: princess of the native people whom he gains by a miraculous exploit involving feats of strength, ruse, rape, athletic prowess and/or the murder of his predecessor. The heroic son-in-law from a foreign land demonstrates his divine gifts, wins the daughter, and inherits half or more of the kingdom. Before it was a fairy tale, it was the theory of society.

MARSHALL SAHLINS, "The Stranger-King, or Dumézil among the Fijians," 1980

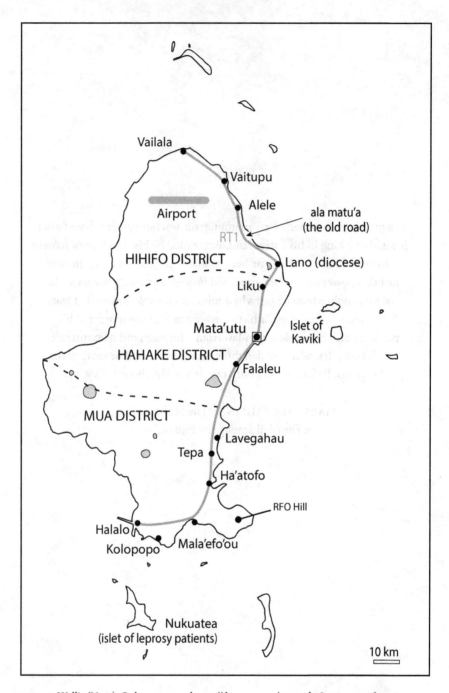

Vailala

Vaitupu

Alele

Airport

ala matu'a
(the old road)

RT1

HIHIFO DISTRICT

Lano (diocese)

Liku

Mata'utu

Islet of
Kaviki

HAHAKE DISTRICT

Falaleu

MUA DISTRICT

Lavegahau

Tepa

Ha'atofo

RFO Hill

Halalo

Kolopopo

Mala'efo'ou

Nukuatea
(islet of leprosy patients)

10 km

MAP 3. Wallis (Uvea). © d-maps.com. https://d-maps.com/carte.php?num_car=64III.

19. King David

A good story is a temptation.

JACK HART, *Storycraft*, 2011

For a long time, I believed that Dr. David had died in Abong-Mbang at the end of the war. The Dutch anthropologist Peter Geschiere, who spent time in the region in the 1970s and wrote what would become a classic work on witchcraft among the Makaa, had told me that he thought David was buried in Abong-Mbang, though he was not certain. Geschiere's main informant in the field was born during this period. He was born on the side of the road halfway between his mother's village and Abong-Mbang's maternity ward because his mother had set out too late. The people of the region clearly remembered the time when pregnant women went to the hospital. Geschiere had also told me that "people in the 1970s said that students used to bring their school notebooks to the tomb of 'Colonel David' so they would get good marks on their exams,"[1] though he recommended I take this with a grain of salt.

This would have made a good story; in fact, I published it just as it was told to me in an article. It would have immediately called to mind Joseph Conrad and Rudyard Kipling, and other similar colonial stories of humanism and excess, of isolation, of failure, of madness and violence, of mimicry and magic. One necessarily thinks of Colonel Kurtz, of his report for the "International Society for the Suppression of Savage Customs," written on the banks of a river in a remote post in rubber-producing Congo, and of the post-scriptum he scrawled at the bottom of the last page: "Exterminate all the brutes!"[2] Reading Koch's or Colonel David's words, which are enthusiastic and tired at the same time, one obviously thinks that there was a little bit of that, that they were never far from drawing a line through the page, from drawing a line through everything. And one is tempted to make use of the analogy, to write that "Conrad's *Heart of Darkness* resonates through every page," as the *New York Times* did in its review of *Fordlandia*.[3] The parallel with fiction raises a rather profound question, central to the cultural history of European imperialism, which is precisely that of the circular relationship between historical narratives, fictional narratives, and colonial subjectivities. Both Conrad and Kipling were inspired by figures who were "kings" of the bush, including the "White Rajah" James Brooke, a both real and mythical hero of Victorian England who founded a dynasty of regents in the Sultanate of Sarawak, on the island of Borneo. "There is only one place now in the world that two strong men can Sar-a-*whack*," say the two heroes of Kipling's "The Man Who Would Be King," before leaving to found their Freemason kingdom somewhere in "Kafiristan."[4] Paul Voulet and Julien Chanoine, the two officers of the Colonial Army who arrived in West Africa in 1898 (the very time Conrad published his novel) for an exploration that should have led to the conquest of Chad but which instead ended in a bloody march, had read Julius Caesar's *The Gallic Wars*. Generations of colonial administrators (and then historians) would play with the metaphor of the "emperor without a scepter."[5] I don't know if Koch, whose pen was more literary, had read Kipling, or Céline, or André Gide, and I know that David was not a great reader, but they both left for Africa at a time when the continent was already a cemetery of utopias, deposed kings, and colonial scandals of all kinds, where fiction and journalism had laid bare the fine words of European humanism. The Conradian theme fascinates me, like everyone, but it is in fact a little too fascinating. I am often told: "Your story about Dr. David, it really feels like Colonel Kurtz." I want to reply: that is precisely the problem.

The story would have been too good but also completely false. It took me a little time to verify things, to find the correct date of birth for Jean Joseph David (his medical thesis indicates 1903 instead of 1902); the records of his birth, marriage, and death; and his military file, accessible by dispensation at the Defense Historical Service in Vincennes.[6] I learned that, in fact, Jean Joseph David died in the suburbs of Paris in 1969, after having ended his career outside the army as a medical sales representative for a small pharmaceutical company where he was in charge of relations with Africa in particular—and that I would have to untangle this magic tomb confusion while hoping that no one would notice the mistake in my article.

In doing this research—which consisted of spending time on the internet, searching for David or Koch in the white pages, targeting the South of France because I know from experience that colonial doctors often retired in the sun, targeting the Île-de-France region because I know from experience that colonial doctors often retired in Paris, sending a few letters, giving up and starting over again—I tried searching for "[all words] Jean Joseph David" in the catalog of the Bibliothèque interuniversitaire de médecine (University Medical Library), in Odéon. The seventh result out of twenty-eight, after textbooks of all kinds and a doctoral thesis in biochemistry in 2013 called "Modulation du potentiel angiogène des progéniteurs endothéliaux humains" (Modulation of the angiogenic potential of human endothelial progenitors), was a record for a *thèse d'exercice*, the equivalent of an MD thesis, defended in 1994 by Geneviève Royannez-Genevey, a general practitioner established in Drôme: "Le 'Roi David' ou l'œuvre d'un médecin français aux îles Wallis" ("King David," or the work of a French doctor in the Wallis Islands). The thesis was written under the supervision of Jean-Pierre Neidhardt at the University of Lyon I. The introduction is half a page long:

> During our medical activity in Wallis and Futuna, we had the opportunity to discuss our predecessors with the medical team. Their memories rarely went back more than ten years. Only one name, buried in the collective memory, came up regularly, that of the man who had been nicknamed 'King David.' In our work, it seemed interesting to us to show how a practitioner, while carrying out his medical role, went beyond his functions and put in place the basis of the contemporary structures of Wallis, a small French archipelago lost in the middle of the South Pacific.[7]

From that point on, I added *Wallis Futuna* to *David* in search engines, and everything went much more quickly. I learned that Dr. David was posted in the protectorate of Wallis and Futuna from 1933 to 1938. He was, as in Haut-Nyong, a doctor and governor. He had published a few articles on his time there, which were actually rather easy to find. His stay had a profound impact on Wallis, to the point that he appears, with a photo, in the island's historical and tourist guides, in a novel, and in several academic works.[8] The researchers in Oceania who worked on David and the history of Wallis never made the link with Cameroon.

The emperor had therefore been king a few years earlier on a Pacific island somewhere between the New Hebrides and Tonga. I concluded (1) that I had certainly been a little light on the fact-checking for my articles, but that I had not been too mistaken in suggesting that there was some megalomania in this story, and (2) that all this was promising, since, after just a few minutes in front of my computer, I discovered the satellite images of Wallis, its turquoise waters, its two hotels, its expatriate blogs, and its rugby pitches.

20. Uvea, Desert Island

AÉ PORT DE WALLIS HIHIFO. Two letters had been blown off the roof of the airport; I do not know how long ago. It's strange to say, but it made me happy, these missing letters, after thirty hours on a plane and a few days spent in New Caledonia. It is as though the sign were saying: welcome to a place where everything is falling apart, where moss grows on the buildings of the French Republic; welcome to a garden island, far from Nouméa, its real estate boom, its racist jokes, and its dead lagoons.

Accounts of arriving in Wallis are always pretty much the same. The island is tiny, as wide as an airfield. A paved road crosses it from north to south, with a roundabout in the middle. There is no real center, nothing that resembles a city, just a beautiful black stone cathedral set on the bank of the lagoon, next to the royal palace, the prefecture, and the pier where the ships dock. Everything is green, red, and calm.

Every five or ten years the major French newspapers publish an article on Wallis and Futuna, which always says pretty much the same thing. The pitch is simple: to quote the latest one, which appeared in *Le Monde* in September 2014, Wallis and Futuna is "a small piece of France where three kings reign."[1] When it comes to details, however, opportunities for surprise are not lacking, making Wallis (known as Uvéa in the local language) and the two islands of Futuna, located more than two hundred kilometers away, a great site for anthropologists.

First, there is the political system, in which the French Republic (represented by an administrator superior with the rank of prefect) coexists with a customary regime, the so-called royalty, which is officially recognized and subsidized by the French Republic. To summarize briefly, the king of Wallis, who bears the title of Lavelua, is at the top of an administrative pyramid of authorities (ministers, district chiefs, then village chiefs). He is in fact a sovereign elected (and eventually dismissed) by a college of notables, who choose him from a group of pretenders to the throne, themselves "descendants of kings," as they are members of the four noble families of the island. Constantly reinvented, the royal institution adapted both to the massive conversion of the archipelago to Catholicism in the nineteenth century and to the transformations caused by French control of the island, first in the form of a colonial protectorate and then, after 1961, with the status of an overseas territory. In practice, while the prefect is the official head of the territory, the influence of the king, his Council of Ministers, and the chiefdoms remains considerable, whether it is to end a strike, arbitrate a conflict, cut off the electricity, close the airport, or send an unpopular French foreign aid worker back to France. The Lavelua remains above all the "cornerstone" of a social organization and a system of representation, based on a set of rites, constraints, prohibitions, privileges, and hierarchies;[2] in short, of an extraordinarily lively Wallisian culture that is part of everyday life, which locals refer to as custom. It takes the form of spectacular ceremonies that follow the rhythm of religious, agricultural, and political calendars, in which exchanges of money, multicolored mats, tubers, and roasted pigs are organized around the king and the consumption of kava, and which are a godsend for visiting journalists.

The role of the Catholic religion is the other aspect of the island's political history and cultural life that is impossible to miss. On the world map of missionary miracles, Wallis easily competes with the center of Cameroon. The island converted in its entirety after the arrival of the Marist fathers in 1837, in a context of internal and regional tensions in which the king saw in the mission a timely ally and a protector against Tongan (and Protestant) ambitions on the archipelago. In the second half of the nineteenth century, a fairly famous Marist "theocracy" was established in which the chiefdom and the mission came together to control social organization (and customs in particular) through a codified set of rules and fines, and to make use of the system of customary chores to build churches, the cathedral, and the royal palace.[3] The Marist mission has remained deeply integrated into Uvean society, through a local clergy trained in great numbers. It remains a "third power" that is essential, which has both enabled and complicated the exercise of French control on the island, and which continues, for example, to provide all primary education on the island. Several of the first missionaries thus became mythical figures in the local pantheon: among them, St. Peter Chanel, who died a martyr in Futuna; Father Battaillon, the "apostle" who converted the island; and Bishop Poncet, who became the first bishop of the island in 1936 and who is now buried in the cathedral. When I arrived at the airport in June 2014, I had in my luggage his *Histoire de l'île Wallis* (History of Wallis Island), a beautiful old-fashioned book whose pages I had to separate with a letter opener, published in 1972 by the Société des océanistes (Society of Oceania Researchers).[4] It is in the mission's archives, I had heard just about everywhere, that all of the island's memory could be found.

Poncet's book provides some explanations regarding the island's third political curiosity, known to only a few historians: the fact that, during the first half of the twentieth century, the representatives of France in Wallis were almost exclusively doctors. The formula tested by David in Haut-Nyong was therefore a well-established tradition in Wallis, where the idea of colonization by doctors, imagined by theorists of the empire such as Hubert Lyautey (to whom we owe the famous "Send me four doctors, I'll send you a battalion in return"),[5] was made into a system. The anomaly is explained by Wallis's marginal status on the map of the French Empire. For a long time, the territory had neither a doctor nor a colonial administration worthy of the name. French control under the protectorate established in 1844 remained purely diplomatic and was limited to a few visits by navy ships. Added to this from 1888 onward was the presence of a "resident," who was in fact a low-ranking colonial administrator acting as a flag bearer, with no police, secretary, or "residence" other than a makeshift hut.[6] In terms of medicine, there were only the visiting navy doctors, who carried out some tasks during their stopovers. In this context, the sending of a doctor who also played the role of administrator (or the opposite) was not part of the great imperial or humanist plan but in fact a request of the missionaries, who began early in the twentieth century to "dream," wrote Bishop Poncet, of a "doctor-administrator" and joined King Vito Lavelua in making repeated requests to the French authorities. The dream came true in 1905: the first "doctor-administrator" from the Colonial Army arrived, inaugurating a form of medical governorate that would remain in force until the 1950s, with a few interruptions.[7] David would be the fifth of these "doctor-administrators."

The colonial administration never made any secret of the tactical side of this formula: "You will present yourself as a doctor in order to win the sympathy of the population," explained the governor of New Caledonia to Dr. Viala in 1906. "When the *lavelua* and his chiefs see that you have not come mainly to impose taxes and live off the country, but that you are able to do good in a disinterested way, they will easily succumb to your influence."[8] The plan did not really work but nevertheless made it possible to obtain from the Wallisian government the payment of an annual fee (the first tax in the history of the island) "as a token of recognition for the concession of a doctor-administrator." The medical presence called for by the mission, granted by France and paid for by the Uveans, was thus immediately caught up in a negotiation between the three powers of the island, which joined forces to recognize its simultaneously disinterested and strategic character. The doctor-administrator formula was abolished shortly after the Second World War. An army colonel, called to the rescue in the 1950s following some political incidents, felt it was a shame: who would have dared to challenge "a resident who cares for everyone, is a friend to everyone, to the elderly and often sick missionaries, to the king and ministers whose wives he helps to give birth and whose children he treats, to the entire population who needs him?"[9] Only a doctor, Colonel Fray explained to the authorities in Nouméa, was "capable of exerting a powerful moral influence over the masses," thanks to "the powerful attraction and influence he was able to exert around himself." Wallis was made to be governed by doctors: "This solution is the only logical one, the only one that responds to the particular character of the island."[10]

The functioning of the health system remains one of the island's most endearing quirks today, as though it were the continuation of the strange story of the medical utopia in the present tense. While the island does not have any private doctors or a pharmacy, hospital consultations, treatments, medication, operations, dental prostheses, glasses, and evacuations to Nouméa and France remain completely free of charge for all. It is not even possible to pay: the hospital simply does not have a cash register. Wallis: the land where health was not a commodity.

Along with the hotel delegation that picked me up after the plane landed, I stopped at the City Dia supermarket, which had just opened in the small shopping center in Mata-Utu, the main town on the island where I would be spending a few weeks. It took me only a few minutes to realize that I would be going completely broke during my stay. Beer costs three or four times what it does in Paris; the only fruits for sale were apples imported from New Zealand; only the chip aisle and the sardines in oil made me feel a little more comfortable. I was about to realize that Wallis is a strange economic universe, partly "a-monetary" while having long integrated cash into the ceremonial exchanges that regulate social and religious life.[11] In practice, there are French foreign aid workers (the *papalagi*) who, a major English newspaper reported spitefully in 1996, take "vastly overpaid holidays" on the island;[12] some two thousand local employees (for about eight thousand inhabitants), mainly in the public sector; and a small commercial sector dominated by a handful of importers in a monopoly situation. The opening of Dia had just triggered a small earthquake by promising to slash prices. Wallis offers a journey to another world that makes Abong-Mbang look like a cosmopolitan capital. There is no market, just a few often empty restaurants; tourism is almost nonexistent and exports completely nonexistent; there are no taxes, no social security, no Revenue de solidarité active (guaranteed income supplement); the police wear shorts and the wearing of seat belts is not officially mandatory; there are no mobile phones, street vendors, or public space, and no land registry, for that matter.[13] Agriculture, livestock farming, and fishing are almost completely cut off from the money economy: without a garden and without friendly or family ties necessary to be part of the barter and donation networks, it is complicated to even find a fresh mango, banana, or fish to eat.

The other thing that struck me during my ride in the hotel's pickup truck was the abandoned houses, all with gaping holes, bare walls, and torn-off roofs. I was going to add "unruly lawns," but it's exactly the opposite: the ruins are the centerpiece of flowered lawns. There was a terrible cyclone in 2012, but the empty houses are above all a sign of the flight of Wallisian youth, who are leaving for New Caledonia and mainland France to study or work. The birth rate has collapsed, local employment opportunities are scarce, and population figures are slowly falling; between 2003 and 2013, the number of inhabitants dropped by two thousand, bringing the total population back to the level of the early 1980s. At the same time, there are more than twenty thousand Wallisians and Futunians in New Caledonia, heirs to a long history of labor migration initiated by the French authorities after the Second World War to provide labor for nickel mines, and an even longer history of mobility throughout the South Pacific. Just before we arrived at the hotel, we passed by a gas station. There were two pumps, the meters of which have been stopped for years, both situated in the middle of what is now a grassy expanse, a bit like a contemporary sculpture. I wrote in my notebook that Wallis, with its empty houses and greenery, is kind of like Detroit, without the cold wind (I had been at the University of Michigan a month earlier to present on the story of Dr. David); a little like Tahiti, without the luxury hotels; a little like Africa, without the people.

It was here that I would have to search for traces of Dr. David. I had tried to do things in the correct order before arriving, by contacting the Wallis and Futuna delegation at the Ministry of the Overseas in Paris. The name

Dr. David "said something" to Vano Panaï, the delegate who met me in his office on Oudinot Street, within the walls of the former Ministry of the Colonies. He explained his comment about David by saying "he reigned, or rather, he spent time, in Wallis. He was very authoritarian." He seemed convinced that the elders on the island were going to remember him. As for the archives, it was going to be more complicated: those of the Residency (as the prefecture was called in colonial times) had been burned for the period before the Second World War, but there were still those of the Health Agency, because it was Dr. David who had built the hospital, and those of the diocese. The most important thing was to follow protocol. I had started off well by contacting Panaï, and by announcing myself immediately to the prefect, the Cultural Affairs Service, and the bishop.

Prior to my departure, I had explored a second lead: the Oceania researchers who had worked on Wallis. It was a rather pleasant task, which consisted in sending email upon email to friends of friends, allowing myself to be led closer and closer until I reached "those in the know." In this case, it was Jean-Claude Roux, a retired geographer from the Research Institute for Development, author of a state doctoral thesis of unparalleled scope (over one thousand pages) on "micro-insularity" in Wallis and Futuna, directed by Gilles Sautter, an important figure in the geography and Africanism of the 1970s and 1980s.[14] The study initially focused on the question of the migration of Wallisians to New Caledonia, but three quarters of the thesis was in fact devoted to history. It was in this work that I had found long passages on "Resident-Regent David." Roux had relied on an in-depth survey of Wallisians and on a myriad of archival holdings, including those of the High Commission of the French Republic in Nouméa (the former colonial government), where there was an "Office of Wallis and Futuna," which held the reports sent by residents posted in Wallis to the governors of New Caledonia on whom they were hierarchically dependent.[15] In 1981, an elderly colonial administrator ran this "somewhat abandoned" office (Roux never ran into anyone there),[16] where reports piled up in a disorderly fashion, among them hundreds of pages written by Dr. David. Roux had dived into these piles, which constituted extraordinary sources for a history of the three islands. For a long time, I had hoped to find them again—they were documents that had not reached Paris—and for this reason I had written, in the weeks before my departure, to nearly the entire organizational chart of the High Commission of the Republic in Nouméa, without any success (by which I mean, without any reply). There was one last possibility: that Roux had given his work files to the Société d'études historiques de Nouvelle-Calédonie (Society of Historical Studies of New Caledonia [SEHNC]), an association of history

enthusiasts based in a small building in the old center of Nouméa, which pub-
lishes a good newsletter several times a year.

I took advantage of my stopover in Nouméa to go through these archives
and take hundreds of photos, without actually reading any of the documents.
With Gabriel and Violaine Valet, the two volunteers who run the SEHNC, I
found a great deal to discuss. Violaine's father had been a high-ranking colonial
doctor, and the couple had lived for fifteen years in Yaoundé, where Gabriel,
a botanist, was dean of the Faculty of Science. They asked me about their old
house, opposite the French high school, and together we reminisced about the
"country," adopting a Cameroonian accent. The French overseas territories, in
the colonial era and then that of cooperation, were conducive to "Afro-Pacific"
trajectories like theirs; you do not have to be an opportunistic historian, given
the current interest in "connected histories," to find them everywhere. Entire
careers have been spent examining the improbable connections that linked
Nouméa or Port-Vila to Libreville or Yaoundé, such as David, Koch, and Pape,
the three main doctors of Haut-Nyong, all of whom passed through the South
Pacific. While walking near my bed-and-breakfast, located in the Vallée des
Colons (Valley of the Settlers), I came across a school called Candide Koch,
named after the doctor's mother, a schoolteacher of Italian origin who had
married his father, a Franco-Mauritian, in Nouméa. The Valets' career follows
the same trajectory, like that of Raymond Mayer, an anthropologist specializing in Wallis who works at the University of Gabon, with whom I exchanged
emails prior to my departure; that of Claude Wetta, a French former foreign
aid worker in Cameroon, who had just left the Wallis Health Agency when I
met him in Paris; or that of the nurse anesthetist sent by the French government who stayed with me at the hotel, Françoise, who had lived in Douala for
a long time. On verandas that all look alike, we shared a common nostalgia,
we compared the indigenous peoples and the climates, loves and accents, the
fruits of the garden, the colors of the earth, the costs of living and the rainy
seasons. David probably never stopped seeing Abong-Mbang as another Wallis,
though I do not know whether he considered it better or worse, but I spent my
time thinking about Cameroon.

Investigations like this are like a treasure hunt. During my stopover in Nouméa, the Valets referred me to Dr. Jean-Marie Papilio, the first (and so far, only)
Wallisian doctor, who made time for me on the patio of a café between two
appointments (he consults in Wallisian, because 70 percent of his patients are
Wallisian). For him, this Dr. David mainly brings to mind "his grandfather,
who used to say, 'King David' with great respect." He remembers lantern-lit
evenings, when there was no TV, when his grandparents used to tell him about

all of this. In any case, he recommended that I speak to his sister, Bernadette, who runs the Cultural Affairs Service in Wallis, promising me a warm welcome. I had already contacted her, on the independent advice of at least three people in France. I had not yet arrived in Wallis and already I was going around in circles.

It may seem obvious, but Wallis is a very small world. As a place where it is hard to drive for more than fifteen minutes without passing a place a second time, and where one can count all the houses on the territory on Google Maps without much effort, it produces a rather striking scale effect. It is not simply a microcosm, in the sense of a miniature world that would reveal more "general" dynamics, of a society reduced as if by homothetic transformation, but rather a space whose minuscule size constitutes its *particularity*, as reduction of scale does not behave in a linear manner. My story can thus do without adjectives and big words: in the 1930s, the "colonial" presence was reduced to one or two people, "France" had a first name (Jean Joseph, in my case), and "traditions" were in permanent negotiation. The political system (and to begin with, the appointment of the king) states in a perfectly transparent manner how it functions as a role-playing game (with rules that are themselves adaptable), with each player assuming provisional and multiple identities, creating almost complete uncertainty, especially for a visiting observer, as to what comes under function, heredity, essence, use, accident, or illusion. One can say, in order to reassure oneself, that the Wallisian monarchy is part of a "truncated descent line" system described in Polynesia by a venerable anthropologist in the 1950s.[17] However, the fact remains that the kings and queens of Wallis bear the title provisionally, that a vacant throne is not exceptional (the throne was vacant when I wrote these lines), that "custom" has been perpetually contested and reinvented since at least the beginning of the nineteenth century, and that this political philosophy has been extended to French authority, which has been reduced to the customary, also provisional and revocable, title of *lesita* (resident) and *kovana* (governor)—read these words aloud. The Wallisian exception in this respect is quite normal. Everyone wears one (or more) hat(s), which they change regularly, and no one really knows what game they are playing. Prefects who try to rationalize all this usually get back on the plane quite quickly. A good report on the television channel France Ô summarized it well: "The king is a blur."[18]

The size of the island combined with its remoteness is also the main reason for its most astonishing feature: the fact that it has remained resistant to development, as though it were indifferent to the economic and cultural trajectory of modernization (including when it comes to diagnosing failure or what comes next). Too tiny to offer a market for anything, too distant to export, the island depends economically and materially on a strange compromise with France, which rests on a series of fictions about the future (the strategic interest of the island, maybe one day; the political role of the Wallisian minority on the New Caledonian chessboard, maybe one day; offshore mining resources, maybe one day; the export of rugby stars, maybe one day; tax evasion, ~~maybe one day~~), but economic takeoff is not one of them. Residents from France, followed by generations of French foreign aid workers, have hit a brick wall over the difficulty of "developing" Wallis, whether through agricultural cooperatives, luxury hotels, frozen fish, or nuclear testing, and over the ability of Wallisian society to persist in its particularity while transforming itself.

So, they find a way through by using the right plays on words. Seasonal articles on Wallis in the French press always adopt a joking tone. David, quoted by Roux, was amused to note that "the principal resource of the protectorate has long been the issue of postage stamps" (the philatelic interest of the island has never been denied since).[19] More philosophically minded, one of his predecessors put it nicely when he wrote that Wallis is "a big word for a little thing."[20] The lesson deserves to be taken seriously, for it harks back to a point of tension in the dialogue between history and the social sciences: general categories (social classes, laws of economics, cultural spaces, systems of transmission of political power) are often "all too capricious clothing in which thought is draped."[21] In my opinion, historians such as Paul Veyne are right to suggest that we should do without these categories and think of history in minor terms, as an "idiographic science," curious about specificity and the "rarity" (*raritas*) of facts that "persist in keeping their individuality" precisely because they are historical.[22] Wallis would be a case study that would have no instance of any generality, except, as in Roux's work, that of "micro-insularity" itself.

I have drawn a practical corollary from this for my investigation, which I often repeated to myself to pass the time: if what you work on is insignificant, you risk falling off the map. Traveling for three short weeks in search of the traces left by a man who spent five years on an island of a few thousand inhabitants eighty years ago, without being too eager to form a scientific opinion on "Polynesia," "colonialism," or the "Pacific," I had to prepare myself to hit a brick wall, too.

After spending my first Sunday at the hotel, I began my investigation with an appointment with Bernadette Papilio, who explained to me that the archives of the Residency no longer exist. They had been "summarized and destroyed" and the general inspector of the archives who had been sent from Paris had been "very sorry" to discover this. She was nonetheless full of ideas and contacts and suggested I start by going to see a former soldier, Juan Bustio, who, if I remember correctly, was in charge of veterans and recruitment for the army in a sort of internet café opposite the island's gymnasium, the "cyber-base." He, too, was an ex-African. When he met me, he kindly admitted that the name "David" did not say much to him, but he did have a piece of advice: "Check Wikipedia."

Protectorate of Mata-Utu, January 29, 1938
Wallis and Futuna

French Resident

No. 8
Subject: End-of-Assignment Report
The resident of France in the Wallis and Futuna Islands
to the commissioner general of the French Republic in the Pacific Ocean
I have the honor to share with you the end-of-assignment report that
you asked me to write before my final departure from the protectorate.

As you specified in your telegram No. 144 of September 13, 1937, I have
only endeavored "to highlight the political, economic and social situation upon my arrival compared to my departure, and also to indicate
suggestions and opinions on the program to be followed to continue the
work begun and to strengthen French influence in these distant islands."

Signed: DAVID

21. Chronicles of the Golden Age

According to the archives, the story of David's time in Wallis is much the same as that of David's time in Cameroon. It was like a rehearsal, in the theatrical sense of the term, like a draft, a trial run, a preview.

Dr. David sailed for the Pacific on June 2, 1933. He had just returned from a long posting in the Levant, where he was a doctor in Raqqa, Syria. This had been his first posting and he had distinguished himself by his drive, athletic abilities, and organizational skills, making use of them, notably, to set up a sanitary blockade on the border with Iraq against an approaching cholera epidemic. His superiors noted that he was "willing" to be assigned to "distant posts" and that he had only a "very moderate taste [. . .] for the more down-to-earth aspects of the profession of the army doctor."[1] Arriving in Nouméa in July, he entered Wallis lagoon on September 13, 1933, on board the *Bucéphale*, a Messageries maritimes (Maritime Transport) steamer which serviced the island three times a year, via Port-Vila in the New Hebrides. He left a little over four years later, after having put the finishing touches on his end-of-assignment report, sixty concise pages filled with tables of figures and nice rhetoric, a chronicle of an unprecedented transformation of the island. This report would circulate in Paris: "This report [. . .] is the work accomplished by Dr. David as it was at the time of his departure, work clearly carried out by him without affectation, without stylistic embellishments," wrote Governor

Marcel Marchessou in his preface; it is "one of the most wonderful colonial successes that I have had the liberty to observe."[2] A typed version of it now rests in the Archives d'outre-mer in Aix-en-Provence. On the binding, the title is inscribed in gilt letters: "L'œuvre du docteur David à Wallis et Futuna" (The work of Doctor David in Wallis and Futuna).

When David arrived, it was not the time for grandiloquence. His predecessor, Dr. Renaud, had been removed in haste along with his family by a navy aviso after being targeted in an assassination attempt, the details of which have never been clarified (or really confirmed, for that matter). He had taken sides in the succession crisis that followed the death of King Sosefo Lavelua in March 1933 and found himself isolated, caught up in a conflict between princely factions,[3] after having lost the support of the mission and gained the hostility of the island's only trader, Julien Brial, an adventurer from the Pyrénées-Orientales who had married a Wallisian woman of royal lineage, Aloïsia. A handful of "troublemakers" had been exiled to the Loyalty Islands in retaliation, but the prestige of France, as they said in Paris, had been seriously damaged. The crisis was just as serious in terms of the economy. Residents had so far failed in this domain, encountering (they said) the "absolute indolence" of the Wallisians and leaving behind them quickly forgotten dreams of coffee, cocoa, peanut, or cotton plantations.[4] Copra (the fat extracted from dried coconuts) remained the island's only exportable resource, but its price fell with the Great Recession, and the coconut groves had just been invaded in 1931 by a species of large beetle that arrived from Asia via the Samoan islands, the coconut rhinoceros beetle, which ravaged the trees by devouring their leaves. Production had collapsed and traders in Fiji were no longer buying, the shipping route having been suspended for fear of contagion.[5]

Dr. David's mission was, first, to get the situation back on track, if possible by maneuvering more skillfully than his predecessor, who had even been reproached by the king for "not properly caring for the sick."[6] The governor briefed him prior to his departure from Nouméa. There was no question of simply acting as a "flag bearer": the Wallisians had to be told that "France has made great sacrifices [. . .] [and] considers on the contrary that it has an essential duty to help its protégés to improve the conditions of their lives by guiding them with its advice."[7] He was counting on his skill and resolve, and, if necessary, the use of punishments and deportations, "the only sanction that makes an impression on the natives,"[8] David noted shortly after his arrival.

In the very first weeks of his time in Wallis, David got started on the copra issue. Diagnosis: the collapse of production was due to "the laziness of the natives who refuse to clear their property," except in the district of Mua (in the south of the island), where "the land is fertile and the inhabitants are more hard-working."[9] Solution: a little science (David had met a tropical agronomist in the New Hebrides who specialized in the subject) and a lot of authority. His plan to "revive the country's economic situation," he explained two months after his arrival, called for "the natives to spend a full day [per week] looking for rhinoceros beetles" and to destroy them on sight. "Every Monday I go in person [. . .] to a village randomly selected from the list to inspect the work of the natives. Severe penalties are imposed by the king to reprimand unwillingness." Also, the entire population of each village was to devote "one week per month" (with Tuesday being the first day of the week) to clearing fallow coconut groves for the "six to seven months" needed to restore them to good condition. To diversify crops, David conducted a little trial and proposed introducing castor bean, a tropical plant whose seeds produce castor oil. He sent some earth to New Caledonia to have it analyzed in the laboratory and had three thousand square meters planted on the lands of the Residency. "If the results are as satisfactory, as I hope they will be, I will force [someone added the annotation: "in their interest"] every landowner to have a castor bean plantation."

An increase in tax revenue was also urgently needed. Since 1916, the island had been subject to a head tax, which represented the only revenue in the budget, apart from taxes on copra exports (and postage stamps). "A fortnight after my installation, the chiefs came to warn me that, given the current poverty of the country, the collection of the tax in its entirety seemed impossible to them. I replied that I would hold them responsible and that if I was not satisfied I would deport some of the least effective among them." David's "tactic," as he put it, was to intervene at the source and strictly plan copra production, the only means the villagers had of obtaining money: "In order to protect them from themselves and force them to work, I myself set the number of tons of copra each district is required to supply per week. Every Saturday evening [. . .] the three *pule* [the chiefs of the three districts, also known more specifically as *faipule* or *faipule palokia*] come to report to me on the work done in their district, papers in hand." And David insisted on being present during transactions with the shopkeepers who bought their produce. Otherwise, "the attitude of the population is satisfactory," wrote David on arriving. "The natives seem gentle and submissive to their chiefs [. . .] . I take every opportunity to put myself in contact with them."

David's economic interventionism gradually bore fruit, making relative peace possible. He negotiated and obtained a reduction in the head tax from the governor in 1934, which was greeted by "an explosion of joy in native circles."[10] The population remained poor, with no money to buy sugar or soap, but "25,000 larvae" of rhinoceros beetles were killed every week and collected in baskets by the women,[11] and the villages regularly managed to deliver more than the required quantities of copra. In April 1934 David began to regret not noticing that his measures to bring in tax revenue had caused "some distress": the chiefs had forbidden the villagers to buy anything and forced them to sell "pigs and poultry for next to nothing in order to raise enough money," while some were made to work on credit, and "fifteen inhabitants of Hihifo are still cutting stones for a Chinese man who settles their tax bill."[12] David continued to use threats to fight against the "wasting" (i.e., local consumption) of coconuts, which were used as a source of drinking water and above all as a staple food for the island's many pigs (which served mainly as currency and as luxury items), and proposed making the cultivation of manioc "mandatory" in order to feed them. At the same time, however, David employed multiple strategies to improve the standard of living of the Wallisians, attacking the donations required by the mission (a "true tithe," he wrote in April 1934), negotiating an increase in the purchase price of trochus (shells collected from the lagoon for their mother-of-pearl), and demanding in vain that the governor take action on the price of copra, purchased at 300 francs (or even 150 francs if it was not dried) per ton from the Wallisians by the exporter and sold at 836 francs to the industrialists in Marseille. "The means at my disposal to improve this defective situation are few [. . .] and the fate of our natives seems to me very precarious this year," sighed David.

A first miracle occurred thanks to the effects of a law passed in Paris on August 6, 1933, which David, who was well informed, was granted permission to apply in the protectorate. The Loi sur les oléagineux (Oilseed Act) was one of the main protectionist measures taken by France during the Great Depression to support the colonial economy in the face of the global fall in the price of raw agricultural materials.[13] At the beginning of the 1930s, the collapse of the price of peanuts, the primary output of French West Africa, had caused concern far beyond the business community. In a colony like Senegal, peanuts were the mainstay of development policies, sealing an alliance between the colonial administration and the local politico-religious elites (the Mouride brotherhood in particular) that appeared to guarantee social peace and political stability.[14] According to Albert Sarraut, the minister of the colonies who tabled the bill, the collapse of prices threatened colonial order, heralding a "decivilization" of the natives returning to "their primitive life,"[15] future anger, and even repercussions for national defense, as, in addition to being a source for peanuts, Africa was a source for infantrymen. Supported by the Senegalese deputy and first African elected to the Chamber of Deputies, Blaise Diagne, Léon Blum, and 480 of the 527 deputies, the law introduced exceptional customs duties on imports from abroad of "fruits and oilseeds, fats and their derivatives"[16] and foresaw using part of this customs revenue to subsidize peasants and producers in the French colonies. This measure of imperial preference caused panic in Marseille's oil and soap factories, which obtained some of their supplies from outside the French colonies and feared that their costs would skyrocket. For the liberal historian Jacques Marseille, the law would even become a textbook case of the archaism of the French imperial economic model. Between the risk of a rise in the price of soap and the very future of the *pax franca* in Africa, the choice was easy to make. In the far reaches of the Pacific, the Wallisians were not asking for too much: as exclusive producers of fats (copra and castor oil), they obtained from the new law an unexpected windfall of around 100,000 francs per year, the equivalent of the island's total budget in the early 1930s.

However, the governor and David agreed that there was no question of distributing such a sum directly to the locals. The "rational application of the Oilseed Act [which] may be sufficient to restore to this whole country the modest welfare to which it is entitled" was to use the money "collectively"—that is, under the management of Dr. David.[17] In March 1935, when the first payment was announced, a Native Welfare Society was created for the purchase of materials, seeds, fertilizer, and food, to be distributed as "bonuses in kind."[18] It should be recalled that native welfare societies had become widespread throughout the empire, after having been tested first in Algeria and then in peanut-producing Senegal (from 1907 onward).[19] The native welfare societies never resembled the agricultural cooperatives run for and by peasants that they were supposed to be. In the context of colonial rule, they functioned at best as a tool for controlling cash crop farming, steered by the colonial administration and financed by a "contribution" in the form of a tax (as would be the case from 1937 onward for coffee and cocoa in Haut-Nyong); at worst, and quite commonly in Africa, native welfare societies were the "district commander's slush fund."[20] In Wallis, the use of credits was not limited to direct support for copra production. David planned to introduce a herd of cows, which could clear the land and fertilize the soil, and buy barbed wire to pen them in, as well as sheet metal and cement to build drinking water tanks (and thus reduce the consumption of "drinking" coconuts). He also planned to distribute tools, farming implements, and fertilizers to Wallisians, as well as cartridges for hunting rats and bats. The magic of the subsidy did the rest: from 1935 onward, guano, shovels, picks, machetes, and sacks of rice abounded on the island. David, for his part, bought himself a sidecar motorcycle (he said "motorbike" in his report).

The second miracle would take a little longer to occur. Copra production recovered, and its prices rose starting in 1935, first modestly, then sharply at the end of 1936, fetching more than 1,000 francs per ton of dry copra when bought from Wallis—an increase of more than 300 percent. Disposable income for the Wallisians followed the same curve. At the end of his stay, David calculated that the income per taxable person rose, after tax, from 132 francs in 1933 to 749 francs in 1937.[21] For the castor beans, success was slow in coming: caterpillars attacked the plantations, the machines were not delivered, and the Wallisians were reluctant to hand-shell the tons of seeds produced, but this was not the point. The island was undergoing a small material and economic revolution, and the Residency's accounts were in the green. Bailed out by tax revenue, it could create "new budget items to intensify [its] action and extend [its] influence."[22]

David sent reports to Nouméa three times per year when the *Bucéphale* would dock at the island to unload supplies to the traders and load copra for the return voyage. Depending on the ship's itinerary, it could be as long as six months before the reports were read in Nouméa, and never less than a month.[23] To prevent correspondence from taking years to carry out, David asked the governor to have the ship remain in the Mata-Utu harbor for "three or four days," time enough for him to read and answer his mail.[24] I imagine that he typed everything himself. Very few Wallisians spoke French, and there is never any mention of a typist, the only other "colonists" on the island being the telegrapher, his wife, and the trader (an Australian, who replaced Julien Brial after he left for New Caledonia). The reports are sober. Trimester after trimester, one reads the uncertain chronicle of a sojourn that has not yet become a "success" or a "successful experiment"; not everything had yet been put on the right track and dressed up in big words about France, medicine, and civilization. There is little variation in the format of the reports. Chapter 1, "Situation politique" (Political situation), very long at the beginning of his posting and then subsequently laconic, discussed David's relations with the royalty and the chiefs of the island. Chapter 2, "Attitude de la mission mariste" (Attitude of the Marist mission), detailed his quarrels and his arrangements with the fathers and inspired the governor, anxious to ease tensions, to make some worried annotations. Chapter 3, "Situation économique" (Economic situation), always the most substantial, was devoted to copra, castor oil, and the Native Welfare Society; in the margins the governor gave his opinions on maize, manioc, and the hunting of flying foxes. Other sections that appeared regularly included those on the operation of the wireless station, the condition of the wharf (the pier), the Burns Philp trading post, and the yield of the Residency's farmland, but curiously, there is almost nothing about health, apart from allusions to the illnesses of a few notables and the construction site of the hospital, which was begun on the heights of Mata-Utu in January 1934.

The chapters on public education are more extensive. As soon as he arrived, David launched a project that had been dear to his predecessors: he set up a French school for "about one hundred children of both sexes, most of them descendants of chiefs" to "raise following French methods a certain number of young people who will later be called on to play leading roles in their country."[25] French was hardly spoken on the island at the time, the teaching being entirely in the hands of the mission and carried out in Wallisian. After a first term in 1934, everything seemed to be going well: the telegrapher's wife, a trained teacher, oversaw the classes; the sons of princes, ministers, and chiefs flocked to French lessons every day; the girls learned how to sew; and the mission kept its distance. It had "kept its promise [not to interfere] and there are no obstacles hindering the development of the school."[26]

Finally, there was a chapter on sports. "I have formed a small soccer team of some of the children from our school," David wrote in April 1934. "Matches will be held upon each visit of the warship, and it may be possible next year, after agreement with the Fédération calédonienne des sports athlétiques [Caledonian Athletic Sports Federation], to send the Wallisian team on a tour of Caledonia."[27] This familiar-sounding story allowed David to write an account of his progress through his reports. He never forgot to add the paragraph on sports. "A sports complex is [. . .] in the process of being organized, but only children are employed in its construction; the rest of the population being reserved for more useful work,"[28] wrote David in August 1934. The sports complex was completed in May 1935, with "in addition to the soccer field, [. . .] a track for running, a jumping pit, a grandstand (native style), and a shower room."[29] In 1936, "two new stadiums are under construction in the southern and northern districts of the island," and David was also planning "the construction of a basketball court and the forming of women's teams for next year."[30] The role of sports as a means of training bodies and creating disciplined subjects is well known to historians of colonialism.[31] In Wallis, David was therefore pleased to see that "young Wallisians are beginning to bend to team discipline" and that "a somewhat primitive, but well understood shower room welcomes new athletes after their efforts and [allows] them to appreciate the benefits of personal hygiene, which is still little valued in Wallis."[32]

Soccer gave a rhythm to ordinary times (training on Thursdays, games on Sundays) and extraordinary times (parties and arrivals of boats). It heralded a more general transformation of the body's techniques, but at the same time, because of the general enthusiasm for it (soccer was the "great fashion,"[33] wrote David in December 1936), it remained a zone of uncertainty in which hierarchies and norms were always in danger of collapsing. Between the lines, one can read that the Wallisian practice of soccer, initiated a few years earlier by the sailor Alain Gerbault (known as Selepo), who had spent time in Uvea after his ship was damaged, remained marked by an undisciplined taste for physical and technical challenge (I was told in Wallis that "playing like Selepo" today means dribbling sequences "à la Maradona"[34]). A connection to time and the world was also played out through soccer: soccer served as a test of greatness; it was a practice of comparison and connection with the outside world; it was a support for projection into the future and provided a measure of the progress made between passages of the warships, whose teams would disembark each time to face the "Wallisian team." The "excellent form of the new native sportsmen" was backed up by figures, as in the final report written at the beginning of 1938: "The various final scores of matches with French warships mark the slow ascent of our beginners. Defeated, indeed, by five goals to zero in 1935, then by five to two in 1936, the Wallisian team was narrowly beaten in 1937, after a fairly balanced game and only by three goals to two."[35] They were nearly there.

David's social agenda and ambitions for reform took shape in retrospect— that is, at the time he drafted his final report, written in the form of a well-crafted "before-and-after" narrative. It has been known since the time of Aristotle that the reversal of fortune, the turning of misfortune into happiness, is the fundamental form of narrative, as well as the key to a well-told story. I do not know if David knew his classics, but his final report is a model of the genre, reminding us that narrative is a strategic tool used by colonial powers.[36] The Wallisians, he explained at the beginning of the chapter devoted to the social situation, represented "the lowest level of the social ladder among the populations of Oceania [. . .] . The various social programs generally organized in the colonies to raise the intellectual and moral level of the natives, to improve their physical conditions of existence, to humanize their character and customs, were indeed very little developed in the protectorate. The Health Service, despite a meritorious effort, remained insufficiently equipped; public education, left entirely in the hands of the mission, proved to be very defective; as for the projects of hygiene and social interest, they were purely and simply nonexistent."[37]

A "program designed to bring about this desirable improvement in the social status of the native population" thus had to be implemented, aimed at "extending education, encouraging sports, reorganizing the Native Medical

Assistance service, and carrying out various hygiene and sanitation projects."[38] This was followed by an inventory of the results obtained, the expansion of the school and the imminent sending of the most studious pupils to New Caledonia, sports, the doctor's personal project to "send lazy and unruly youth to [a] school of courage and discipline,"[39] and finally the organization of health care.

Real medical action had remained timid for a long time. At the beginning of his stay, David seemed to have had little time for the sick, few medicines, only one nurse, a shabby dispensary on the edge of a swamp, and a rather vague knowledge of the state of health of the island. He had as his road map a 1909 publication by Dr. Viala, the island's first doctor-administrator, who had laid out in the *Annales d'hygiène et de médecine coloniales* (Annals of colonial hygiene and medicine) an inventory of the "medical geography" of the island that was not too alarmist.[40] At the beginning of the century, European medicine was practically absent, but the Wallisians were well disposed toward vaccination; malaria had spared the island, and the "race" was robust.[41] The local pathology was dominated by skin diseases of all kinds and by filariasis, a somewhat mythical disease in the history of colonial medicine, which, by disrupting the lymphatic circulation, causes elephantiasis, edemas of the lower limbs or of the genitals. The disease gave doctors opportunities for miraculous operations and spectacular photographs.

As a sign of both his goodwill and his ignorance in the field of health, one of David's first measures involved the declaration of births and deaths:

> By comparing our 1933 register with that of the mission, I was able to realize that ours was incomplete, as the natives are not very willing to accept this constraint. For the births, I therefore warned the village chiefs that I would hold them personally responsible for any failure to comply with this order (two have already been dismissed for this reason). For deaths, I made death certificates compulsory and warned the fathers that they should not proceed with any burial without first presenting a burial permit signed by me. (This also to make me aware of the main causes of mortality among the natives, as not all of them come to see the doctor).[42]

The country was small enough that it was possible to count everyone; 1933 would be year zero of a new mode of government, based on files, lists, tables, curves, and randomization.

It is as though we have already read what followed. In addition to the construction of the hospital, David multiplied "attempts to generalize European medicine," overcame competition from local practitioners, and decided to go "meet the patients"[43] by traveling the island by sidecar motorcycle and by establishing two dispensaries, one in the north and one in the south. He made mother and child welfare his priority, forbade the use of native doctors and witch doctors during childbirth, and appointed nineteen matrons, one per village, whom he instructed in basic hygiene. He had a maternity ward and a nursery built at the hospital, and puerperal fever was relegated to the annals of the past. He created a camp for leprosy patients in the island's interior in 1935, with a chapel, subsistence crop plantations, and regular distribution of tools, food, and lamps to convince the sick to remain. Eleven of the twenty-one leprosy patients on the island settled there. Once the major work on the hospital and roads was completed, David began a program of village reconstruction, with a new model of housing, with separate kitchens and cut stone slabs. Seven fifty-thousand-liter cisterns ensured a supply of drinking water.

In short, Wallis was beginning to resemble a small bio-political utopia, where everything was done to "preserve the vitality of the population and encourage it to abandon its very harmful habits."[44] In early 1938, David was able to dream of making a liar out of Dr. Viala, who, when he had left the island in 1909, announced that Wallis's isolation, geographical makeup, and small size would "reduce to the state of utopian any hope" of "economic development."[45] In the end, the opposite was true: "The isolation of the archipelago, so often deplored, can on the contrary only contribute to the success of our humanitarian plans, because it will allow us to introduce in successive stages the benefits of civilization and to exclude from it all that the still-primitive peoples cannot assimilate without damage."[46] One had to think about the "pretty children who brighten the villages," an "irrefutable testimony of the beautiful vitality of the race," and take stock. Once the social programs were fully developed, the population of Wallis would grow "in considerable proportions" and spread to the rest of Oceania, where the islands were depopulated. And "we must not lose sight of the fact," concluded David, "that the Wallis-Futuna group is one of the rare Oceanian possessions where the Polynesian type has been preserved in all its strength." David invented for the island a destiny as model colony, racial reserve, and experiment in civilization.

The contrast between this and the dreadful image of 1933 is all the more powerful as there is something of a blank in the archives that I consulted. In the documents left by Roux in Nouméa, which are stored in polystyrene boxes like those used to keep fish fresh, there are no quarterly or annual reports written after the end of 1936. The last year of David's stay does not seem to have been reported as such. There is a hiatus that takes us directly from the hesitant reports of 1933, 1934, 1935, and 1936 to the edifying account written at the beginning of 1938, which would end up, with its gilt-letter binding, in the archives of Aix-en-Provence (after some time, presumably, spent in the library of the Ministry of the Colonies).

In the time it takes to blink.

To count to three.

The island is transformed.

ON OCTOBER 11, 1937, at around 9 a.m., the colonial aviso *Rigault de Genouilly*, a 104-meter steamship that had left the shipyards five years earlier, crossed the Uvea Pass with more than 125 men on board. A flotilla of pirogues came to meet it to guide its movements. On board the ship were the governor and the head of the Health Service of New Caledonia, who had come on an inspection mission. As the steamer approached Mata-Utu, the view was striking: on the hill, a large building of cut stones dominated the island and looked out over the sea. It was the new hospital.

Captain-Doctor David went aboard to greet them along with Monsignor Poncet and a delegation of Wallisian dignitaries. Everyone disembarked at 2 p.m. The governor's first visit was to the hospital, "one of the jewels of Mata-Utu." It "marks in a tangible way," Governor Marchessou wrote upon his return, "the progress made in Wallis by the administration of the protectorate":

> Prior to 1933, the natives put up the strongest resistance to any work of public utility. It was with great difficulty that we were able to obtain the vague maintenance of a poor channel of communication with them. Nor did they take into account the advice given to them by the French resident for the improvement of their food and cash crops.
>
> At present, a beautiful five-meter-wide road, sandy and very smooth, allows one to drive from the north to the south of the island, passing through all the villages on the east coast. The coconut groves, which constitute the main wealth of the natives, are well maintained, new crops: castor bean, corn, manioc, taro, etc. have been established in each district. Cement cisterns are becoming more and more numerous; there will soon be some in every village. These results have not been achieved without resistance from the natives who thought that the French resident did not have to worry about making them work; he is there, they thought, to wave the French flag and to collect the taxes that the population would like to pay.

This is not how Dr. David understood his duty. Today he has the satisfaction of seeing that the people of Wallis recognize the benefits brought to them by our French resident.[47]

The delegation of Governor Marchessou (who had previously lived in Africa himself and knew about manioc and yams) drew crowds for three days. The visit was in fact planned to coincide with the celebrations marking the centenary of the arrival of the first Marist fathers on the island. In the preceding weeks, David had had the road extended to the extreme south of the island, to Kolopopo, near the place where Father Bataillon had landed one hundred years earlier. He had demolished the huts that were in the way, rebuilt the village square, and built a "Great Hall."[48] On October 12, the whole island, more than three thousand people who had arrived on foot starting the day before, gathered for the centenary Mass, celebrated by the bishop, who was assisted by two Wallisian priests, followed by a Kava ceremony with the French authorities and the ship's officers. The governor had no words to describe the "shimmering colors," the "grandeur of the ceremony," and the quality of the play performed by the seminary students, a historical reenactment of the arrival of the missionaries.[49] On the thirteenth, a "considerable crowd" attended the blessing of the hospital by the bishop;[50] on the fourteenth, the authorities, general staff, and officers of the ship met one last time with the entire population of the island at "the stadium perfectly equipped by [David]" to attend a "great native feast" with a dance performance and Kava ceremony.[51] At noon, after a final lunch at the residence, the aviso weighed anchor while firing twelve cannon shots.

David had three to four months remaining before his departure, time enough to get his papers in order and write his report.

EXTRACT FROM THE PROGRESS REPORT ON COLONEL DAVID
1938—Will return to France after four-and-a-half years in Wallis. An inspection of this archipelago in October 1937 by the governor and me showed what important work had been carried out from the administrative and political point of view, as well as from the medical point of view—Was entered in the 1938 promotion list for the rank of Major-Doctor.

Nouméa, February 28, 1938. Lt-Colonel-Doctor. Director of the Health Service.

Signed: [illegible]

22. *I te Temi* o Tavite (In the Time of David)

I got Blaise (Pelesio) Hoatau's name from Jean-François Vrignaud, alias François Robin, a teacher of economic and social sciences who taught at the Wallis high school and then became a novelist. I had met with him in Paris because his latest novel, *Le Résident d'Uvéa* (The Resident of Uvea), tells the story of the island's doctor-administrators, with a short passage on Dr. David.[1] I had left our meeting with a short bibliography and a few names of former students who might have memories to share, including Blaise, whom "everyone on the island knows" and who works at the Direction de l'équipement (Infrastructure Department), just across from the gymnasium, the cyberbase, and the shopping center (in Wallis, everything is just across from everything). I had to go through several steps to find him, as he has retired. But, indeed, everyone knows Blaise. I asked a young lady who was smoking in front of the infrastructure building where to find him. She took me to a secretary, who took me to the young man who replaced Blaise, who borrowed a car from a colleague to lead me to Blaise's house, in the village of Ahoa, where we found his daughter, who in turn took her car to lead us to another house, which Blaise was in the process of renovating. His face lit up immediately when I told him that "Jeff" (Jean-François) had sent me. We made an appointment for the weekend, and our little procession of three cars set off again on the dirt road that winds between the plots of land, then dispersed when we met the asphalt. I expected a lot from this meeting, because Blaise was one of the rare contacts who had not been recommended to me five or six times by all the authorities on the island as a compulsory step in my research. It is always good to get off the beaten path.

Blaise Hoatau was born in 1952, which means he lived through the protectorate era. "In the flesh,"[2] he said: he had gone hungry, because at that time, before the island had gained the status of Overseas Territory, there was no subsidy from Paris to alleviate the food shortages that followed the cyclones. He also lived through the time of copra production, when he had to collect coconuts with the other schoolchildren to pay for the sacks of rice in the canteen and the fuel for the mission's truck. "We were forbidden to eat the coconuts. Forbidden. [. . .] We had to dry the copra, put it in sacks, and sell it to a company." He lived through the time when only twenty students per age group on the whole island entered the sixth grade in the seminary at Lano. He also lived through the time of compulsory military service, when all the young people of the island went for a year to Caledonia or to Paris; in his case, he was sent to the artillery, at the Suippes camp, near Châlons-sur-Marne. He learned about the time of Dr. David from his mother, who was born in 1919: "It was the time when she was just married, in the years 1933–1934, before the Second World War."

He continued: "My mother used to tell me that it was thanks to this guy that the roads were able to be built. He wanted to do rational things, you know. A road with gutters, a shoulder, pavement, there you have it. Roads that would be maintained." Blaise likes to talk about roads. They were his profession for twenty-seven years, spent in the Department of Public Works as a topographer, "doing roads, leveling work, work for airports, in schools, topographical surveys all over the place." He was also part of the team that worked on the beautiful 1 / 25,000 scale IGN map that I had in my bag (the whole island fits on one map). So, David's road construction was of direct interest to him, because David had "disrupted the land," by plotting the road "on the fly," cutting properties in half without knowing (or caring). Years later, there is still no law that defines the public domain, and it is not clear who owns the road, whether the owners of the land were compensated or expropriated, or what the width, the "right of way," and the "construction limits" of the road are. To put it in technical terms, "it's totally unclear." For Blaise, the first Wallisian topographer, all this meant hours spent negotiating and explaining whenever a ditch had to be redone or a guardrail put up. These were things he had not learned in France, at the École nationale des sciences géographiques (National School of Geographic Sciences) in Forcalquier, but it fell to him to deal with them because he was perfectly bilingual, something which made him known all over the island.

The road network has since been expanded, which makes the location of the original roads somewhat less clear, but Blaise is sure that the "RTI," the road that runs along the east coast, where most of the population is located, in the path of the trade winds, is the one that was laid out by David. It connects Hihifo, the district in the north, to Mua, in the south, via the mission of Lano and Mata-Utu, the "capital." And in David's time, it was "up to each village to do the maintenance": each village was given a segment of road, which was then subdivided by family, each one being responsible for a fifty-meter stretch in front of their house. Blaise's mother and her neighbor had their "piece." They had to put sand on it, "clear" it, clean the ditch, and plant tufts of vetiver to hold the earth in place. "They had to maintain the road. That's all there was to it."

Before saying our goodbyes, we took a short walk along the road together, and Blaise told me a little about the embankment, the ditch, the shoulder, and the fifty meters that his mother had to cut regularly. It rained a lot while we were talking, and the ditch flooded. Well aligned on the embankment, he showed me the tufts of vetiver, which are still used to prevent erosion. I had heard this word before, in a commercial for perfume or shower gel; here, it is known as *kasiahi*. It is a plant that is very well known to the Wallisians because it is made into scented oils, and the older people all know that it was David who had had them plant it. It looks like the ornamental grasses that landscapers tend to put in parks all over Europe in recent years. Blaise also told me how sand was put on the road by the bagful; it was taken from a beach between Mata-Utu and Liku that has since disappeared. They then began using coral extracted by bulldozer, which hardened like cement as it dried, and finally, "with the environmental movement," stone. It was noon, and I was very glad I had rented a car because it was too hot to walk.

However, David's preferred mode of transportation, as Blaise had learned from his father-in-law, was the motorcycle, or more precisely, the sidecar motorcycle. David was known for this all over the island, and one can imagine that he enjoyed himself, the wind in his hair on his beautiful sand road lined with vetiver. When they heard the sound of the engine, the children would come running to breathe in the smell of gasoline, a smell that was new at the time, like that of vetiver roots. (I would add that smell is a very important sense in Wallis.[3] You need only inhale in the airport lobby or any administrative office, where everyone wears a necklace of flowers, or to peruse the shelves of the huge perfume shop in Mata-Utu, or talk to the Wallisians about the way that French foreign aid workers smell, to realize that the island is an olfactory landscape.)

I would often think back to what Blaise told me about roadside maintenance. Grass grows quickly in the tropics, but the landscaping in Wallis is
beautifully maintained, as though it were a sort of garden island. One morning, toward the end of my stay, the whole team at my hotel was busy trimming
the roadsides, some cutting, others raking, including the side that runs along
the sea. They were doing it the way you do housework, without thinking about
it. "It's for the mosquitoes," they told me when I came to say hello. Maybe it's
true, maybe there are health regulations, or maybe this maintenance is also
related to land issues and is a means of establishing ownership. However, the
adoption of this practice has also been attributed to David. Mikaele Tui, one of
the Wallisian specialists on the culture and the history of the island, explained
it to me after my stay there: "The French are often surprised that the lawns are
so well maintained . . . It was David who taught us [. . .] . David decided that the
roadsides needed to be maintained. When I was twelve or thirteen, I remember
that there was one day a week when we had to clean the roads. It was David
who started it, and we did it without thinking about it."

This discussion about lawns expresses a particular type of relationship between past and present, a way of linking them, that plays an important role
in my study. It could be said, although it is not really my approach, that these
lines are about David's *memory*. Historians often add an extra chapter to their
works devoted to commemorations linked to their object of study—that is to
say, to the present uses of the fragment of the past they have written about
and reconstructed, chapters devoted to monuments, to "memory places," to
historiographical production, to memory "wars" sometimes; in short, to explicit forms of reconstruction and summoning of the past from the present,
which we are able to keep at a distance, or at least distinguish from historical
work proper. This approach in terms of memory is important, but it has several shortcomings. It favors explicit discourses; it is often hemmed in by ready-
made questionnaires on politics, the state, and the nation; it presupposes that
one always knows in advance what will be commemorated or forgotten; and it
does not change much in the way history itself is written. Another way of pos-
ing the question of memory is to say that the past "shapes" the present, haunts
it, that the past is a present absence—a specter, a ghost, an echo, or sometimes
a trauma. In this way, the past is given a capacity for initiative, which acts on
the people of the present sometimes in spite of themselves, and the researcher
is above all a seeker of metaphors to describe this phenomenon.[4] This is not
what I am trying to do here, either. Rather, I am rather interested in forms of
material, proven, tangible presences from the past, but the existence of which
we are not aware of in advance. I make unexpected encounters with traces the

starting point of my investigations and not an "opening chapter" or an epilogue as in a *real* history book.

It is in this way that my approach is archaeological.[5] It is not just an analogy, nor a statement to be taken to the letter, in the sense that I would use carefully dated material fragments to fill in gaps in the archives, much as oral interviews are sometimes used as "complementary" sources, which, once rigorously critiqued, would allow the historical past to be reconstructed in a more accurate and richer way. The detour through traces (or through interviews, for that matter) does not serve as *witness account*, does not establish a *triangulation* that would allow access to a truer past; it is rather a way to ask the question of past and present differently, to think about their intertwining and mutually engendering relationship. For archaeology, at least in the way that this discipline has reinvented itself in recent years around the question of the "contemporary past," has something fundamental to say about this. Archaeologists, wrote Laurent Olivier following Lewis Binford, do not discover the past. No matter what time period they come from, whether Greek antiquity or the Second World War, archaeological remains are part of the present world, the here and now, and are contemporary to us—that is the condition of their existence. Archaeologists, by definition, are archaeologists of the present, and their subject is "the material of the past which fills the entire mass of the present."[6] Their knowledge of the past is never direct or immediate but is based on an understanding of the material transformations that time makes on things in the *present*.

The power of archaeology lies in the surprises that excavations hold, which "bring out the part of the unknown, or the unrepresented, that is ingrained in the reality of our world,"[7] where historians' reflections on what is remembered and what is forgotten often go around in circles, by commenting at length on "forgotten" events that we know in advance to have been "forgotten," which is to say, they have not been forgotten at all. This aporia is evident in the history of French colonialism, which should always be looked back on as a forgotten past. Rather than use the archives to diagnose the limits of memory (or the opposite) in a world that one would imagine as "essentially known or at least entirely knowable,"[8] for my study, I wanted to draw inspiration from the work of the historian Nancy Hunt, to leave room for surprise, for stumbling, for the discomfort that comes from the irruption of traces in the present,[9] those traces that make the past come out by their presence, that make events in the past historical facts "posthumously,"[10] to borrow a term from Walter Benjamin. The method, therefore, in my view, is about wandering, guided tours, car rides, what geographers call a "nonrepresentational" approach,[11] which is based on the shared perception of the landscape—objects that we touch, plants that we smell, fruits that we taste—rather than on the somewhat-worn ritual of "face-to-face" sociological interviewing or ethnographic "observation."

The second consequence, which concerns the writing of history more directly, consists in realizing that the place of the past is not the past itself, but the present and the present alone.[12] Whether we are dealing with archives in polystyrene boxes in an association building in Nouméa, digitized newspaper articles, retired surveyors, or cement cisterns, the access they give to the past is conditioned by the fact that we can relate to them, that they are there with us, whether they be in good condition or damaged, complete or incomplete. The past that they "contain" does not really exist outside this connection, and the historical narratives that make us believe the contrary, by erasing the multiple mediations that allow it to happen, are mystifications. Our knowledge of the past can only be *relational*, that is to say, according again to Laurent Olivier, a knowledge based on our particular relationship—us, here, now—with the remains of the past that we have been given to comprehend.[13] This is why it is necessary to speak *simultaneously* of the archive and the archivist, of the content of the documents and the logic of their conservation and destruction, of the always extraordinary accident that brought them to us. That is why it is necessary to speak *simultaneously* about Blaise, about Dr. David, and about the steps taken on the road. This is something of the lesson that archaeology has to offer to history and memory studies, from which archaeology can no longer be distinguished. Benjamin said it in a beautiful fragmentary text: "In this sense, for authentic memories, it is far less important that the investigator report on them than that he mark, quite precisely, the site where he gained possession of them. Epic and rhapsodic in the strictest sense, genuine memory must therefore yield an image of the person who remembers, in the same way as a good archaeological report not only informs us about the strata from which the findings originate, but also gives an account of the strata which first had to be broken through."[14]

Pelesio (Blaise), when he spoke about Dr. David while chewing his tobacco, always called him "Tavite," the Wallisian version of the first name David (pronounced tah-vee-tay). Since Blaise knows the whole island like the back of his hand, all its potholes and speed bumps, we visited the cisterns that Tavite left behind, the *tane cima* as they say here, even those that have been demolished; the now-vanished soccer stadium, invaded by vegetation and dwellings, which was by the sea, in the place known as Tobiano, at the foot of the hill with the hospital on it; the fields in the *toafa*,[15] the often infertile land covered in scrub in the island's interior where Tavite had tried to grow *pinati*, peanuts, apparently without much success. The character has become the marker of a series of stories, objects, and places, condensed into a five-word phrase that accounts of his time on the island are peppered with:

> When I was little we used to talk about [. . .] "the time of Tavite" . . . *I te temi o Tavite*. The time of David, in the era of David: *I te temi o Tavite*. It was a common phrase at the time. When we talked about a road: *I te temi o Tavite*. When we talked about a plant: *I te temi o Tavite*. He brought peanuts to plant in Wallis, he brought a lot of things to plant in Wallis, vanilla . . . He was the one who advised to drink lemongrass in case of fevers. Because he was a doctor, too.

This "time of David" is not a segment of the past that we remember; it is not a "story," a chapter with a beginning and an end. It is vetiver and the RTI, the smell of gasoline and the sound of the lawnmower; it is something that exists only by being actualized—through arguments over the laying of a pipe, a hospital strike, a cup of lemongrass, a first name. It is not a recollection but rather a "replay," a repetition, a reappearance. It is like a song. The time of David is not a dating, it is a provenance.[16]

23. Doctor Machete

The other thing Blaise told me about, which would often come up during my conversations in Wallis, were the large machetes that Tavite had introduced on the island: "Resident David paid people. Their compensation was an ax and a machete, which they called *hele faka lesita*. In local translation, it means 'a machete handed out by the *lesita*, the resident.' It's a machete distributed by the government. So, it stuck, you can ask any Wallisian of my age, what's a *hele faka lesita*? and he'll tell you, it's that. [. . .] At the end of every month, you'd go and get your machete. Because he had some to hand out."

I asked Blaise if he had one so I could see what it looked like. He did have one, of course (everyone has this type of machete handy, indispensable if only to cut open a coconut), and I took a photo of him with his machete in hand. He posed somewhat solemnly, looking off into the distance. In the archival material, David called them "Sabatier knives" and counted that he distributed 1,480 of them free of charge during his stay,[1] thanks to funds from the Oilseeds Act, to clear the coconut groves, prepare the fields, and clear the construction sites for the road and the hospital.

This story about machetes made me want to look for them everywhere, to follow them around the island, to do their "social biography." This method is a bit "fetishistic,"[2] as Arjun Appadurai and Nancy Hunt wrote. In the two weeks that followed, I found myself asking to see these machetes, weighing them, tapping their blades, asking questions. "A machete à la Resident. We still say that today," explained Siolesio (Sioli) Pilioko, the former director of the Service des affaires culturelles (Cultural Affairs Service), in the middle of a dream garden with pine, coconut, and fruit trees. The machete sums up the image of David, who embodies the generic function of "resident," a metonymy of an age of plenty, when new things, knives, machetes, shovels, crowbars, arrived by the hundreds and were distributed both free of charge and based on merit, and "everyone was happy." I took more photos, including one of Sioli Pilioko pretending to cut a tuft of vetiver. "It's with these machetes that we built the RTI," Atoloto Uhila, an old man who knew David when he was a child, told me. Of course, even though I tried every time to pretend that I did not know what the significance of this machete was, I did not do a good job of hiding my joy, so there was always the risk that I was the one creating the link between past and present, and that people only answered my questions to try to make me happy, a classic bias when a researcher asks questions. All these stories of traces could simply have been a by-product of my questionnaire, a trick. At least, that is what I thought until I went on TV.

Somewhat by chance, on the last Sunday of my visit to Wallis, I met a journalist from France Télévisions Wallis-et-Futuna, Lagimaina Hoatau. He was sitting next to me at the big meal that followed the Mass and Kava ceremony on the Feast of Saints Peter and Paul in a village in the northern district of Hihifo—an enormous buffet of stewed pork, fish salad, and rosé wine, all at 10 a.m., in the presence of the bishop and the notables of the district. There was a delegation of priests from all over the Pacific visiting the island, and Lagi thought I was one of them until we started talking about David. Then he began to tell me all kinds of stories, and we ended up doing a little report together on the subject for the television news.

A small aside is in order here: television plays a unique role in Wallis, which merits a study in itself. France Télévisions is based in Wallis, on the hill known as RFO,[3] and produces bilingual programs in French and Wallisian, including two news programs per day. Wallisian journalists are good, both technically and editorially, and as is the case elsewhere, Facebook and streaming increase the audience for the channel's reports. What makes the *Wallis et Futuna 1re* newscast a rather extraordinary institution has partly to do with the scale of the island. Every day, three villages with a total of eight thousand inhabitants are the subject of two fifteen-minute newscasts, which means that, whatever the subject, one always knows the person on the screen, either in person or by association. For doctoral students, researchers, international volunteers, and interns of all kinds who spend a few weeks on the island, this almost always guarantees a good-quality report on their work, whether it is an audit of the water supply network or a botanical survey—a few minutes of celebrity that make grandparents in France happy, except that the intern (or, in my case, the historian) is always already "known," if only by their scooter or car, before going on TV. In the evenings, people often gave me an account of what I had done during the day, if I had been in the south, to the diocese, or to the supermarket.

For our report, Lagi suggested taking me along the RTI, to the archives in Lano, and then to the hospital in Sia. To get some good shots, he had me walk back and forth, in the II a.m. heat, shooting me up close and from afar, zooming in on my shoes, treading the pavement "of this road that we owe to Resident David," as the voice-over would say. He had the idea for a scene at the little shop in Wallis where I liked to go to get supplies, the kind of shop that reminds me a little of Africa (as long as you ignore the prices), where you can find everything: soap, household products, bread, cold drinks, sardines, batteries, farming tools, and all varieties of corned beef, the local dish. Lagi's instructions were to walk into the shop, without letting anyone know in advance, and ask if I could buy these *hele faka lesita* to make use of the element of surprise, a bit like on *Cash Investigation*.[4] So, off we went. The surprise did not go as planned: I was the only one who was a bit thrown off. I had the impression that the women working in the shop were getting to know me pretty well and that they were used to interviews, and Lagi, with his France Télévisions pickup and his camera on his shoulder, is well known to everyone. I asked the question at the counter, adopting a kind of Cameroonian accent that earned me some mockery from my family, and of course I was offered without the slightest hesitation a *hele faka lesita*, which cannot be confused, explained the woman at the counter, with the other models of machete and ax available for purchase. However, she had no idea why it is called that, so I explained it to her, and through her, to the whole island. And that was a wrap on our little scene.

At the hospital, we just wandered around filming a few things. The "David building," as Father Jaupitre (who is one of the most knowledgeable people on the island) calls it, one of the memories of the island that he showed me at the diocese, is at the summit, with an old flamboyant tree in front. It is a U-shaped building that opens onto the sea, with a view of the lagoon, the islets, and the open sea, and a wraparound porch, like in the old hospitals in Africa. Today, the hospital is mainly housed in new multistory buildings built around and below the original building, some of which are air-conditioned. There is nothing that directly evokes history, no stela, no plaque, no names on the pavilions. To the right of the building is a villa in ruins where I had wandered around a few times, taking pictures of old switches, rusty ventilators, and vegetation that has started to grow. This had been the house of the head doctor back in the time when he lived at the hospital, back when the military doctors knew how to do everything and remained posted here for many years at a time. Today, a large part of the medical staff comes for short rotations of a few months, from France or New Caledonia, and lives in the hotel. This is cheaper in terms of salaries, less difficult than expatriation, and more attractive for doctors, but for long-term follow-up, and contact with and knowledge of the patients, it is more complicated. "You have to change doctors every three months," people often complain. It would have been too good if the house had been David's, the perfect ruin of a lost modernity, the wreckage of the bygone days of an authoritarian but less distant medicine, which put taking care of people before cost. But the house was built in the 1950s.

David's building now houses the maternity ward. There are quite a few people in the rooms, mats on the floor, fabrics and pretty cushions, fans, women from Wallis and women from Futuna, the other island, located several hundred kilometers from Uvea and connected to it by a small plane that flies twice a week. Medical service is rather limited in Futuna and there is no maternity ward, as it would be too expensive to maintain a gynecologist, a surgeon, and an operating room (the minimum necessary requirements to avoid complications or to perform a caesarean section) for about fifty births per year. The Health Agency of Wallis and Futuna therefore asks the women of Futuna to come to Wallis, paying for their air travel, accommodation, and meals, for their four-month ultrasound, and then for a whole month before their due date, to wait for the birth.

It is a coincidence, but I cannot get over it: for a whole month, pregnant women in Futuna live in the maternity ward with a female companion, who usually sleeps on the floor or on a bench, just as in the Haut-Nyong Medical Region, except in 2014. I had learned about the existence of this arrangement before coming, through discussions with the former director of the Agence de santé de Wallis-et-Futuna (Wallis and Futuna Health Agency), Claude Wetta, a former French foreign aid worker in Cameroon. "Fed and housed for a month": in a strange hybridization that made me feel superstitious, the flagship project of Dr. David's Abong-Mbang period is being carried out here and stated in the same terms, seventy years later, in the hospital he had built on the other side of the world. Of course, the logic is different. The medical utopia of Haut-Nyong was a public health operation, even a demographic policy, a way of combatting death by protecting women from work, the village, and the patriarchy. The transfer of the women of Futuna also has its share of utopia, that of free health care by airlift, where one can hop across oceans to give birth, but it responds instead to a very contemporary concern for safety: to manage risk, to allocate resources rationally, and to give all women in the republic's territory roughly equal opportunities to be well looked after in case of complications on D-day. Perhaps the issue is also a legal one, for that matter, a way for the administration to "cover" itself; one would have to verify when giving birth in Futuna became an intolerable risk. What is certain is that in Dr. David's time, and for a long time afterward, the women of Futuna gave birth in Futuna.

In March 2015, in the run-up to International Women's Day, the Wallis TV news put together a nice report on "pregnant women from Futuna." It seemed a bit unreal, a journey through time and space, a little as though a TV crew had come to film the Abong-Mbang maternity ward in 1942 and then posted it all on Facebook. The report showed women getting bored spending a month in the hospital, "endless days, even weeks," they said, which they spent napping, singing, and looking after other women. They said they were "obliged" to be there. The lucky ones had family in Wallis, and the others, their companion, the only person allowed to stay with them. For several years, the Health Agency has been talking about offering Futunian women temporary housing in order to free up beds and make their stay less "medical," but the project "is no longer one of the current priorities," explained the journalist. This is how the report ended, with a shot of a baby sleeping in the background.

The report about me aired several days after my departure.[5] "The initial feedback is positive, many people appreciate this window on the recent history of Wallis, and others have finally learned who this famous Tavite was," Lagimaina wrote to me. I like the version with the Wallisian voice-over, even if I do not understand any of it. The language is singsong, and the subtitle is pretty: *Hisitolia*. I did not manage to save it when it was streaming, but there is one thing I wish I could check: I do not think that David was ever referred to as "King David." During my weeks in Wallis, however, it is a question that I asked as systematically as the one about machetes. Blaise had used the expression spontaneously, and I seized the opportunity on the fly: "Did you say King David? Was it a nickname?"

24. Becoming King, Part I

COUP D'ÉTAT AT THE DISPENSARY

"Learn the language as quickly as possible." On August 19, 1933, Governor Bernard Siadous provided David with some advice in the letter outlining his mission: "I have reason to believe that the current interpreter is largely responsible for the difficulties encountered by Dr. Renaud; put only limited trust in him; try to find out whether he deserves the esteem of the population, whether he has not annoyed it by his behavior, whether he is holding grudges. The sooner you can do without him, and the sooner you will remove the mask that the interpreter will fashion, whether voluntarily or otherwise, for the people you will be administrating from your true face."[1]

The time has come to tell the most astonishing of David's stories: that which took place in Wallis. It is the story of a resident who accepted a role that was a little too prominent for him, who married a princess, and who made all the men aged eighteen to fifty-nine living on the island work on his construction sites. It is the story of a doctor who became king, or who was made king, without anyone being really sure, without anyone really understanding why. It is a story that is told in Wallisian, a story from which David himself seems to be fading away. To use the words of the historian Romain Bertrand, it is a question of understanding the vernacular production of the colonial moment: not the Wallisian appropriation or reception of a modernity that would have arrived with David, but rather the entrenchment of David in Wallisian ways of governing and pronouncing authority, strength, wealth, and success. In short, it is a question of understanding his integration into a local (and itself, changing) lexicon of power.[2] This in no way detracts from the talent of his French incarnation—on the contrary—but the character of David is in part a Wallisian invention, the fruit of a collective political compromise. It is the story of a quid pro quo, of a working misunderstanding, to use Marshall Sahlins's very Polynesian expression.[3] It is the story of a man who believed that he was stepping outside his role but in fact only occupied the place that had been prepared for him.

The only photo of David in Wallis was published in one of his articles with the caption "The doctor-administrator on tour." He appears in shorts and sandals, cigarette in his mouth, on the handlebars of his sidecar motorcycle, with two shirtless children standing next to him, arms at their sides.[4] There is no one in the passenger seat. I think about this because the way in which I have told the story of "Resident David's work" so far, his extraordinary transformation of the island through agriculture, medicine, and soccer, is a bit dishonest. I have given a very colonial account of it, which even David would not have approved of. It erases a whole series of actors; firstly, the Wallisian notables, but also the entire hierarchy of "native government," the missionary institution, and the Chinese and Australian traders who also pulled the strings and gave the doctor room to maneuver. It conveys the impression of a face-to-face encounter between a man of action and a passive population. It conveys the impression that there was no one by David's side.

The Wallisians I met had different theories about who the passenger in David's sidecar would have been. For Manuele Lisiahi, a political figure on the island (he sat in the Territorial Assembly for thirty years and presided over it for some time) who was born a few months before the doctor arrived in 1933, the passenger would have been his father-in-law, Sosefo Vale Faka Aga, whom David had lured away from the seminary in Lano to become his new interpreter shortly after his arrival. It was he, Sosefo, who gave the orders on the road construction sites. "He was the one who Dr. David got to say, 'Do this for me, do that for me' to the workers."[5] When David had meetings at the chiefdom, he would go pick up Sosefo from his village of Gahi, seating him in the sidecar of his motorcycle.

In August 1933, during his three-week stopover in Nouméa, David had time to speak with his predecessor, Dr. Renaud, to go over a few reports and get an idea of the political landscape on the island, the crisis that had chased Renaud out, and what would have to be done to turn things around. The colonial world made a ritual of this kind of changing of the guard, in which one exchanged a few mediocre recipes for governing; advice on the houseboy or the cleaning woman; a few pointers on allies, clients, and enemies; and banalities on the customs and the abilities of the locals. Governor Siadous and the two doctors no doubt agreed that France's power should be put on display; in his first letter, David asked that naval warships be sent into the Wallis lagoon frequently to demonstrate "to the natives that the government has not forgotten their error, that it has an eye on them."[6]

However, the main issue was more subtle. Before even approaching Wallis, David also knew that he would be alone, with his gun but without police, with a small boat that would not go far as his only means of escape. Like his predecessor, he was reminded that he had "no means of coercion" and that a "show of force could put [him] in a difficult situation."[7] He had also read, in different versions, short introductions to Wallisian customs and the political system, for example in the writings of the missionaries or in the article by Dr. Viala. He knew that he would have to deal with an elderly king who was without great influence and not especially well disposed toward the Residency, Mikaele Lavelua, who presided over a Council of Ministers which the resident attended in a consultative capacity when it met. The Council, or Royal Fono, was composed of seven ministers, each from families who held the position hereditarily, including a prime minister who bore the title of *kivalu*. David probably had in his notes the names of the three district chiefs, the *faipule*, and the eighteen village chiefs who carried out orders and presided over the local assemblies, the *fono*. He also knew that, in practice, the king's hands were often tied by his Council of Ministers, which had the power to depose him, and that the authority of the Marist mission was considerable; in fact, the prestige of the king and of the chiefs depended on how close their ties with the mission were. Finally, he understood, like his predecessors, that power is performance, that the only authority he would have would be that which they would allow him to have, that he would have to rely on intermediaries and local ways of doing things, and that in this case the hierarchy of power (chieftainship, noble families, mission, Residency) in Uvea was demonstrated, ratified, and possibly contested during well-regulated ritual interactions, including the renowned Kava ceremony.[8] This ceremony, which followed Mass on religious holidays, consists of sharing a drink prepared from the roots of the kava (*Piper methysticum*, a plant with mild psychotropic effects consumed throughout this region of the Pacific) with notables and guests. The residents likely had their own small file on the subject. The Kava is a sacred ceremony whose most solemn moment is the distribution of the cups following a complex order that demonstrates the rank of those present, the first and last cup being the most prestigious. Attention had to be given to appearances, as David knew:

When, on the morning of September 13, 1933, the steamer *Bucéphale*, on which I had passage, dropped anchor facing Mata-Utu, I was [. . .] perfectly aware of the kinds of difficulties that had always beset my predecessors [. . .] . However, when the special agent [the telegrapher Alexis Bernast] came aboard and, after introducing himself, told me with great annoyance that all the chiefs, including the king and the prime minister, were refusing to welcome me at the landing [. . .] , I felt a certain anxiety at this early manifestation of hostility. After consulting with my agent, I asked him to inform the King that I was postponing my landing until the early afternoon, and that I therefore hoped that he would have all the time he needed to present himself, along with his Council, at the indicated place, failing which [. . .] I would temporarily suspend payment of the discretionary allowance he was accustomed to receiving each month.[9]

Everyone was at the landing when David disembarked a few hours later. But the new resident went from one disappointment to another when he visited the royal palace: "Received without the slightest deference, served fifth in the kava, I realized without any difficulty the place and role that would be assigned to me in the future."[10] Perhaps he was thinking of what Dr. Renaud had written a few months earlier: "I do not know [. . .] if the role of the resident in Wallis is to serve as the whipping boy for half a dozen savages, but in any case that is exactly the place we occupy."[11]

No one wanted confrontation, however. Following the Renaud affair and the punishments that had resulted, the ministers and chiefs feared for their roles, and the mission called for a return to calm. Most important, David understood that a trustworthy person was the one calling the shots: the prime minister, to whom he referred as *kivalu*. He had just returned from a stay in New Caledonia where he had made a good impression on the governor, a rather rare trip at the time, which likely made him an exceptional notable, a modern man, one might say, initiated in the ways of the world and noticed by the colonial administration. He was "an active man, quite intelligent, and very much listened to,"[12] who seemed to willingly carry out the resident's orders, while discreetly taking advice from the mission, wrote David. He was "the only [notable] who works and has responsibilities,"[13] while the king, who was ill as well as worn out, was happy to simply preside over ceremonies. One can see that David liked him and vice versa: in his first letter, David proposed that the prime minister's bonus be increased by one hundred francs a month. On November 26, David was able to write in his first report that "the present situation is favorable, but it is only the beginning, and the memory of the recent deportations encourages the natives to remain calm. I intend to form a definitive opinion during the five long months that separate me from the next mail collection. The attitude of the Marist mission will certainly influence the course of events."[14] The *Bucéphale* arrived as expected three days later to collect the mail. Before the boat left again, David had just enough time to add, on a separate sheet of paper:

DEATH OF THE KING OF THE WALLIS

The King of the Wallis died today November 30 at 6 p.m. after a short illness (bronchopneumonia). The necessary measures have been taken and the officers of the *Bucéphale* attended the ceremony.

ELECTION OF THE NEW KING

I will proceed with the election of the new king once the tax is collected in its entirety (end of next week).

I will likely choose Minister Kulitea, the brother-in-law of the current *kivalu*, whom I mentioned at the beginning of my political report. He is a man in his fifties, intelligent, active, who could do very well if he wants to.[15]

"This death," David later wrote, "would have unimaginable consequences."[16] What followed took place at the dispensary. On December 5, a few days before the final date set for the payment of taxes and the election of the new king, the nurse came to see him to inform him of "the general satisfaction caused by the temporary abolition of a regime that many Wallisians abhorred because of the abuses it engendered."[17] "Public opinion," his nurse explained, was "in favor of maintaining the status quo"—that is, the continuance of a period *without a king*. Other Wallisians asked him, "Is it so necessary to have a king?"[18] David wanted to ensure that he understood clearly: "A little surprised by this sudden change of heart, and fearing flattery from my Wallisian employee, I decided to question my patients myself."[19] During his consultations, the doctor therefore "secretly" asked his patients to sign a petition if they were in favor of "annexation" (note that the clinical setting acted as a voting booth, a "political technology of individuals,"[20] to use an expression of Michel Foucault's, which would not have surprised anyone on an island where an unclear distinction between government and medicine was a basic principle). David obtained thirty-three signatures in two days and sent the news by cable to Nouméa.

In the days that followed, the Council of Ministers, which could not agree on any candidate, agreed to postpone the appointment of a king under the influence of *kivalu*, who assured David of his "cooperation."[21] In each district, David organized large public *fono*s to explain the project: the three district chiefs added their signatures, as did 214 men and 107 women, "not counting the village chiefs," all of whom signed. A rumor circulated on the island for a time: "Don't sign any more, the French will force you to become soldiers and kill the Catholic religion. The fathers are refusing confession and communion to supporters of the new regime." However, David obtained formal denials from the fathers during their Sunday sermons by reassuring them that he was not planning to overturn the morality laws, which prohibited divorce and punished adultery.[22] I have never seen the terms of the petition, signed by a total of 399 people, but it is clear that it literally called for "annexation": the end of the protectorate regime, the abolition of the monarchy, and the establishment of a regime in which the resident would directly preside over a Wallisian government responsible for executing his decisions. Nouméa did not officially reply to David's letters and cables, no doubt fearing the reaction of the mission, of which no member or student signed.[23] The governor simply suggested extending the informal arrangement in force, in which David presided de facto over the Royal Fono, an "efficient" system, he explained, because it was "easier for a resident to preside over a native council than to advise a stubborn and unintelligent king."[24] But for David, there was no doubt in April 1934 that "the annexation is virtually complete: everyone is waiting for it, many are hoping for it. Given the insignificance of all the chiefs, their versatility, and their frequent bad faith, annexation [. . .] seems the only regime likely to bring order to Wallis once and for all." And, to "avoid any return to the old regime," the governor of Nouméa also validated David's proposal to share the king's salary among the main chiefs.[25]

The news opened up unexpected political possibilities. David himself could not believe it: "The country has gone almost without transition from one extreme to the other: open hostility has given way to a surprising docility." He wondered whether this "complete reversal" was not a manifestation of the "extreme versatility of the Polynesian character."[26] However, it was likely the result of tensions, rivalries, and hesitations within the princely families, which largely escaped David's notice. The vacancy of power for a few days or weeks is nothing exceptional. Given the circumstances, it may also have been a way for the Wallisians to catch their breath. In the midst of the copra crisis, under pressure to pay their taxes, they may have been hoping to escape the customary expenses that would accompany the coronation of the king. In practice, "while awaiting annexation," David found himself presiding over the Council of Ministers. He seemed overwhelmed by his own authority, which allowed him to launch major projects: "Since the departure of the last boat, I have thus been able to have several thousand stones cut for the hospital, to revive the (long-abandoned) destruction of the *Oryctes rhinoceros*, to start clearing the coconut groves, and to have the first elements of a leprosarium put in place."[27]

The island remained in a gray area regarding the king until September 1935, when Governor Siadous arrived on a warship for an inspection tour. David prepared an agreement for him to sign, which canceled without explicitly saying so the protectorate treaties signed in the nineteenth century, decreed the abolition of the role of king, and assigned all governing powers to the resident. It was the "definitive abolition of the absolute monarchy," a "small peaceful revolution,"[28] wrote David, who imagined himself the liberator of the Wallisians from their leaders.

25. Becoming King, Part II

THE WALLISIAN ART OF GOVERNING

As David and Monsignor Poncet would tell it, the success of the "resident-regent's" major projects policy was due to the fact that he suddenly had "free rein" to command,[1] enabling "the French government to finally administrate the whole country and to develop humanitarian projects at will."[2] This is somewhat true, but so is the opposite. The modernizing turn taken by the island marked, on the contrary, the establishment of new ties between the chiefdoms, mission, and French Residency, the weaving of a web of alliances and new dependencies, which owe as much to the actually quite fascinating tactfulness of Dr. David as to the logic, agendas, desires, and value of certain actors, starting with the hundreds of men who began to break rocks at the beginning of 1934. These men were more than mere mediators of "colonial power." One must go a step further: it is Tavite who must be seen as the transmission belt of a vernacular mode of government.

"On the first day of each month," wrote David a few weeks following his arrival, "I hold a meeting in the school hall, attended by the king, ministers, and village chiefs. I present them with a program of work, make my observations and, most important, I explain the reasoning behind what I am asking of them. This is an innovation that I rely on a great deal, as it allows me to see them often, all together, and to give them my advice directly. I am starting to speak the language a little and am hoping to do without the services of the interpreter shortly."[3] Even before the death of King Mikaele, the power of the resident was based on the practice of the *fono*, a customary institution of deliberation that was henceforth marked on the calendar.

The elders who remember the time describe it like this: "He was always passing through the chiefdom," Sister Malekalita Falelavaki told me, over a bowl of strong Nescafé in the beautiful home of the Mua nuns. Her father was the village chief in Kolopopo and had explained to her that David went to "meetings": "He came to gather his chiefs and that's how he passed on the subjects for the *fono*."[4] In this way, David combined inspection visits, organized "rationally," he said, accompanied by sanctions if necessary, with regular attendance at district and village *fonos*, the best forums for negotiation, public speaking, and the ritualization of consent. The omnipresence of the resident, soon to be traveling by motorized vehicle, was less a taste for direct democracy, which would short-circuit the hierarchy of the chiefdom, than a way of giving it new strength by making it the exclusive channel for the extraction of labor, the collection of taxes, and the redistribution food and goods. "All my efforts are toward making the chiefs aware of their role," wrote David in 1934. In this way, he obtained the allocation of a share of the head tax, previously levied for the king by the village chiefs in proportion to the number of taxable persons, thus giving them the means to maintain their place in ceremonial exchanges, in which authority was measured by ostentation and gifts of wealth. "Spokesmen for the ministers, these small chiefs have a very important role and they must scrupulously enforce the decisions taken at the *fono*,"[5] he explained to the governor. For Sioli Pilioko, who told me all of this, David "took on the role of the king, who, with his Council, carried out community projects in the districts. Every Sunday after Mass, the *faipule* [district chiefs] would gather the village chiefs to present the week's work to them. David saw that the Wallisians were courageous workers."

The massive recruitment of workers, in this context, was not a miracle linked to the intrinsic strength of the colonizing power, but in fact it set in motion another Wallisian social institution, the *fatogia*—that is, the system of customary chores. Participation in work ordered by the chiefs—notably, preparations for ceremonies—was in fact a fundamental obligation, which the mission had taken advantage of since its installation on the island, not without causing tensions. It is based on a performative mode of belonging to the village, a unit that was not strictly territorial in nature. As the anthropologist Sophie Chave-Dartoen explains, "It is by providing the chief with services in the name of his household that each villager, with his land and all the co-residents, becomes attached to the community thus formed. At the same time, he recognizes the authority of the 'village chief.'"[6] David's originality consists in having redirected the institution of chores toward "works of general interest" in the colonial sense of the term (it goes without saying that services intended to build chapels or prepare celebrations were also perceived as benefiting the community), and in having pushed it to the extreme limit of what was tolerable. The exceptional intensity of the work, made possible through the use of imported tools and food, strengthened rather than weakened the community ties and the relationships of authority on which they were based, at least initially.

David is also remembered for this in the present. Today, the question of the *fatogia* is a stumbling block in debates on custom, in terms of deploring its loss of importance in a nostalgic way, highlighting its heaviness and archaism in the name of modern individualism, and defending its specificity in the face of the *papalagi* who obviously understand nothing about collective life. "It is our identity," Sioli Pilioko told me.[7] Alice Fromonteil, who is writing an anthropology thesis on oral literature in Wallis and who guided me in my first steps on the island, had spoken to one of her informants, Patita Lakina, for me before I arrived. "David" made him think, of course, of the authoritarian guy who built the hospital in Sia but also of a report he had just seen on TV, on the organizational problems of the Pacific Mini-Games, the big event of 2013 on the island, for which "volunteers" (I put quotation marks because the operation apparently cost quite a lot) had to be brought in from New Caledonia, because of a lack of sufficient volunteers available on site. It irritated him somewhat: "All they had to do was to go through custom and the Catholic mission to get volunteers in Wallis. Everyone would have been a volunteer."[8] They should have gone through "people who are used to having volunteers," not through the authorities of the French state, be it the prefect, the senator, the deputy, or the territorial councillors, with their big salaries and their big cars. "You have to ask the priest, you have to ask the chiefdom. [. . .] At that point [people] accept because it's for the good of the population." Even though he would never have dared to speak of "volunteers," David understood this, much better than his predecessors, who never succeeded in mobilizing people for "government projects," to the point of provoking a small revolt in 1926 that was calmed by the arrival of a warship.[9]

The question of work and its control through the chieftaincy weighed on David's relationship with the mission. David's relations with the ecclesiastical superior, Reverend Father Fillion, and the other missionaries were courteous from the outset and would remain so. Young Jean Joseph had been taught by the Marists and passed for a good Catholic. He and the missionaries invited each other for lunch, helped each other out, and gave each other fish and containers of milk, and the doctor spared no effort for the fathers. However, they had a number of points of contention, as had been the case since the beginning of the protectorate.[10] The mission required parish tithes and benefits in kind from its faithful; its control of morals and religious practice, supported by a kind of militia, was strict (attendance at Mass was obligatory under penalty of punishment); and it was also an important economic player, subject to taxes and duties, that owned shops, plantations, and land (one sixth of the island in fact, it was said at the time). The Wallisian fathers formed a respected elite, and the missionaries themselves, often bilingual, had acquired a knowledge of Wallisian society that was not comparable to that of the residents who disembarked there. As Jean-Claude Roux recounted, tensions had sometimes bordered on nervous breakdown, especially when the resident doctors were frankly anticlerical, in a context in which both sides were glorified by the island's isolation (the bishop on whom Wallis depended was installed in Tonga and, where the Residency was concerned, connections with Nouméa, Paris, and Tahiti were often unpredictable). David knew that he was walking on eggshells, and a section of his reports to Nouméa detailed his grievances against the mission and his maneuvers to limit the hold it had. "Perhaps you think, Mr. Commissioner General, that I am going a bit outside the scope of my duties?" he asked to test the waters.[11]

David focused his efforts on the issue of customary chores, demanding and then legally requiring, via an agreement signed when Governor Siadous was appointed in 1935, that the "mission cease to rely on the authority of the chiefs in its dealings with the faithful";[12] in other words, that it rely solely on individual goodwill and offerings and that it leave the resident with exclusive control of the chiefdom as a conduit for organizing collective works or calling for contributions in kind. Efforts had to be made, David explained, to "free [the chiefs] from the hold the mission had over them."[13] David had a talent for blowing hot and cold: he complained to the governor about the "medieval" procedures of the mission while recognizing its sovereignty in matters of morality;[14] he deprived it of the power to levy taxes in cash or in kind, while directly financing the repair of the roof of the church at Mata-Utu; he regulated the work of children in boarding schools but promoted the expansion of a girls' school run by the nuns; and he prevented the missionaries from resorting to customary chores while personally ordering major works for their benefit, including the reconstruction of the facade of the church in Mua and preparations for the 1937 centennial. In return, David benefited from the more or less benevolent neutrality of the missionaries, who supported the construction of the hospital by making available to him a masonry expert, Wallisian Father Petele Hamale, whose "simple presence among the laborers influenced the strong-willed and allowed the first building to be finished without trouble or conflict for the sixteen months that the project lasted."[15] Their understanding became downright "cordial" with the arrival of the new ecclesiastical superior, Alexandre Poncet, who disembarked from the *Bucéphale* in June 1936 with a letter from Pope Pius XI making him the first bishop of the new apostolic vicariate of Wallis and Futuna.[16] In his book, Poncet recalled a resident who was cunning like a fox, who tried to diminish and at the same time make use of the prestige of the mission in the eyes of the Wallisians, but to whom the country and the church were indebted in the end.[17] For Sister Malekalita, the time was even a blessed one, when "the chiefdom, the upper administration, and the diocese worked together for the common good of the people."[18]

According to David's writings and the admiring annotations of the governor, all the resident's maneuvers, the way he navigated between the mission, the ministers, and the workers on his building sites, were nothing but "subterfuge," "ability," and "perseverance."[19] However, by reading between the lines, one can see there was someone else operating in the background, the person who was in fact David's double, whose role was uncovered by Roux: the "zealous" and "energetic" Kivalu.[20] David called him by this name (or by his first name, Atoloto), but he was in fact the *mukoi* minister (normally the lowest rank in the hierarchy, the *'aliki fau*) who was promoted in June 1933, following the Renaud affair, to the highest rank, that of *kivalu*, at the cost of a breach of customary protocol (which reserved the title and the preeminent place of *kivalu* for a single family clan).[21] With his position and somewhat usurped title, the *kivalu/mukoi* shook "tradition" at its very foundations. It was he who made the resident's projects and alliances possible, if he did not inspire them directly. When David, at the beginning of his stay, drew lots for the villages to go inspect, it was with Kivalu that he carried out these inspections.[22] When David succeeded in getting the chiefs to adopt his program of major projects, it was "thanks to the real support that Kivalu never stopped giving [him] in all of these meetings."[23] When he negotiated the de facto annexation of the protectorate, it was Kivalu, the one to whom "according to custom, the appointment of a new king fell," who was "fully committed to the idea of not electing one."[24] When the island was being transformed by major construction projects, it was "the personal authority of the prime minister [that was] the basis for these improvements."[25] When it was necessary to crack down, it was to the *kivalu/mukoi* that he would say, "I saw that something was wrong."[26] And the rest followed, mainly customary fines payable in pigs. When David rewrote the constitution of the protectorate in 1935,[27] he was careful to get the governor to endorse the change in customary protocol, which placed the *mukoi* (called Kivalu by David, clearly a generic title) at the head of the Council of Ministers, relegating the Kivalu family to lowest rank and inscribing in law a strange way of putting merit and people before genealogy and titles. Such a shift, Poncet noted, was "completely at odds with Wallisian tradition."[28] It was a way, wrote David, of "definitively consecrating the predominant place that the administration intended to keep for this faithful servant."[29] He would be able to remain first among ministers while at the same time retaining his family title of *mukoi*. David installed him in Sagato Soane, the royal palace, right next to the Residency.

And when Mukoi, now prime minister for good, died one day in November 1936, it was with great sadness and white gloves that David honored him, in formal dress.[30] The entire population was there for a solemn ceremony, except for the Reverend Father Fillion, whose absence confirms that Mukoi was indeed the architect of the change in the sphere of influence on the chiefdoms from the mission to the administration. Mukoi may have been the passenger in the sidecar, but I realized this too late and too far from Wallis to investigate. When David said *I*, he meant *we*.

26. Becoming King, Part III

KICKING CUSTOM TO THE CURB

There is a story that people always tell as soon as you mention the name Tavite, an anecdote that sums up the figure. It is nowhere in the archives, and Poncet does not mention it in his book. This is the version told by Pelesio (Blaise), who heard it from his father-in-law:

> PELESIO (BLAISE) HOATAU: One day, there was some village work being done [in Falaleu]. I'm married to a girl from Falaleu, so my father-in-law is from Falaleu. According to custom, it's the young people who do the outdoor work, when it comes to planting, when it comes to building roads. And it's the old people who make kava in the meantime. Always, always, it was like that. It's hard to imagine old people carrying around machetes and crowbars. In our custom, it's always the young people who do that.

> And when King David arrived, he saw the people of Falaleu around the *tanoa*. He came and he kicked the *tanoa* over.

> GUILLAUME LACHENAL: The *tanoa*, what's that?

> PELESIO HOATAU: The *tanoa* is the dish for kava. He kicked the *tanoa* over and he stomped on it! He said, "When I said that everyone works,

it's not the old people who come to make kava and the young people who work, it's everyone!"

There are several versions of this story. The main elements do not vary: during major construction work (likely the building of a cement cistern) in Falaleu, the coastal village just south of Mata-Utu, David came across a group of people who were not working and who were quietly drinking kava. The resident got angry and overturned and trampled on the *tanoa*, the sacred wooden container in which the kava was prepared. One waits for a moment for a response equal to the insult, a violent reaction, but nothing happened. Everyone got up and went to work.

Some versions suggest a kind of egalitarian gesture, against a background of antagonism between elders and young people, a way of taking the side of the young, the common people (*tu'a*) against the chiefs and nobles (*'aliki*). The scenario of a hegemonic alliance between the imperial state and the social inferiors (i.e., the dominated), sometimes to the point of overturning sociopolitical hierarchies, is recurrent in colonial situations.[1] In other versions, the problem is mainly that everyone was participating in the Kava and no one was working. But, in essence, all versions agree: David's gesture was a "total affront" to the chieftaincy, an insult to Wallisian custom, a profanation, which earned its author a black mark against his name. Because of this episode, "he was seen rather badly," Blaise said. The "oral tradition," as they say, remembers this in particular about David: "He's the one who stomped on the *tanoa*," "He stomped on the kava," "That sums up the figure: he did whatever he wanted, you know!," "He put his foot in it, so to speak." They tell you this as a matter of course in Wallis, in a supermarket parking lot, between two doors, at a banquet table, or while mowing the lawn.

Seen from a distance, one could view David's gesture as a colonial contempt for local tradition. A sacred custom? David shrugged his shoulders, kicked the kava dish, and shouted at the notables. His kicking of custom to the curb would also have been understood in the figurative sense: the virtual annexation of the island, the disruption of protocol with the enthronement of the lowest ranking minister as prime minister (*kivalu*), the dismissal and deportation of chiefs from one end of the island to the other, or the "Westernization" of the Council of Ministers that David would organize at the end of his stay by assigning each of the customary ministerial titles a "portfolio" in due form. One would be minister of coconut groves, another of the preservation of the Polynesian arts, one of the police, another of hygiene, and all under the direction of Mukoi, putting an end to "the courtiers and parasites."[2]

However, David's relationship to custom was in fact much more complex. The resident was always worried about validating his own authority in the political language of Wallis, starting by paying attention to his place at the Kava during *katoaga* (customary ceremonies). The one he was assigned at his first Kava "deeply wounded" him: receiving the fifth cup was a "public insult." Shortly after his arrival on October 2, 1933, David set about "remedying the situation." Invited to the Royal Kava on the Feast of Christ the King, David asked to see the king to thank him for his invitation and then told him that he would attend on one condition: that he be given the cup of honor, the first, to which only kings and bishops were normally entitled. As David noted in his account of this meeting, "The amazement that was painted on his face immediately informed me of the place that in all good faith he attributed to the resident in the hierarchy of the island's notables." David insisted and made veiled threats. The king withdrew, consulted his ministers, and had the Kivalu deliver his "categorical" refusal. David insisted and made more direct threats before the prime minister came back to him, "this time to deliver royal consent." David would later realize that this was the first turning point of his stay. The power struggle "publicly marked [. . .] the new direction of a once immutable policy and a made a population that was naively attached to its customs and was easily impressionable sense that another authority was going to reveal itself alongside the royal authority."[3]

Rank during Kava ceremonies would remain a little obsession for David, who therefore fully appreciated the sacred and political nature of the beverage. Things became even more complicated from 1936 onward, when Wallis became a full-fledged diocese. David's negotiations with Bishop Poncet mainly concerned the protocol to be adopted for placement at the Kava; the new bishop took long notes on the matter in his notebooks. The two men agreed on a pact of nonaggression, with the resident suggesting that he could politely give the bishop the place of honor at the *katoaga* organized by the government, such as the one on July 14, and vice versa during mission celebrations. For the parish feasts of patron saints, they would alternate turns or try to drink the first cup at the same time. And David advised the bishop not to attend the Kava ceremonies given in honor of the warships, where the first cup goes to the commander, to avoid having to witness the salaciousness of the sailors.[4]

For above all else, David feared that he would be mocked. During one of his first tours in Hihifo, the Northern District, David found himself confronted with "about a hundred natives who all declared themselves to be physically unfit"[5] and therefore exempt from taxation. "The majority of these patients were mostly frauds, which I set out to identify. General discontent was expressed immediately: the health check was carried out amid the annoying laughter and hurtful reflections of the assembly and I had to endure, in particular, the rude invectives of a particularly excited Wallisian." Small incidents of this kind occurred frequently at the beginning of David's stay, to the point of creating an "extremely difficult situation." One of them initiated David to the subtleties of the levels of the *faka 'uvea* language:

> That same week, during consultations at the dispensary while I was administering to two young girls, I noticed that my nurse seemed irritated with one of them. When I asked him about the reasons for his anger, I received the following explanation: there are two different words in the Wallisian language to express the French "yes:" *io* and *koe*. *Io* is used in common conversations, between people of the same rank, *koe* is a deferential term, applied to chiefs and nobles. One of the young girls had used the respectful expression in answering me and her very surprised comrade had said to her, in substance, the following: "Why do you say *koe* to the resident? You know that only chiefs and fathers are entitled to it: to the resident, you say *io*."

Fortunately, wrote David further on, repeated medical tours and "the honorable place now reserved for the resident in official ceremonies did not fail to deeply impress the multitude" and eventually gave "a fairly favorable turn" to relations with the population. He now drank kava in the royal position.[6] The custom that David had insulted in Falaleu was also the one that created his authority. It had been necessary to go through this so that people could speak to him as they would to a chief—a Wallisian one.

I think that the resident-doctor's kick must be seen as a gesture that was ultimately fundamental, an "elementary form of [. . .] political life,"[7] which had to do with the relationship between authority and transgression. The anthropologist Marshall Sahlins has written a famous text on the subject, which is part of an important debate in the discipline.[8] For political anthropology, power (and especially royal power) is in fact to be sought outside and beyond society; it is not inherent to the human community but finds its source outside it, in barbarism, witchcraft, the divine, or nature (one could say that economics occupies this place today). Examples abound, whether in Greek or Roman myths, in the Polynesian world, or in African societies in which sovereignty is closely linked to the world of the invisible. "Power reveals and defines itself as a rupture of the people's own moral order."[9] It is based on a transgression—a loved one annihilated, a brother murdered, a kava stomped on. Seen in this light, the account of the Falaleu incident (which echoes similar myths in Wallis and other Pacific islands)[10] validates, rather than undermines, David's authority, as power "is a usurpation, in the double sense of a forceful seizure of sovereignty and a sovereign denial of the prevailing moral order. Rather than a normal succession, *usurpation itself is the principle of legitimacy.*"[11] It is this mechanism—usurpation as a principle of legitimacy—that underlies the authority of a recurring figure in the Pacific and beyond: that of the "stranger-king."

27. Te Hau Tavite

The question arises: was David ever king? There are two answers. The first is not very complicated: no. Resident David was never enthroned king, never took the title of *lavelua*, never occupied the royal palace. He put an end to a system that had been in place, for better or for worse, since 1450, which is no small feat in terms of "overturning of custom," but custom would in fact survive, with a new king appointed in 1941, and history would label David's time on the island an "interregnum." The term, which appears on the official lists of Wallisian monarchs, is modest and retrospective (it was not used once in David's time, when the abandonment of the title *lavelua* seems definitive). From the pen of Monsignor Poncet, who divided his *Histoire de l'île Wallis* into chronological chapters according to residents or kings in office, and who titled the chapter dealing with David's time there "interregnum," it even sounds like something of a cutting remark.[1]

The second answer is more interesting and is in fact suggested by the anthropological literature on the region. That answer is: it is a bit of a gray area. During the discussions I had in Wallis, one of my questions on this subject always fell flat: "Were people being ironic, calling him King David?" That was my first hypothesis, but in all likelihood, I was missing something. I had thought that the expression might have come from the missionaries, from David himself, or from one of his successors, that it was a more or less mocking allusion to the colonial myth of the "white rajah." For example, Bishop Poncet was amused by the fact that David had taken advantage of the presence of an airplane on board a warship (a seaplane, I suppose) to go on an aerial tour of "his kingdom."[2] David himself played with the idea in his correspondence and articles, and "King David" appears as such in commemorative publications.[3] But the origin of the term seems to have in fact been Wallisian, and irony had little to do with it. Dr. Jean-Marie Papilio was the first to tell me: "He was called King David, the Wallisians said that to elevate him. It was with respect, admiration, he was the magician, the white doctor." For Blaise, "you can't say it's pejorative. It's not pejorative. He was almost like a king." For Sioli Pilioko, "we didn't call him that to his face, it was a bit taboo."

When I asked the question in French, the typical answer was rather pensive, an amused or weary sigh, as though the respondents were saying to themselves, "Te Hau Tavite . . ." On an island where speaking French is a generational marker, a sign of youth, it is in these singsong words that the expression exists. At the banquet on the Feast of Saints Peter and Paul that I mentioned earlier, Lagimaina, the journalist from France Télévisions, introduced me to his neighbor to the right, Atoloto Uhila, one of the island's most notable elders, who was eight years old when David left Mata-Utu. It was a nice surprise, because I had been told about him, and speaking to him was one of my "goals" for my last week there. It was the end of the meal, and the three of us were facing the empty bottles, with Lagi sitting in the middle and interpreting, as if everything had been organized that way on purpose. To talk about Tavite, Atoloto said three words, counting them on his fingers: *toketa, lesita, hau.* Thumb, index, middle finger. Doctor, resident, king. "Te Hau Tavite—King David," Lagi translated for me, "is a title that he acquired through sheer hard work. His approach made him worthy of [being called] a king," which is something I had often been told in other words. "He was very active when it came to custom, so there was an amalgamation, it gave him the status of a king."[4]

"King" is the common and somewhat ethnocentric translation of the title and concept of *hau* in Wallisian, *lavelua* being the title taken by the elected official installed on the throne, by which he is addressed (a bit like saying "majesty") and which becomes that person's name. The word and the thing *hau* come from Tonga. They were imposed on Uvea in the fifteenth century with the conquest of the island by Tongan warriors, whose descendants constitute, broadly speaking, the noble lineages of the island.[5] Wallis gradually freed itself from Tongan tutelage, but, to put it simply, the Wallisian monarchy comes from elsewhere.

The concept of *hau* originally referred to a specific form of authority, that of the "warlord," the conquering hero; however, the term *hau*, used in Wallis,

Rotuma, Tonga, Fiji, and the Cook Islands, can, depending on the context, be confused with the sacred and hereditary royal function (as is the case today in Wallis) or duplicate it.[6] Noble heredity and seniority are only a necessary, but not sufficient, condition to become *hau*. In addition to belonging to the higher caste, it is necessary to show the charisma of a leader and the strength of a warrior, in particular, "the ability to defeat a rival in a man-to-man fight." Even though, from the nineteenth century onward, usage gave to the term *hau* a less specific meaning in Uvea, which invariably (and independently of acts of war) designates the king in office bearing the title of *lavelua*, and even though the Marist theocracy had stabilized a system of transmission of power that no longer left room for usurpation by force, the royal office in Wallis is based at least in part on this concept of warlike and charismatic authority. Moreover, the king is, among other considerations, appointed or dismissed on the basis of his personal leadership qualities. Genealogies are formal on this point: one can *become hau* by force, cunning, or labor; acquire a noble status; and pass it on to one's descendants.[7]

Another thing that is always said about Tavite is that he was tall, strong, and handsome. This is not told as an anecdote but rather said as a confirmation and explanation of his authority. The first time I heard this, it was a bit surprising. Bernadette Papilio, the director of the Cultural Affairs Service, told me that "everyone knows him. Everyone remembers his authority, his personality. He had a strong personality; he had an imposing physique. He was handsome, he was a handsome man, he had a lot of things going for himself, you know."[8] Even the nuns I interviewed confirmed that he was a "large man." The compliment is not insignificant on an island where the average man (or woman) is a "man and a half," as they say in the rugby world. The Wallisians are gigantic, a cliché that WHO corpulence studies confirm and that has led to the island being closely watched by the major French rugby clubs.[9] The grandfather of the immense Jonah Lomu is Wallisian, like the Taofifénua brothers from my childhood in Grenoble or the Toulouse center and winger Yann David (the coincidence of the surname is fortuitous). Physical strength counts a lot in Wallis, Bernadette explained to me, all the more so because "at the time, everything was physical, so it made an impression."

One of the richest interviews I have conducted regarding David is the conversation I had with Jean-Baptiste Mulikihaamea. He was a major figure on the island, and at the time of my visit he was president of the Conseil économique et social (Economic and Social Council), an important political body responsible for linking the Superior Administration and the chiefdom. Prefect Michel Aubouin, who met with me as soon as I arrived in Wallis, immediately advised me to see him; he got all the anecdotes he knew about David, "a sort of legend here, who was as strong as a giant," from him.[10] Jean-Baptiste was not to be missed. He was easy to find: he ran a small grocery store at the main crossroads of Mata-Utu, identifiable by its old mango tree and signpost, one of the only ones on the island, with arrows pointing in all directions. He came from a large family with Tongan ancestry, and his father was the *lavelua* Leone Manikitoga, whose coming to the throne in 1941 had ended the interregnum. Leone, who was a few years younger than David, had been "noticed" for his qualities by the resident at the end of his stay.

For our interview, Jean-Baptiste (he insisted that I call him by his French first name) had prepared files and newspaper clippings. Our discussion began like this: "We always called him King David. We don't know where he's from, that's why I'm interested [in chatting with you]. All I know is that he was named while in Africa, in Algeria, that's where he left from. He arrived in Wallis. We don't know this gentleman's measurements, but he was about 1.90 meters tall. That's tall, because most Wallisians are very, very tall."[11]

He showed me a photo of David published in an old newspaper, *Malamanei* (The world), printed in New Caledonia for the Wallisian community, in an article he himself had written: "The figure, you can see how he is; when he came ashore, he was in uniform, the uniform of the officers of the time, the pants with boots that went all the way up to here [to the knee]. He had a distinctive feature: he always carried his gun with him, hanging there, like the cowboys, and he always had a whip attached to his belt. At the time, the Wallisians thought: 'A white man walking around with a whip and pistols, to do what?'"

They used to watch him shoot coconuts with a pistol when he got up in the morning. "We spied on him. And [the Wallisians] noticed that every morning he went out shirtless and did his physical training." He had made a bench and dumbbells out of coconut trunks. The Wallisians said, "He's not that strong, and when he wasn't around, they would try to do what he had been doing. Well . . . those who tried almost killed themselves, almost got crushed by the weights . . . But he could do it a dozen times; it was like nothing."

The nickname "King David" was not meant as a put-down, Jean-Baptiste explained: "People nicknamed him that because he presided over everything, and he also worked! He wasn't out there slacking off. As far as we know, he started at seven in the morning and went to bed at seven or eight at night. But, all day long, he went here, he went there, he went everywhere: he was tireless, this guy."

The second reason, the one that really counts, goes back to the kava-kicking incident in Falaleu. The important aspect of this episode, Jean-Baptiste explained to me, was less the gesture itself than the reaction of the chiefs and nobles who had just been insulted. "Someone could have stood up in the middle of it with a machete or a stick and knocked him out. But who's the guy who could outmatch him . . . because they already knew him." They already knew "his strength": David was "an expert in Greco-Roman wrestling, in French boxing," continued Jean-Baptiste, and the old people who knew him said that, at the time, during festivities, David "got people to wrestle" him, the Wallisian way, where "the first one to hit the ground" lost. "They tried to measure up to David, but no one ever succeeded. I think the guy, if he came here from Africa, he's not just anyone, he must know how to wrestle. [. . .] They never managed to take David down." This was why—simply because he was the strongest— they called him Te Hau Tavite.

I do not fully grasp the reference to David's supposed African origin, but what is certain is that David was strong, and that this strength was common knowledge, like his pistol and his whip. Jean-Baptiste also told me that one day David allowed himself to get carried away with speeding, sending his motorbike into the ditch, and then got it out alone, lifting it with both arms, before setting off again in front of the Wallisians who had hoped to see the resident come to them, tail between his legs, to ask for help.

He was hardworking, exceptionally hardworking; he was strong, exceptionally strong; and his authority had been tested in hand-to-hand combat. He was feared and admired. According to the anthropological corpus on the subject, it does not take much more than that to be *hau*.[12] One last lead: Sister Malekalita also told me that "King David" was so named because he was a descendant of a royal family (in France, she implied). Then her account began to drift, getting mixed up with the biblical story of King David (as a reminder, he too is big and strong; he spies on the wife of one of his generals from his patio and seduces her, sends the general to war and his death, then asks God for forgiveness for his sins). My own memories are even more confused because I did not have a digital recorder with me that day, especially since the story of King David (from the Bible) echoes Wallisian myths about men spying on women at the bath (a national sport, according to oral tradition).[13] But the important thing to bear in mind is that Te Hau Tavite is a biblical expression, which appears in the Tongan and Wallisian translations of the Bible, and that it is possible that the expression thus preexisted Resident David, who has come, in a way, with his charisma and his thirst for women and power, to actualize the Davidian myth.

In short, I will probably never know the whole story, if people really called him *hau*, and who, but it would be a contradiction to see in the evocations of this all-powerful and hardworking resident cute, somewhat naive memories, a kind of nostalgia for the colonial, an alienated first-person account of the golden legend of the great officers of the empire. Rather, they should be read as a vernacular means of talking about authority, drawing on a category widely shared in Polynesian space.[14] David's power did not derive from "colonial domination." His authority was the result of a test of strength, a commensurability of powers, whose arbiters were the Wallisians themselves, who established the rules, the language, and the way the points would be counted. Industriousness (*fa'a gāue*), for example, is a crucial measure of the greatness of individuals in Uvea.[15] In other words, the hierarchy of power does not exist outside the test of power but rather is derived from it. Such a performative means of establishing a consensus on authority not only opens up the possibility of giving supreme power to a foreigner but even makes the "stranger-king" (dear to Marshall Sahlins) a standard figure whose strength rests precisely on his connection to the outside, to ships, to guns, to the mana of other ancestors.[16] The possibility of David being enthroned king was likely never discussed, but in principle, there was nothing to prohibit it. In addition to the Tongan origin of the institution and the royal lineages of Wallis, people remember that in 1926, in a context of crisis and contestation of customary chores, Alain Gerbault (known as Selepo) had almost been proposed as king, also because of his extraordinary charisma, his good looks, his eloquence, his love of the locals, and his mana, demonstrated by his ability to have warships come to his rescue.[17] Being made king was an honor in appearance only. In fact, it was a way of putting someone in their place—that of the foreigner.[18]

And then Tavite was handsome. Manuele Lisiahi and his wife, Falakika, daughter of David's interpreter, Sosefo, have proof of this: "At the end of his stay, he left with one of the Brial girls. Sofia. [...] That girl was really beautiful."[19] Sophie (or Sofia) Brial was the daughter of Julien (Suliano) Brial, the island's French trader, a powerful figure in the 1920s, who was taking some time off in Nouméa when Dr. David passed through. Brial had married Aloïsia, a Wallisian woman from a royal family who would be crowned queen in the 1950s. Brial's children and grandchildren were among the most important political figures on the island, especially Benjamin, Sofia's brother, who was the deputy for Wallis for more than thirty years. In the 1930s, Sofia had spent some time in Nouméa as well before returning with her sister to Wallis, where she and the young resident became close. Sofia had been educated "*à la française*" and Jean David was the only "French" company she could find on the island. She was a rather bold girl (the parish priests said she looked like trouble, but this can be read as a kind of compliment) who had been kicked out of the Nouméa Scouts because she "frequented young men."[20] Jean was in his thirties, single and curious; Sofia was twenty-one, bilingual and resourceful; and both of them were on a desert island. The story had something inevitable about it. Julien Brial, having been informed of what was going on, took the news badly. The affair had worried the governor and the bishop, both of whom vowed not to send any more single residents to the island. David and Sofia were married in 1936 before a missionary; then David took Sofia with him to France. The civil registry tells us that he married her in a civil ceremony in 1939 in the suburbs of Paris. Spiteful tongues say that he used her to gain the "approval" of the chieftaincy.

The Brials' house was next to my hotel in Liku. It is an imposing colonial house, with a concrete pier for boats. Nyvé, the hotel manager, told me pensively, drawing on her cigarette, that Sofia was a very beautiful woman, round and pale I imagine, as this is what is considered to constitute feminine beauty here. She became a princess.

28. Tavite Lea Tahi (David-Only-Speaks-Once)

There is another theory about the empty seat in the sidecar, the most common one in fact: it was filled by a dog. It sat next to David, it never left his side, and it scared the life out of the Wallisians. It was a "big dog," or even two dogs according to some, "German shepherds."[1] The dog does not appear in any photographs, has no name, and is nowhere to be found in books and archives, but Wallisians do not forget to include it in their portraits of the doctor-administrator. With his dog baring its teeth and the doctor cracking his whip, another side of David emerges, another plane of his biography: stories of humiliation, threats, and violence, which are told in a somewhat dazed, ambiguous fashion.[2]

David wore his pistol on his belt, with the grip pointing outward, in the manner of George Patton, as the old Wallisians, who had seen the story of the American general (one of the great figures of the Second World War) in the 1970 film *Patton*, had told Jean-Baptiste. It seems that the film shows Patton, a handsome athlete, trousers tucked into his boots, a great leader and a megalomaniac, shooting at German planes with a revolver, just like David with his coconuts in the morning. That was his style. "He became the Geronimo of Wallis," says Blaise. He was a cowboy and an Indian chief.

His whip was mysterious. When a Wallisian asked him why he was always walking around with his whip, whether it was to hit people on the back, David had said: "Stand there, don't move, we'll bet, I'll knock your *manu* off, bring your *manu* down with the whip." The *manu* is the piece of cloth that the men in Uvea wear around their waist. It is tied by folding it up like a bath towel. "It's not possible," they told David, "you'll have to whip the poor guy . . ." And with one flick of the whip, crack, he knocked the *manu* off. "Unbelievable," concluded Jean-Baptiste, who told me the story. The prefect also told me that David "undid *manu* with his whip." Without overinterpreting, one can view this story as a metaphorical representation of the fact that David was skillful, both literally and figuratively, that he was the strict but fair type. I do not know what to make of the fact that the Wallisian in the story found himself naked at the end; the image of a *manu* falling off is the very essence of ridicule in Wallis.[3] One can imagine the astonishment and the laughter.

Wallisians have a whole collection of anecdotes like this. On the last evening before I left, Michel (Mika), father of the France Télévisions journalist Lagimaina, told me all the stories he knew about David—"rumors," he warned.[4] The first story began on the construction site of the RTI, which in Wallisian is called the old road (*ala matu'a*). The old man who told it to him was eighteen or nineteen years old at this time and "was enlisted" for the construction work. That day, a young woman walked past the workers. She was the Wallisian "wife" of Bernast, the telegrapher and administrative clerk at the Residency, David's only assistant (Bernast's French wife, the teacher, was still on the island, which of course troubled the missionaries). The young laborers called out to her: "Hey-hey, you're beautiful, you're fine." Bernast heard about this, got angry, and went to get David, who came back with his dog to sic it on the young laborers "who teased the woman." Michel speaks quickly, but I was recording:

Among them was a man named Pulu, who was the father of a former king—his son later became king. The old man, he wouldn't stand being chased by the dog. He went to David's house. Before he left, he cut off a piece of wood, like the wood behind you, bamboo, about this big, about a meter or less. That's what he told me, the old man. He went to David's house, King David's house. He went to his house. When he got there, there was a little gate, there was a chain that kept him from opening the gate . . . He took the chain off, and the dog jumped on him. With one move, he put the wood in the dog's mouth, turned around, and put his knee on the dog to paralyze it and he wanted to kill the dog.

David showed up, with his gun.

The old man said to him, "Shoot! Shoot me! I'll kill your dog first. I'll kill your dog." And he was standing there with his piece of wood, doing this with his knee here—that's what the old man told me—he stuck his knee here, he turned the dog around, the dog was completely paralyzed.

Michel reenacted the fight, the screams, the guy's wringing the dog's neck:

MICHEL HOATAU: And David said, "Let go or I'll kill you!" "Kill me! *Mate! Fa Pa!* Come on, kill me!" And David dropped his gun. The old man said, "*Mole Tui!*" That means, "Don't ever forget!" That's Pulu: "Don't ever forget this, don't do it again or I'll kill you." David was completely weakened because he saw that his weapon had gone to pieces, that his dog was screwed, you know. Without the dog, there was no David. That's what all the old people say, "Without the dog, there's no David." He was tall, over two meters, he was a huge man, but without the dog, he was nobody.

GUILLAUME LACHENAL: What was it, the phrase in Wallisian?

MICHEL HOATAU: *Mole he kuli, mole he Tavite.* No dog, no David.

David's dog, who was finally spared, was "as nasty as he was," Emeni Simete explained to me.[5] Emeni's name appears in the acknowledgments of Jean-Claude Roux's thesis, as a "young jurist" who had helped him go through the archives at the mission.[6] Since then, Emeni has become a prosecutor in Nouméa, and he had a lot to tell me. He came to see me one evening at my hotel (Wallis, one of the last places on Earth with no mobile phones, is a bit old-fashioned: you make vague appointments, you go to people's houses, and if they are not there, you wait for them to come back). We had been put in touch by his brother-in-law, Jacques Pambrin, one of Bernast's descendants. Emeni's stories contrast sharply with those of Jean-Baptiste and Blaise, and with Poncet's book. They are based on a never-published manuscript written in Wallisian by a seminarian from Tonga, Mikaele Toga. It is a sort of counterhistory of the island of Wallis, a largely unstructured series of short stories, rawer than the versions of the missionaries. No one had ever told me about this text, which Emeni did not bring with him. The David described by Mikaele Toga was not just authoritarian or charismatic. He was even bigger trouble than that. He punished people by locking them in the toilet. He deported chiefs. He hit women.

Mikaele Tui, deputy director of the Cultural Affairs Service, spoke in the same vein. According to him, David's dog was the ultimate insult to Wallisians. Dogs are poorly regarded, the "scum of the earth,"[7] and to sic one on Wallisians to frighten them was a supreme humiliation, a disgrace, all the more so if they were nobles, as in the story of Pulu's fight. By comparison, kicking the kava was almost respectful. The dog was more than a weapon or a tool; it was a double, an alter ego. It was David's strength but also, ultimately, his weakness; it embodied the fact that his power was (also) illegitimate, or at least had become so at a certain point. No dog, no David, as the saying goes. All it would take was a good, strong blow to the throat with a stick to undo everything.

Another account suggests that David was at the mercy of the island's strongmen. I heard several versions of this story, a little muddled, often without conclusion. It took place one day at the hospital construction site, where David had ordered a large mango tree to be uprooted. The tree had already been cut down, but he wanted the stump removed. It was a huge job, and a largely pointless one, in the opinion of the locals. A large hole had been dug, supported by wooden crossties, so that the entire taproot could be pulled out at the base. Among the conscripted laborers were two "giants," both from the village of Alele, in the district of Hihifo, in the north of the island, which is still considered to be the most rebellious area of the island. One of them was known for causing several incidents: Fale Mana—stocky, strong, always ready for a fight. The other was called Misaele. They were there, not really working, giving David dirty looks, with the more or less obvious intention of challenging him. David did not get flustered and asked them to go down into the hole, a way of asserting his authority and perhaps testing the strength of the two giants. They went down, gave each other the signal, and, with their immense strength, uprooted the stump in one try. "Congratulations! That's it for today, everyone can go home." David must have realized that the two men were not stupid or weak, which meant he would not be able to control them by force. To reward them, he gave them his jacket, some sweets, a bag of rice, and a bag of flour, and then took them back to Hihifo. Once they arrived, the two companions got out of the Jeep (or the sidecar). And then something unexpected happened: one in front, the other in the back, they lifted the vehicle, which David was still in. The story ends with this image: the French resident high above the ground, his wheels spinning in the air, the engine revving, and the two giants laughing. I find this story to be a good allegory of "colonial power": a fragile and bizarre compromise, in which the physical balance of power that was the basis of authority was always in danger of being reversed, in which the demiurge in a white helmet always seemed to be on the verge of falling into powerlessness and ridicule.

Tui told me all this in Terminal 2 of the Charles de Gaulle Airport, shortly after my return to France. I took the RER (Regional Express Network) commuter train to the airport to meet him as he was heading to board his flight for the long journey back to Uvea. Standing next to his luggage trolleys, Tui remained allusive, but he confirmed my impression: the end of David's stay was complicated. "It was going to end badly,"[8] and David left at the right time. "It could have cost him his life," and his definitive departure enabled him to avoid that solution. This is a sharp departure from the amused, vanilla-and-lemongrass-scented evocations of King David. Allusions to his violence often recur, in the archives as well as in people's accounts—in particular, an episode in which he allegedly hit women.[9] I cannot, of course, prove anything, but from the way he was spoken of at the time and from the way he is remembered, it must be believed that the man was remarkably violent, even for a colonial soldier, even for a leader, even for a male in the 1930s. Violent, not just "authoritarian."

The contrast between the different versions is not only a question of point of view, although it certainly cuts along cleavages particular to Wallisian society (just as, in Haut-Nyong, he could be adored by schoolchildren and women, feared by the elderly and men of working age, and hated by missionaries and plantation owners). The fact that David had many faces is not a matter of a difference in "perspective," as though all one needs to do is determine where different points of view overlap in order to arrive at a true picture of him. Firstly, the accounts probably refer to different moments during David's time in Wallis, and his status changed between 1933 and 1938. The doctor became king, or became nothing, as the days went by, as he became enthusiastic, bored, and carried away. More fundamentally, there is the simple fact that there is not just one David. Not only must his biography demonstrate that he is a plural subject, as sociologists say, but it must go further, following Jean-François Bayart on this subject. One must try to make it a "biography without subject,"[10] kaleidoscopic and fragmentary, an *abiography* that expresses an awareness that every life has several dimensions, makes use of several frameworks in different space-time planes that coexist but do not coincide. The biographical subject, the individual, is not indivisible; it can only be grasped through moments, practices, and processes of individuation without coherence or aim. One must renounce the biographical illusion, which in a broader sense includes microhistorical strategies that see the individual as a clue, a revealer of entities or phenomena of a higher order (his time, his society, henceforth made coherent and intelligible). Using the framework proposed by Jean-François Bayart, this study of Dr. David can be read as a way of "thinking about the unfinished state of societies, the incompleteness of the structures and practices that institute them, the overlapping of the constituent durations of their own historicity, the coexistence within them of a plurality of spaces/times, the ambivalence of relationships of domination, the synergy between coercion and hegemony."[11] Tavite was resident and *hau*, calm and violent, skilled and clumsy, loving and hateful, loved and hated. "He was too strict, but he really loved the people." I can no longer find in my notes whether someone told me this in Africa or in the Pacific. Incoherent, just like what has been called colonialism.

I wondered whether it is even more complicated than that. The stories about Tavite take the form of Wallisian myths, as Alice Fromonteil, who is doing her thesis on the subject, immediately pointed out to me. Anchored in a place, they always begin with the name of a village, generally that of the narrator. Their intrigues—stories of usurpation, physical strength, cunning, sagacity—echo older myths; they get mixed up with other stories about, for example, the time Americans spent on the island during the Second World War, or about other residents (for example, a resident in the 1950s exasperated the Wallisians by demanding that the trees they cut down be uprooted).[12] In short, it would be nonsensical to use them as "evidence," even though I do, to some degree.

One night, while writing this chapter, I watched the movie *Patton*, the script for which was written by Francis Ford Coppola, who would later adapt *Heart of Darkness* to make *Apocalypse Now*. The Conradian elements in *Patton* are obvious, the rise and fall narrative arc is perfect, but most troubling is the resemblance between David and the American general, played magnificently by George C. Scott: his pants tucked into his boots; his riding crop in his hand; his kepi; his Colt on his belt with its ivory grip; his white dog, the only being who remains faithful to him when everyone else abandons him, after he was relieved of command for having slapped a traumatized soldier who no longer wanted to fight (a fit of anger that would cost him dearly, a bit like David's "blow-ups").[13] A number of Wallisians told me about David's Jeep, which he never had, unlike Patton, who spends half the film in his. Patton, poet and emperor, beautiful loser and half crazy, believed in reincarnation. In a famous scene, in the middle of the ruins of Carthage, he remembers being Hannibal, and in another scene, Napoleon's general. "I fought in many guises, many names / but always me."[14] I seriously wonder whether, as Jean-Baptiste suggested to me, it was really this film that people were telling me about when they spoke about David, if Patton was the original and David, the fictional character.

Patton is David, who was himself many other Wallisian and Tongan warlords, and perhaps also Colonel Kurtz, with stories confirming, explaining, and inspiring each other; a myth decoding other myths. And what if each of the Wallisian narratives, like Marshall Sahlins's Pacific mythologies, was "basically an episode which, in its own way, tells the same story, and even if there are variations, the overall framework remains the same?"[15] François Hartog, following Sahlins, proposed to "show how Fiji" was itself a source of history—that is, to take seriously the specific way in which the heroic history of the Pacific islands defines a regime of historicity proper, in which "the divide between [past and present] which inaugurates Western history did not exist," in which descendants incarnate their ancestors and "the past is a vast reservoir of models of action," containing "everything from myths of origin to recent memories."[16] This would require a more thorough knowledge of Wallisian mythology than my own, but perhaps by following Hartog's proposals, one could understand how the stories about David (and the unfolding of the events themselves) include a whole series of elements from before and after his time on the island; how "events do not occur, they recur; they are not unique, they are repetitions"; and how, therefore, his *hisitolia* is necessarily also still current, on an island where, like the "islands of history" of Sahlins's Pacific, "the past can only be experienced in the present," where the future has always already happened.[17]

I DID NOT EXPLAIN all this to David's children, whom I met in France. It would have been a bit complicated. But his daughter liked the story of the dog in the sidecar. She explained to me that he had tamed animals everywhere he went, failing only with crocodiles. It seems that in Syria, he tamed a wolf.

When David left Wallis, he was not able to take his dog with him. He left it behind. Tui wondered with a smirk if it was eaten, but it seems unlikely to him, as it was not really part of local custom; rather, it would have been its master who would have been eaten, like St. Peter Chanel, Martyr of Futuna. I imagine the dog wandering alone on the island. Maybe it was killed, maybe it died of old age, maybe it has descendants. The island is full of mean dogs that chase scooters and are kept at a distance through the use of big sticks.

The other thing that this David left behind is a first name. "David has even become a first name," Lagimaina explained to me during our festive meal. The name in question, Tavite Lea Tahi, is in fact based on Tavite, the biblical name, that means "David-word (*lea*)-one (*tahi*), David-only-speaks-once." Wallisian first names are often poetic; for example, Lagimaina means "clear sky." "Tavite Lea Tahi is a name you don't give to just anyone," Lagimaina explained to me with a smile. "It has to be someone strong; if he's a weakling, you find him a second first name." Tavite Lea Tahi is for the strong-willed, who "inspire respect," as the euphemism does a nice job of putting it. This name sums up the authority of the character, in all its dimensions, both usurped and legitimate, charismatic and established; it refers directly to the class of the *'aliki* (nobles):

it's the name of the one who has the last word, because he is the strongest, because he is the chief, because he is above the laws and rules of the common people, because he is the most handsome, because he speaks well, because he speaks the truth. All of this in the same person. "We listen to him, but no one responds."[18] David speaks only once.

The day I left, Nyvé took me to the airport in the hotel pickup truck, in the pale light of the early morning. I was wearing a clean shirt and a necklace of flowers around my neck, which I had kept in the fridge since the day before, as people do here. We lost sight of each other as I checked in my luggage. When I found her in the parking lot, among all the people in necklaces saying goodbye, she asked me where I had been. It was a pity, Nyvé told me, she had just been talking to Tavite Lea Tahi, her cousin, I could have met him. He had come to drop people off, he was over there, leaving again. I stood on my tiptoes, trying to see where he was. All I saw was a couple of people in the distance, under the streetlights, and a pickup truck with the headlights on leaving the parking lot. I had missed Tavite.

29. Doctor Disaster

There is a clandestine story about David. It is a story that you hear in bits and pieces, that people tell without finishing their sentences, while putting out their cigarettes. When it's being told, you put down your pen. Those who tell it do so without being asked. It is a story not to be remembered because those who lived through it wanted to forget it. "The old man who told me this," said Michel Hoatau, after having told me all his anecdotes about David, "he was suffering when he told me this; he said, 'I'm telling you this, but it's not pleasant for me, because what I saw . . . no . . . dogs, guns like that. No, no . . . I can't.'" Of course, there are those who say that without David there would be no road, those who talk about the "positive effects," but that makes Michel smirk a little. Those people are not the ones who suffered under a "dictatorship that did a lot of harm." Those people were probably too young to work and just good at playing soccer.

The side of this story that is out in the open, which comes through in the publications, concerns "forced labor"—that is, the mobilization of the population for major projects. Monsignor Poncet uses the term in his book. He politely reproaches the doctor for "his methods," the progressive downward spiral of an organization initially presented as a "provisional effort" before taking on "the appearance of a permanent mobilization of the population, whose various tasks were obligatorily set for each day of the week."[1] The system "seemed to be truly opposed to the basic freedom owed to every human being."[2] The results were all that counted, the bishop acknowledged in his book, the kilometers of road built, the stone hospital, the cement cisterns, and the whitewashed churches. But even so, he protested in 1937: could the program not be lightened a little, to give the natives a little rest, as the preparations for the centenary were literally exhausting them? "They will rest with my successor," David had replied.[3] This short sentence has remained. Other recent Wallisian publications are a little more frank: Mikaele Tui speaks of a "dictatorial period," a resident with "questionable methods," who thought he was "the supreme authority of the island";[4] Virginie Tafilagi, of "a tyrannical man who terrorised the population."[5]

The terms "dictatorship" and "forced labor" are misleading, as I have already explained. The support of the chiefdoms for David's project was tangible, recruitment was channeled through the local institution of the *fatogia*, and, after the initial strong-arming, I am not aware of any use of force; moreover, it is not clear that this would have worked in David's favor, even if he was armed with a six-shooter. This is a classic equation in colonial situations: consent and coercion, affection and violence, desire and obligation, are not mutually exclusive.[6] Wallis was ruled with a whip and a soccer ball. However, the arrangement was fragile—and extraordinarily costly. Evidence suggests that, at the end of David's stay, generalized mandatory labor threatened the very foundations of Wallisian society.

The construction sites were not really in full swing until 1936, once copra production was resumed. Men were mobilized on several fronts: the last hospital buildings were being completed, the cement cisterns were being raised, the church in Mua was being rebuilt, and, above all, "road construction was being continued methodically throughout the island."[7] There were apparently no dark clouds on the horizon. The arrival of materials through the Native Welfare Society provided the workers with tools and payment, and the missionaries were content to sit back and admire the spectacle, from which they also benefited. "The resident is always heavily involved in the work," wrote the bishop in July 1936, and "the work of transforming the terrible old dirt path that connected Hihifo to Mua into a beautiful, wide road continues. Dr. David is still on good terms with the mission; he often comes to Lano and has invited us to lunch on July 14. He recently married a daughter of Mr. Brial, the former trader of Wallis in a religious ceremony; he plans to stay here for another year. May we never have any serious difficulties with the administration."

Poncet even specified: "It is in full agreement with the resident that this work is carried out under the direction of the chiefs."[8] The tone changed as the months went by, however, even if the alliance was never questioned. The centenary of the mission was coming up, and David's intervention was crucial in securing the passage of a warship that would give pomp and circumstance to the ceremonies. During 1937, when the twenty-six kilometers of road were finally completed, the situation appears to have degenerated.

"Our people no longer have time for confession," complained Father Marquet to the ecclesiastical superior of the General House of the Marist Brothers in a letter dated May 1, 1937. "One must work for the government constantly until nightfall; one must make copra even when there is no more; one must work for the glory of a gentleman who earns at least 50,000 francs a year; must they 'work themselves to death,' as he says?"[9] The first time I read this letter, in the archives of the Marist Fathers in Rome, a magnificent building in the Monteverde district, with a view of the city in the May sun, it made an impression on me. It was the first time I had seen a written source confirm that the situation had perhaps been more tense than the official stories suggested. Father Marquet continued: "He punches men and women and even the sick. Lenin-style authoritarianism, pride that cannot withstand any criticism. Extreme fear regarding the spiritual outweighing the temporal, the resident appearing inferior to the bishop and only receiving the second kava. What a misery that people are sent here without any oversight, who can do whatever they want here, and who are always believed."

The same Father Marquet had, in previous years, always been pleased with the resident, "an active and energetic man, very well disposed toward us and frank," he said a year after his arrival.[10] His letter is a bit like a nervous breakdown. One can read the fatigue and exasperation between the lines, the need to let go, with the eternal conflict between mission and administration in the background—none of this is really new. But other indications suggest that this was not all, that the situation deteriorated over the course of 1936—and continued to do so until David's departure in 1938.

From the time he arrived in Wallis on Ascension Day of 1936, Monsignor Poncet recorded his impressions—the chronicle of masses, first communions, rains, winds, lunches at the Residency, and his progress on the typewriter—in his notebook every day. On June 12, he wrote: "Last night, the resident gave the order to stop the singing we were doing for 'Ala mata' [the wake] of a person who died yesterday near the Mata-Utu dispensary. He was not obeyed. Result: this morning, he severely rebuked the chiefs, dismissed Kulitea and Petelo Mamio (Pule de Hahake), sentenced them and all the people who had taken part in the wake to two months' labor, and ordered the treatment of [Mukoi?] stopped for three months."[11]

The doctor likely had trouble sleeping—the flu, the whistling trade winds, the singing under his windows—to the point where he punished his favorite chief, Mukoi; dismissed two others; and sentenced everyone to forced labor. Invited to the bishop's palace, he apologized twice in a row. "Real illness," noted Poncet, who asked the nun who worked at the hospital about it. The doctor had "problems with his wife." She had been sent to Nouméa to her father, Julien Brial, who screened her mail and refused to let her go to France. For the past few months, David had been "bored in Wallis," he confided to the bishop. His marriage in March had been hasty, as Sofia was very ill at the time and at risk of dying. She survived, and since then, David did not really know what to do. "All this explains why he is nervous."[12]

Some Wallisians complained to Lano, the temperate bishop. On July 1, 1936, David once again pushed some of the chiefs and part of his government aside. This practice was beginning to veer sharply away from Wallisian customs. On July 14, a "providential" rainfall spared the bishop from having to travel for the festivities;[13] David had demanded that he be the first of the two to be served at the Kava. Mukoi's death in November weakened David a little and led to new ministerial reshuffles (with the *kivalu* regaining his position). The bishop had been in Futuna for several months at this time and was unaware of what was happening in Wallis. In short, I have the impression of a growing tension, of a mechanism that was getting jammed from mid-1936, but for a long time, all I had were hints, nothing very solid, a bit like what had happened in Haut-Nyong. These included a few memories, like those of Sioli Pilioko, who recounted how opponents of King David like her grandfather were exiled from one end of the island to the other, their children left behind to be adopted by siblings, and Poncet's notes from 1937 on chiefs sentenced to hard labor for several months for not having delivered enough copra, and on the story of the beaten women.[14] There was also the letter from an exasperated Father Marquet, written after David left, which emphasized that the resident was "an *out-of-control* tyrant, ruling by kicks and punches, putting people in prison on mere suspicion. He turned Wallis into a barracks, if not a labor camp. [. . .] He could not withstand the slightest observation or criticism; he was becoming a raving lunatic."[15]

In the archives of the diocese in Lano, there is a copy of a report, filed with the correspondence of Monsignor Poncet, which is titled "Rapport présenté respectueusement par Mgr Poncet, vicaire apostolique des îles Wallis et Futuna, à Son Excellence le Gouverneur de Nouvelle-Calédonie: Objet: Le travail forcé à Wallis" (Report respectfully presented by Monsignor Poncet, Vicar Apostolic of the Wallis and Futuna Islands, to His Excellency the Governor of

New Caledonia: Subject: Forced labor in Wallis).[16] It is typewritten, no doubt by Poncet himself, dated May 1939, a little more than a year after David's departure. When I read it, I immediately thought, "This alone was worth the airplane trip!" I read the report several times during my stay. I liked coming to work at the archives in Lano, where I sat at the desk of Bishop Fuahea, the first Wallisian bishop. Nothing had been touched since his death in 2005, not even his photos or his cologne. I even tried to progress as slowly as possible so that I could come back and spend several afternoons in this way. The secretary, Mahilina, stayed with me to keep an eye on me (you can see her in the background in the TV report on "Wallis and Futuna Première"). We chatted in the air-conditioning while I photographed the archives page by page.

"At first, I was hesitant to believe what I heard." Upon his return from Futuna in August 1936, Poncet found the Wallisians "overburdened with chores."[17] He complained to David, who replied "that this was a 'big push'; after the centenary celebrations (October 1937), the natives will rest." When the celebrations were over and the work did not stop, David then said, "They will rest with my successor." Upon his departure, his replacement, Dr. Lamy, also a doctor in the Colonial Army, immediately gave the entire population a full month's rest before resuming the program of major projects developed by David, the workload lightened by one week off per month. There was no real lull in sight, however, and a growing concern about conditions on the island. It was this, as well as the opportunity to create an unconciliatory inventory of King David's work, that seems to have prompted the bishop's letter. The report cautions that it "does not aim to criticize any person or intentions" but only to provide the governor with "some information."[18] In substance, the report is a twenty-five-page indictment of the major projects carried out by the administration. It attacked the former resident while providing a slightly better assessment of Dr. Lamy. "The courteous and benevolent manner in which he behaves [with the Wallisians]," Poncet specified, "contrasts in every respect that of his predecessor."[19]

It all began, explained Poncet, in 1936. "The present organization of work, so different from what it was until very recently, was introduced almost imperceptibly in 1936–1937, without prior public notice, under the guise of exceptional work requiring considerable manpower, but presented as a temporary effort."[20] To the traditional rhythm of collective work carried out in the villages—the growing of subsistence crops, fishing, net making, the building of houses—had long been added the contribution of gifts in kind to the king and the mission and participation in church construction. The new organization developed by David and then renewed by Lamy completely changed everything. Each day of the week was devoted to a compulsory task for all men aged eighteen to sixty years "under threat of punishment."[21] Mondays were earmarked for work on construction sites, stone cutting, and the provision of materials; Tuesdays and Wednesdays, the collective clearing of coconut groves; Thursdays, subsistence crops; and Fridays and Saturdays, the preparation and sale of copra. The bishop pretended to be searching for the right words: how was this different from "slavery"? Had a regulation that provided for "endless" compulsory work every day of every week of every year of the "existence of an able-bodied man" been put in place anywhere else? "Does a comparable social reality exist elsewhere?" The system was "unheard of," concluded Poncet. "It effectively suppresses any freedom the native has in the use of his time."[22]

But Poncet's concerns were not about principles: the most serious apprehension concerned the very reproduction of the labor force, indeed, the very survival of the island. It was one thing to recruit workers for the building sites, but they still needed to be fed and their absence from the fields must not affect food production—the classic issue, dear to Marxist historians, of the link between agricultural productivity and the extraction of surplus labor. In Uvea, the equation was solved "traditionally" in a way, by a social institution, the so-called *kainaki* service, which supplied provisions (in the form of prepared food) to the workers on a construction site or to the chiefdom. Prior to the Christianization of the island, the term referred to the obligation of each village to take turns feeding the nobles (*'aliki*) and the king.[23] It is one of the obligations men have to the community, which in modern times has become a kind of tax in kind whenever there are collective projects or major festivals. As Poncet explained in his report, forced labor on a large scale brought about the resumption of the practice of *kainaki* while at the same time completely throwing it off balance. Whereas the *kainaki* remained a onetime obligation, limited to the village or district where the collective work was taking place and moderated by a system of rotation between families, food baskets now had to be delivered to the administration every day of the week and, in addition, had to be brought from one end of the island to the other, depending on where the construction sites were located. The preparation and transport of the baskets, sometimes over fifteen to twenty kilometers, took up most of the time of the workers who were not on the construction site. The island must seem immense when workers are required to cross it under the blazing sun with a basket of yams on their back.

The model, obviously, was not sustainable, even if the tools and fertilizers of the welfare society (including the *hele faka lesita*) allowed for an increase in agricultural productivity. David's main solution was to use the administration's budget to buy sacks of rice with which to provide a ration to the conscripted laborers.[24] But the imbalance went deeper than this. The generalization of forced labor posed "serious disadvantages from the point of view of the feeding of the natives," wrote Poncet at the beginning of a paragraph in which every word was hard-hitting. Quite simply, there was a threat of "scarcity" or even "famine." The Wallisians feared that they would soon run out of food, and Poncet was willing to believe them; he feared "dire consequences." David himself admitted that he did not see the famine coming and that he underestimated the work required to grow subsistence crops. With one short day devoted to the crops, families had barely enough time to get to their plot, where they had previously spent several days in a row. Workers exhausted from the previous day's work no longer had the strength to get up early and found themselves in the fields at the hottest hours of the day. The construction schedules did not take into account the growing and harvesting seasons, and entire yam harvests were lost. Large-scale fishing was being abandoned and skills forgotten because people could not follow the rhythm dictated by the sea and the weather. Poncet wrote, "The current system of forced labor can only result in dire consequences."[25] He was concerned about the long term: the notorious clearing of coconut groves (the colonial antidote to the Wallisians' "slackness") in fact disrupted the multiannual cycles of voluntarily leaving lands fallow in order to fertilize them and caused entire areas to be lost to cultivation, with no possibility of remedying this for decades. "This point was reportedly brought to the attention of Dr. David, who chose to ignore it," Poncet noted.[26] The proof was undeniable, and the bishop seemed sorry to see the mission benefiting from the system despite itself. To cope with demand for copra and food, flights were becoming more common. The island as described by Poncet seemed to be teetering on the brink. "There are living documents of the ancient Polynesian civilization [. . .] which, if we are not careful, may soon disappear."[27]

Naturally, Poncet had a thousand reasons to complain about the doctor-administrators, especially about this David who had married badly, who "never graced the church with his presence,"[28] not even for Christmas Mass, and who never ceded his place in the Kava, and apparently planned to do so only once he had left the island. However, reading the report is nonetheless edifying in that it suggests a threat to the cultural reproduction of Wallisian society, in the anthropological sense of the term. One of Michel's anecdotes (he calls them "tips," which he learned from his grandfather and his father) confirms this, by stating in what is doubtless a metaphorical fashion the anxiety that David's reign brought to bear on village and family life:

When [my grandfather] left for work in the morning, he would leave so early that the kids were still in bed. And in the evening, when he came home, the kids were already in bed. This meant that practically all parents, especially fathers, didn't see their kids. Impossible. I mean, he could see them sleeping, but he couldn't wake them up. He'd leave, he'd kiss them goodbye before leaving, but that was it. I think we can sum it up like that. It's something that still shows what the mood was like back then.

His wife said something in Wallisian, and he confirmed it.

> Everyone was tired, it's true. There wasn't much to eat, a bit of rice, but it was rationed, rice was rationed. No one could bring in anything to eat. When there was breadfruit . . . there was no one left to work the plantations. There were no more fields, no more banana trees, no more taro, no more *kape* [a tuber that is a close relative of taro], no more yams. Everybody was busy working. Only the women stayed at home, went fishing, took care of the children. It was Tavite who was in charge. Ah yes, he was demanding.[29]

This was also the time of David, a time of hunger, of families who no longer saw each other, of women who did everything, of fields abandoned to go break rocks or shell castor beans. David imposed an arbitrary rhythm on life, one without seasons, which prevented it from following the rhythm of the taro plantations and the trade winds; he projected another space onto the island, one in which the micro-geographies of fields, burnings, and fallows were broken up. Children no longer saw their parents; the day continued into the night; lands were burned and cultivated at times of rest; fishing nets were no longer woven; plantations were no longer sown; stories were no longer told in the evening; there was no time to go to Mass anymore. The almost mythical tales about King David that have since blossomed and are remembered today are perhaps a way, as François Hartog, taking inspiration from Marshall Sahlins, wrote, of domesticating the event, of moving the crisis back into the past, of "warding off the unbearable disarray of what was happening."[30]

David's knowledge, that of his books on agronomy and his account ledgers, was ignorance. This can be gleaned from the writings of Poncet, who liked to highlight that David did not understand anything about yams.[31] One can even sense it in the reports written by David, who discovered at the end of his stay that caterpillars were devouring all the castor oil plants,[32] or that the coconut trees appeared to no longer be producing, provoking a "coconut scarcity,"[33] and was then told that this was a natural rhythm that everyone had always been aware of.

In Wallis, the king is responsible "for the life and survival of the *fenua* (country)."[34] He is held accountable for the vitality of the island, the fertility of the land, the riches of the sea, but also for cyclones and disasters, which may justify his being deposed. A network of correspondences is established between his person, his acts, and the state of the country. The interface between God(s) and men, the status and power of the *hau*, are at once sacred, social, and ecological. This is a classic aspect of Polynesian anthropology, well described in the Wallisian instance by the anthropologist Hélène Guiot. In particular, along with chiefdom, the king assumes "the responsibility for the proper functioning of the *'ulufenua*,"[35] a concept that refers to the earth's resources, both vegetable and mineral, which are also the substance of life. The harmony of the world depends on the good health (*ma'uli*, in the sense of fertility and vitality) of the *'ulufenua*—thanks to God, thanks to the king, who is the guardian of the island's lands and forests, and finally, thanks to the respect of all the customary obligations and prohibitions. During the Kava ceremonies, the ritual is thus addressed to the *hau*, invoking divinity through him:

> Ke hakea te tai
> Ke ma'uli te 'ulufenua
> Ke hifo lahi te vai
> Ke tou 'ofa mo agatonu ki te 'atua
> Malo!

> May the sea be full of fish
> May the *'ulufenua* [that which gives birth to the earth] be lush
> May the rain fall abundantly
> May we love and be righteous before God
> Thank you![36]

It should be remembered that this is how David was addressed when he received the first cup of kava. In other words, Te Hau Tavite likely did not escape an assessment of his person in terms of the health and vitality of the island, human and nonhuman alike. Wallisian conceptions of "public health" or "the environment" are intrinsically linked to those of the person and the power of the *hau*. The equivalency works both ways. We can imagine that David's economic and agricultural successes, his fine speeches, his workforce, the distribution of machetes, the fertilization of poor soil with imported guano, the agreement he arranged with the mission, and the rhinoceros beetles that were burned by the basketful mutually confirmed each other as signs of harmony and vitality; conversely, the invasions of caterpillars, the signs of scarcity, the exhaustion and anger of the men, the drying up of the coconut trees, the nervousness of the resident, the empty chair at Mass, and the kicks to the kava all stemmed from the same imbalance.

It is difficult to be precise, but the general mobilization of the island in preparation for the mission's centenary in 1937 has left some traces in the oral and environmental memory of the island. The elders report that, to speed up the production of victuals for the grand ceremonies (*katoaga*) planned for the governor's visit, part of the *vao tapu*, the sacred forest that climbs toward the crater lake Lalo, was burned and used for cultivation at this time. This constitutes one of the first encroachments in human memory on the taboo forest, considered to be the domain of the gods and the source of life for the *fenua*, the uses of which were strictly codified and placed under the responsibility of the *hau*.[37] In short, this constituted the breaking of a major taboo, carried out under pressure and perhaps on David's instructions; it was certainly under his responsibility, whether or not he had ordered this to happen. Already in August 1936, the bishop noted on his return from an excursion to the lake with the seminarians that "the old forest that was once *tapu* was almost entirely burned down for planting a little over six months ago: the resident Dr. David found out too late to prevent it."[38] It is hardly surprising, then, that things with David "ended badly." "You know that here the leaders are responsible for disasters," Lagimaina told me in our first conversation. I answered him with a falsely ingenuous question: if things ended badly with David, what was his disaster? The silent famine of 1936 to 1938? The lands no longer producing as well as they had in the past?

David's disaster is impossible to miss. The books discuss it and the elderly remember it. It was the "great fever" that ravaged Wallis beginning in mid-1936, known in Wallisian as *fiva lahi* (the word *fiva*, from the English word "fever," is used throughout Polynesia). The doctors called it typhoid fever, a disease hitherto unknown on the island but familiar to hygienists at the beginning of the twentieth century. At the time, it was known to spread in an epidemic fashion in prisons, barracks, or trenches, where people were crammed together, and that it is caused by a bacterium (*Salmonella typhi*) transmitted by food or water contaminated by the fecal matter of the sick or of "healthy carriers." Although it rarely occurred in "native settings," colonial clinicians were familiar with its symptoms: a high and irregular fever, "coated" tongue, rose spots on the body, extreme despondency and stupor (typhoid state), prostration, delirium, pain, and violent diarrhea, followed by death in one case out of three, with there being little that could be done.[39]

On the eve of his departure for Futuna in August 1936, Poncet noted hastily: "A visit to the hospital, full of sick people: two women and a child appear in a desperate state; Suliano [illegible] (about fifteen years old) and Vito (thirteen years old), seminarians, have a high fever. It is the typhoid epidemic. I bless the sick in all the wards."[40] Upon his return, he took stock of the damage: "Still a dozen people sick with typhoid in the hospital. Suliano was cured and has returned to the seminary. I also learned of the deaths of Mukoi (the prime minister) and Kivalu (the former *pule* of Hihifo). Today we learned of the abdication of King Edward VIII of England."[41] The Wallisian nurse at the hospital (the only one on the island) had also died, "a victim of his devotion."[42] On December 20, the bishop ordered three days of public prayer to bring an end to the extensive loss of life. In his year-end report, written at the same time, David reported nothing except the sad death of Mukoi, his mentor, friend, and protégé, of a "short infectious illness."[43]

In January 1937, the epidemic resumed with greater intensity. The bishop asked the fathers to warn their faithful, to undertake to identify those affected, and to "have them taken to the hospital in Sia at the first sign of illness."[44] On January 28, David went to see the bishop. With eleven dead in ten days, the epidemic was undergoing a "resurgence," and it was time to take "energetic measures to stop the epidemic." He decided to build an "isolated camp" for the sick near the hospital, surrounded by unscalable fences, and to send the convalescent to the island of Kaviki, a sandbank just opposite Mata-Utu. He would have bathrooms installed in each house and asked the monsignor to "propagandize to make people accept these regulations willingly, especially those concerning the camps for the sick and convalescent."[45] Isolating the sick and the survivors (who were still capable of transmitting the infection) was the only option for fighting the epidemic: the vaccine invented at the end of the nineteenth century was expensive, and David "showed no intention" of using it, the bishop later wrote.[46] Confinement in camps, as with trypanosomiasis (or today, Ebola), is primarily a preventive measure at the population level. Therapeutically, affected individuals had nothing to expect from internment except a strict diet and were required in any case to rely on personal resistance, luck, or providence to have any hope of survival. The camp for the sick (which oral memory seems to identify with the "hospital toilets," the *fale siko*, from *fale*, "home," and the English "sick"[47]) was rapidly put into operation, with three large huts and a total of eighty beds. David kept his statistics on deaths and complications (intestinal hemorrhage and perforation of the peritoneum) and got angry when patients who were already dying were brought to him. A French nun took care of the sick, and Father Marquet came to give last rites and communion—too often, as far as David was concerned, as he feared that this might weaken the patients.

The small islet of Kaviki also filled up. There were soon about sixty people in isolation there, grouped in huts according to their districts of origin. It was Poncet who was worried this time: young men and women were living side by side "without any supervision," and the seminarians were at risk of "losing their vocation."[48] It should be remembered that the islets that dot the lagoon are considered to be "other spaces" in Wallis,[49] therapeutic places where the wind soothes and whets the appetite, still frequented today by pregnant women, enchanting sites of pilgrimage and relaxation, which were coveted for a time by Club Med and where entire villages come to "camp," to fish or work to maintain the sites, for days on end, following specific rules and taboos. However, they are also considered spaces of escape and exclusion: until the 1970s, Nukuatea was the "Islet of the Leprosy Patients," based on an idea of David's or his successor's, and only a few years ago a dangerous madman, convicted of homicide, was exiled there and chased the French foreign aid workers who went to the islet to enjoy the beaches. With its white sand, Kaviki is particularly beautiful (Canal + staged a fake rugby match there to make it look good in a report). I swam there one evening, but it was a bit of a foolish undertaking (three thousand meters there and back, without being able to touch my feet to the bottom to take a rest). At the time of the epidemic, the isolation was total: food was brought in by boat, visitors were not allowed to eat or drink while there, nothing was allowed to be transported back to the big island, and every Sunday, missionaries traveled there to celebrate Mass.[50]

However, the epidemic persisted, and the list of deaths grew longer. The nun was so overworked that David could no longer bear it, so he decided to send her to Futuna. "The poor sick have nothing with which to treat themselves: they drink herbal tea without sugar. We can find money to buy wood and sheet metal for chicken coops, pigsties, farms, built with beautiful cut stones brought from ten kilometers away, but we have nothing for the upkeep of the hospital," complained Father Marquet.[51] All *katoaga* were forbidden in order to prevent the population from gathering.[52] Vaccines, paid for in part by the mission, finally arrived in May. The entire population was vaccinated, and no new cases occurred. "It seems that this is the end of the epidemic, which had caused at least one hundred deaths since June 1936,"[53] Poncet noted on June 24, 1937. The island would be able to prepare for the centenary.

DAVID'S INTERPRETATION OF the epidemic was very conventional, as old as public health: the blame lay with the victims. For his part, he counted 124 deaths, a disaster he attributed to the "primitive" character of the country, "devoid of water cisterns and the most basic hygiene," and to the Wallisians who "carefully" hid the sick so that they would not be sent to the camp, who brought them too late, in "a full state of physical decay," and who continued to come "clandestinely in the middle of the night" to feed and even force-feed them, compromising the success of the doctor's treatment plan.[54] But Monsignor Poncet provided another version of events in his 1939 report, suggesting that it was the "undernourishment" caused by forced labor that weakened "the natives' power of resistance."[55] Jean-Claude Roux reported that "some witnesses [. . .] also blamed the water tanks built for a praiseworthy purpose at the instigation of the Resident,"[56] the contamination of a cistern being a very effective means of spreading the disease, described at the time in military camps in New Caledonia, for example. This seems somewhat unlikely in the case of this epidemic (there were many outbreaks within families), but popular epidemiology, in blaming David's cisterns, may not have been completely wrong. Typhoid, which was unknown in Wallis before 1936 and which almost certainly came to the island aboard the same boat as Monsignor Poncet on Ascension Day, is not a "primitive" disease secreted by the carelessness and ignorance of the locals but an epidemic of modernity. As David's colonial comrades knew, in the tropics it affected mainly soldiers and sailors. It is an epidemic of kitchens and collective latrines, to put it briefly, and it hit the college and seminary of Wallis hard. The disaster had come to the island with cement, machetes, and the sidecar motorcycle.

With 124 deaths, close to 5 percent of the total population, including many young people, the *fiva lahi* is perhaps the worst epidemic in the history of the small island. It was not a question of David, who grieved like all the others, having been overwhelmed. He did everything he could with the energy and courage that he is known for. I have even been told that Sofia almost died, and that he treated her, saved her, and then married her afterward. But according to the Wallisian conception of the sovereign's responsibility for the harmony and vitality of the country, David was responsible for the epidemic he fought to control, which coincided with the famine, the peak of the recruitment of forced labor, and the frenzy of building and clearing land to prepare for the governor's arrival. For the doctor was not only a doctor; he was also resident and king, head of public works, and justice of the peace. It was, in a way, the same tragedy as would occur in Haut-Nyong—history would repeat itself once again. When it came time to tally the numbers for his final report, the colonial doctor had to face the facts: after four years of medical government, the figures were not good.

"If we consult only the story the numbers tell, the results of this vast over-all program seem rather discouraging. A close look at the figures shows that 462 deaths were recorded from 1934 to 1937 compared with 454 in the period 1930–1933, an increase of eight deaths," David explained in his final report.[57] He did what he could with the statistics. The birth rate barely moved, and infant mortality stagnated at a very high rate (around twenty deaths per one hundred births), despite progress in maternal and child care. In 1937, the population balance was in fact the worst it had been since 1932. The cause of "this initially disappointing finding" is not difficult to identify: it was typhoid. The epidemic had "distorted the results," he concluded.[58] This sentence was also worth the trip. Typhoid had distorted the statistics, as if this had not occurred in the real world, as if the truth lay elsewhere, in the beautiful story told to the governor, in the unraveling dream David clung to. Utopia does not fit well with reality.

PART III.
EPILOGUES

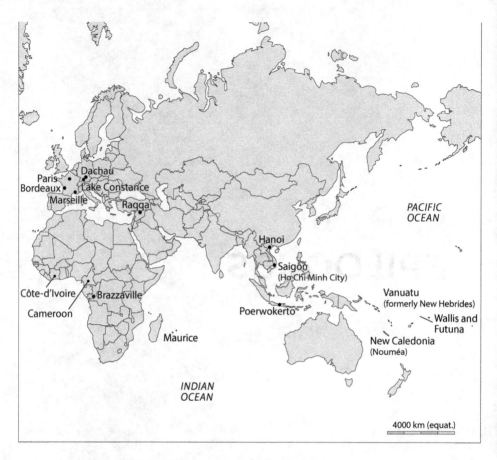

MAP 4. Places mentioned. © d-maps.com. https://d-maps.com/carte.php?num_car=3503.

30. Afelika (Africa)

"You have to mention the day Dr. David left," Jean-Baptiste Mulikihaamea told me.

JEAN-BAPTISTE MULIKIHAAMEA: If I may say so, it was truly national mourning in Wallis. Because we did a *kataoga*, a Royal Kava due to his rank. And, among Wallisians, when a figure speaks, [he speaks] at the end of the Kava. [This speech] has been described a little—it's too bad, we couldn't find the . . .

GUILLAUME LACHENAL: The transcript . . .

JEAN-BAPTISTE: But they say he gave his farewell speech in front of the palace. There was a sea of people, from what my father told me, everyone was crying their eyes out, everyone was crying. And all David said was that he was sorry. "If I have treated you badly, please forgive me. What I have done was not done out of pride, out of wickedness. I did it for you, to teach you to take responsibility for yourselves. If I did not do enough for you . . . this is what I have been able to give you. And I know that for generations, I will not be around anymore, but I know that everyone . . . always . . . [will remember]." The proof is, it's 2014, and we're still talking about this figure.

GUILLAUME: And he spoke in Wallisian?

JEAN-BAPTISTE: He spoke in Wallisian. He gave his speech in Wallisian, because he spoke it fluently. It's too bad that they weren't able to transcribe it. He didn't need an interpreter. He learned all on his own.[1]

On February 4, 1938, the *Pierre Loti*, the replacement for the *Bucéphale*, which had run aground on a reef in the New Hebrides, brought David's successor, Dr. Lamy, to Wallis. The new and former residents spent a few days together, the time required for an initiation "to the Wallisian world,"[2] a big party, a farewell speech, and a lunch with the bishop. On February 8, the *Pierre Loti* left for the New Hebrides, taking Jean Joseph David and his wife, Sofia, with it.[3]

"*Deo Gratias*," wrote Father Marquet as they say at the end of Mass, "the air was no longer breathable, at least here in Mata-Utu. [. . .] What will his successor be? They leave, the mission remains."[4] David's boat trip lasted a good two months. When he disembarked in Marseille on April 29, the island at the other end of the world had already gone back to work, as the new doctor-administrator resumed the plans laid out by David. After having taken a relaxed approach during the early weeks, Lamy traveled to the villages to explain that it was necessary to "persevere with David's policies,"[5] and he began by having stones cut for the hospital and for the new leprosy camp on the large islet of Nukuatea. His time in Wallis was a success: the goodwill of the Wallisians was confirmed, his authority was solid, the demographic indicators were improving, and he was able to rely on the *kivalu* put in place by David (this was Leone Mulikihaamea, Jean-Baptiste's father, who would be made *lavelua* in 1941). In the report he submitted in May 1939, Monsignor Poncet worried about the continuation of the regime of forced labor and tried to settle a score with Tavite, but Nouméa replied that France was at war, and everyone had to make sacrifices. The matter was closed.[6]

David would not be in touch too often. There is just one handwritten letter in the archives of Monsignor Poncet; in fact, this was the only private correspondence I had access to throughout this entire investigation. It contains his well wishes for the year 1939. The text is difficult to decipher because the ink has gone through the paper with the result that the front and back of the letter are superimposed:

PARIS, JANUARY 6, 1939.

Monsignor,

Please allow me, although it is unfortunately not possible for me to be among the first to present you with my well wishes for the New Year, to do so at least with all [illegible].

Rest assured that the former resident to Wallis makes very sincere well wishes for the conduct of your apostolate and the prosperity of your educational projects.

I hope [illegible] that your projects concerning your colleges will come to fruition and that the very beneficial activities of the Marist mission will undertake [illegible] new.

Please be kind enough to remember me to your French and Wallisian missions and to pass on to them my most cordial wishes.

As for me, a deposed king, for the time being in service in a colonial infantry regiment in Paris, I am making the best of a bad situation, and I am striving to stock up on the science of health . . . and on patience, in view of new colonial postings, probably in Africa . . . unless the Maginot Line decides to offer me the cozy shelter of its concrete bunkers.

Believe, in any case, whatever clement or merciless skies will shelter me in the years to come, believe that I will never forget this small and endearing country that is Wallis, and if you have the opportunity, tell your followers that my affection for them was not [illegible] and that [they] remain deeply rooted in my memory.

In eight or nine months' time, I shall be leaving France again. I will remain full of courage and spirit, but I do not think I will find native populations so worthy of interest any time soon.

Receive, Monsignor, with my thanks for the very trusting welcome that I always received in your missions, the assurance of my respectful devotion.

David[7]

The Wallisians I met were unaware of what had become of their "deposed king." I believe that the nostalgic tone of his wishes would not have surprised them—the curiosity, attachment to the *fenua*, humor, politeness, fair play, and even the "class" of the *lesita* left their mark on the island. Jean-Baptiste's article, "Te temi o Tavite," published in 1979 in *Malamanei*, would cement this memory: David "really loved the country"; he "went to drink kava in the villages." The article, full of somewhat mysterious anecdotes translated by Alice Fromonteil, describes him as one would speak of a king, feared and calm, whose charisma came from the heavens (*lagi*). The French-language version published alongside the Wallisian text is completely different, but it also ends by evoking the "giant" who wore a Colt on his belt and who "gave of himself without any personal profit and this for the well-being of the Wallisians"; "his severity remains legendary." Surrounding the article, there are advertisements for a Citroën dealership and a perfume shop in Nouméa; just below the Wallisian text, complete with a photo of helicopters from the film, is an ad for *Apocalypse Now*. Here too, the back and the front are superimposed.[8]

People were curious when I told them that I knew what David had done in Africa, that he had been there planting cocoa, laying out roads, building hospitals and soccer fields, doing "the same as here." During interviews, they talked about it among themselves, translating each other. I understood only one word that kept coming up, "Afelika," the transliteration of Africa—I found it nice. All they knew was that he had left, without leaving any children or heirs, and they had never heard anything more about him. "It's like that, Ta-vite disappeared." They knew more or less that Sophie had settled in Paris and had become a restaurant owner in the Montparnasse district or something like that, that David had died in the 1970s, that Sophie had come back alone and died here, and was buried with the rest of the Brial family, which includes a queen and deputies. I was always the one who revealed that they had divorced very quickly, that David had made his life without her. As Nyvé told me at the hotel, the story was a bit taboo.

BACK IN FRANCE, DAVID was awarded medals. He had brought back excellent marks from the Pacific, which got people talking about him in the offices of the Ministry of the French Colonial Empire on rue Oudinot. In New Caledonia, Governor Marchessou was enthusiastic about David's end-of-stay report and wrote a glowing preface to it during his stopover in Nouméa at the end of February 1938.[9] On December 31, David was awarded the silver medal of the Academy of Medicine, where his work had been noted in 1937 in a report on child welfare in the colonies.[10] Shortly thereafter, he received the Medal of Epidemics, likely for his battle against typhoid. David's time in Wallis became a "French endeavor" worthy of expanding beyond Oceania, where the colonial press had already been reporting on the miracles accomplished by the doctor.[11] He set about writing a long article for the *Revue des troupes coloniales* (Colonial Army review), which would be published in August 1939.[12] David presented the article one evening in the spring of 1939 in the large amphitheater of the Faculty of Medicine of Paris, as part of a series of conferences on the "great tropical endemics" organized by Louis Tanon, a professor at the Faculty who assiduously relayed colonial initiatives to the Parisian medical world (notably, he was one of the lobbyists for the Jamot mission). "The colonial project about which I have the honor of speaking to you this evening," David began, "concerns a rather unknown French possession, situated in the middle of the Pacific Ocean, about twenty thousand kilometers from Paris, and which has the unique characteristic at the present time in our colonial empire of being administered by a doctor."[13] His talk reviewed the ethnology, history, geography, and diseases of the island before focusing on the "French endeavor": the political incidents that gave full powers to the doctor, the art of government in the *fono*, economic action, and the progress made everywhere. He concluded with confident projections: "In 1942, the health and social organization of the country will be entirely complete."[14] The lectern had had all the great names of colonial medicine stand before it, including General Blanchard, the inspector of the Colonial Health Service, who had inaugurated the 1939 session. For Major David, who had graduated at the bottom of his class from the Pharo a few years earlier, this was a triumphant return. It got him into the good books of the directors of the Health Service, which had just found the ideal candidate for the Haut-Nyong experiment.

The small Wallisian utopia found an unexpected reverberation by becoming, after the fact, an experiment in government by medicine, the standard-bearer of the Colonial Health Service and even of French medicine itself. David's pen lent itself well to this. In the conclusion of his article in the *Revue des Troupes coloniales*, he dreamed of the "overpopulation" to come in the protectorate, of its "most flourishing economic and demographic situation" which would allow, once a maritime crossing system was set up, the installation of the "vigorous" Wallisians in other Pacific possessions. In this instance, he was a visionary. "Whatever it may be [. . .], a colonial doctor will preside over this destiny. His task remains a difficult one," he concluded by quoting Viala, the first of the island's doctor-administrators, but "his efforts will never be in vain and they will always be pleasant to him, in that they will also result in spreading and strengthening, among primitive populations, love and admiration of France, their protective nation."[15] Just below the article is a drawing, a caricature with neat features. It depicts a doctor of the Colonial Army in shorts and white shirt, sitting on his trunk. Sitting cross-legged in front of him are two shirtless Polynesians, a man and a woman. Beside him, there is a guard with a spear. On the doctor's head, there is a crown.

It was David's son who gave me a photocopy of this article, which also includes photos of the sidecar motorcycle, a soccer match, and Wallisian warriors. The drawing left me a bit perplexed. It suggests, like the allusion to the "deposed king" in the letter to Poncet, that David himself did not know whether to take the story of the king seriously. It suggests an ironic distance, a form of split nested within the very narrative of the good doctor who subdues the savages and brings about the advent of civilization. As Romain Bertrand reminds us with regard to the Spanish conquest of the Philippines, the world did not wait for us to doubt, laugh, or be eaten up by remorse.[16] In fact, I believe that David's adventure was from the outset lived in the second degree, as a rehearsal, parody, and actualization of a tale of a civilizing mission and stranger-king (of which the Victorian white rajah is only a local, European version, itself the product of a working misunderstanding). By superimposing several layers of misunderstandings, performative myths in which everyone only half believes but which nevertheless inform historical practice and shape subjectivities, the episode avoids a critique of propaganda as a distortion of the "real." The real story is not hidden behind David's big words about France and the legendary laziness of the Wallisians. He knew that these commonplaces had to be mastered to please the governor, and it is impossible to know whether he was smiling at his own excesses or whether he was truly impassioned—likely both. To borrow a Polynesian lesson from Marshall Sahlins, practice is shaped by myth (which serves as a matrix of subjectivation, or self-making, and a repertoire of action) and for myth (which incorporates elements of this), without regard for the origins of this myth.[17] David the half king played a game the codes of which were both those of the imperial republican gesture and those of the big men of the Pacific. His role of "leader" followed several scripts at the same time, between Lyautey, Eugène Jamot, and the *hau* of Uvea.[18] He was a figure whose blood, to quote George Patton, his cinematographic double (inspired by a general who literally thought he was King Arthur),[19] had already been spilled "countless times among the stars."[20]

In his thesis on Wallis, Jean-Claude Roux concluded that Commander David had "perhaps succeeded too well,"[21] meaning that he and his successors were intoxicated by the unexpected success of his interventionist model, based on forced labor and the abolition of royalty, which in fact brought the island to an impasse. The residents who succeeded him until the late 1950s referred to David in their writings as an effective but excessive modernizer, admirable but impossible to imitate. Although Wallis would soon turn its back on the "David policy," the remark rings true when you know the rest of the story. At the end of September 1939, David took in his luggage for Cameroon a dream that he was very close to realizing. His "hubris," like that of Captain Cook when he arrived in Hawaii and willingly accepted the divine role that was offered to him, "was as much Polynesian as it was European," Wallisian above colonial. Like Cook in Hawaii, when he arrived in Haut-Nyong, "he had years of experience [. . .] as a 'kind of superior being.'" Like Cook, he seemed to "walk through his death scene with a certain dream-like quality."[22] He was once again *hau* when he listened to the children of Abong-Mbang sing a song to his glory, in a voice that was too enthusiastic, during the torchlight processions.

David neither died nor was buried in Abong-Mbang; the blue, white, and red tomb in the tall grass just above the school is not his. He met his second wife, Elizabeth de Louvencourt, who was then the wife of Dr. Perves, another local medical officer there.[23] When old Evina in Abong-Mbang told me that David had sent Dr. Perves to the front with the Free French Forces so he could take his wife from him, I thought, "like King David in the Bible." Their first son was born in Algiers in May 1944, and they married in Saint-Mandé at the end of 1945, once David had settled his divorce from Sophie, who had spent the war in France. Elizabeth was an aristocrat, daughter of a count.

In Algiers, to whence he was repatriated, David met Dr. Charbonnier, a young fellow colonial doctor who was about to travel to Wallis to take on the position of doctor-administrator and who was taking advantage of the wait for the boat to spend some time at the municipal library. David briefed him, explained to him the protocol at the Kava, the importance of demanding a place in the choir at the church, and undoubtedly gave him an idea of the bishop's personality, as well as those of the other fathers, King Leone, and Sosefo the interpreter; he told him all the things "that never appear in official reports."[24] I do not know what information the Algiers Gaullists had about Wallis at the time, but the situation there was particularly uncertain. Cut off from the world, the island was initially Vichyist, the ill-considered idea of Monsignor Poncet and Dr. Vrignaud, who was governing at the time, prior to the simultaneous arrival of the American army and a new Gaullist resident doctor in May 1942.[25] In the middle of the Pacific War, the installation of an American base with about five thousand soldiers was a major event for the island, which saw its subsistence problems solved by an avalanche of dollars and corned beef. The Wallisians discovered tanks, Jeeps, and plane crashes. The American Golden Age covered up and erased the traces of Tavite, starting with his roads, all of which were bulldozed, and his herd of cows, of which only a few head soon remained (the American intelligence service, led by an archaeologist, Major Soper, noted all the same that he was the only Frenchman to have left his mark on the island, through his style, which was "extremely energetic [. . .] from sunrise to sunset").[26] The brief American period is today the subject of a small museum in Wallis, with collections of uniforms and Coca-Cola bottles, which veterans sometimes come to visit; it is the only official "memory place" on the island outside of the Catholic monuments. The passage of the *Amelika* is probably the most talked-about episode in the history of Wallis. The historian Frédéric Angleviel, for example, refers to a kind of cargo-cult.[27] The landing (and the escapades) of thousands of soldiers shook the country and disrupted the economy. Subsistence crops and coconut groves were abandoned. Until 1947, recurrent unrest, linked to Wallisian demands for annexation by the United States supported by American officers, forced Resident Charbonnier and King Leone to scramble to maintain the French protectorate. In his memoirs, Charbonnier recounted all this, as well as his attempts to grow cotton and cocoa. He noted, without providing details, that he owed a great deal to the advice of "David, known as emperor."[28]

HAVING ARRIVED AT THE Nouméa airport, I said goodbye to Jean-Baptiste Mulikihaamea by the baggage carousel. We had known in advance that we were going to be on the same flight from Wallis. Like almost everyone else on the Airbus, we wore necklaces of flowers and shells. I had time to check on takeoff: the missing letters on the front of the airport had been replaced, which makes it look more serious, and less romantic.

I conferred with Jean-Baptiste while waiting for our bags to arrive, as there was also an elderly lady on our plane, thin, beautiful, with big white hair: Thérèse (Telesi) Brial, Sofia's sister and David's ex-sister-in-law. We had also known for a few days that she would be on our flight (in Wallis, everyone knows who from the island is going to take a flight on the plane), and Jean-Baptiste had told me that he would take the opportunity to introduce us. In a way, I had never been so close to King David. I could have gone over and said hello, talked to her about my research, told her that it was I who had been to her house in Liku, that her children had turned me away kindly. I could have asked her what she knew about her former brother-in-law, what her sister had said about him, asked her if the family had any papers, if there was a photo of him on the wall or in an album at the Brials'. In a way, that would have been the finishing touch on my investigation, the intimate moment. However, Jean-Baptiste's advice was to leave her alone. Telesi looked tired; it was not even eight o'clock in the morning, and everyone's mind was already elsewhere. The past would remain in its place, now thousands of miles away.

I took my leave of Jean-Baptiste, promising to put him in contact with David's family in France so that they could exchange documents and photos. I discreetly threw my flower necklace in the trash, to avoid having to give it to the environmental inspectors who screen the arrivals. A few months later, I learned about Jean-Baptiste's death via Facebook. The cameras of France Télévisions and all the island's authorities were there for his funeral, at the big cathedral in Mata-Utu.

31. Dachau, Indochina

For the soldiers of the Free French Forces, the war did not end with the Liberation (with the exception of the African soldiers, including many Cameroonians, who were sent back to their countries of origin to "whiten" the troops marching across France). This was the case for David, who was "reintegrated into the ranks," first in the Political Affairs Department of the Commission for the Colonies in Algiers, and then, at the end of 1944, in the First Army, fighting in the Battle of Alsace. He spent the winter in Belfort, where he was in charge of evacuation hospital number 413 while fighting raged in the snow and cold, in Mulhouse and then in Colmar. One can find a trace of him in the index of a volume on military history, *Les vaincus seront les vainqueurs: Les Français en Allemagne (1945)* (The defeated will be the victors: The French in Germany [1945]), by Jean-Christophe Notin, which retraces the last conquests of the Free French forces of General Leclerc and the First Army led by General de Lattre de Tassigny.[1] It is at the time of the liberation of the Dachau camp in the south of Germany in May 1945 that David appears. The American army had quarantined the camp as soon as it was "liberated" on April 29, because of a typhus outbreak that was wreaking havoc there. Thousands of French citizens, mostly Resistance fighters, were held inside in terrible conditions and were secretly sent supplies by French soldiers. Shortly after the Armistice, General de Lattre had secured from the American generals (including the famous Patton) the possibility of evacuating the French prisoners on one condition: that none should return to France before the end of the quarantine, around May 25. A massive operation was then launched to transport around five thousand deportees from Dachau and its satellite camps to the islands of Mainau and Reichenau on Lake Constance, which had been chosen for the quarantine. It was Lieutenant-Colonel-Doctor David who was in charge of the medical aspect of the operation and was responsible for organizing treatment in the castle, hotels, and villas of the two islands, which had been emptied of their wealthy inhabitants.

Colonel David was back on a garden island, a "paradise for deportees" as a local historian would later say,[2] in an "enchanting landscape" where everything was crystal glasses, fine wines, silver cutlery, and too-soft beds.[3] Once again, there was evidence of "his tireless activity": managing the arrival of thousands of deportees in a few days, testing and triaging those infected with typhus, those infected with tuberculosis, and the others, making lists, issuing orders, planning, rationing, and barely resting.[4] His talents as a leader of men, as a "sensitive" leader, as Jean-Claude Roux said, once again caused people to notice him and were mentioned in several publications on the evacuation of Dachau.[5] General-Doctor Melnotte, who headed the First Army's Health Service, was quite clear in his praises: "His reputation was underrated. A tireless organizer, with a rare energy, and an unstoppable will, Lieutenant-Colonel-Doctor David has once again proved himself to be the man for difficult situations and quick solutions with happy results if not of a rigorous administrative orthodoxy. Many deportees owe their lives and health to his ceaseless efforts."[6]

The islands became a showcase for the French army, visited by high-ranking officials and photographers, where concerts and shows were held beginning at the end of May; a wonderful Bastille Day celebration was held there on July 14, 1945. The hospital also housed a "biological and therapeutic research center,"[7] which David helped to equip, where malnutrition and the treatment of it were studied. Once again, he found himself in charge of a strange place, where medicine was the subject of a publicly staged experiment—a *Demonstrationobjekt*, as they say in German.[8] The arriving deportees were walking skeletons; several of them fell dead from the truck that brought them from Dachau. The work carried out in Mainau enabled three Parisian doctors to publish a reference book, *La Dénutrition: Clinque—biologique—therapeutique* (Malnutrition: Clinical—biological—therapeutic). In it, they thanked David for his "constant benevolence."[9] The book is difficult to read. It discusses bodies that resembled those of the "oldest old," generalized edema, extreme wasting, diets, rations to be increased gradually, and cases where there was nothing to be done. David would later tell his family about the deportees who went back to France with their pockets full of porcelain and silverware. It is difficult to say what the two islands showcased, Nazi horrors or life restored; it is rather the same uncertainty as with the sleeping sickness camps of the colonies.

In Madouma, as in Mainau, a general and his wife would pass by from time to time to shake hands with and distribute candy to leprosy patients and deportees alike. I do not know whether David thought about the Ayos or Kaviki camps, about his own colonial experience with men who were emaciated and gray, if there was the same smell and the same sleepless nights; I do not know whether he "made the connection." I do not want to add to it, to compare the incomparable, but there are many connections between the two stories. There were concentration camps that were called by that name in German Haut-Nyong; the founder of Ayos, Philalethes Kuhn, was one of the first German doctors to join the NSDAP—the Nazi Party[10]—and the first three Allied doctors to enter Dachau were colonial doctors from Leclerc's Second Armored Division, which they had joined from Cameroon. They may have visited the camp laboratory that had just been deserted by Claus Shilling, an eminent specialist in tropical diseases who was familiar with the sleeping sickness camps of Brazzaville, corresponded before the war with the great French colonial physicians, and ended up being hanged in 1946, condemned by an American court for his experiments on prisoners.[11]

After a year spent in the Ministry of Prisoners, Deportees and Refugees, followed by a stint at the military hospital in Fréjus, David was promoted to the rank of colonel-doctor in October 1947, just before leaving for Dakar to serve in French West Africa. He was appointed to a position that suited him: director of public health for the colony of Côte d'Ivoire. One can imagine him happy to leave the winter and the barracks behind him to return to Africa and take up such prestigious duties. Abidjan was a nice posting: Côte d'Ivoire was the jewel of French West Africa, in the heart of "useful" Africa intended for progress and civilization. The colony had been affected by the world conflict. The "war effort" of Free France had resulted in a rubber rush in the area (and, the same causes producing the same effects, in a resurgence of sleeping sickness),[12] in a generalized recourse to forced labor, and in an explosive political situation, between the nationalist and trade union mobilizations of the Africans and the hardening of the colonizers' attitudes, with some of them envisioning a southern US-style secession.[13] However, the territory was also in the process of inventing a destiny for itself as a modern colony. The port of Abidjan was a permanent construction site, from which wood and cocoa were exported; migrant workers were pouring in from Upper Volta; and the dynamism of Ivorian planters and entrepreneurs promised economic development that was without equivalent in the rest of French Africa. Throughout the empire (which became the French Union in 1946), a political and economic turning point was being reached. The time had come for the "modernization of overseas territories" through massive investments by Paris in colonial infrastructure under the leadership of technocrats and experts of all kinds. The Fonds d'Investissement et de Développement Economique et Social (Economic and Social Investment Fund; FIDES) financed a planned program to ensure the economic takeoff of the colonies through special credits.[14] In Côte d'Ivoire, as was the case elsewhere, public health, the improvement of which was thought to be a necessary condition of development, received unprecedented support (albeit modest compared with the credits devoted to port, road, and rail infrastructure), allowing for construction and purchase of vehicles. Credits from FIDES aside, health was one of the high-priority items in the local budget and saw constant growth. The funds devoted to health quadrupled between 1944 and 1948, reaching nearly 20 percent of the colony's total budget. In 1949, David announced a "record figure," with, for example, 62 percent of construction expenditures having been allocated to health.[15] David could dream big: colonial medicine finally appeared to have the means to achieve his ambitions.

The colonel-doctor was acting from a script that he knew well, that of medicine as "social hygiene," which he had directly helped inspire during his visits to Haut-Nyong, the Brazzaville Conference, and Algiers. Moreover, it was Marcel Vaucel, the instigator of the Haut-Nyong experiment, who directed the Health Service of the Ministry of the Overseas of France after a heroic performance in the war at the outposts of colonial Gaullism. In theory, the principle was clear: to resolve by mass preventive action the demographic problem that was hampering development, and at the same time to make medicine a tool for transforming African populations and people by educating them in hygiene, sports, and modern domestic life. Côte d'Ivoire, where the demand for agricultural and industrial labor appeared insatiable, seemed like a textbook case. In practice, David's work doubtless moved away from what he liked best: the conversations under coconut trees, the soccer matches, the agricultural experiments, the discussions concerning the future of the colonies. Apart from the inevitable "rapports annuels du Service de santé de la Côte d'Ivoire" (annual reports of the Côte d'Ivoire Health Service, which were composed of hundreds of pages of tables of figures with comments), I have few sources on his time in Abidjan, but it seems likely that the days of an officer of his rank were first and foremost bureaucratic. He headed a service that included dozens of European public servants; more than fifty "African doctors" trained at the Dakar Medical School; five hundred nurses, midwives, and orderlies; and hundreds of employees of all kinds, including eleven secretaries and typists in his own offices in Abidjan.[16] He managed a budget of several hundred million CFA francs, to be negotiated and voted on. He made concrete mixers run all over the country, where new dispensaries and hospitals were sprouting up like mushrooms. He had no time or inclination to write about Haut-Nyong or Wallis, his small personal successes. The few letters he wrote that that I have read are short and dry and talk about payment issues, the amount of sales, and late telegrams.[17] The rest, I imagine: young children at home, millions to manage, the chauffeur and the houseboys, receptions at the governor's house, running water, the telephone, electricity, all the trappings of adult life.

For a doctor like David, who was misunderstood and powerless in Wallis and Abong-Mbang, the new postwar situation, in which public health was one of the foundations of colonial policies and no longer just a philanthropic facade, seemed to fulfill the old dream of social medicine. The doctors' missions were framed in the broadest possible terms: nutrition, health education, early childhood, work, and housing finally fell within the scope of colonial state intervention under the heading of "medico-social action." The optimistic, even utopian tone of the planners echoed the experimental projects of the 1930s, as if this time it were a question of carrying out trials such as the "Medical Region" on a large scale, building on their success.

In Côte d'Ivoire, David found a model colony in terms of maternal and child welfare, where since 1943 the Health Service had been pursuing a policy of "housing" pregnant women similar to that of the Haut-Nyong experiment (prior to this, only women in towns who lived near a maternity ward were targeted by maternal and child welfare).[18] The initiative was likely modeled on the Cameroonian experiment when the Gaullists took over French West Africa. The governor of Cameroon, Pierre Cournarie, had taken over the post of governor-general of French West Africa in 1943, when Vaucel moved to Algiers. The principle was to allow women living outside towns to give birth in maternity wards by summoning them one month before the birth to "housing centers" where they were fed and housed. In practice, they were screened in the villages, registered, and obliged to come under penalty of sanctions imposed on their husbands; people described the women as having been "rounded up."[19] The doctors had initially presented the new policy as a success, in exactly the same terms that had been used for Haut-Nyong. The internment of thousands of women enabled newborn babies to gain three hundred to five hundred grams in birth weight, a 1944 report estimated.[20] General-Doctor Sicé had referred to the experiment in his article on the "social role of the colonial doctor," inflating the figures at the same time (according to the article, babies had gained six hundred grams in birth weight).[21]

However, the reports David found on his desk when he arrived in Abidjan revealed a situation that was much less bright. Starting in mid-1946, pregnant women had stopped coming to the housing centers. Alarmist letters were piling up: maternity camps were "literally deserted" in most regions. At the time, the reason for this seemed obvious to everyone: it was a repercussion of the passing of a law on May 7, 1946, in Paris, which gave citizenship to all subjects of the empire and at the same time abolished the Code de l'indigénat, which had defined the legal status and obligations of the "natives," including the obligation to obey doctors' orders. In practice, the doctors said, it had become impossible to compel Africans, who were now avoiding their rounds and ignoring their summons like they were mere "scraps of paper,"[22] whether they be for childbirth or sleeping sickness. The "primitives," who understood nothing of the law that was passed too quickly, imagined that they were now free from all discipline; all public health action threatened to collapse, and the "future of the race" was in danger. Complaints came from doctors all over Africa and were relayed to high-ranking officials in Paris, a sign of a real crisis and a hollow demonstration that the "adherence" (quotation marks required) of populations to colonial medicine had hitherto been based on the coercive regime of the Native, with its lashes of the whip, its fines, and its endless lists of offenses.[23] "*Dépré tia*" ("force is finished"), said the Lobi women in the northwest of the country, mocking the doctor, and it would now be necessary to "transport us by car or pay us" if they were to go to the housing center.[24] "The white man is no longer in charge, we are free to do what we want, etc., our women can give birth wherever they please," said the men.[25] "Persuasive coercion" was no longer possible, said the doctors.[26]

After his first year in Côte d'Ivoire, David himself realized that the hemorrhage was persisting, with several thousand fewer deliveries in maternity wards. His report included several pages of testimonies from African doctors in charge of rural subdivisions, who were also annoyed to see carefree rural women ignoring the authority conferred on them by being men and being "evolved." Their complaints summed up the political crisis, in the broadest sense of the term, that was affecting postwar Côte d'Ivoire, beyond the simple distrust of colonialism. According to them, women no longer obeyed their husbands, who no longer obeyed the canton chiefs, who no longer obeyed the administrators, who no longer obeyed the (African) doctors—the troubles spanned gender, class, and race. The Ivorian woman found "the housing center to be lifeless, monotonous, despite all the well-being she derives from it and which she does not notice."[27] She was even demanding "comfort."[28] The match appeared to have been lost.

David's diagnosis, however, was fairly accurate. He quickly dismissed the most eagerly awaited and reassuring interpretation, found in all the writings of colonial physicians on the subject: that of a misinterpretation of the 1946 law, the error, the misunderstanding produced by a premature reform for still-childish minds, the only way to make the women's refusal conceivable. No, said David, there had to be something else, something material: the fact that the housing centers were often in a pitiful state, without running water, mattresses, or blankets, and were too far from the villages, requiring women in the ninth month of pregnancy to walk fifty kilometers to come and rest. "It is likely that women in Brest would have similar reactions if they were to give birth in Morlaix, and this, despite the advantage of the railway," David wrote. "It is therefore up to us to modernize our methods," he concluded, to create centers near the big villages with midwives and not just matrons, and to organize a transport service by truck. And, as usual, this was to be initiated with an experiment, applying the program "in one or two pilot districts."[29]

The statistics recovered in 1948, although it is not known whether the experiment was attempted. "This general recovery is due in part to a beginning of a cooling of political passions, but above all to the efforts and activity of all the personnel who were committed to fighting against the population's disaffection with regard to our action," said David shortly before his departure.[30] The numbers would jump in the 1950s, even though the medicalization of childbirth remained limited to the cities and a few large missionary structures, and there would be no more talk of housing centers. David's time in Côte d'Ivoire (where two people who had spent time in Haut-Nyong, Dr. Koch and Dr. Pape, worked in the service) marks the pinnacle of his career as an administrator. It was at the same time a test of reality, an initiation in the end of empire. Medicines had never been so effective, trucks and Jeeps were crisscrossing the bush, but one mechanism had seized up, the one that used to fill leprosy camps, sleeping sickness camps, and maternity wards. It was a time of DDT and of disorder. French colonialism appeared to be entering an era of emotional insecurity, in which doctors discovered that their benevolence was repaid with indifference, even hostility. One would expect him to be angry, but David seems to have been quite well prepared for this troubled time, phlegmatic in his analyses, and almost aloof when he quoted in his reports the exalted pages of younger doctors who called for a return to order.

The years David spent in Abidjan, between late 1947 and the mid-1950s, were times of turmoil. Strikes, "agitations," and mobilizations were increasing. In early 1948, Paris appointed a "hard man," Laurent Péchoux, to the post of governor, with instructions to mercilessly combat the Rassemblement Démocratique Africain (African Democratic Rally, or RDA) nationalist party, which culminated in several bloody repressions. The army opened fire on the crowd on several occasions, causing a total of about one hundred deaths. Hundreds of activists were imprisoned without trial, many of them women. The affair even caused a stir in Paris.[31] Péchoux wrote a long letter of thanks to David upon his departure, praising his exceptional qualities and saluting his action during the "events" during which the Health Service had had to undertake a "heavy task," without any more being said on the subject. He concluded by stating that he hoped to see David again soon in Côte d'Ivoire.[32]

The subsequent part of the story took place in Indochina. Colonel David's second tour of duty in French West Africa, doubtless at the head of the organizational chart, was canceled on April 25, 1951. "This superior officer has been designated to continue his service in the Far East," reported the *Journal officiel*.[33] Many other colonial doctors were mobilized, as David was, in response to the Indochinese conflict, depopulating the health services in the rest of the French Union. The Expeditionary Force had just been taken over by de Lattre de Tassigny, the charismatic leader of the First Army, in which David had served. In the mess hall in Indochina, he was called by the nickname "King Jean," or sometimes "DDT," to poke a little fun at him.[34] Colonel David landed in Saigon on June 13, 1951. He ran the Grall military hospital, one of the most important in Indochina, and chaired the Medical Repatriation Commission, which filled the hospital ships leaving for Marseille—a post that must have allowed him to observe what war did to bodies and minds. From April 1952, he was deputy director of the Health Service of the Far East Ground Forces. As he had done in the past, he gave this role his all. The general-doctors who noticed him ran out of ways to say that David was a great leader, an elite officer of impeccable righteousness and elegance. He was made an officer of the Legion of Honor in October 1953, shortly after his return, and received other citations and war medals related to his action in Indochina. In Paris, he attended the École des hautes études militaires (School of Advanced Military Studies), the last hurdle preventing him from being promoted to the rank of general-doctor, for which he had been insistently proposed since 1951.[35]

One can see how the story might have ended: a top position in Africa, stars on his kepi, and perhaps a marble plaque, later on, at the entrance of a hospital or ministry. But Indochina was tough. In July 1952, his wife and children were at Cap Saint Jacques, the seaside resort near Saigon where the army had a base and sanitarium, when the Vietminh attacked at lunchtime, killing twenty people, including a young captain-doctor and his family.[36] The gilded cage at Cap Saint Jacques, where officers liked to go for a beach holiday, had been transformed into a horrific scene. Madame David de Louvencourt was only wounded, but the massacre left its mark. David's resilience appears to have been definitively broken. It was definitely not a misunderstanding or a misinterpretation: the natives had changed; they no longer appreciated the games at the stadium; they had no love or admiration for their protective nation; they fired on doctors. David's daughter, who told me some of this story, explained that her parents were "not supporters of French Algeria," that they had seen independence coming without anger or sadness, that her father had kept dear friends from his time in Côte d'Ivoire, that he said that African nurses were often better than his French colleagues. However, Indochina was the straw that broke the camel's back. He had had enough of the colonies, the heat and humidity, the years far away from France, the administration, the troubles. What followed was a return to the southern suburbs of Paris, early retirement in 1955, and death in 1969. Colonel David would not become a general.

32. The Light Riots

September 2007. There had been no power in Abong-Mbang for four months. The school year had just started. A brief return of electricity, between Tuesday, the eleventh, and Thursday, the thirteenth, had raised the anger a notch, with the population accusing Aes-Sonel, the national electricity supplier that has been privately owned since the late 1990s, of having restored power just long enough to send out the electricity bills. Friday the fourteenth was a day of anger. The population of Abong-Mbang gathered en masse and descended on National Highway 10, blocking access to it with barricades to demand the return of light. The barricades were lifted late in the night after a long negotiation. Prefect Sylvestre Essama promised electricity would be restored by Sunday at noon and discreetly called in a detachment of the Groupement militaire d'intervention (Military Intervention Group), one of the best equipped and most feared security forces in the country, specializing in armed robbers, terrorists, and raids of all kinds. Sunday came and went without power being restored, and the prefect issued a new statement announcing the return of electricity for noon the next day.

On Monday at noon, there was still no power. At the bilingual high school in Madouma, the large concrete complex built on top of the graves of victims of sleeping sickness, opposite the entrance to the old camp, the tension was mounting. At 1:30 p.m., the students left the school, crossed the dike, and headed toward the city, passing by the hospital. They joined a crowd of young people from the middle schools, the technical high school, and the classical high school, which occupies part of the school complex built in David's time. Together they sang the national anthem and advanced toward the Nyong River to once again block access to the road to the East. The city's motorcycle taxis, perhaps fifty of them, led the way, with the noise of the engines and shouts. Just past the market, they ran into Military Intervention Group policemen, who threw tear gas, fired warning shots, and beat up a motorcycle taxi driver. Young people wore pans on their heads, their faces painted with charcoal; some threw stones. The prefect was there, with all the police forces. Hit by a stone, he pulled out his pistol, which he carried on his belt like a cowboy. Facing him were some students, who put their hands up.

"Kill me! *Mate! Fa Pa!* Go on, kill me."

The prefect opened fire. A high-ranking police officer opened fire as well. A dozen demonstrators fell to the ground. Two students in uniform, Bertrand Marcel, aged seventeen, and Jean Jaurès, aged fifteen, were hit, one in the neck, the other in the chest. They were taken to the clinic operated by the nuns a little farther down. They had just enough time to receive the last rites, and then they died. I have heard a lot about this double murder, and it is always recounted the same way. "It was like the film," one of the Abong-Mbang FC soccer players I met with Valentin in 2014 explained to me at the end of training. "The bullets came from the prefect's hands."

Word of the deaths spread fast. Groups returned to the prefecture, looted it, and set it on fire. They also set fire to the prefect's residence, the small 1927 castle where David and the other district commanders had lived. The prefect's family managed to escape via the swamps and hide. I am told that millions of CFA francs and red mercury, a metal with mysterious powers prized by practitioners of witchcraft, swindlers, and politicians, were found in the residence. There was even a room inside made entirely of sheet metal, which would not burn, that contained secret documents. Everything was looted: the wine, the goats, the chickens. All that remained were two pigs "wandering around the yard," wrote the journalist Édouard Tamba in his impressive account of the "light riots," which I am summarizing here. A few photos accompanied his articles that appeared at the time in *Le Messager* (The messenger), the flagship newspaper of the Cameroonian opposition, founded in Douala by Pjus Njawe.[1] They show the blackened frame of the former prefecture, a colonial building with a veranda and stone walls. In 2012, the first time I went to Abong-Mbang, it had been replaced by a new nine-story cinder block building. In the photo, in front of the ruins, there was a pile of burnt paper, which was still smouldering.

In 2014, when Valentin, Madame Ateba, and I met with the prefect who had taken over the post, he was somewhat apologetic. I had explained to him that I was interested in the history of one of his distant predecessors as leader of Haut-Nyong and that I wondered if there were any archives anywhere. "You know that the old prefecture burned down and so did the archives. If it hadn't burned down, we'd be looking at documents from the 1930s, the 1940s, right now," he apologized. It became a running gag during the visits I made with Valentin: my work had gone up in smoke before it had even started. Madame Ateba's daughter, Gisèle Rouly, laughed at me: "It's not your book that burned in there, it's your *books!*" The sub-prefect who met with me in 2015 had confirmed that there were no remaining documents anywhere: "Our archives have been consumed by the insurgents." Tamba had also written about this in his articles. Abong-Mbang had lost "its memory."[2]

The charred documents may have contained a piece of the history of the medical experiment in Haut-Nyong—files, telegrams, pay slips, windows into the daily life of the doctor-governors, and perhaps competition results, passes, traces of middle school students or the army of Cameroonian auxiliaries, which are now invisible. They would have allowed me to tell this story better, without always using the same threads, the quarrels between administrators and missionaries, or the contrast between relationships and memories. The light riots left a hole right in the middle of my research, a pile of ashes.

However, I think that the issue must be examined the other way around. Perhaps the meaning of my investigation lies in its voids, in its blanks, in its imposed silences, in these files that were burned and then washed away by the rain. Archives, whatever they may be, speak as much about what they record as about what they exclude. Their existence is primarily the result of a subtraction, like any archaeological remains. They are, as Michel Foucault said, "the law of what can be said," they are what has not been destroyed, or not completely destroyed, following an operation (keep/discard) analogous to the one that creates the garbage cans or waste disposal sites that make archaeologists, the "ragmen of the past," happy.[3] The problem is therefore not that history is "mutilated knowledge,"[4] as first-year undergraduates learn, but rather that we must make room for the history of this mutilation (which is the necessary condition for the existence of the witnesses of the past, who are accessible to us only because the rest has disappeared) in the investigation and the recounting of it.[5] The condition of archives—preserved or destroyed, monumentalized or neglected, classified, kept secret, forgotten, flooded, trampled—also carries a message; their "form" also has a "content." Archives are "subjects" as well as "sources," to use a distinction made by Ann Stoler; one must allow oneself to be led by them, rather than "mining" them (what a sad expression, by the way).[6] They are always contemporary to us, always historical, and contain nothing of the past that is not also always part of our present. They do not come from the past but from a shelf; they are with us, extant by miracle or accident, even when they come out of the bunkers of the National Archives, like everything that is uncovered during a dig. It is in this sense that our view of archives must be, once again, archaeological, attentive to their transformation over time, to the hazards and disturbances that bring them to us. As the historian Luise White wrote, the gaps, the fissures, even, in the archives, so familiar to historians of contemporary Africa, are not an "obstacle" but rather a "complement" to historical investigation; it is necessary to "see messy archives for what they are, fragmented records of shambolic events, of false starts and donor-driven policies and impossible development schemes and missed opportunities."[7]

The documents that burned behind the cordon of soldiers, in the silence after the riot, do not only testify to the rage that followed the deaths of Marcel and Jaurès. In fact, they suggest, by their very absence, a possible conclusion to my story, perhaps its most important message. The two high school students had marched to demand what David and his colleagues had promised them, in their authoritarian, violent, and sometimes ridiculous way, but had promised all the same: light, development, "emergence," to use the Cameroonian expression. The promise that one day they could lead a "normal life for a human being," as the people of Messamena said as they remembered Dr. Koch, is buried with many other futures in Cameroon, privatized like Sonel, abandoned like the coffee plantations, but not completely forgotten. It is a demand for equality and inclusion, a deferred dream, "expectations of modernity" that cannot be considered a mere irony, by shrugging one's shoulders, by laughing at those somewhat crazy colonial doctors and the children who believed them.[8] Nostalgia is a way of keeping possibilities alive. The political attention we owe to this is my first conclusion, the first moral of my story.

There are other ways to relate this story to the present. It can be read as a plea for social medicine, a plea, one that went unheeded in this case, for an approach I believe is valuable, that of a medicine that believes that intervention in the "social determinants" of health is indispensable, that there is nothing natural about inequalities in the face of illness and death, and that it is the mission of doctors to uncover the social and political mechanisms that produce them, as opposed to the naive belief that biomedical "innovation" will solve health problems one by one, without the need for any changes in the world order.

David's adventures can also serve as a clinical case. They are a reminder that megalomania is an occupational hazard for doctors, both in the past and in the present, which takes exuberant forms in the tropics. The corridors of hospitals and humanitarian organizations are rife with anecdotes on the subject. The story is over the top but ultimately banal. It reminds us that the colonial experience often resembled, even in its most abject aspects, an "entirely baroque and ridiculous circus."[9]

Finally, one can read this story as a cautionary tale. However, it would in this case not be a tale of hubris and nemesis, the story of an overambitious man who violated a duty of restraint, wanting to transform nature and teach others how to live, despising their knowledge and values, before being punished by the gods for his arrogance. No; rather, it would be a Pascalian meditation, the story of a man who thought he was king when he was shipwrecked on an unknown island, without understanding that there was an expectation of quid pro quo.[10] It would be a lesson about power and the impotence that goes with it, in which the desire to know and to control is pathetic, in which arrogance is rewarded with ridicule, and in which the people, contrary to Pascal's parable, are not fooled: they can laugh, threaten, and remember. They know that power is by definition usurpation, and that sovereignty is a form of banishment, a principle that also presides, as Sahlins suggests, over the "subterranean history of our own democracies."[11] Like David, our sovereigns can never be sure that the wheels of their carriage are touching the ground. They are always alone on their island, never understanding why everyone around them is laughing.

"BECAUSE CAMEROON IS STRONG," a statement that is often understood first and foremost in the absurd, Prefect Essama was promoted after the riots, made "secretary general or something like that," or at least, that is what they say in Abong-Mbang. He always denied opening fire that day, claiming that he had in fact taken a digital camera out of his pocket. Madame Ateba told me that she had negotiated with the authorities for the release of the student prisoners by raising her voice, something with which she has experience. However, because "the old men of the East are strong" too, a statement that is often understood first and foremost to refer to witchcraft, the former prefect, who was passing through Abong-Mbang on the night of August 11, 2009, on a trip to the East, had a car accident and died on impact. "He died where he killed." Case closed. "The people said: let him come back, we'll see." There is no need to say anything further. These "complicated" matters are discussed only through silence or euphemism.[12] Let's just say he did not see the logging truck parked at the side of the road at the Mampang bend just on the other side of the Nyong.

What remains of that story is his navy-blue Mercedes, folded in four. The wreck remained for several years on the side of the road, right in the middle of the city center, on the way to the market, on the very site of the light riots. We took our time passing in front of it when we were there, casting sidelong glances at it like everyone else. In 2015, the police brought it back to the brigade compound. There it remained, perhaps for fear that someone might take it and appropriate the stories of violence, magic, and death folded up in the smashed-in sheet metal. There it remained, like a cumbersome, suspicious piece of the past that was impossible to obliterate, a mocking monument to those who govern us, who treat us, and who kill us.

Afterword

Postcard from a COVID-free Island

On July 16, 2021, as the Delta variant of SARS-CoV2 was about to spoil the summer for most countries in the northern hemisphere, the South Pacific island of Wallis was officially declared COVID-free. The state of emergency in Wallis had been short-lived: the beginnings of an epidemic led to fears of the worst in March 2021, with the Alpha variant causing the first deaths. The island's limited health infrastructure, aging population, and high prevalence of diabetes and obesity (among the highest in the world) sounded like the makings of a catastrophe. However, rapid confinement, good contact tracing, and a massive vaccination campaign with the support of health care workers from mainland France limited the death toll to seven, and the last case was reported on April 27. The COVID pandemic, it seems, has reunited Wallis with its destiny as a health utopia.

It is astonishing that French government spin doctors have not made more of the success stories of the French Pacific islands even as the press the world over has been celebrating the achievements of Jacinda Ardern, the prime minister of New Zealand, whose record is not better. In Wallis, 2020 was a COVID-zero year. The secret of the islanders' success was simple: in March 2020, the Wallis authorities decided to cut off the island from the world, suspend all passenger flights, and repatriate by way of a large cruise ship, which doubled as a floating quarantine center in the lagoon, any Wallisians who wished to return home. Since then, all people entering the island are subject to a strict fourteen-day quarantine. All hotels on the island, including the one where I spent a month five years ago while conducting research for this book, were requisitioned for this purpose. Wooden palisades were added to isolate the rooms and guards posted to ensure that no one escaped. The islanders themselves were the first to demand strict measures: when a traveler tested positive in October 2020, a "collective of the people's interests," assembled at the airport to block it off. [1]

Even though management of the epidemic was a fiasco in Paris, as it was in most of Old Europe, France surely knew what it took to defeat COVID. With its police officers in shorts, its French prefect, its baroque political system, and its tiny hospital, the case of Wallis proves it: France has the capacity to be as efficient as Hong Kong, New Zealand, or Taiwan. Using the same approach, New Caledonia, a postcolonial dependency of France in the midst of a political crisis, has done even better than Wallis, with no deaths reported to date among its nearly 300,000 inhabitants, as has American Samoa. But no one seems interested in making this known. Perhaps the political commentators specializing in COVID who have appeared by spontaneous generation on television sets around the world simply do not know what to say about these pandemic outliers, which have in common that they are political oddities inherited directly from the time of colonial empires. Their success leaves only two possible conclusions, both equally difficult for critical social science to swallow. The first is that the most anachronistic colonialism is as effective a strategy against a pandemic as the progressive (and perhaps idealized) democracy of New Zealand. The second (which I personally favor) is that enlightened leadership, political decisions, and community engagement ultimately count for little in the face of contingencies of luck, virology, and insular island geography.

Wallis is a country where "public health dictatorship"—a phrase the entire world discovered during the pandemic—has long been a constitutional principle: the island was ruled almost exclusively by doctors like Dr. David during the first half of the twentieth century. In a strange irony, the island finds itself in a peaceful and promising situation on the pandemic front (though this is perhaps fragile, as neighboring Fiji faces a major outbreak of COVID's Delta variant) at precisely the same time when France is tearing itself apart in the face of COVID's fourth wave and government measures to make vaccines mandatory. As I write these lines in France, vaccination centers are being ransacked and antivax activists are dreaming of being "resistance fighters" in the face of "public health totalitarianism," taking this stupidity so far as to don yellow stars. During a demonstration last week, an idiotic sign hijacked the ARBEIT MACHT FREI gate of the Dachau concentration camp with the slogan THE VACCINE PASSPORT SETS YOU FREE.

These obscene references to the past, which are so present in the public debate on COVID in France, encourage us to play carefully with the register of similarities and "lessons of the past." An excess of history is no more desirable than amnesia. *The Doctor Who Would Be King,* the story of an exceptional public health regime that describes hubris and medical impotence in the face of the forces of epidemic and capitalism, foreshadows the present in an almost-too-obvious way. All of the elements are there: doctors whispering in the ears of rulers before taking those rulers' place; an epidemic suspending the laws of civil life and economics; the government submitting to the higher value of "health"; and experts who do not seem to know what to do with their unexpected power. The medical megalomania that runs through this book has found a perfect incarnation in the French COVID-19 landscape: Dr. Didier Raoult, the Aix-Marseille professor of medicine famous for his weekly videos in a style that is at once scholarly, populist, and incensed and who propelled hydroxychloroquine onto the world stage, to the point of captivating Donald Trump, might be understood best as a mediocre Dr. David-turned-YouTuber. Raoult clearly embodies the colonial genealogy of the messianic, uncouth, grumpy doctor, both technically (hydroxychloroquine is an old "tropical" drug "rediscovered" for use against COVID-19) and biographically. Didier Raoult's career has been built around scientific and academic cooperation with French-speaking African countries. The professor of medicine was born in Dakar, Senegal, during the time of the French Empire and often says that he is "crazy about Africa." He is the son of the colonial doctor André Raoult, an important figure in the health service of the Colonial Army of the 1950s, who undoubtedly knew Dr. David.[2]

The tragicomedy of experts and self-described "very stable geniuses" trying to govern the COVID crisis thus seems reassuringly familiar. The impression that the characters and the dramatic structure of the epidemic have passed through history intact is fascinating, but I think we should be wary of this "concordance of times," as the medieval historian Patrick Boucheron has said.[3] The lessons of the past—accounts of plague, influenza, or cholera that medical historians everywhere (myself included) rushed to give at the beginning of the pandemic—are sometimes decoys. Perhaps the role of historians is also to disturb the reassuring feeling of déjà vu. Perhaps the role of history is, as the great historian Marc Bloch suggested, to help us not to "think in terms of yesterday"[4] but to understand the present in what is new, different, unheard of, and banal at the same time—in this case, a pandemic that never ends, that has lost the thread of its own history, that no longer resembles the standardized narratives of historians, and that thwarts and shifts our critical certainties about bio-politics and the "public health dictatorship."[5] For this reason, the most useful histories of epidemics are perhaps the most bizarre ones: those that have no beginning, no end, and no moral, like that of Dr. David's epic.

Global Health Heroism in East Cameroon

Not much is known about COVID-19 in Abong-Mbang, Cameroon. Cameroonian newspapers reported that the city's mayor, Charmant Oyal, was infected at the beginning of the epidemic, causing panic, and then nothing more was said. As with many places in Africa, Abong-Mbang is off the radar of health surveillance, the population is very young, hospitals are rarely visited, oxygen tanks are absent, tests are rare, and vaccines are even more so. To estimate the impact of the virus in a region such as East Cameroon will take extensive investigations or a catastrophic evolution (always possible, unfortunately). This ignorance about COVID is paradoxical because, since the beginning of the 2000s, East Cameroon has been a hotbed of global health interventions, a land crisscrossed by international health scientists, where knowledge essential to the understanding of pandemic risk was produced, and not just because the region is known for its trade in the pangolin (an animal emblematic of the global conservation crisis that featured centrally in the early origin stories of the COVID-19 pandemic).

Global interest in East Cameroon dates back to the late 1990s. The discovery in Cameroon of two atypical HIV strains—HIV-1 group O and HIV-1 group N—which caused AIDS but were genetically different from previously known variants, to the point of confounding diagnostic tests, set off a scramble for samples from Cameroonian patients.[6] A dozen international teams raced to the capital city of Yaoundé, forging partnerships with local researchers and doctors. The hunt for the virus had industrial stakes (a new strain of HIV potentially could mean a patent) but scientific ones also: the Cameroonian variants of HIV promised to solve the question of "the origin of AIDS." Several teams were interested in HIV-like viruses, or SIVs, that were circulating among local monkeys and apes and took samples from animals in zoos, primate sanctuaries, and markets where primate carcasses (so-called bushmeat) were sold. The hunt for the virus led to several spectacular discoveries, widely reported by the international media. Comparisons of the genetic sequences of human and simian viruses discovered in Cameroon, especially in chimpanzees, made it possible to demonstrate that the country was the "birthplace of HIV," which appeared in the human species following several cross-species transmission events or spillovers. In 1999, the American virologist Beatrice Hahn was able to announce at the leading American virology conference that the "puzzle of HIV origins was solved," largely thanks to the Cameroonian virological data.[7]

Another scientific narrative took over from this passion for finding the origin of AIDS: that of the risk of a new pandemic emerging in the future, caused by an HIV-3 or HIV-4 strain. The consumption of bushmeat in Cameroon, the virologists explained, exposed the local populations—and the rest of the planet—to the future emergence of an unknown virus, and everything had to be done to monitor and prevent this risk. That hypothesis directly echoed the security turn in global health and the constitution of what Nick King calls the "emerging diseases worldview."[8] In the late 1990s the mission of health interventions in southern countries no longer was to free populations from disease, misery, and backwardness, as in Dr. David's time, but to monitor and control a few hot spots at the human-animal interface where new pathogenic threats were likely to emerge. In this context, Cameroon's appeal to scientists and their funders was enhanced: the country's eastern forests had chimpanzee and gorilla populations that were accessible to scientists (at a time when other Congo basin countries were in political crisis) and obviously threatened by the timber industry, corruption, and hunters' guns, making the region a unique place to understand primate-human viral traffic and to seal an alliance between conservationists and virologists to denounce the destruction of nature and biodiversity by loggers, poachers, and villagers on the hunt for meat. The Abong-Mbang road thus became the major axis of bushmeat tourism in Africa: virologists, journalists, and photographers found the primate carcasses they needed to feed their viral apocalypse stories. Examples include David Quammen's airport bestseller *Spillover* ("the powerful, prescient book that predicted the COVID-19 coronavirus pandemic," according to its publisher) and Nathan Wolfe's *The Viral Storm*, as well as the spectacular *Eating Apes* by Dale Peterson and *The Last Great Ape* by Ofir Drori and David McDannald.[9] Drori and McDannald's description of the Spartan hotel room in Abong-Mbang, in which it is hard not to read a variant of Teju Cole's "white savior industrial complex," has become a cliché of this literature.[10] From *New Yorker* features to TED conferences to articles in *Science* and *Nature*, the viruses of East Cameroon made it possible to write a global health success story in the 2000s. The research conducted in Cameroon played a pioneering role in the development of public health approaches applied in the following decade to the Ebola, Zika, and coronaviruses. More than sixty years after the Haut-Nyong experiment, Ayos, Abong-Mbang, Messamena, Lomié, and, farther away, Ngoila, Yokadouma, and Mouloundou have once again become a territory of projection and imagination, caught between utopia and dystopia, for epidemiological experts the world over.

These research programs are admirable, both from an entrepreneurial point of view (they have absorbed millions of dollars in funding from the US biodefense program, agencies such as the French Agency for Research on AIDS and Viral Hepatitis (ANRS) in France, and the Google Foundation) and from a scientific point of view, since the development of noninvasive techniques for sampling viruses from wildlife, with the help of local populations and scientists, as well as advances in the phylogenetic study of sequences, has allowed for a fascinating mapping of viral reservoirs. They also deserve severe criticism: First, they conceive of pandemic risk within the framework of a "politics of disgust."[11] The emergence of viruses is a narrative of transgression (between humans and primates) of natural, racial, and political boundaries, in which African culinary practices and migration appear as pathogenic forces to be monitored and contained, with a few nuances to make this outlook TED-compatible. Second, the biosecurity model ignores the historical, political, and technological factors, beyond simple zoonosis, that make viral emergence possible; the example of HIV—for which the decisive role of iatrogenic transmission through injections during the colonial era, particularly in Cameroon, is now established—is a textbook case.[12]

That the saga of virus hunters unfolded in the very locations of the Haut-Nyong experiment (and other heroic and sometimes disastrous attempts by colonial doctors to eradicate sleeping sickness) invites another critical remark. Rather than describing virus hunting as an enterprise of stigmatization, surveillance, and extraction (which it undoubtedly is), I propose to see this way of practicing global health as a form of spectacle and refined inaction in which the relationship to reality is ultimately distant—to the point of being disturbing. It is clear, after twenty years of efforts to make Cameroon the laboratory of "viral forecasting" to "prevent the next pandemic," to use the slogan of virus hunter Nathan Wolfe,[13] that the results (like the limited success of global efforts in "pandemic preparedness" in the pre-COVID era) are minimal in terms of public health. Seen from the forest villages of East Cameroon, where people are dying, untreated, from perfectly common, identified, and treatable diseases such as HIV and tuberculosis, the obsession of virologists with future viruses and Disease x is even more obscene. There seems to be a disconnect between the hype for viral forecasting (despite results that have been superficial at best) and a disastrous reality, both in terms of health and politics.

In Cameroon, the hubris of the virus hunter is combined with a kind of nihilism, in the sense that the star scientists themselves acknowledge that nothing can be done to prevent the next pandemic, given that local cultures and extractive capitalism are such impossible forces to fight—with a few nuances to make this discourse TED-compatible. Nothing can be done in East Cameroon, but this seems to be one more reason to intensify the race for virological scoops, smart projects, and good stories. Nothing can be done, but this is hardly a problem when public health is redefined as spectacle and as fiction—or perhaps the right word is, again, *utopia*. In the nihilism of the new heroes of global health, whose enthusiastic storytelling seems haunted by a hatred of the present, a bit of the spirit of Haut-Nyong blows through. Perhaps Dr. David has been reincarnated.

SAINT-DENIS, FRANCE, JULY 27, 2021

I would like to thank my publisher at Le Seuil, Bruno Auerbach, who convinced me that this story could become a book and who patiently guided its writing. This text takes elements from an article published in 2010 in the journal *Annales* (vol. 65, no. 1 [2010]: 121–56), for which I had benefited from the advice of Emmanuelle Sibeud and Antoine Lilti.

I am immensely fortunate and honored to be published by Duke University Press, as part of the book series curated by Nancy Hunt and Achille Mbembe. Their inspiring influence permeates every line of this book. I owe so much to their research and writings over the years. I would like to thank Elizabeth Ault of Duke University Press, who made this translation possible; the anonymous readers; the editorial staff; and Cheryl Smeall for her beautiful work translating both the poetic and the technical.

The idea of an archaeology of medicine in Africa owes much to the conversations I have had over the years with Wenzel Geissler, often joined by John Manton, Ann Kelly, Aïssatou Mbodj-Pouye, and Noemi Tousignant. The joyful inspirations of Nancy Hunt and Vinh-Kim Nguyen have been particularly precious to me, and I can also testify to the legendary generosity of Peter Geschiere, who provided me with his comments on various versions of this text. Rachel Wadoux was the first reader of the final version of the manuscript, and I thank her for her contribution.

I would like to thank the participants in the seminars and conferences in which I presented drafts of this work for their suggestions, notably at the Department of Social Anthropology at the University of Cambridge (2016), at the Dreaming of Health and Science in Africa conference at Hinxton Hall (2015), and at the University of Michigan, where I am particularly grateful to Martin Pernick, Gabrielle Hecht, and the organizers of the 2014 Global Reach Lecture.

I owe a huge debt of thanks to Alice Fromonteil, whom I had the good fortune to meet in Wallis through the good offices of Niko Besnier and Claire

Moyse, for her help on site, her company, her translations, her rereadings, and the references she gave me, from Sahlins to Pascal. For all their advice prior to my departure, I thank Valelia Muni Toke, Jean-Claude Roux, Julien Clément, Claude Wetta, Raymond Mayer, Jeff Vrignaud, Michel Naepels, Warwick Anderson, Denise Sabourin, Robert Laufoaulu's parliamentary attaché Valérie Cauvin, as well as Paino Vanai, the representative for the Wallis and Futuna Islands at the Ministry of the Overseas. In Nouméa, I would like to thank Bertrand Lequien, Anne Leizour, Gabriel and Violaine Valet, Robert Kernion, Jean-Marie Papilio, Max Sheckelton, and Frédéric Angleviel. On the *fenua*, my thanks go to Prefect Michel Aubouin, Benjamin Gérard, Chanel Telipini, and all the services of the Superior Administration. Bernadette Papilio Halagahu at the administration of the Cultural Affairs Service guided the first steps of my research, and Mikaele Tui was an exceptional conversation partner upon my return. For their welcome at the diocese in Lano and access to its archives, I express my gratitude to Bishop Ghislain de Rasilly, Father Jaupitre, and Mahilina Sako. For their welcome, I thank the director of the Health Agency of Wallis and Futuna, Alain Soeur, and the general supervisor of the hospital of Sia, Serge Pruneau. I thank the late Jean-Baptiste Mulikihaamea, Blaise Hoatau, Manuele Lisiahi, Falakika Lisiahi, Petelo Logologofolau, Sapeta Logologofolau, Bruno Arrigoni, Juan Bustio, Jacques Pambrun, Samino Folonka, Siolesio Pilioko, Kimi Seo, Emeni Simete, Sister Suliana Muni Toke, Sister Malekalita Falelavaki, Geneviève Royannez-Genevey, Atoloto Uhila, and Mika Hoatau for their precious testimonies and advice. Lagimaina Hoatau offered me the pleasure of being on TV and above all many reflections on the story of King David. Finally, thanks to Nyvé and the whole Moana-Hou team.

In Cameroon, I thank Élise Wang Sonné, her son Daniel Claude Wang Sonné, and Jean Lucien Ewangue for giving me access to Wang Sonné's archives and allowing me to evoke his memory. My first visits to Abong-Mbang and Kwoamb were on a trip I took from Ayos, where I had the chance to work as a team with John Manton and Joseph Owona Ntsama, who was responsible for making that project work. We were greatly helped by Daniel Ze Bekolo and Kombang Ekodogo, as well as by the director of the hospital during our visit in 2012, Dr. Amougou. For their testimonies and advice, I thank Madame Ateba Mvodo, née Ngono Émilienne; the late André Ateba; Gisèle Rouly; the prefect of Haut-Nyong and the sub-prefect of Abong-Mbang; Jean Marie Evina Mevaa; Williams Evina; Nkoé Valère; Engoga Joseph; Claude Nang Bigouak; Milong Zoa, Tamare Zoa, and the Zoa family in Messamena; Dr. Prince Bayebane; Dr. Denis Nsame; the sub-prefect of Messamena, Désiré Abena Milongo; and Father Georges Rey; as well as Sister Danuta and Sister Tatiana of the Little

Sisters of Ayos for their hospitality. For their support over many years and during this project, my thanks go to the Paul Ango Ela Foundation and its director, Kalliopi Ango Ela; my friends Richard Njouom, Sébastien Pion, Fred Eboko, and Yves Eyaa; and the whole team of the Institut de recherche pour le développement (Institute of Development Research) in Yaoundé, especially Bruno Bordage, Mohamed Elomo Molo, and of course, Valentin Angoni.

Several people helped me to find the traces of the colonial doctors of the Haut-Nyong experiment in the archives. I thank Jean-Paul Bado, Pierre Marie David, Tamara Giles-Vernick, Eric Jennings, Vincent Bonnecase, Jean-Marie Milleliri, Jean-Michel Damas, Jean Goasguen, and André Borgomano for their tips, as well as the archivists who helped me. I also thank Michèle Guy for the remedial course on the King David of the Bible. The families of the doctors involved welcomed my project with great kindness. I thank the children of Dr. David, as well as Héléne Choumara, Yves Pape, Jeanine Hermet, and finally Catherine Koch, whom it was so enriching to meet. I hope to live up to the trust they put in me.

My research has benefited from the support of the Institut universitaire de France (University Institute of France) and the SPHERE laboratory, the lab's directors, Pascal Crozet and Sabine Rommevaux, and its administrator, Virginie Maouchi.

All remarks made in this book are my opinion alone and I am solely responsible for any errors that may be found therein.

INTRODUCTION

Book epigraph: Jonathan Lethem, *The Fortress of Solitude: A Novel* (New York: Doubleday, 2003).

1 This quote is taken from Edward Said, *Culture and Imperialism* (New York: Knopf, 1993), n.p. For another version, see Joseph Conrad, *Jeunesse*, followed by *Au cœur des ténèbres*, trans. André Ruyters (Paris: Gallimard, 2005 [1925]), 92.

2 Erwin Heinz Ackerknecht, *Medicine at the Paris Hospital 1794-1848* (Baltimore: Johns Hopkins University Press, 1967), 154. The hygienist literature contains numerous examples of medical utopias, including Benjamin Ward Richardson, *Hygeia: A City of Health* (London: Macmillan, 1876), and Walter J. Carr, "Annual Oration on Life and Problems in a Medical Utopia," *Lancet* 201, no. 5205 (1923): 993–1001.

3 Wang Sonné, "Approche historique de la gestion de la Région médicale du Haut-Nyong (Cameroun), 1939-1948," in *Treating Illness: Historical Routes*, ed. Antonio Guerci (Genoa: Erga Edizione, 1998), 371–83.

4 "Discours prononcé par Mr le gouverneur général Richard Brunot en conseil d'administration le 17 janvier 1940," *Journal officiel du Cameroun*, no. 483 (February 1, 1940): 118.

5 Wang Sonné Archives, Haut-Nyong file, Wang Sonné, "Interview avec Joseph Dobo, dit Le Droit. Dimpan, par Messamena. 15.12.92."

CHAPTER 1. A SHOWCASE FOR COLONIAL HUMANISM

1 Peter Geschiere, *The Modernity of Witchcraft: Politics and the Occult in Postcolonial Africa*, trans. Peter Geschiere and Janet L. Roitman (Charlottesville: University Press of Virginia, 1997), 27–34.

2 Treaty of Versailles, Part I, Covenant of the League of Nations, article 22, accessed August 26, 2019, https://avalon.law.yale.edu/20th_century/leagcov.asp#art22.

3 Michael D. Callahan, *Mandates and Empire: The League of Nations and Africa, 1914-1931* (Brighton, Sussex: Academic Press, 1999); *A Sacred Trust: The League of Nations and Africa, 1929-1946* (Brighton, Sussex: Academic Press, 2004).

4 Philippe Bourmaud, "Internationalizing Perspectives: Re-reading Mandate History through a Health Policy Lens," *Canadian Bulletin of Medical History* 30, no. 2 (2013): 15.

5 Guillaume Lachenal, "Médecine, comparaisons et échanges inter-impériaux dans le mandat camerounais: Une histoire croisée franco-allemande de la mission Jamot," *Bulletin canadien d'histoire de la médecine* 30, no. 2 (2013): 23–45.

6 Albert Calmette, préface, in Gustave Martin, *L'Existence au Cameroun: Études sociales, études médicales, études d'hygiène et de prophylaxie* (Paris: Émile Larose, 1921), v–vi.

7 Gustave Martin, "L'organisation médicale allemande au Cameroun," *Bulletin de la Société de pathologie exotique* 12 (1919): 531.

8 Martin, *L'Existence au Cameroun*.

9 Charles Jojot, "Le secteur de prophylaxie de la maladie du sommeil du Haut-Nyong (Cameroun)," *Annales de médecine et de pharmacie coloniales* 14 (1921): 423–42.

10 This health-related division aside, the subdivision of Akonolinga (downstream from Ayos) would not be reattached to the Haut-Nyong region.

11 Ranked thirty-fifth out of forty, he did "not apply himself," according to his service records: Service Historique de la Défense (Defense Historical Service) (Vincennes, hereafter SHDV), GR 2000 Z 205, 01707, "Dossier personnel Colonel David, Joseph Jean" (1966); according to other sources, he placed second to last: André Borgomano, "Le Roi David—Ancien de Santé navale," *Bulletin de l'ASNOM* 94, no. 127 (2014): 49–52.

12 Eugène Jamot, "La maladie du sommeil au Cameroun," *Bulletin de la Société de pathologie exotique* 18 (1925): 762–69.

13 Société des Nations, *Procès verbal de la 19ᵉ session de la Commission permanente des mandats* (Geneva: Société des Nations, 1930), 120.

14 Lachenal, "Médecine, comparaisons et échanges inter-impériaux"; Guillaume Lachenal and Bertrand Taithe, "Une généalogie missionaire et coloniale de l'humanitaire: Le cas Aujoulat au Cameroun, 1935-1973," *Le Mouvement social*, no. 227 (2009): 45–63; Jean-Pierre Dozon, "Quand les pastoriens traquaient la maladie du sommeil," *Sciences sociales et santé* 3, nos. 3-4 (1985): 27–56.

15 The decree creating a "permanent mission of sleeping sickness prophylaxis" appeared in the *Journal officiel* of July 10, 1926.

16 Callahan, *Mandates and Empire*, 146–48, 260n19.

17 Société des Nations, *Neuvième Session 8-25 juin 1926: Rapports des puissances mandataires, soumis au Conseil de la Société des Nations et examinés par la Commission permanente des mandats* (Geneva: Société des Nations, 1926), 74.

18 Société des Nations, *Neuvième Session 8-25 juin 1926*, 74.

19 The film, directed by Alfred Chaumel in Cameroon, was distributed under several titles and in several versions, including *Le Réveil d'une race* (1931) and *La mission Jamot au Cameroun (1926-32)*. It was first shown at the Théâtre des Champs-Élysées in 1930. The version I am citing is that released in 1939 with sound added (15 mins., Archives de l'Institut Pasteur). On the filming and the reception of the film, see "Cinéma éducateur et propagande coloniale à Paris au début des années 1930," *Revue d'histoire moderne et contemporaine*, nos. 51-54 (2004): 135–51.

Epigraph: The *Report on the Haut-Nyong Region* is from Archives nationales du Cameroun, Yaoundé (National Archives of Cameroon, Yaoundé, hereafter cited as ANY), Affaires politiques et administratives (Political and Administrative Affairs, hereafter cited as APA) 12040 (ca. 1939), cited in Wang Sonné Archives, Haut-Nyong file, "Divers." The reference is incomplete, but this document was likely Dr. David's first report, written at the end of 1939.

1 Robert Koch, Max Beck, and Friedrich Karl Kleine, *Bericht über die Tätigkeit der zur Erforschung der Schlafkrankheit im Jahre 1906/07 nach Ostafrika entsandten Kommission* (Berlin: J. Springer, 1909).

2 Peter Geschiere, *The Modernity of Witchcraft: Politics and the Occult in Postcolonial Africa*, trans. Peter Geschiere and Janet L Roitman (Charlottesville: University Press of Virginia, 1997), 30 n6.

3 ANY, APA, Lieutenant-Colonel-Doctor Cartron, "Rapport annuel: Année 1938; Service de santé; Cameroun français. B.—Partie médicale" (1939), 110, 119.

4 [Pierre] Millous, "Le traitement de la maladie du sommeil au Cameroun," *Annales de médecine et de pharmacie coloniales* 34 (1936): 967.

5 *Rapport annuel du Gouvernement français sur l'administration sous mandat des Territoires du Cameroun pour l'année 1930* (Paris: Imprimerie générale Lahire, 1931), n.p. The image is reproduced in *Togo-Cameroun: Magazine mensuel*, no. 5 (1931): 233, http://gallica.bnf.fr /ark:/12148/bpt6k6260907b/f37.image.r=Togo%20Cameroun.

6 Claude Legaïac, "Ayos," *Togo-Cameroun: Magazine mensuel* January (1930): 25, http:// gallica.bnf.fr/ark:/12148/bpt6k9734452p/f33.image.r=Togo%20Cameroun.

CHAPTER 3. MADAME ATEBA

1 On the importance and ambiguities of the involvement of women's groups in the single party, see Jean-François Bayart, *L'État au Cameroun* (Paris: Presses de la Fondation nationale des sciences politiques, 1979).

2 Wang Sonné, "Les Auxilliaires autochtones dans l'action sanitaire publique au Cameroun sous administration française (1916–1945)" (PhD diss., Faculty of Letters and Human Sciences, University of Yaoundé, 1983), 285–93.

3 Interview between Wang Sonné and Simon Somis, Madouma, June 15, 1981, transcribed in Wang Sonné, "Les Auxilliaires autochtones dans l'action sanitaire publique au Cameroun," Annexe, viii.

4 For a summary of this link between medical therapy and witchcraft (and on medicine as witchcraft, in terms of both care and violence), see Nancy Rose Hunt, "Health and Healing," in *Oxford Handbook of Modern African History*, ed. John Parker and Richard Reid (Oxford: Oxford University Press, 2013), 377–95. On this topic, see also Megan Vaughan, "Healing and Curing: Issues in the Social History and Anthropology of Medicine in Africa," *Social History of Medicine* 7, no. 2 (1994): 283–95; Vinh-Kim Nguyen, *The Republic of Therapy: Triage and Sovereignty in West Africa's Time of AIDS* (Durham, NC: Duke University Press, 2010), in particular, on accusations relating to the treatment of HIV, see pages 80 and 98; Luise White, *Speaking*

with Vampires: Rumor and History in Colonial Africa (Berkeley: University of California Press, 2000).

5 Here, I am using Julie Livingston's words about the diagnosis of cancer in Botswana: Julie Livingston, *Improvising Medicine: An African Oncology Ward in an Emerging Cancer Epidemic* (Durham, NC: Duke University Press, 2012), 165.

6 On the link between witchcraft and anthropophagy, see Peter Geschiere, *The Modernity of Witchcraft: Politics and the Occult in Postcolonial Africa*, trans. Peter Geschiere and Janet L. Roitman (Charlottesville: University Press of Virginia, 1997), 12–15.

7 Author interview with Nkoé Valère, village chief of Madouma, May 2015.

8 Interview between Wang Sonné and Simon Somis, Madouma, June 15, 1981, transcribed in Wang Sonné, "Les Auxilliaires autochtones dans l'action sanitaire publique au Cameroun," Annexe, vii.

9 Author's notes, conversations held at the Ayos hospital, March 2012.

10 The year 2013 had been marked in the Central African Republic by the outbreak of a civil war linked to the rebellion launched by Séléka, which came from the north of the country to attack Bangui, also destabilizing the secure situation in eastern Cameroon. We spoke at a time when massacres were taking place in Bangui and when the French military was organizing Operation Sangaris. Bangui is connected to the rest of the world by the road that passes through Abong-Mbang, where we saw convoys of military and humanitarian equipment passing through. The reference to Libya refers to the military intervention that took place in 2011.

11 Claire Chazal is a French television journalist and was formerly a news anchor on the French national television network TF1.

CHAPTER 4. ADVOCATING FOR A REGIME OF EXCEPTION

Epigraph: Institut de médecine tropicale du Service de santé des armées (Institute of tropical medicine of the military health service; hereafter cited as IMTSSA), box 174, Pasteur-Vallery Radot, "Rapport d'inspection sur le fonctionnement de l'Assistance médicale indigène en AEF et au Cameroun" (1939), 40.

1 Jean-Paul Bado, *Eugène Jamot, 1879–1937: Le médecin de la maladie du sommeil ou trypanosomiase* (Paris: Karthala, 2011).

2 Charles Assalé, "L'inauguration du monument du docteur Jamot," *La Gazette du Cameroun*, no. 142 (1937): 1–3.

3 Centre des archives d'outre-mer (Center for overseas archives; hereafter cited as CAOM), Agence économique de la France d'outre-mer (AGEFOM) 1002 / 3512, Commissariat de la République française au Cameroun, *Bulletin d'informations et de renseignements*, no. 29 (January 19, 1939).

4 Jacques M'Bape, "La mort du médecin-colonel Jamot," *La Gazette du Cameroun*, no. 138 (1937): 4–5.

5 Philalethes Kuhn, "Die Schlafenkrankheit in Kamerun," *Medizinische Klinik* 27 (1914): 1131–35.

6 Eugène Jamot, "La maladie du sommeil au Cameroun," *Bulletin de la Société de pathologie exotique*, vol. 18 (1925): 769.

7 Jean-Pierre Dozon, "Quand les pastoriens traquaient la maladie du sommeil," *Sciences sociales et santé*, 3, nos. 3–4 (1985): 27–56.

8 Albert Calmette, "Rapport au sujet des instructions sanitaires de M. le gouverneur général Carde et du programme de développement sanitaire des Colonies," *Bulletin de l'Académie de médecine* 95 (1931): 1029.

9 Governor Marchand, "Arrêté déterminant les infractions spéciales à l'indigénat par application du décret du 8 août 1924," *Journal officiel du Cameroun*, no. 107 (1924): 33.

10 Cited in "Courrier de l'Afrique équatoriale. Cameroun. Vie administrative," *Annales coloniales* 25, no. 112 (August 11, 1924). The statute was abolished in 1925 and reinstated in 1934: Governor Repiquet, "Arrêté du 18 août 1934 érigeant le centre d'instruction d'Ayos en poste administratif indépendant, relevant directement du Commissaire de la République," *Journal officiel du Cameroun*, no. 343 (1934): 622–23.

11 CAOM, SG Togo-Cameroun, box 30, file 261, "Proposition locale tendant à attribuer l'exercice des pouvoirs disciplinaires aux médecins chargés de la lutte contre la maladie du sommeil" (1924).

12 League of Nations Health Organization, *Minutes of the International Conference on Sleeping Sickness, Held in London at the Colonial Office from May 19th to 22nd, 1925* (Geneva: League of Nations, 1925); *Report of the Second International Conference on Sleeping Sickness, Held in Paris, November 5th to 7th, 1928*, CH 743 (Geneva: League of Nations, Health Organization, 1928), 7.

13 Decrees issued by the governor of Cameroon February 19, 1938, and March 1, 1938.

14 Émile Roubaud, "E. Jamot (1879–1937)," *Bulletin de la Société de pathologie exotique* 30 (1937): 340.

15 "Échos d'outre-mer et des terres étrangères," *Annales coloniales* 39, no. 2 (January 10, 1938): n.p.

16 Archives nationales du Cameroun, Yaounde (ANY), Lieutenant-Colonel-Doctor Cartron, "Rapport annuel. Année 1938. Service de santé. Cameroun français. B.—Partie médicale," 1939, 70.

17 ANY, Cartron, "Rapport annuel: Année 1938," 73.

18 ANY, Cartron, "Rapport annuel: Année 1938," 73.

CHAPTER 5. A FRENCH DREAM

1 Léonard Sah, "Activités allemandes et germanophilie au Cameroun (1936–1939)," *Revue française d'histoire d'outre-mer* 69, no. 255 (1982): 129–44.

2 Institut de médecine tropicale du Service de santé des armées (IMTSSA), box 174, Pasteur-Vallery Radot, "Rapport d'inspection sur le fonctionnement de l'Assistance médicale indigène en AEF et au Cameroun."

3 From the time of its founding by Louis Pasteur at the end of the nineteenth century, the Pasteur Institute played a major role in French colonial policy. In addition to centralizing research on various aspects of tropical medicine, the Pasteur Institute trained military doctors planning on a colonial career. The institute funded the creation of numerous semiautonomous outposts in the colonies from Saigon to Brazzaville, collectively called the overseas Pasteur Institutes. For an overview, see Bruno Latour, *The Pasteurization of France* (Cambridge, MA: Harvard University Press, 1984);

Anne Marie Moulin, "Patriarchal Science: The Network of the Overseas Pasteur Institutes," in *Science and Empires*, ed. Patrick Petitjean (Dordrecht, Netherlands: Kluwer Academic, 1992), 307–22. For background information on PVR, see Anne Simonin, "Le Comité médical de la Résistance: Un succès différé," *Le Mouvement social*, no. 180 (1997): 159–78, as well as PVR's memoirs: Pasteur-Vallery Radot, *Mémoires d'un non-conformiste: 1886–1966* (Paris: Grasset, 1966).

4   Commissariat de la République française au Cameroun, *Bulletin d'informations et de renseignements*, no. 29 (January 19, 1939).

5   Pasteur-Vallery Radot, "Pourquoi le Cameroun doit rester français," *Revue des deux mondes* 109, no. 15 (September 1939): 401.

6   A prestigious French monthly magazine, founded in 1829.

7   Pasteur-Vallery Radot, "Pourquoi le Cameroun doit rester français," 388, 401.

8   Pasteur-Vallery Radot, "Les Instituts Pasteur d'outre-mer," *La Presse médicale* 21 (1939): 410, 413.

9   Archives de l'Institut Pasteur, Paris (Archives of the Pasteur Institute, Paris; hereafter cited as AIP), box IPO-B-10, Institut Pasteur du Cameroun, Noël Bernard, "Lettre à Marcel Vaucel" (June 12, 1939).

10 AIP, IPO-B-10, Institut Pasteur du Cameroun, Pasteur-Vallery Radot, "Lettre à Marcel Vaucel" (March 7, 1939).

11 AIP, IPO-B-10, watercolors.

12 AIP, IPO-B-10, Institut Pasteur du Cameroun, Marcel Vaucel, "Lettre à Pasteur Vallery-Radot" (September 7, 1939).

13 IMTSSA, box 107, Lieutenant-Colonel-Doctor Vaucel, "Rapport annuel: Année 1939; Service de Santé: Cameroun français. B.—Partie médicale" (1940), 163.

CHAPTER 6. HAUT-NYONG MUST BE SAVED

1   "Discours prononcé par Mr le gouverneur général Richard Brunot en conseil d'administration le 17 janvier 1940," *Journal officiel du Cameroun*, no. 483 (February 1, 1940): 118.

2   Albert Sarraut, *La Mise en valeur des colonies françaises* (Paris: Payot, 1923). On colonial humanism and the notion of "mise en valeur" (improvement), see Alice L. Conklin, *A Mission to Civilize: The Republican Idea of Empire in France and West Africa, 1895–1930* (Stanford, CA: Stanford University Press, 1997); Gary Wilder, *The French Imperial Nation-State: Negritude and Colonial Humanism between the Two World Wars* (Chicago: University of Chicago Press, 2005), 43–117. For an economic and political discussion, see Catherine Coquery-Vidrovitch, "Colonisation ou impérialisme: La politique africaine de la France entre les deux guerres," *Le Mouvement social*, no. 107 (1979): 51–76.

3   Sarraut, *La Mise en valeur des colonies françaises*, 94–95.

4   Jules Carde, *Discours prononcé par M. J. Carde, gouverneur général de l'AOF à l'ouverture de la session du Conseil de gouvernement, décembre 1927* (Gorée, Senegal: Imprimerie du gouvernement général, 1928), 42, transcribed in Raymond Gervais and Issiaka Mandé, "Comment compter les sujets de l'Empire? Les étapes d'une démographie impériale en AOF avant 1946," *Vingtième Siècle* 3, no. 95 (2007): 30.

5   Vincent Bonnecase, *La Pauvreté au Sahel: Du savoir colonial à la mesure international* (Paris: Karthala, 2011), 34–40.

6　Centre des archives d'outre-mer (CAOM), Agence économique de la France d'outre-mer (AGEFOM) 888, file 2538, Eugène Jamot, "Rapport de la mission Jamot" (1930), 80.

7　Liverpool School of Tropical Medicine (LSTM), TM/18/3/35, Société de pathologie exotique, "Procès-verbal de la Commission de la maladie du sommeil (réunie le 11 janvier 1939 au ministère des Colonies)" (1939), 9.

8　Société de pathologie exotique, "Procès-verbal de la Commission de la maladie du sommeil" (1939), 9.

9　Gervais and Mandé, "Comment compter les sujets de l'Empire?"

10　Peter Redfield, *Life in Crisis: The Ethical Journey of Doctors Without Borders* (Berkeley: University of California Press, 2013), 49, 185; Bertrand Taithe, "Reinventing (French) Universalism: Religion, Humanitarianism and the 'French Doctors,'" *Modern and Contemporary France* 12, no. 2 (2004): 147–58.

11　Jean Jaurès (1859–1914), the first leader of the French Socialist Party, has remained since his assassination one of the most important historical figure of the French Left. The reference to the governor of Cameroon is from Commissariat de la République française au Cameroun, *Bulletin d'informations et de renseignements*, no. 29 (January 19, 1939).

12　Jean Koufan, "Socialism in the Colonies: Cameroun under the Popular Front," in *French Colonial Empire and the Popular Front: Hope and Disillusion*, ed. Tony Chafer and Amanda Sackur (New York: St. Martin's Press, 1999), 203–17.

13　Bibliothèque François-Mitterand (François Mitterand library), Richard Brunot press file, FOL-LN1–232 (3597), "Un gouverneur général qui a compris son rôle: M. Richard Brunot au Cameroun, 25 mai 1939" (1939).

14　Wang Sonné Archives, Haut-Nyong file, Wang Sonné, "Interview avec Joseph Dobo, dit Le Droit. Dimpan, par Messamena. 15.12.92."

15　Wang Sonné, "Interview avec Joseph Dobo, dit Le Droit. Dimpan, par Messamena. 15.12.92."

16　Wang Sonné, "Interview avec Joseph Dobo, dit Le Droit. Dimpan, par Messamena. 15.12.92."

17　Archives de la Congrégation des Pères du Saint-Esprit, Chevilly-Larue (Archives of the Congregation of the Fathers of the Holy Spirit, Chevilly-Larue; hereafter cited as Arch. CSE), 2J1.11b / 107508, "Note du Dr Weber (01.01.1939)" (1939).

18　Arch. CSE, 2J1 11b, Yaoundé/Divers, "Correspondances des Pères de Messamena, 1935–1953" (1939).

19　Dr. Weber, "Considérations pratiques sur les '2ᵉ période irréductible,'" *Trypano*, no. 3 (1941); R. A. Weber, "Marcel Vaucel, 'La maladie du sommeil au Cameroun' (*Revue des sciences médicales, pharmaceutiques et vétérinaires de l'Afrique française libre*), tome 1, no. 2, oct. 1942," *Médecine tropicale* 4 (1944): 260–62.

CHAPTER 7. LESSONS IN MEDICAL ADMINISTRATION

Epigraph: Archives nationales, Yaoundé (ANY), Affaires politiques et administratives (APA), 10.999, Dr. Jean Joseph David, "Région médicale du Haut-Nyong: Rapport de gestion" (1942), 70.

1　Wang Sonné Archives, Haut-Nyong file, "Notes diverses (*Journal officiel du Cameroun*)"; Service Historique de la Défense, Vincennes (SHDV), GR8 YE 58129, "Dossier personnel Lagarde Sylvain Roger" (1941); SHDV, GR8 YE 107110, "Dossier personnel Gailhbaud Fernand Marie" (1954); SHDV, GR 2000 Z 201, 00030, "Dossier personnel Koch, Henri Louis Gustave" (1957); SHDV, "Dossier personnel Colonel David, Joseph Jean" (1966).

2 Peter Geschiere, *Village Communities and the State: Changing Relations among the Maka of South-Eastern Cameroon since the Colonial Conquest* (London: Kegan Paul International, 1982), 194.

3 For an account of the rallying of Cameroon behind Free France, see Didier Etaba Otoa, *Le Cameroun libre avec les Français libres: 1940* (Yaoundé: Presses de l'UCAC, 2000).

4 Eric T. Jennings, *Free French Africa in World War II: The African Resistance* (New York: Cambridge University Press, 2015), 95.

5 Examples include Paul Bert, Claude Bernard's student, who was appointed resident-general of Annam-Tonkin in 1886; Jean-Marie de Lanessan, governor-general of French Indochina (1891–94); and, in Madagascar, Victor Augagneur. Laurence Monnais-Rousselot, *Médecine et colonisation: L'aventure indochinoise, 1860–1939* (Paris: CNRS Éditions, 1999), 326–29. Another example, in Algeria, is military doctor Auguste Warnier, who was prefect of and then deputy for Algiers between 1871 and 1875. He was known for his commitment to a virulent policy of colonization, based on the dispossession of land. Jacques Léonard, *La Médecine entre les savoirs et les pouvoirs: Histoire intellectuelle et politique de la médecine française au XIXe siècle* (Paris: Aubier-Montaigne, 1981), 324–27.

6 ANY, APA, David, "Région médicale du Haut-Nyong: Rapport de gestion," 57.

7 ANY, APA, David, "Région médicale du Haut-Nyong: Rapport de gestion," 58.

8 ANY, APA, David, "Région médicale du Haut-Nyong: Rapport de gestion," 40.

9 Action Plan for 1940, cited in David, "Région médicale du Haut-Nyong: Rapport de gestion," 2.

10 ANY, APA, David, "Région médicale du Haut-Nyong: Rapport de gestion," 9.

11 ANY, APA, David, "Région médicale du Haut-Nyong: Rapport de gestion," 7.

12 ANY, APA, David, "Région médicale du Haut-Nyong: Rapport de gestion," 39.

13 ANY, APA, David, "Région médicale du Haut-Nyong: Rapport de gestion," 8.

14 Action Plan for 1940, cited in ANY, APA, David, "Région médicale du Haut-Nyong: Rapport de gestion," 43.

15 Action Plan for 1940, cited in ANY, APA, David, "Région médicale du Haut-Nyong: Rapport de gestion," 43.

16 Action Plan for 1940, cited in ANY, APA, David, "Région médicale du Haut-Nyong: Rapport de gestion," 44.

17 Action Plan for 1940, cited in ANY, APA, David, "Région médicale du Haut-Nyong: Rapport de gestion," 44.

18 ANY, APA, David, "Région médicale du Haut-Nyong: Rapport de gestion," 48.

19 ANY, APA, David, "Région médicale du Haut-Nyong: Rapport de gestion," 48.

20 ANY, APA, David, "Région médicale du Haut-Nyong: Rapport de gestion," 45.

21 ANY, APA, David, "Région médicale du Haut-Nyong: Rapport de gestion," 56.

22 ANY, APA, David, "Région médicale du Haut-Nyong: Rapport de gestion," 49.

23 ANY, APA, David, "Région médicale du Haut-Nyong: Rapport de gestion," 50.

24 Nicolas Bancel, Daniel Denis, and Youssef Fates, eds., *De l'Indochine à l'Algérie: La jeunesse en mouvements des deux côtés du miroir colonial, 1940–1962* (Paris: La Découverte, 2003); Jacques Cantier, "Un enjeu essentiel: Vichy et les jeunes dans l'Empire français," in *L'Empire colonial sous Vichy*, ed. Jacques Cantier and Eric Jennings (Paris: Odile Jacob, 2004), 91–115; Phyllis M. Martin, *Leisure and Society in Colonial Brazzaville* (Cambridge: Cambridge University Press, 1995).

25 ANY, APA, David, "Région médicale du Haut-Nyong: Rapport de gestion," 2.

26 Action Plan for 1940, cited in ANY, APA, David, "Région médicale du Haut-Nyong: Rapport de gestion," 44.

27 Memorandum of the District Commander, April 8, 1942, cited in ANY, APA, David, "Région médicale du Haut-Nyong: Rapport de gestion," 52.

28 ANY, APA, David, "Région médicale du Haut-Nyong: Rapport de gestion," 53.

29 ANY, APA, David, "Région médicale du Haut-Nyong: Rapport de gestion," 58.

30 ANY, APA, David, "Région médicale du Haut-Nyong: Rapport de gestion," 62.

31 ANY, APA, David, "Région médicale du Haut-Nyong: Rapport de gestion," 71.

32 ANY, APA, David, "Région médicale du Haut-Nyong: Rapport de gestion," 76.

33 ANY, APA, David, "Région médicale du Haut-Nyong: Rapport de gestion," 81.

34 ANY, APA, David, "Région médicale du Haut-Nyong: Rapport de gestion," 92.

35 ANY, APA, David, "Région médicale du Haut-Nyong: Rapport de gestion," 92.

36 ANY, APA, David, "Région médicale du Haut-Nyong: Rapport de gestion," 105.

37 ANY, APA, David, "Région médicale du Haut-Nyong: Rapport de gestion," 100.

38 ANY, APA, David, "Région médicale du Haut-Nyong: Rapport de gestion," 97.

CHAPTER 8. PARADISE: A GUIDED TOUR (DECEMBER 2013)

1 Roland Barthes, *Mythologies*, trans. Richard Howard and Annette Lavers (New York: Hill and Wang, 2012), 66.

2 Barthes, *Mythologies*, 66.

3 He was in fact a Spanish engineer named Marélo.

4 Allusion to the zones occupied by environmental activists in contemporary France, particularly that at the proposed site for a new airport in Notre-Dame-des-Landes, near Nantes.

5 Archives de la Communauté du Saint-Esprit (Arch. CSE), 2J2.6 / 109722, *Journaux de communauté de la léproserie d'Abong-Mbang*, three notebooks (1948–68).

6 "Avec la mission Lorraine-Congo: 'Nous partons pour le pays des Pygmées,'" *Le Figaro* (November 7, 1952). Consulted in Arch. CSE, 2J1.14a6 / 107539.

7 Henri Joseph Armand Chefdrue, born March 16, 1883, in Pointe-à-Pitre. See Véronique Hélénon, *French Caribbeans in Africa: Diasporic Connections and Colonial Administration, 1880–1939* (Basingstoke, England: Palgrave Macmillan, 2011).

8 One of the organizations to contest this view is Doctors Without Borders. See especially the recent report: Doctors Without Borders, *Out of Focus: How Millions of People in West and Central Africa Are Being Left Out of the Global HIV Response*, accessed June 15, 2020, https://www.msf.org/sites/msf.org/files/2016_04_hiv_report_eng.pdf.

9 Jan Vansina and the American Council of Learned Societies, *Oral Tradition as History* (Madison: University of Wisconsin Press, 1985), 45, http://hdl.handle.net/2027/ heb.02676.

10 Chantal Biya was born in Dimako in Haut-Nyong. The saying is that she gets her beauty from her mother, Rosette, who was Miss Bertoua 1967. For a political portrait, see Fred Eboko, "Chantal Biya: 'Fille du peuple' et égérie internationale," *Politique africaine*, no. 95 (2004): 91–106.

CHAPTER 9. A REAL-LIFE EXPERIMENT

Epigraph: Personal archives of Catherine Koch, Captain-Doctor Koch, "Rapport sur l'agriculture et l'élevage à Messamena (31 décembre 1943)" (1943), 138.

1 On the idea of experimental politics and the experimentalization of government, see Lion Murard and Patrick Zylberman, "De l'hygiène comme introduction à la politique expérimentale (1875–1925)," *Revue de synthèse* 105, no. 115 (1984): 313–41; Christophe Bonneuil, "Development as experiment," *Osiris* 14 (2001): 258–81.

2 Archives nationales du Cameroun, Yaounde (ANY), Affaires politiques et administratives (APA), 10.999, Dr. Jean Joseph David, "Région médicale du Haut-Nyong: Rapport de gestion" (1942), 109.

3 Institut de médecine tropicale du Service de santé des armées (IMTSSA), box 252, Commission de la maladie du sommeil, "Séance du 28 mai 1941: Compte-rendu de la lutte contre la trypanosomiase [pour l'année 1939]" (1941), 14.

4 The Cross of Lorraine was the symbol of Free France.

5 Henri Koch, "Le petit bétail chez les Badjoué et Bikélé de Messaména," *Bulletin de la Société d'études camerounaises*, nos. 13–14 (1946): 27–108; Henri Koch, "Proverbes badjue et bikele," *Bulletin de la Société d'études camerounaises*, no. 5 (1944): 31–52.

6 IMTSSA, box 115, Médecin-chef de région, "Étude sur l'administration médicale directe d'une région démographique éprouvée, 18 janvier 1944" (1944). I never managed to find this other report: Médecin-capitaine Soubde, chef de la subdivision de Messamena, "Extrait d'étude médico-administrative de la subdivision de Messamena, 1940–1946," Archives of the IRCAM (Institut de recherches scientifiques du Cameroun [Institute of scientific research, Cameroon]), Yaoundé, file H, Haut-Nyong, cited in Peter Geschiere, *Village Communities and the State: Changing Relations among the Maka of South-Eastern Cameroon since the Colonial Conquest* (Boston: Kegan Paul International, 1982), 161.

7 For a historiographical overview of the subject, see Anne Hugon, "L'historiographie de la maternité en Afrique subsaharienne," *Clio*, no. 21 (2005), http://clio.revues.org /document1466.html.

8 IMTSSA, box 107, Lieutenant-Colonel-Doctor Vaucel, "Rapport annuel: Année 1939, Service de Santé. Cameroun français. B.—Partie médicale," 1940, 453.

9 ANY, APA, David, "Région médicale du Haut-Nyong: Rapport de gestion," 10.

10 Vincent Bonnecase, *La Pauvreté au Sahel: Du savoir colonial à la mesure internationale* (Paris: Karthala, 2011), 34–40.

11 Personal archives of Catherine Koch.

12 IMTSSA, box 272, "Cameroun, Région médicale du Haut-Nyong—Rapport au sujet d'une expérimentation de la diététique sur l'évolution de la lèpre" (1944); "Lettre de Marcel Vaucel au médecin-chef poste médical de Doumé" (April 1, 1940).

13 Personal archives of Catherine Koch.

14 IMTSSA, Vaucel, "Rapport annuel: Année 1939," 234.

15 IMTSSA, Vaucel, "Rapport annuel: Année 1939," 234.

16 Guillaume Lachenal, *The Lomidine Files: The Untold Story of a Medical Disaster in Colonial Africa*, trans. Noémi Tousignant (Baltimore: Johns Hopkins University Press, 2017).

17 The final report on the experiment can be found in Thomas Arthur Manly Nash, *The Anchau Rural Development and Settlement Scheme* (London: Colonial Office, 1948).

18 Cambridge University Library, Royal Commonwealth Society Library, Institute of Education Collection, "Sleeping Sickness Service Survey in the Anchau Corridor, c.1940," Y301IU / 34-62 (1940), accessed October 12, 2015, http://janus.lib.cam.ac.uk /db/node.xsp?id=EAD%2FGBR%2F0115%2FY301IU%2F34-62.

19 Marcel Vaucel, "La maladie du sommeil au Cameroun" (1942), manuscript (personal archives of Jean-Pierre Eouzan, Yaoundé).

20 Marcel Vaucel, "La maladie du sommeil au Cameroun," *Revue des sciences médicales, pharmaceutiques et vétérinaires de l'Afrique française libre* 1, no. 2 (1942); "État de la maladie du sommeil au Cameroun en 1939," *Annales de l'Institut Pasteur* 67, no. 3 (1941): 212; "L'état de la maladie du sommeil au Cameroun," *La Presse médicale*, nos. 102-3 (1941): 1282.

CHAPTER 10. THE INVISIBLE MEN

1 In the words of James Scott, who describes the major development projects (in the scientific, statist, and modernizing sense of the term) of the 1930s to the 1970s as attempts at ordering and identification designed to make societies and environments legible, so that they could be manipulated by the state and its experts. James C. Scott, *Seeing like a State: How Certain Schemes to Improve the Human Condition Have Failed* (New Haven, CT: Yale University Press, 1998), 2.

2 Institut de Médecine Tropicale du Service de Santé des Armées (IMTSSA), box 115, Médecin-chef de région, "Étude sur l'administration médicale directe d'une région démographique éprouvée, 18 janvier 1944," 1944.

3 Simon Schaffer, *The Brokered World: Go-Betweens and Global Intelligence, 1770-1820* (Sagamore Beach, MA: Science History Publications, 2009); Kapil Raj, *Relocating Modern Science* (London: Palgrave Macmillan, 2007); Walima T. Kalusa, "Language, Medical Auxiliaries, and the Re-interpretation of Missionary Medicine in Colonial Mwinilunga, Zambia, 1922-51," *Journal of Eastern African Studies*, 1, no. 1 (2007): 57-78; Mari Webel, "Medical Auxiliaries and the Negotiation of Public Health in Colonial North-Western Tanzania," *Journal of African History* 54, no. 3 (2013): 393-416; Benjamin N. Lawrance, Emily Lynn Osborn, and Richard L. Roberts, eds., *Intermediaries, Interpreters and Clerks: African Employees in the Making of Colonial Africa* (Madison: University of Wisconsin Press, 2006).

4 Wang Sonné, "Les Auxilliaires autochtones dans l'action sanitaire publique au Cameroun" (PhD diss., Faculty of Letters and Human Sciences, University of Yaoundé, 1983).

5 Wang Sonné, "Les premiers 'médecins africains' camerounais: L'évolution d'une élite autochtone au service de l'action sanitaire française au Cameroun (1932–1950)," *Revue scientifique et technique* 6, no. 3 (1989): 91–110.

6 Wang Sonné Archives, "Notes diverses (*Journal officiel du Cameroun*)," n.p.

7 Lucie Zouya Mimbang, *L'Est-Cameroun de 1905 à 1960, de la mise en valeur à la marginalisation* (Paris: Harmattan, 2013), 267–68.

8 Personal archives of Catherine Koch, Captain-Doctor Koch, "1945: Programme de travail Société de prévoyance (instructions aux moniteurs)" (1945).

9 Archives nationales du Cameroun, Yaounde (ANY), Affaires politiques et administratives (APA), 10.999, Dr. Jean Joseph David, "Région médicale du Haut-Nyong: Rapport de gestion" (1942), 65.

10 Personal archives of Catherine Koch, Captain-Doctor Koch, "Rapport sur l'agriculture et l'élevage à Messamena (31 décembre 1943)," 1943, n.p.

11 All quotations are from Wang Sonné, "Notes diverses (*Journal officiel du Cameroun*)," n.p.

12 Peter Geschiere, *The Modernity of Witchcraft: Politics and the Occult in Postcolonial Africa*, trans. Peter Geschiere and Janet L. Roitman (Charlottesville: University Press of Virginia, 1997), 28; Peter Geschiere, *Village Communities and the State: Changing Relations among the Maka of South-Eastern Cameroon since the Colonial Conquest* (Boston: Kegan Paul International, 1982), 169–89.

13 Wang Sonné Archives, Haut-Nyong file, "Interview avec Joseph Dobo, dit Le Droit. Dimpan, par Messamena. 15.12.92."

14 Mimbang, *L'Est-Cameroun de 1905 à 1960, de la mise en valeur à la marginalisation*, 184.

15 Wang Sonné Archives, Haut-Nyong file, "Interview avec Effoudou Rodolphe de Marqueyssac [*sic*], Atok, juillet 1993."

CHAPTER 11. SOCIAL MEDICINE, FRENCH-STYLE

1 Iris Borowy, "International Social Medicine between the Wars: Positioning a Volatile Concept," *Hygiea Internationalis* 6, no. 2 (2007): 13–35.

2 Richard De Nancy, *Discours sur les études du médecin et sur les qualités nécessaires à l'exercice de sa profession* (Lyon, France: Imprimerie de Durand et Perrin, 1825), 39.

3 "Die Medicin ist eine sociale Wissenschaft, und die Politik ist weiter nichts als Medicin im Grossen." The original quote appeared in Rudolf Virchow, "Der Armenarzt," *Die Medicinische Reform*, no. 18 (Nov. 3, 1848): 125, and was reprinted in *Gesammelte Abhandlungen aus dem Gebiete der öffentlichen Medicin und der Seuchenlehre* (Berlin: Hirschwald, 1879). On this aspect of Virchow's work, see Ian F. McNeely, *"Medicine on a Grand Scale": Rudolf Virchow, Liberalism, and the Public Health* (London: Wellcome Trust, 2002).

4 On this point, see Steven Feierman, *Peasant Intellectuals: Anthropology and History in Tanzania* (Madison: University of Wisconsin Press, 1990); Megan Vaughan, "Healing and Curing: Issues in the Social History and Anthropology of Medicine in Africa," *Social History of Medicine*, 7, no. 2 (1994): 283–95.

5 Paul Weindling, "Social Medicine at the League of Nations Health Organization and the International Labour Office Compared," in *International Health Organizations and*

Movements, 1918-1939, ed. Paul Weindling (Cambridge: Cambridge University Press, 1995), 134-53.

6   Sunil S. Amrith, *Decolonizing International Health: India and Southeast Asia, 1930-65* (Basingstoke, England: Palgrave Macmillan, 2006), 27.

7   He provided a satirical (and anti-Semitic) description of the League of Nations in Louis-Ferdinand Céline, *L'Église* (Paris: Denoël et Steele, 1933). Many of his writings from this time are collected in Louis-Ferdinand Céline, *Semmelweis et autres écrits médicaux* (Paris: Gallimard, 1977).

8   Amrith, *Decolonizing International Health*, 21-46.

9   Lion Murard and Patrick Zylberman, "La mission Rockefeller en France et la création du Comité national de défense contre la tuberculose (1917-1923)," *Revue d'histoire moderne et contemporaine* 34 (1987): 257-81.

10 Lion Murard, "Designs within Disorder: International Conferences on Rural Health Care and the Art of the Local, 1931-1939," in *Shifting Boundaries of Public Health: Europe in the Twentieth Century*, ed. Susan Gross Solomon, Lion Murard, and Patrick Zylberman (Rochester, NY: University of Rochester Press, 2008), 149.

11 Murard, "Designs within Disorder," 155-57.

12 *Rapport sur la socialisation de la médecine dans la Chine rurale . . . par le Dr. C. C. Chen . . .* (Conférence intergouvernementale des pays d'Orient sur l'hygiène rurale, Bandoeng, 1937) (Geneva: Organisation d'hygiène de la Société des Nations, 1937), 25.

13 Kirk Arden Hoppe, *Lords of the Fly: Sleeping Sickness Control in British East Africa, 1900-1960* (Westport, CT: Praeger, 2003).

14 Glen Ncube, "The Making of Rural Healthcare in Colonial Zimbabwe: A History of the Ndanga Medical Unit, Fort Victoria, 1930-1960s" (PhD diss., Department of Historical Studies, University of Cape Town, 2012).

15 Shula Marks, "Common Sense or Utopian Dream? Part I: South Africa's Practice of Social Medicine between 1940 and 1955 in Transnational Perspective" (conference held in Basel, Switzerland, September 13, 2011); Shula Marks, "South Africa's Early Experiment in Social Medicine: Its Pioneers and Politics," *American Journal of Public Health* 87, no. 3 (1997): 452-59.

16 There is a great deal of literature on the Office du Niger. See, most notably, on "homoculture" and the demographic evaluation of the experiment, Vincent Bonnecase, *La Pauvreté au Sahel: Du savoir colonial à la mesure international* (Paris: Karthala, 2011), 137-42, and, more generally, Jean Filipovitch, "The Office du Niger under Colonial Rule: Its Origin, Evolution, and Character (1920-1960)" (PhD thesis, Department of History, McGill University, 1985); Monica M. Van Beusekom, *Negotiating Development: African Farmers and Colonial Experts at the Office du Niger, 1920-1960* (Portsmouth, NH: Heinemann, 2002).

17 See, for example, Fonds reine Élisabeth pour l'assistance médicale aux indigènes du Congo belge-Foreami, "Rapport annuel: Année 1938," Brussels (1939), 12.

18 John L. Hydrick, *Intensive Rural Hygiene Work in the Netherlands East Indies* (New York: Netherlands Information Bureau, 1944); Romain Bertrand, *État colonial, noblesse et nationalisme à Java* (Paris: Karthala, 2005), 396.

19 Intergovernmental Conference of Far-Eastern Countries on Rural Hygiene, *Report of the Intergovernmental Conference of Far-Eastern Countries on Rural Hygiene, held at Bandoeng, Java, August 3rd to 13th, 1937* (Geneva: League of Nations Health Organization, 1937); Annick Guénel, "The 1937 Bandung Conference on Rural Hygiene: Toward a New Vision of Healthcare," in Solomon, Murard, and Zylberman, *Shifting Boundaries of Public Health: Europe in the Twentieth Century*, 62–80.

20 Pierre Dorolle and Françoise Favre, *Histoire de vie: Propos recueillis par Françoise Favre* (Martigny, France: Pillet, 2000).

21 J. L. Hydrick, *Hygiène rurale intensive et éducation hygiénique: L'œuvre entreprise par le Service de la santé publique des Indes néerlandaises, par J. L. Hydrick, . . . Traduction française du Dr P. M. Dorolle, suivie d'un Commentaire sur l'œuvre d'hygiène rurale intensive à Java* (Hanoi: Gouvernement général de l'Indochine, Inspection générale de l'hygiène et de la santé publique, 1937), 70.

22 Helen Tilley, *Africa as a Living Laboratory: Empire, Development, and the Problem of Scientific Knowledge, 1870–1950* (Chicago: University of Chicago Press, 2011), 16.

23 William Malcolm Hailey, *An African Survey: A Study of Problems Arising in Africa South of the Sahara* (London: Oxford University Press, 1957 [1938]), quoted in Tilley, *Africa as a Living Laboratory*, 5.

24 Louis Tanon, "Préface," in *Les Grandes Endémies tropicales: Études de pathogénie et de prophylaxie* (Paris: Vigot, 1930), 1:i–ii.

25 On this subject, see Murard, "Designs within Disorder."

26 Christophe Bonneuil, "Development as Experiment: Science and State-Building in Late Colonial and Postcolonial Africa, 1930–1970," *Osiris* 15 (2000): 258–81.

27 Hydrick, *Intensive Rural Hygiene Work in the Netherlands East Indies*, 41.

CHAPTER 12. LIFE HAS RETURNED

1 Service Historique de la Défense, Vincennes (SHDV), GR 2000 Z 205, 01707, "Dossier personnel Colonel David, Joseph Jean" (1966).

2 Personal archives of the David family, "Relevé des notes du médecin colonel David" (1953).

3 Personal archives of the David family, "Relevé des notes du médecin colonel David" (1953).

4 Personal archives of the David family, "Relevé des notes du médecin colonel David" (1953).

5 "Inauguration du stade Chefdrue à Abong-Mbang," *Le Cameroun libre*, no. 216 (September 10, 1943).

6 Dorothy Shipley White, *Seeds of Discord: De Gaulle, Free France, and the Allies* (Syracuse, NY: Syracuse University Press, 1964).

7 Author interview with Jean Marie Evina Mevaa, May 26, 2015.

8 "Fête prévue le dimanche 5 décembre," *Le Cameroun libre*, no. 220 (November 19, 1943).

9 Adolphe Sicé, "L'Assistance médicale en Afrique noire française," *Africa* 14, no. 1 (1943): 27. For an account of Lord Lugard in the context of international debates on colonial policy, see Véronique Dimier, "Politiques indigènes en France et en Grande-Bretagne dans les années 1930: Aux origines coloniales des politiques de développement," *Politique et sociétés* 24, no. 1 (2005): 73–99. On the institute, see Benoît de

L'Estoile, "L'anthropologue face au monde moderne: Malinowski et 'La rationalisation de l'anthropologie et de l'administration,'" *Genèses* 17, no. 1 (1994): 140–63.

10 Sicé, "L'Assistance médicale en Afrique noire française," 32.

11 Institut de médecine tropicale du Service de santé des armées (IMTSSA), box 115, Médecin-chef de région, "Étude sur l'administration médicale directe d'une région démographique éprouvée, 18 Janvier 1944," 1944.

12 "Concours du jeune footballeur," *L'Éveil du Cameroun*, June 5, 1943.

13 On the health issues discussed at Brazzaville, see Danielle Domergue-Cloarec, "Les problèmes de santé à la Conférence de Brazzaville," in *Brazzaville, janvier-février 1944: Aux sources de la décolonisation*, ed. Institut Charles-de-Gaulle and Institut d'histoire du temps présent (Paris: Plon, 1988), 57–169.

14 I am referring here to the assessment of Frederick Cooper, *Decolonization and African Society: The Labor Question in French and British Africa* (Cambridge: Cambridge University Press, 1996), 177–83.

15 "Plan d'hygiène sociale et d'assistance médicale, recommandation de la Conférence africaine française de Brazzaville," reproduced in IMTSSA, box 115, "Instruction du Commissaire aux colonies, Comité français de libération nationale, no. 1283 Colslg / 88.4, 18 juin 1944" (1944).

16 "Plan d'hygiène sociale et d'assistance médicale, recommandation de la Conférence africaine française de Brazzaville."

17 Paul-André Rosental, *L'Intelligence démographique: Sciences et politiques des populations en France (1930-1960)* (Paris: Odile Jacob, 2003), 77–100.

18 Paul Rabinow, *French DNA: Trouble in Purgatory* (Chicago: University of Chicago Press, 1999), 84. On mass blood transfusion as developed in Algiers, see Edmond Benhamou, "L'organisation de la réanimation-transfusion en Afrique française pendant la guerre," *Bulletin de l'Académie nationale de médecine* 129 (1945): 195–98.

19 *La Conférence africaine française: Brazzaville, 30 janvier-8 février 1944* (Paris: Ministère des Colonies, 1945), 67.

20 IMTSSA, box 115, "Instruction du Commissaire aux colonies, Comité français de libération nationale, no. 1283 Colslg / 88.4, 18 juin 1944."

21 Centre des archives d'outre-mer (CAOM), AFFPOL 2295, file 3, " Procès verbal du 5 février 1944" (1944).

22 IMTSSA, box 115, "Instruction du Commissaire aux colonies, Comité français de libération nationale, no. 1283 Colslg / 88.4, 18 juin 1944."

23 I borrowed this expression from Dominique Pestre, "Le nouvel univers des sciences et des techniques: Une proposition générale," in *Les Sciences pour la guerre, 1940-1960*, ed. Amy Dahan and Dominique Pestre (Paris: Éditions de l'EHESS, 2004), 14.

24 CAOM, AFFPOL 2295, file 5, "Tableau des départs," 1944; "Dossier personnel Colonel David, Joseph Jean."

25 J. F. Brock, "A Physician's Visit to Central Africa," *South African Medical Journal* 19 (1945): 34–38. "In one area of French Equatorial Africa where the disease had been most resistant, serious consideration was being given to the appointment of a medical man instead of an Administrator as District Commissioner in order that no red-tape should hinder the primary objective of reducing the incidence of sleeping sickness" (37).

26 Charles Roquebain, "L'Afrique équatoriale française et le Cameroun pendant et depuis la guerre," *Annales de géographie* 55, no. 299 (1946): 188–95. "Pure philanthropists, hygienists, and ethnologists are considering the cessation of all industrial enterprises in very sparsely populated regions: they would gladly entrust the administration of these territories—sorts of human reserves—to doctors and agricultural instructors. Nice job!" (195).

27 Adolphe Sicé, *L'AEF et le Cameroun au service de la France* (Paris: PUF, 1946); Marcel Vaucel, *La France d'outre-mer dans la guerre: Documents* (Paris: Office français d'édition, 1945).

28 IMTSSA, box 73, Anonymous, "Le service de santé aux colonies depuis le début de la guerre," 1944.

29 "Les réalisations de la France combattante au Cameroun sous mandat français," in *Notes documentaires et études*, no. 6, Série coloniale-II, January 25, 1945, 17.

30 Marcel Vaucel, *Médecine tropicale* (Paris: Flammarion, 1952).

31 "Freedom from Disease in the Tropics," *Lancet* 246, no. 6369 (1945): 373; Elsie May Bell Grosvenor, "Safari through Changing Africa," *National Geographic Magazine* 54, no. 2 (1953): 145–98.

32 SHDV, GR 2000 Z 201, 00030, "Dossier personnel Koch, Henri Louis Gustave" (1957).

33 SHDV, "Dossier personnel Koch, Henri Louis Gustave."

34 Archives de la Communauté du Saint-Esprit (Arch. CSE), 2J1 11b, Dr. Raymond, "Lettre à la Mission catholique de Messamena" (April 10, 1947).

35 IMTSSA, box 110, Colonel-Doctor Vaisseau, "Rapport annuel: Année 1948; Service de la Santé publique; Cameroun français" (1949), 114.

36 IMTSSA, box 115, Marcel Vaucel, "Suppression de la Région 'médicale' du Haut-Nyong: Lettre au haut-commissaire de la République française au Cameroun, 27 Octobre 1947" (1947).

CHAPTER 13. COLONEL DAVID WILL BECOME A GENERAL

1 Author conversation with Nkoé Valère, village chief of Madouma, May 26, 2015.

2 Doc Gynéco was a major French hip-hop artist in the late 1990s, known for his laid-back vocal style.

3 Koppo (featuring Funkys, Daryx), "Back Back," on *Si tu vois ma go*, Blick Bassy, 2004.

4 Archives nationales du Cameroun, Yaounde (ANY), Affaires politiques et administratives (APA), 10.999, Dr. Jean Joseph David, "Région médicale du Haut-Nyong: Rapport de gestion" (1942), 109.

5 Michel Foucault, *Discipline and Punish: The Birth of the Prison*, trans. Alan Sheridan (New York: Vintage, 2012), 364.

6 I am referring here to a somewhat simplistic reading of Foucault, who in fact described bio-politics as a minimal form of government, based on the adherence of individuals and their constitution as moral subjects, rather than as a disciplinary or even totalitarian intervention.

7 "3rd European Colloquium on Ethnopharmacology, 1st International Conference of Anthropology and History of Health and Disease, Programme 01.06.1996," accessed November 10, 2019, http://ethnopharma.free.fr/colloque3/ingpro1.html#socio.

8   Wang Sonné, "Approche historique de la gestion de la Région médicale du Haut-Nyong (Cameroun), 1939–1948," in *Treating Illness: Historical Routes*, ed. Antonio Guerci (Genoa: Erga Edizione, 1998), 371–83.

9   Wang Sonné, "Approche historique de la gestion de la Région médicale du Haut-Nyong," 380.

10 Nancy Rose Hunt, "Being with Pasts: A Preface," in *Traces of the Future: An Archeology of Medical Science in Africa*, ed. Paul Wenzel Geissler, Guillaume Lachenal, John Manton, and Noémi Tousignant (Bristol, UK: Intellect, 2016), 9–13 (12).

11 Nancy Rose Hunt, *A Nervous State: Violence, Remedies, and Reverie in Colonial Congo* (Durham, NC: Duke University Press, 2016); Nancy Rose Hunt, "Espace, temporalité et rêverie: Écrire l'histoire des futurs au Congo belge," *Politique africaine*, no. 135 (2014): 115–36.

CHAPTER 14. THE MISSIONARIES' NIGHTMARE

1   Archives de la Congregation des Peres du Saint-Esprit, Chevilly-Larue (Archives of the Congregation of the Fathers of the Holy Spirit, Chevilly-Larue, 2D54 A, Résumé de journaux de communautés, fascicule 1 (Doumé), Mission de Lomié, "Résumé du journal, 28 novembre (1941)" (1941).

2   Arch. CSE, 2D54 A, "Résumé du journal (sans date)" (1942).

3   Arch. CSE, 2D54 A, fascicule 11 (Lomié), Mission de Lomié, "Journal (sans date)" (1942), 104.

4   Arch. CSE, 2D54 A, "Journal (21 décembre 1941)" (1941).

5   Arch. CSE, 2D54 A, "Journal (26 septembre 1942)" (1942).

6   Arch. CSE, 2J1 11b, Yaoundé / Divers, "Correspondances des Pères de Messamena, 1935–1953" (1942).

7   They were also known as "monitors." Arch. CSE, 2D54 A, Résumé de journaux de communautés, fascicule 9 (Messamena), Mission de Messamena, "Résumé du journal (sans date)" (1943).

8   Arch. CSE, Yaoundé / Divers, "Correspondances des Pères de Messamena, 1935–1953."

9   Mission de Lomié, "Résumé du journal, 28 novembre (1941)."

10 Peter Geschiere, personal communication. The denunciation of Masonic "plots," particularly by members of the Catholic hierarchy, is a recurrent theme in present-day Cameroonian debates on the moral and political corruption of the regime.

11 Arch. CSE, 2D54 A, Résumé de journaux de communautés, fascicule 11 (Lomié), Mission de Lomié, "Journal (3 novembre 1942)" (1942).

12 Arch. CSE, 2D54 A, fascicule 1 (Doumé), Mission de Doumé, "Résumé du journal (sans date)" (1941).

13 Philippe Laburthe-Tolra, *Vers la lumière? Ou le Désir d'Ariel: À propos des Beti du Cameroun; Sociologie de la conversion* (Paris: Karthala, 1999).

14 Arch. CSE, 2J1.14a6, Mission de Doumé, "Rapport sur le district de Doumé, avec carte, pour le bulletin des Œuvres" (ca. 1952).

15 Lucie Zouya Mimbang, *L'Est-Cameroun de 1905 à 1960, de la mise en valeur à la marginalisation* (Paris: Harmattan, 2013), 187.

16 For a more general discussion of colonial missionary-administrator relations in Africa, see James P. Daughton, *An Empire Divided: Religion, Republicanism, and the Making of French Colonialism, 1880-1914* (Oxford: Oxford University Press, 2006).

17 Mongo Beti, *Le Pauvre Christ de Bomba* (Paris: Robert Laffont, 1956).

18 Wang Sonné Archives, Haut-Nyong file, "Interview avec l'abbé François Xavier Nnanga, curé d'Esseng, né en 1923 à Lomié, juillet 1993."

19 Arch. CSE, 2J1 11b, Père Stintzi, "Lettre au docteur Koch du 23 février 1943" (1943).

20 Arch. CSE, Yaoundé / Divers, "Correspondances des Pères de Messamena, 1935-1953."

CHAPTER 15. THE DARK WATERS OF THE HAUT-NYONG

1 Archives nationales du Cameroun (ANY), Affaires politiques et administratives (APA), 10.999, Dr. Jean Joseph David, "Région médicale du Haut-Nyong: Rapport de gestion" (1942), 120.

2 Institut de médecine tropicale du Service de santé des armées (IMTSSA), box 111, Colonel-Doctor Farinaud, "Rapport annuel. Année 1944" (1945), 161.

3 Service Historique de la Défense, Vincennes (SHDV), GR8 YE 58129, "Dossier personnel Lagarde Sylvain Roger" (1941).

4 SHDV, GR 8YE 107110, "Dossier personnel Gailhbaud Fernand Marie" (1954).

5 IMTSSA, box 115, Médecin-chef de région, "Étude sur l'administration médicale directe d'une région démographique éprouvée, 18 janvier 1944," 5.

6 ANY, APA, David, "Région médicale du Haut-Nyong: Rapport de gestion," 102.

7 Peter Geschiere, *The Modernity of Witchcraft: Politics and the Occult in Postcolonial Africa*, trans. Peter Geschiere and Janet L. Roitman (Charlottesville: University Press of Virginia, 1997), 30.

8 This recap is based on the work of Peter Geschiere, "European Planters, African Peasants, and the Colonial State: Alternatives in the *Mise en Valeur* of Makaland, Southeast Cameroun, during the Interbellum," *African Economic History*, no. 12 (1983): 83-108.

9 "Les travaux publics au Cameroun en 1926," *Bulletin général de l'Agence des colonies* 20, no. 225 (1927): 1060.

10 The flourishing of coffee plantations and the ambiguous position of the administration are well analyzed in Lucie Zouya Mimbang, *L'Est-Cameroun de 1905 à 1960, de la mise en valeur à la marginalisation* (Paris: Harmattan, 2013), 252ff.

11 Mimbang, *L'Est-Cameroun de 1905 à 1960*, 263.

12 J. Koufan, "Socialism in the Colonies," in *French Colonial Empire and the Popular Front: Hope and Disillusion*, ed. Tony Chafer and Amanda Sackur (New York: St. Martin's Press, 1999), 203-17.

13 Bibliothèque François-Mitterand, Richard Brunot press file, FOL-LN1-232 (3597), "Un gouverneur général qui a compris son rôle. M. Richard Brunot au Cameroun, 25 mai 1939" (1939).

14 The texts of these decrees are reproduced in *Rapport annuel du gouvernement français sur l'administration sous mandat des territoires du Cameroun pour l'année 1938* (Paris: Imprimerie Cogery, 1939).

15 The system of "mandatory public service" was reorganized by the decree of December 26, 1938. *Rapport annuel du gouvernement français sur l'administration sous mandat des territoires du Cameroun pour l'année 1938*, 203.

16 ANY, APA 10 / 422 F, December 11, 1939, cited in P. Geschiere, "European Planters, African Peasants, and the Colonial State," 94.

17 APA, ANY, David, "Région médicale du Haut-Nyong: Rapport de gestion," 82.

18 ANY, APA 10 / 422 F, December 11, 1939, cited in P. Geschiere, "European Planters, African Peasants, and the Colonial State," 94.

19 ANY, APA, David, "Région médicale du Haut-Nyong: Rapport de gestion," 82.

20 ANY, APA, David, "Région médicale du Haut-Nyong: Rapport de gestion," 82.

21 Archives de la Congregation des Peres du Saint-Esprit, Chevilly-Larue (Archives of the Congregation of the Fathers of the Holy Spirit, Chevilly-Larue, 2J1 11b, Divers, "Correspondances des Pères de Messamena, 1935-1953."

22 This quotation is contained in the first sentence of the decree of November 17, 1937.

23 ANY, APA, David, "Région médicale du Haut-Nyong: Rapport de gestion," 84.

24 ANY, APA, David, "Région médicale du Haut-Nyong: Rapport de gestion," 84.

25 Geschiere, "European Planters, African Peasants, and the Colonial State," 96.

26 On the use of forced labor in the context of the war effort, see Richard A. Joseph, *Le Mouvement nationaliste au Cameroun: Les Origines sociales de l'UPC* (Paris: Karthala, 1986), 62–70; Eric T. Jennings, *Free French Africa in World War II: The African Resistance* (New York: Cambridge University Press, 2015), 217–48.

27 ANY, APA, David, "Région médicale du Haut-Nyong: Rapport de gestion," 119.

28 Mimbang, *L'Est-Cameroun de 1905 à 1960*, 284.

29 ANY, APA, David, "Région médicale du Haut-Nyong: Rapport de gestion," 119.

30 The figure concerns children aged fifteen days to two years. IMTSSA, box 115, Médecin-chef de région, "Étude sur l'administration médicale directe d'une région démographique éprouvée, 18 janvier 1944," 4.

31 ANY, APA, David, "Région médicale du Haut-Nyong: Rapport de gestion," 71.

CHAPTER 16. RUBBER FOR THE EMPEROR

1 Paul Wendt, "The Control of Rubber in World War II," *Southern Economic Journal* 13, no. 3 (1947): 203–27; Adebayo Oyebade, "Feeding America's War Machine: The United States and Economic Expansion in West Africa during World War II," *African Economic History* 26, no. 26 (1998): 119–40.

2 Eric T. Jennings, *Free French Africa in World War II: The African Resistance* (New York: Cambridge University Press, 2015), 179–216. On the harvesting of rubber from forests in Central Africa and the similarities between the two rubber "ages" at the beginning of the twentieth century and during the Second World War, see Tamara Giles-Vernick, *Cutting the Vines of the Past: Environmental Histories of the Central African Rain Forest* (Charlottesville: University Press of Virginia, 2002): 159–66; Catherine Coquery-Vidrovitch, *Le Congo au temps des grandes compagnies concessionnaires, 1898-1930* (Paris: Éditions de l'EHESS, 2001), 424–40; Nancy Rose Hunt, *A Nervous State: Violence, Remedies, and Reverie in Colonial Congo* (Durham, NC: Duke University Press, 2016).

3 These were the prices for purchases made locally by European traders. Archives de la Congregation des Peres du Saint-Esprit, Chevilly-Larue (Archives of the Congregation of the Fathers of the Holy Spirit, Chevilly-Larue, 2D54 A, Résumé de journaux de communautés, booklet 12, Mission de Doumé, "Résumé du journal (sans date)" (1944), 129; Archives nationales du Cameroun, Yaounde (ANY), Affaires politiques et administratives (APA), 10.999, Dr. Jean Joseph David, "Région médicale du Haut-Nyong: Rapport de gestion" (1942), 63.

4 Robert Harms, "The End of Red Rubber: A Reassessment," *Journal of African History* 16, no. 1 (1975): 73–88; Raymond Dumett, "The Rubber Trade of the Gold Coast and Asante in the Nineteenth Century: African Innovation and Market Responsiveness," *Journal of African History* 12, no. 1 (1971): 79–101.

5 Other than the "djem and dzimou" peoples of Lomié, these were "the Poum-Poums and the Djems" of Abong-Mbang and the "Bakoumas of Doumé." ANY, APA, David, "Région médicale du Haut-Nyong: Rapport de gestion," 63.

6 Jean Despois, "Les genres de vie des populations de la forêt dans le Cameroun oriental," *Annales de géographie* 55, no. 297 (1946): 19–38.

7 ANY, APA, David, "Région médicale du Haut-Nyong: Rapport de gestion," 63.

8 ANY, APA, David, "Région médicale du Haut-Nyong: Rapport de gestion," 63.

9 On the harvesting of rubber as a means of escape in eastern Cameroon in 1940, see Lucie Zouya Mimbang, *L'Est-Cameroun de 1905 à 1960, de la mise en valeur à la marginalisation* (Paris: Harmattan, 2013), 192. Nancy Hunt recently proposed considering the role of "wandering" in the history of central Africa; see Hunt, "Espace, temporalité et rêverie: Écrire l'histoire des futurs au Congo belge," *Politique africaine* no. 135 (2014): 115–36.

10 J. Despois, "Les genres de vie des populations de la forêt dans le Cameroun oriental," 34.

11 ANY, APA, David, "Région médicale du Haut-Nyong: Rapport de gestion," 119.

12 Arch. CSE, Mission de Lomié, "Journal (sans date)" (1943), 124.

13 ANY, NF 377 / 1, Governor of Cameroon to the district commander of Haut-Nyong, telegram of February 19, 1942, cited in Leonard Sah, "Le Cameroun sous mandat français dans la Deuxième Guerre mondiale" (PhD thesis, Faculté des lettres et sciences humaines, Université Aix-Marseille I, 1998), 484.

14 Jennings, *Free French Africa in World War II*.

15 Arch. CSE, Mission de Lomié, "Journal (sans date)" (1943).

16 Arch. CSE, Mission de Lomié, "Journal (sans date)" (1943).

17 Arch. CSE, Mission de Lomié, "Journal (sans date)" (1944).

18 Arch. CSE, Mission de Lomié, "Journal (sans date)" (1943).

19 Institut de médecine tropicale du Service de santé des armées (IMTSSA), box III, Colonel-Doctor Farinaud, "Rapport annuel: Année 1943; Service de santé; Cameroun français; A.—Partie administrative" (1944), 31.

20 Maryinez Lyons, *The Colonial Disease: A Social History of Sleeping Sickness in Northern Zaire, 1900–1940* (Cambridge: Cambridge University Press, 1992).

21 P[ierre] Millous, "La maladie du sommeil," *Le Progrès médical*, no. 24 (1937): 898.

22 IMTSSA, box III, Colonel-Doctor Farinaud, "Rapport annuel: Année 1946; Service de santé; Cameroun français" (1947); Colonel-Doctor Farinaud, "Rapport annuel:

Année 1945; Service de santé; Cameroun français" (1946); Colonel-Doctor Farinaud, "Rapport annuel: Année 1944; Service de santé; Cameroun français; A.—Partie administrative" (1945).

23 ANY, APA, David, "Région médicale du Haut-Nyong: Rapport de gestion," 73; IMTSSA, box 115, Médecin-chef de région, "Étude sur l'administration médicale directe d'une région démographique éprouvée, 18 janvier 1944," 11.

24 Wendt, "The Control of Rubber in World War II," 208.

25 Raymond Dumett, "Africa's Strategic Minerals during the Second World War," *Journal of African History* 26, no. 4 (1985): 381–408.

26 Mimbang, *L'Est-Cameroun de 1905 à 1960, de la mise en valeur à la marginalisation*, 212.

27 Personal archives of Catherine Koch, Captain-Doctor Koch, "Poste médical de Messamena: Enquête démographique," March 1945, n.p.

28 These data come from the website of the current rutile mining project underway in Haut-Nyong, accessed July 14, 2008, http://www.akonolinga.net.

29 Arthur A. Pegau, *Titanium. Mineral Resources Circular no. 5*, 1956, https://www.dmme .virginia.gov/commercedocs/MRC_5.pdf; "La production de l'étain et du rutile au Cameroun," *Revue internationale des produits coloniaux* (1940): 148–50.

30 J. L. Oudart, "Les pharmaciens coloniaux," *Médecine tropicale* 65, no. 3 (2005): 263–72.

31 Farinaud, "Rapport annuel: Année 1946; Service de santé; Cameroun français," 167–68.

32 It would take about fifteen years to contain this epidemic. It was eventually contained thanks in large part to lomidinization campaigns, which were very intense in the region in the 1950s.

33 The expression comes from the recollections of the colonial doctor Jean Dutertre, "Jean-Marc et la trypano," accessed July 2, 2006, http://perso.orange.fr/jdtr/Jeanmarc .htm. The figure of the "louse" as a metaphor for the mediocre office employee, as seen in Gustave Flaubert and Guy de Maupassant, has been the subject of a fine study: Cyril Piroux, *Le Roman de l'employé de bureau, ou l'Art de faire un livre sur (presque) rien* (Dijon: Éditions universitaires de Dijon, 2015).

CHAPTER 17. "HERE WE ARE THE MASTERS"

1 Eric T. Jennings, *Free French Africa in World War II: The African Resistance* (New York: Cambridge University Press, 2015).

2 All quotes in this paragraph come from the personal archives of Catherine Koch, Captain-Doctor Koch, "Poste médical de Messamena: Enquête démographique," March 1945, n.p.

3 Didier Fassin, "Au cœur de la cité salubre: La santé publique entre les mots et les choses," in *Critique de la santé publique: Une approche anthropologique*, ed. Jean-Pierre Dozon and Didier Fassin (Paris: Balland, 2001), 47–73.

4 Lion Murard and Patrick Zylberman, *L'Hygiène dans la République: La santé publique en France, ou l'utopie contrariée: 1870–1918* (Paris: Fayard, 1996).

5 Philippe Roussin, *Misère de la littérature, terreur de l'histoire: Céline et la littérature contemporaine* (Paris: Gallimard, 2005).

6 Greg Grandin, *Fordlandia: The Rise and Fall of Henry Ford's Forgotten Jungle City* (New York: Metropolitan Books, 2009), 17.

7 Jean-Paul Bado, *Eugène Jamot, 1879–1937: Le Médecin de la maladie du sommeil ou trypanoso-miase* (Paris: Karthala, 2011); Léon Lapeyssonnie, *La Médecine coloniale: Mythes et réalités* (Paris: Seghers, 1984).

8 Graham Greene, *A Burnt-Out Case* (London: Heinemann, 1961); Jean-Paul Sartre, *Typhus* [scénario, vers 1944] (Paris: Gallimard, 2007); Louis-Ferdinand Céline, *L'Église* (Paris: Denoël et Steele, 1933); Paule Constant, *Ouregano* (Paris: Gallimard, 1980); Paule Constant, *C'est fort la France!* (Paris: Gallimard, 2013).

9 All quotes in this paragraph come from Koch, "Poste médical de Messamena: Enquête démographique."

10 Service Historique de la Défense, Vincennes (SHDV), GR 2000 Z 205, 01707, "Dossier personnel Colonel David, Joseph Jean," "État de service."

11 "Le monde colonial," *Annales coloniales*, September 12, 1938, n.p.

12 Warwick Anderson, *Colonial Pathologies: American Tropical Medicine, Race and Hygiene in the Philippines* (Durham, NC: Duke University Press, 2006), 130–57; Bertrand Taithe, *The Killer Trail: A Colonial Scandal in the Heart of Africa* (Oxford: Oxford University Press, 2009), 46–71.

13 SHDV, GR 2000 Z 201, 00030, "Dossier personnel Koch, Henri Louis Gustave" (1957). Notably, he published "Apercu démographique des territoires de l'AOF," *Bulletin médical de l'AOF* 6 (1949): 161–73.

14 "Débats parlementaires—Assemblée nationale—1re seance du 22 mars 1949," *Journal officiel de la République française*, no. 30 (1949): 1673.

15 SHDV, "Dossier personnel Koch, Henri Louis Gustave."

16 SHDV, "Dossier personnel Koch, Henri Louis Gustave."

17 Henri Koch, *Magie et chasse dans la forêt camerounaise* (Paris: Berger-Levrault, 1968).

18 Henri Koch, *La Médecine de l'espérance* (Paris: Maloine, 1967), 120.

CHAPTER 18. KOCH! KOCH!

1 The French term that Madame Zoa used was doubtless meant to designate another type of feline here, something like a panther.

2 The diagnosis of a social and emotional crisis (possibly manifesting itself in the field of witchcraft) as the cause of epidemics recalls Tamara Giles-Vernick's work on the "end of love" which is described as a cause of the Buruli ulcer epidemic along the Nyong River. Tamara Giles-Vernick, Joseph Owona-Ntsama, Jordi Landier, and Sara Eyangoh, "The Puzzle of Buruli Ulcer Transmission, Ethno-Ecological History and the End of 'Love' in the Akonolinga District, Cameroon," *Social Science and Medicine* 129 (2015): 20–27.

3 Wang Sonné Archives, Haut-Nyong file, "Interview avec Mbouk Mvom Marc Claude, décembre 1992."

4 The production of ethnographic works by administrators and doctors was habitual in colonial Africa: Emmanuelle Sibeud, *Une science impériale pour l'Afrique? La Construction des savoirs africanistes en France, 1878–1930* (Paris: Éditions de l'EHESS, 2002).

5 Johannes Fabian, *Out of Our Minds: Reason and Madness in the Exploration of Central Africa* (Berkeley: University of California Press, 2000).

6 Personal archives of Catherine Koch, Captain-Doctor Koch, "Poste médical de Messamena: Enquête démographique," March 1945.

7 Koch, "Poste médical de Messamena: Enquête démographique."

8 Koch, "Poste médical de Messamena: Enquête démographique."

9 Author interview with Father Georges Rey, Abong-Mbang, May 27, 2015.

10 All quotes from the personal archives of Catherine Koch, Henri Koch, "Les Serpents," n.d.

CHAPTER 19. KING DAVID

Epigraph to part II: Marshall Sahlins, "The Stranger-King, or Dumézil among the Fijians," *Journal of Pacific History* 16, no. 3 (1981): 115.

Epigraph to chapter 19: Jack Hart, *Storycraft: The Complete Guide to Writing Narrative Nonfiction* (Chicago: University of Chicago Press, 2011), 233.

1 Peter Geschiere, personal communication, 2008.

2 Joseph Conrad, *Heart of Darkness* (Minneapolis, MN: Lerner, 2015), 48.

3 Greg Grandin, *Fordlandia: The Rise and Fall of Henry Ford's Forgotten Jungle City* (New York: Metropolitan Books, 2009); Ben Macintyre, "Dearborn-on-Amazon," *New York Times*, July 16, 2009, https://www.nytimes.com/2009/07/19/books/review/Macintyre-t.html.

4 Rudyard Kipling, "The Man Who Would Be King," in *The Man Who Would Be King, and Other Stories* (Oxford: Oxford University Press, 1999), 252. "The Man Who Would Be King" was first published in Rudyard Kipling, *The Phantom 'Rickshaw, and Other Tales* (Allahabad, India: A. H. Wheeler, 1888). Works on the "White Rajah" are numerous; see, notably, Nigel Barley, *White Rajah* (London: Little, Brown, 2002).

5 Bertrand Taithe, *The Killer Trail: A Colonial Scandal in the Heart of Africa* (Oxford: Oxford University Press, 2009), 131; William Benjamin Cohen, *Rulers of Empire: The French Colonial Service in Africa* (Stanford, CA: Hoover Institution Press, Stanford University, 1971); William Benjamin Cohen, "The French Governors," in *African Proconsuls: European Governors in Africa*, ed. Lewis H. Gann and Peter Duignan (New York: Free Press, 1978), 19–50; William Benjamin Cohen, *Empereurs sans sceptre: Histoire des administrateurs de la France d'outre-mer et de l'École coloniale* (Paris: Berger-Levrault, 1973).

6 Service Historique de la Défense, Vincennes (SHDV), GR2000 Z 205, 01707, "Dossier personnel Colonel David, Joseph Jean" (1966).

7 Geneviève Royannez-Genevey, "Le 'Roi David' ou l'œuvre d'un médecin français aux îles Wallis" (Thesis, Faculté de médecine Lyon-Sud, Université Claude Bernard–Lyon I, 1994), 1.

8 See François Robin, *Le Résident d'Uvéa* (Paris: Harmattan, 2012); Philippe Godard, *Wallis et Futuna* (Nouméa: Éditions Mélanésia, 1983); Richard Rossille, *Le Kava à Wallis et Futuna: Survivance d'un breuvage océanien traditionnel* (Talence, France: Centre de recherches sur les espaces tropicaux, 1986); Jean-Claude Roux, *Wallis et Futuna: Espaces et temps recomposés; Chroniques d'une micro-insularité* (Talence, France: Centre de recherche sur les espaces tropicaux, 1995); Malia Sosefo Drouet-Manufekai, ed., *Tāvaka*

lanu'imoana: Mémoires de voyage (Nouméa, New Caledonia: Agence de développement de la culture kanak, Centre culturel Tjibaou, Comité de recherche historique Tāvaka, 2009); and Nancy Pollock, "Doctor Administrators in Wallis and Futuna," *Journal of Pacific History* 25, no. 1 (1990): 47–67; as well as, more recently, André Borgomano, "Le Roi David—Ancien de Santé navale," *Bulletin de l'ASNOM* 94, no. 127 (2014): 49–52.

CHAPTER 20. UVEA, DESERT ISLAND

1 Nicholas Six, "Wallis et Futuna, petit bout de France où règnent trois rois," *Le Monde*, September 5, 2014. Journalists never tire of this. In February 2000, *Le Figaro magazine* ran the headline "Les derniers rois de France" (The last kings of France); in 1989, *Le Monde* titled an article "Les trois derniers rois de France viennent de vivre leur revolution" (The last three kings of France have just had their revolution); and in the same year, *La Croix* published "Trois rois pour la république" (Three kings for the Republic). "L'île où les cochons sont rois" (The island where pigs are kings), joked *Le Nouvel Observateur* in 1981: "In Wallis, the most beautiful lagoon in the Pacific, the Republic subsidizes and respects the sacred order of the coconut tree. . . ." All quotes from *Wallis-et-Futuna: Dossier de presse* (Paris: FNSP, Centre de documentation contemporaine, 1952–2000). I wrote these lines before President François Hollande's visit to Wallis in February 2006, which generated an avalanche of articles of the same kind. I cannot resist citing the account of the local news that spoke of a "Doctor Hollande" at the bedside of the archipelago: Patrick Ferrante, "François Hollande à Wallis et Futuna: Coutume, avions et or bleu," France télévisions Wallis et Futuna 1ere, 23 février 2016, accessed March 1, 2016, http://la1ere.francetvinfo.fr/wallisfutuna/2016/02/23/francois-hollande-wallis-et-futuna-coutume-avions-et-or-bleu-334489.html.

2 Sophie Chave-Dartoen, "Le paradoxe wallisien: Une royauté dans la République," *Ethnologie française* 32, no. 4 (2002): 643. This article provides a recent and concise portrait of the archipelago.

3 Frédéric Angleviel, *Les Missions à Wallis et Futuna au XIXe siècle* (Talence, France: Centre de recherche des espaces tropicaux, 1994).

4 Alexandre Poncet, *Histoire de l'île Wallis: Le Protectorat français*, vol. 2 (Paris: Société des océanistes, 1972).

5 According to Anne-Marie Moulin, this sentence appeared in a letter (or a telegram) addressed to General Gallieni, who was in Madagascar at the time: Anne-Marie Moulin, *Le Médecin du prince: Voyage à travers les cultures* (Paris: Odile Jacob, 2010), 345n2. See also Paul Doury, "Lyautey et la médecine," *Histoire des sciences médicales* 35, no. 3 (2001): 305–14.

6 Jean-Claude Roux, "Pouvoir religieux et pouvoir politique à Wallis et Futuna," in *États et pouvoirs dans les territoires français du Pacifique: Nouvelle-Calédonie, Polynésie française, Vanuatu, Wallis et Futuna; Schémas d'évolution* [Proceedings of two days of workshops, Paris, May 7, 1985], ed. Paul de Deckker and Pierre Lagayette (Paris: Harmattan, 1987), 69.

7 Poncet, *Histoire de l'île Wallis*, 51.

8 Letter from the governor to Dr. Viala, May 8, 1906, cited in Nancy Pollock, "Doctor administrators in Wallis and Futuna," *Journal of Pacific History* 25, no. 1 (1990), 52.

9   Wallis, Archives de l'administration supérieure (Archives of the Superior Administration), Colonel Bray–Commmandant supérieur des troupes du groupe du Pacifique, "Rapport confidentiel à monsieur le gouverneur de la Nouvelle-Calédonie et dépendances. Objet: Îles Wallis et Futuna" (1953), 7.

10 Bray, "Rapport confidentiel à monsieur le gouverneur de la Nouvelle-Calédonie et dépendances," 6.

11 Chave-Dartoen, "Le paradoxe wallisien."

12 Oswald Iten, "Trouble Brews in Pacific Paradise," *Guardian*, July 31, 1996.

13 The mobile phone made its first appearance on the island at Christmas of 2015, a year and a half after my time there.

14 Jean-Claude Roux, "Espaces coloniaux et société polynésienne de Wallis-Futuna (Pacifique central)" (PhD diss., Université de Paris I–Panthéon-Sorbonne, 1991). The thesis was published: Jean-Claude Roux, *Wallis et Futuna: Espaces et temps recomposés; Chroniques d'une micro-insularité* (Talence, France: Centre de recherche sur les espaces tropicaux, 1995). In what follows, I refer to the thesis more often because it is searchable. It can be consulted in the Institut de Recherche pour la Développement's digital repository: accessed September 22, 2016, http://horizon.documentation.ird.fr/exl-doc/pleins_textes/divers09-08/36043.pdf.

15 The governor of Nouméa had authority over Wallis and Futuna as commissioner general of the French Republic in the Pacific Ocean.

16 Jean-Claude Roux, personal communication, 2014.

17 Marshall Sahlins, "Differentiation by Adaptation in Polynesian Societies," *Journal of the Polynesian Society* 66, no. 3 (1957): 291, cited in Roux, "Pouvoir religieux et pouvoir politique à Wallis and Futuna."

18 *Uvéa, le flou du roi*, a film by Luc Laventure (RFO, 2008). YouTube, consulted September 22, 2016, https://www.youtube.com/watch?v=aYGus4ytVK8.

19 Cited in Roux, *Wallis et Futuna: Espaces et temps recomposés*, 86.

20 Cited in Roux, *Wallis et Futuna: Espaces et temps recomposés*, 8.

21 Paul Veyne, *When Our World Became Christian, 312–94*, trans. Janet Lloyd (Cambridge, MA: Polity, 2010), 141.

22 Paul Veyne, *Writing History: Essay on Epistemology*, trans. Mina Moore-Rinvolucri (Middletown, CT: Wesleyan University Press, 1984), 63.

CHAPTER 21. CHRONICLES OF THE GOLDEN AGE

1   Service Historique de la Défense, Vincennes (SHDV), SHDV, GR 2000 Z 205, 01707, "Dossier personnel Colonel David, Joseph Jean" (1966).

2   Preface by Governor Marchessou, Nouméa, February 21, 1938, Centre des archives d'outre-mer (CAOM), BIB SOM e648 Dr. David, "L'œuvre du docteur David, 1933–1937, à Wallis et Futuna" (1938), 1–2.

3   Jean-Claude Roux, *Wallis et Futuna: Espaces et temps recomposés; Chroniques d'une micro-insularité* (Talence, France: Centre de recherche sur les espaces tropicaux, 1995), 188–89.

4   Dr. Viala, "Les îles Wallis et Horn: Notes de géographie médicale," *Annales d'hygiène et de médecine coloniales* 12 (1909): 202.

5   Jean-Claude Roux, "Espaces coloniaux et société polynésienne de Wallis-Futuna (Pacifique central)" (PhD diss., Université de Paris I–Panthéon-Sorbonne, 1991), 142–43.

6   Roux, "Espaces coloniaux et société polynésienne de Wallis-Futuna (Pacifique central)," 276.

7   Société d'Etudes Historiques de Nouvelle Calédonie (hereafter cited as SEHNC), Archives Jean-Claude Roux, David folder, Governor Siadous, "12.1. Lettre au résident de France aux îles Wallis et Futuna, 19 août 1933" (1933).

8   SEHNC, Archives Jean-Claude Roux, David, Jean Joseph David folder, "12.4. Rapport trimestriel au commissaire général de la République dans l'océan Pacifique, 26 novembre 1933" (1933).

9   SEHNC, Archives Jean-Claude Roux, David, Jean Joseph David folder, "12.4. Rapport trimestriel au commissaire général de la République dans l'océan Pacifique, 26 novembre 1933" (1933), as well as for the quotes that follow.

10 SEHNC, Archives Jean-Claude Roux, David, Jean Joseph David folder, "12.11. Rapport trimestriel au commissaire général de la République en Nouvelle-Calédonie, 16 août 1934" (1934).

11 SEHNC, Archives Jean-Claude Roux, David, Jean Joseph David folder, "12.5. Rapport annuel au commissaire général de la République dans l'océan Pacifique, 13 janvier 1934" (1934).

12 SEHNC, Archives Jean-Claude Roux, David, Jean Joseph David folder, "12.7. Rapport trimestriel au commissaire général de la République en Nouvelle-Calédonie, 21 avril 1934" (1934), as well as for the quotes that follow.

13 The classic study on this issue is Jacques Marseille, *Empire colonial et capitalisme français: Histoire d'un divorce* (Paris: Albin Michel, 1984). On the 1933 law, see 285–99.

14 Jean Copans, *Les Marabouts de l'arachide: La Confrérie mouride et les paysans au Sénégal* (Paris: Le Sycomore, 1980); Philippe Couty, "Les mourides et l'arachide au Sénégal," *Tiers-Monde* (1982): 311–14.

15 Cited in Marseille, *Empire colonial et capitalisme français*, 289.

16 "Loi du 6 août 1933 tendant à établir des droits de douane sur les fruits et graines oléagineux, les matières grasses et leurs dérivés (Arrêté de promulgation no. 613 C du 21 septembre 1933)," *Journal Officiel* no. 19 du 01/10/1933 (1933): 355.

17 SEHNC, David, "12.11. Rapport trimestriel au commissaire général de la République en Nouvelle-Calédonie, 16 août 1934."

18 SEHNC, Archives Jean-Claude Roux, David, Gouverneur de la Nouvelle-Calédonie et Dépendances folder, "12.12. Lettre au résident de Frances aux îles Wallis et Futuna, 19 octobre 1934. Réponse au rapport trimestriel" (1934).

19 Christophe Bonneuil, "Mettre en ordre et discipliner les Tropiques: Les Sciences du végétal dans l'Empire français, 1870–1940" (PhD thesis [history of science], Université Paris VII–Denis Diderot, 1997), 399–407 and 451–62.

20 Anne Bergeret, "Les sociétés indigènes de prévoyance du Maghreb à l'Afrique Noire: Dérive d'une institution," in *Les Techniques de conservation des grains à long terme*, vol. 3, ed. François Sigaut, Corinne Beutler, and Marceau Gast (Paris: Éditions du CNRS, 1985), 179.

21 CAOM, David, "L'œuvre du docteur David, 1933–1937, à Wallis et Futuna," 41.

22 CAOM, David, "L'œuvre du docteur David, 1933–1937, à Wallis et Futuna," 40.

23 The report of January 13, 1934, arrived on June 6. SEHNC, David, "12.5. Rapport annuel au commissaire général de la République dans l'océan Pacifique, 13 janvier 1934."

24 SEHNC, David, "12.4. Rapport trimestriel au commissaire général de la République dans l'océan Pacifique, 26 novembre 1933."

25 SEHNC, David, "12.5. Rapport annuel au commissaire général de la République dans l'océan Pacifique, 13 janvier 1934."

26 SEHNC, David, "12.11. Rapport trimestriel au commissaire général de la République en Nouvelle-Calédonie, 16 août 1934."

27 SEHNC, David, "12.7. Rapport trimestriel au commissaire général de la République en Nouvelle-Calédonie, 21 avril 1934."

28 SEHNC, David, "12.11. Rapport trimestriel au commissaire général de la République en Nouvelle-Calédonie, 16 août 1934."

29 SEHNC, Archives Jean-Claude Roux, David, Jean Joseph David folder, "12.16. Rapport trimestriel au commissaire général de la République dans l'océan Pacifique, 3 mai 1935" (1935).

30 SEHNC, Archives Jean-Claude Roux, David, Jean Joseph David folder, "12.23. Rapport trimestriel au gouverneur de Nouvelle-Calédonie, 9 août 1936" (1936).

31 This imperial project was fundamentally paradoxical, in that it was always reinvented and diverted, the athletes giving their own meaning and style to their practice, whether it be nationalistic, as among Indian cricketers (Arjun Appadurai, *Après le colonialisme: Les Conséquences culturelles de la globalisation*, trans. Françoise Bouillot [Paris: Payot, 2001], 139–68), or hedonistic, as among the dribblers in Brazzaville (Phyllis M. Martin, *Leisure and Society in Colonial Brazzaville* [Cambridge: Cambridge University Press, 1995]).

32 SEHNC, Archives Jean-Claude Roux, David, Jean Joseph David folder, "12.20. Rapport annuel au commissaire général de la République dans l'océan Pacifique, 31 décembre 1935" (1935).

33 SEHNC, Archives Jean-Claude Roux, David, Jean Joseph David folder, "12.24. Rapport annuel au commissaire général de la République dans l'océan Pacifique, 10 décembre 1936" (1936).

34 An allusion to the Argentinian soccer player Diego Maradona, considered one of the best players in the history of the game, who was known for his outstanding dribbling skills.

35 CAOM, David, "L'œuvre du docteur David, 1933–1937, à Wallis et Futuna," 52.

36 Edward Said, *Culture and Imperialism* (New York: Knopf, 1993).

37 CAOM, David, "L'œuvre du docteur David, 1933–1937, à Wallis et Futuna," 48.

38 CAOM, David, "L'œuvre du docteur David, 1933–1937, à Wallis et Futuna," 48.

39 CAOM, David, "L'œuvre du docteur David, 1933–1937, à Wallis et Futuna," 52.

40 CAOM, Viala, "Les îles Wallis et Horn: Notes de géographie médicale."

41 CAOM, Viala, "Les îles Wallis et Horn: Notes de géographie médicale," 201.

42 SEHNC, David, "12.4. Rapport trimestriel au commissaire général de la République dans l'océan Pacifique, 26 novembre 1933."

43 CAOM, David, "L'œuvre du docteur David, 1933–1937, à Wallis et Futuna," 53.

44 CAOM, David, "L'œuvre du docteur David, 1933–1937, à Wallis et Futuna," 55.

45 CAOM, Viala, 1909, cited in David, "L'œuvre du docteur David, 1933–1937, à Wallis et Futuna," 64.

46 CAOM, David, "L'œuvre du docteur David, 1933–1937, à Wallis et Futuna," 65, as well as for the quotes that follow.

47 SEHNC, Archives Jean-Claude Roux, David folder, Governor Marchessou, "12.26. Tournée du gouverneur commissaire général aux îles Wallis et Futuna, 7 octobre 1937" (1937), 5–6.

48 SEHNC, Marchessou, "12.26. Tournée du gouverneur commissaire général aux îles Wallis et Futuna, 7 octobre 1937."

49 SEHNC, Marchessou, "12.26. Tournée du gouverneur commissaire général aux îles Wallis et Futuna, 7 octobre 1937," 10. See also the account of Monsignor Alexandre Poncet, *Histoire de l'île Wallis: Le Protectorat français*, vol. 2 (Paris: Société des océanistes, 1972), 132–38.

50 Poncet, *Histoire de l'île Wallis*, 138.

51 SEHNC, Marchessou, "12.26. Tournée du gouverneur commissaire général aux îles Wallis et Futuna, 7 octobre 1937," 14.

CHAPTER 22. *I TE TEMI O* TAVITE (IN THE TIME OF DAVID)

1 François Robin, *Le Résident d'Uvéa* (Paris: Harmattan, 2012).

2 Author interview with Blaise Hoatau, Wallis, June 20, 2016, as well as for the quotes that follow.

3 Sophie Chave-Dartoen, "Uvéa (Wallis): Une société de Polynésie occidentale; Étude et comparaison" (PhD thesis [social anthropology and ethnology], École des hautes études en sciences sociales, Paris, 2000), 672–75.

4 Here, I am adding my voice to the criticisms of Vinciane Despret and Emilie Cameron regarding the increased reference to "specters" and "ghosts" in recent anthropological literature: Vinciane Despret, *Au bonheur des morts: Récits de ceux qui restent* (Paris: La Découverte, 2015); Emilie Cameron, "Indigenous Spectrality and the Politics of Postcolonial Ghost Stories," *Cultural Geographies* 15 (2008): 383–93.

5 For a developed and enriched version of the discussion that follows, please see P. Wenzel Geissler and Guillaume Lachenal, "Introduction: Brief Instructions for the Archeologists of African Futures," in *Traces of the Future: An Archeology of Medical Science in Africa*, ed. Geissler et al. (Bristol: Intellect, 2016), 15–30.

6 Laurent Olivier, "Des vestiges" (higher degree research thesis, Université Paris I, 2004), 11.

7 Olivier, "Des vestiges," 12.

8 Olivier, "Des vestiges," 12.

9 "The results may be unexpected, surprising histories with a rambling, bewildering form," warns Nancy Hunt: Nancy Rose Hunt, "Bicycles, Birth Certificates and Clysters: Colonial Objects as Reproductive Debris in Mobutu's Zaire," in *Commodification: Things, Agency, and Identities (The Social Life of Things Revisited)*, ed. Wim Van Binsbergen and Peter L. Geschiere (Münster, Germany: Lit Verlag, 2005), 124. See also Nancy

Rose Hunt, *A Colonial Lexicon: Of Birth Ritual, Medicalization, and Mobility in the Congo* (Durham, NC: Duke University Press, 1999).

10 Walter Benjamin, "On the Concept of History," in *Selected Writings, vol. 4, 1938–1940*, ed. Marcus Bullock and Michael W. Jennings (Cambridge, MA: Belknap Press, 2003), 397.

11 See, for example, John Wylie, "Landscape, Absence and the Geographies of Love," *Transactions of the Institute of British Geographers* 34 (2009): 275–89.

12 Laurent Olivier, *The Dark Abyss of Time: Archaeology and Memory*, trans. Arthur Greenspan (Lanham, MD: AltaMira Press, 2011), 49–50.

13 Olivier, "Des vestiges," 12.

14 Walter Benjamin, "Excavation and Memory," in *Selected Writings: Volume 2, 1972–1934*, ed. Marcus Bullock and Michael W. Jennings (Cambridge, MA: Belknap Press, 1999), 594.

15 Chave-Dartoen, "Uvéa (Wallis): Une société de Polynésie occidentale," 124.

16 In Wallisian, *i* is a spatial operator which can be translated as "in," so that "I te temi" has a spatial connotation.

CHAPTER 23. DOCTOR MACHETE

1 Centre des archives d'outre-mer (CAOM), BIB SOM e643, Dr. David, "L'œuvre du docteur David, 1933–1937, à Wallis et Futuna" (1938), 37.

2 Arjun Appadurai, ed., *The Social Life of Things: Commodities in Cultural Perspective* (Cambridge: Cambridge University Press, 1986), 5, cited in Nancy Rose Hunt, "Bicycles, Birth Certificates and Clysters: Colonial Objects as Reproductive Debris in Mobutu's Zaire," in *Commodification: Things, Agency, and Identities* (The social life of things revisited), ed. Wim Van Binsbergen and Peter L. Geschiere (Münster, Germany: Lit Verlag, 2005), 124.

3 A reference to the name of the French TV and radio network in overseas territories, the Société de radiodiffusion et de télévision pour l'outre-mer, renamed RFO in 1982.

4 *Cash Investigation* is a French television news show that does investigative reports on business and financial topics.

5 For the two reports (broadcast several times in July 2014 and March 2015, respectively, unfortunately not available for longer than a few weeks), see the Wallis et Futuna Ire website: http://la1ere.francetvinfo.fr/wallisfutuna /.

CHAPTER 24. BECOMING KING, PART I: COUP D'ÉTAT AT THE DISPENSARY

1 Service Historique de la Défense, Vincennes (SHDV), Archives Jean-Claude Roux, David folder, Gouverneur Siadous, "12.1. Lettre au résident de France aux îles Wallis et Futuna, 19 août 1933" (1933).

2 Romain Bertrand, "Politiques du moment colonial: Historicités indigènes et rapports vernaculaires au politique en 'situation coloniale,'" *Questions de recherche* 28 (2008), www.ceri-sciences-po.org/publica/qdr.htm. In addition to Bertrand's work on Java (Romain Bertrand, *L'Histoire à parts égales: Récits d'une rencontre Orient-Occident, XVIᵉ–XVIIᵉ siècle* [Paris: Seuil, 2011]), I am inspired by John Walker's counterhistory of the

white rajah of Sarawak (Borneo), which describes how the power of James Brooke and his successors found its source in local representations of authority and in a game of alliances between local actors, in contrast to the Victorian legend that surrounds the Brooke dynasty. John H. Walker, *Power and Prowess: The Origins of Brooke Kingship in Sarawak* (Honolulu: University of Hawai'i Press, 2002).

3 Marshall Sahlins, *Islands of History* (Chicago: University of Chicago Press, 1985).

4 Médecin-commandant J. J. David, "L'œuvre française aux îles Wallis et Futuna," *Revue des Troupes coloniales* 33, no. 265 (1939): 701–28, photo album n.p.

5 Author interview with Manuele Lisiahi and Falakika Lisiahi, Wallis, June 27, 2014.

6 SEHNC, Archives Jean-Claude Roux, David folder, Jean Joseph David "12.4. Rapport trimestriel au commissaire général de la République dans l'océan Pacifique, 26 novembre 1933."

7 "Lettre du gouverneur au résident de France, 9 mai 1931," cited in Jean-Claude Roux, "Espaces coloniaux et société polynésienne de Wallis-Futuna (Pacifique central)" (PhD diss., Université de Paris I–Panthéon-Sorbonne, 1991), 273.

8 For a good description of this, see Dominique Pechberty, "Le Kataoga," *Journal de la Société des océanistes* 106, no. 1 (1998): 75–79.

9 Cited in Centre des archives d'outre-mer (CAOM), BIB SOM e643, Dr. David, "L'œuvre du docteur David, 1933–1937, à Wallis et Futuna" (1938), 2.

10 CAOM, Dr. David, "L'œuvre du docteur David, 1933–1937, à Wallis et Futuna" (1938), 2.

11 Cited in CAOM, David, "L'œuvre du docteur David, 1933–1937, à Wallis et Futuna," 1.

12 SEHNC, David, "12.4. Rapport trimestriel au commissaire général de la République dans l'océan Pacifique, 26 novembre 1933."

13 SEHNC, David, "12.4. Rapport trimestriel au commissaire général de la République dans l'océan Pacifique, 26 novembre 1933."

14 SEHNC, David, "12.4. Rapport trimestriel au commissaire général de la République dans l'océan Pacifique, 26 novembre 1933."

15 SEHNC, Archives Jean-Claude Roux, David, Jean Joseph David folder, "Annexe au rapport trimestriel, 30 novembre 1933" (1933).

16 CAOM, David, "L'œuvre du docteur David, 1933–1937, à Wallis et Futuna," 6.

17 SEHNC, Archives Jean-Claude Roux, David folder, Jean Joseph David, "12.7. Rapport trimestriel au commissaire général de la République en Nouvelle-Calédonie, 21 avril 1934."

18 Alexandre Poncet, *Histoire de l'île Wallis: Le Protectorat français* (Paris: Société des océanistes, 1972), 116.

19 SEHNC, David, "12.7. Rapport trimestriel au commissaire général de la République en Nouvelle-Calédonie, 21 avril 1934."

20 Michel Foucault, "The Political Technology of Individuals," in *Power: Essential Works of Foucault, 1954–1984* (New York: New Press, 2000), 403–17.

21 SEHNC, David, "12.7. Rapport trimestriel au commissaire général de la République en Nouvelle-Calédonie, 21 avril 1934," as well as the quotations that follow.

22 On the role of the mission, see the concordant account of the episode by Poncet, *Histoire de l'île Wallis*, 117.

23 There is no reference to the affair in the governor's letter of March 1934. SEHNC, Archives Jean-Claude Roux, David folder, Governor Siadous, "12.6. Lettre au résident de France aux îles Wallis et Futuna, 16 mars 1934" (1934).

24 SEHNC, David, "12.7. Rapport trimestriel au commissaire général de la République en Nouvelle-Calédonie, 21 avril 1934," as well as the quotes that follow.

25 Via a simple comment, "OK," in the margin. SEHNC, Archives Jean-Claude Roux, David folder, Jean Joseph David, "12.11. Rapport trimestriel au commissaire général de la République en Nouvelle-Calédonie, 16 août 1934" (1934).

26 SEHNC, Archives Jean-Claude Roux, David folder, Jean Joseph David, "12.5. Rapport annuel au commissaire général de la République dans l'océan Pacifique, 13 janvier 1934."

27 SEHNC, David, "12.7. Rapport trimestriel au commissaire général de la République en Nouvelle-Calédonie, 21 avril 1934."

28 CAOM, David, "L'œuvre du docteur David, 1933–1937, à Wallis et Futuna," 10, 19. On "liberation," see p. 26.

CHAPTER 25. BECOMING KING, PART II: THE WALLISIAN ART OF GOVERNING

1 Alexandre Poncet, *Histoire de l'île Wallis: Le Protectorat français* (Paris: Société des océanistes, 1972), 117.

2 Centre des archives d'outre-mer (CAOM), BIB SOM e643, Dr. David, "L'œuvre du docteur David, 1933–1937, à Wallis et Futuna," 1938.

3 Societe d'Etudes Historiques de Nouvelle Caledonie (SEHNC), Archives Jean-Claude Roux, David, Jean Joseph David folder, "12.4. Rapport trimestriel au commissaire général de la République dans l'océan Pacifique, 26 novembre 1933".

4 Author interview with Sister Malekalita Falelavaki, Wallis, June 18, 2014.

5 SEHNC, Archives Jean-Claude Roux, David, Jean Joseph David folder, "12.11. Rapport trimestriel au commissaire général de la République en Nouvelle-Calédonie, 16 août 1934."

6 Sophie Chave-Dartoen, "Le Paradoxe wallisien: Une royauté dans la République," *Ethnologie française* 32, no. 4 (2002): 638.

7 Author interview with Siolesio (Sioli) Pilioko, Wallis, June 22, 2014.

8 Alice Fromonteil, interview with Patita Lakina, Wallis, June 2014, personal communication, as well as the quotes that follow. *Custom* (in the singular) refers broadly to the Wallisian culture and more specifically to the set of hierarchical relations and obligations that defines the chiefdom and kingdom institutions (see chapter 20).

9 Jean-Claude Roux, "Espaces coloniaux et société polynésienne de Wallis-Futuna (Pacifique central)" (PhD diss., Université de Paris I–Panthéon-Sorbonne, 1991), 261.

10 For a summary, see Jean-Claude Roux, "Pouvoir religieux et pouvoir politique à Wallis et Futuna," in *États et pouvoirs dans les territoires français du Pacifique: Nouvelle-Calédonie, Polynésie française, Vanuatu, Wallis et Futuna; Schémas d'évolution* [Proceedings of two-day workshop, Paris, May 7, 1985], eds. Paul de Deckker and Pierre Lagayette (Paris: Harmattan, 1987), 54–80. For the nineteenth century see, in particular, Roux, "Espaces coloniaux et société polynésienne de Wallis-Futuna (Pacifique central)," 30–36, 75–99, 224–27.

11 SEHNC, David, "12.11. Rapport trimestriel au commissaire général de la République en Nouvelle-Calédonie, 16 août 1934."

12 SEHNC, Archives Jean-Claude Roux, David folder Protectorat des îles Wallis et Futuna, "12.19. Lois wallisiennes déterminant certains rapports entre la mission catholique et ses fidèles" (1935).

13 CAOM, David, "L'œuvre du docteur David, 1933-1937, à Wallis et Futuna."

14 SEHNC, David, "12.11. Rapport trimestriel au commissaire général de la République en Nouvelle-Calédonie, 16 août 1934."

15 CAOM, David, "L'œuvre du docteur David, 1933-1937, à Wallis et Futuna," 15-16.

16 Poncet, Histoire de l'île Wallis, 127.

17 Poncet, Histoire de l'île Wallis, 141.

18 Author nterview with Sister Malekalita Falelavaki, Wallis, June 18, 2014.

19 For example, CAOM, David, "L'œuvre du docteur David, 1933-1937, à Wallis et Futuna," 16. Governor Marchessou provided an annotation regarding the management of the Wallisian government: "And this is precisely where Dr. David's ability and perseverance triumph." CAOM, David, "L'œuvre du docteur David, 1933-1937, à Wallis et Futuna," 11.

20 Roux, "Pouvoir religieux et pouvoir politique à Wallis et Futuna," 76.

21 Note, however, that there are debates in the present day in Wallis regarding this issue, and that even Monsignor Poncet was ambiguous about it: Poncet, Histoire de l'île Wallis, 121.

22 SEHNC, David, "12.4. Rapport trimestriel au commissaire général de la République dans l'océan Pacifique, 26 novembre 1933," 5.

23 SEHNC, David, "12.4. Rapport trimestriel au commissaire général de la République dans l'océan Pacifique, 26 novembre 1933," 8.

24 Poncet, Histoire de l'île Wallis, 117n1.

25 CAOM, David, "L'œuvre du docteur David, 1933-1937, à Wallis et Futuna," 9.

26 Author interview with Sioli Pilioko, Wallis, June 22, 2014.

27 SEHNC, Archives Jean-Claude Roux, David folder, Protectorat des îles Wallis et Futuna, "12.18. Réglement du 10 septembre 1935" (1935).

28 Poncet, Histoire de l'île Wallis, 121.

29 CAOM, David, "L'œuvre du docteur David, 1933-1937, à Wallis et Futuna," 11.

30 SEHNC, Archives Jean-Claude Roux, Jean Joseph David folder, "12.24. Rapport annuel au commissaire général de la République dans l'océan Pacifique, 10 décembre" (1936).

CHAPTER 26. BECOMING KING, PART III: KICKING CUSTOM TO THE CURB

1 See Jean-François Bayart's recent work on West Africa: Jean-François Bayart, "Les chemins de traverse de l'hégémonie coloniale en Afrique de l'Ouest francophone: Anciens esclaves, anciens combattants, nouveaux musulmans," Politique africaine, no. 105 (2007): 201-40. And, more generally, on the subject of the colonial period as a "reshuffling of the cards" in colonized societies, see Jean-François Bayart, L'État en Afrique: La Politique du ventre (Paris: Fayard, 1989), 144.

2 Centre des archives d'outre-mer (CAOM), BIB SOM e643, Dr. David, "L'œuvre du docteur David, 1933-1937, à Wallis et Futuna" (1938), 11.

3 For all quotes in this paragraph, see CAOM, David, "L'œuvre du docteur David, 1933–1937, à Wallis et Futuna," 4–5.

4 Archives de la mission de Lano (Archives of the Lano Mission), DVIIId, Poncet, Alexandre Poncet files, "Notes du 17 et du 22 juillet 1937" (1937).

5 CAOM, David, "L'œuvre du docteur David, 1933–1937, à Wallis et Futuna," 14, as well as the quotes that follow, 14–15.

6 According to oral tradition. Author interview with Emeni Simete, Wallis, June 24, 2014.

7 Marshall Sahlins, "The Stranger-King, or Elementary Forms of the Politics of Life," *Indonesia and the Malay World* 36, no. 105 (2008): 184.

8 Marshall Sahlins, "The Stranger-King, or Dumézil among the Fijians," *Journal of Pacific History* 16, no. 3 (1981): 112.

9 Sahlins, "The Stranger-King, or Duzémil among the Fijians," 113.

10 I also refer to Alice Fromonteil's work in progress on oral literature in Wallis, which has collected, translated, and analyzed several myths of stranger-kings and -queens, in which royalty is acquired by cunning or force, and by insulting custom (and in particular, the *tanoa* used to prepare kava). See, in particular, "Lekapai, Tai-Panakihi & l'écaille de la tortue Hagone," "Le voyage de Hina," and "La légende du voyage de Hāvea-Fakatoke vers Pulotu" (Alice Fromonteil, personal communication, 2016).

11 Sahlins, "The Stranger-King, or Dumézil among the Fijians," 80.

CHAPTER 27. TE HAU TAVITE

1 Alexandre Poncet, *Histoire de l'île Wallis: Le Protectorat français* (Paris: Société des océanistes, 1972), chapter 17, 115–22.

2 Poncet, *Histoire de l'île Wallis*, 125.

3 Philippe Godard, *Wallis et Futuna* (Nouméa: Éditions Mélanésia, 1983), quoted in *Tāvaka lanu'imoana: Mémoires de voyage*, ed. Malia Sosefo Drouet-Manufekai (Nouméa: Agence de Développement de la Culture Kanak, Centre Culturel Tjibaou, Comité de Recherche Historique Tāvaka, 2009); Richard Rossille, *Le Kava à Wallis et Futuna: Survivance d'un breuvage océanien traditionnel* (Talence, France: Centre de recherches sur les espaces tropicaux, 1986), 79.

4 Author conversation with Lagimaina Hoatau and Atoloto Uhila, Wallis, June 29, 2014.

5 Mikaele Tui, "La chefferie," in *Uvea*, ed. Elise Huffer and Mikaele Tui (Suva, Fiji: Wallis, Institute of Pacific Studies, University of the South Pacific, Service des affaires culturelles de Wallis, 2004), 8–14.

6 Niel Gunson, "The Hau Concept of Leadership in Western Polynesia," *Journal of Pacific History* 14, no. 1 (1979): 28–49. This is not to be confused with the Samoan *hau* made famous by Marcel Mauss, which signifies "the force in the thing given"—although the terms are no doubt related.

7 Sophie Chave-Dartoen, "Uvéa (Wallis): Une société de Polynésie occidentale; Étude et comparaison" (PhD diss. [social anthropology and ethnology], École des hautes études en sciences sociales, Paris, 2000).

8 Author interview with Bernadette Papilio-Halagahu, June 16, 2014.

9 See, for example, Florence Flament, "Rapport final sur la santé des élèves à Wallis et Futuna: Étude réalisée en mai 2015," WHO, Global School-Based Student Health Survey (GSHS) (2015), accessed September 16, 2016, www.who.int/chp/gshs/gshs-report -wallis-futuna-2015.pdf.

10 Author interview with Michel Aubouin, Wallis, June 16, 2014.

11 Author interview with Jean-Baptiste Mulikihaamea, Wallis, June 21, 2014, as well as the quotes that follow.

12 Sophie Chave-Dartoen's analysis of the importance of personal qualities (bravery, industriousness, technical skills) in the distinction of men is particularly illuminating: Chave-Dartoen, "Uvéa (Wallis): Une société de Polynésie occidentale," 535–46. She relates stories that attribute the origins of royalty (hau) and noble lineages ('aliki) to particularly brave warriors who acquired the status by distinguishing themselves both in combat and in the leadership of their communities (540–41).

13 Dominique Pechberty and Epifania Toa, Vivre la coutume à 'Uvea, Wallis: Tradition et modernité à 'Uvea = Aga'i fenua o 'Uvea (Paris: Harmattan, 2004), 259.

14 Here, I take my inspiration from John Walker's approach in his work on the white rajah of Sarawak, which demonstrates how "Booke's role and position in Sarawak were, in key ways, constructed by local people to reflect their own objectives and priorities." John H. Walker, Power and Prowess: The Origins of Brooke Kingship in Sarawak (Honolulu: University of Hawai'i Press, 2002), xx.

15 Chave-Dartoen, "Uvéa (Wallis): Une société de Polynésie occidentale," 538.

16 The classic article is Marshall Sahlins, "The Stranger-King, or Dumézil among the Fijians," Journal of Pacific History 16, no. 3 (1981): 107–32. For more recent studies that further discuss Sahlins's statements on the universality of the motif of the stranger-king, see Ian Caldwell and David Henley, "Introduction: The Stranger Who Would Be King," Indonesia and the Malay World 36, no. 105 (2008): 163–75; Sahlins, "The Stranger-King, or Elementary Forms of the Politics of Life," 177–99.

17 Jean-Claude Roux, "Espaces coloniaux et société polynésienne de Wallis-Futuna (Pacifique central)" (PhD diss., Université de Paris I–Panthéon-Sorbonne, 1991), 260–67.

18 I thank Marylin Strathern for sharing this remark.

19 Author conversation with Manuele Lisiahi and Falakika Lisiahi, Wallis, June 27, 2014.

20 Archives de la mission de Lano, DVIIId, Poncet notebooks, Alexandre Poncet, "Notes sur la conversation avec le gouverneur Siadous, 25 avril 1936 à Nouméa" (1936).

CHAPTER 28. TAVITE LEA TAHI (DAVID-ONLY-SPEAKS-ONCE)

1 For example, author interview with Sioli Pilioko, June 22, 2014; author interview with Blaise Hoatau, June 20, 2014.

2 On sometimes "dream-like" memories of colonial violence, see Nancy Rose Hunt, "Espace, temporalité et rêverie: Écrire l'histoire des futurs au Congo belge," Politique africaine 3, no. 135 (2014): 115–36.

3 Once again, I thank Alice Fromonteil for informing me of the importance attributed to this clothing technique in Wallis, and about the fact that clownish figures pretend to tie it wrong or make it fall off to get a laugh.

4 Author interview with Michel Hoatau, Wallis, June 30, 2014, as well as the quotes that follow.

5 Author interview with Emeni Simete, June 24, 2014.

6 Jean-Claude Roux, "Espaces coloniaux et société polynésienne de Wallis-Futuna (Pacifique central)" (PhD diss., Université de Paris I–Panthéon-Sorbonne, 1991), ii.

7 Author interview with Mikaele Tui, Roissy-Charles-de-Gaulle, July 9, 2014.

8 Author interview with Mikaele Tui, Roissy-Charles-de-Gaulle, July 9, 2014.

9 Author interview with Michel Hoatau, Wallis, June 30, 2014; author interview with Emeni Simete, Wallis, June 24, 2014; Archives de la mission de Lano, DV IIId, Poncet Notebooks, Alexandre Poncet, "Notes sur la conversation avec le gouverneur Siadous, 25 avril 1936 à Nouméa," April 8, 1937; Archives of the Marist Fathers, Rome, OW 208, Father Marquet, "Lettre à la Maison générale des maristes, 1 mai 1937" (1937).

10 On this notion, I refer you to the essay by Jean-François Bayart, "Annexe méthodologique: Pour des biographies sans sujet," in Le Plan Q: Ethnographie d'une pratique sexuelle (Paris: Fayard, 2014), 141–63.

11 Bayart, "Annexe méthodologique," 162.

12 Wallis, Archives de l'Administration Supérieure, "Lettre du roi et des ministres au gouverneur, 27 octobre 1952" (1952), 3.

13 Franklin J. Schaffner, Patton, 20th Century Fox, 1970.

14   Through the travail of ages,
       Midst the pomp and toils of war,
       Have I fought and strove and perished
       Countless times among the stars.

       As if through a glass, and darkly
       The age-old strife I see—
       Where I fought in many guises, many names—
       but always me.

   This version of the poem, which appears in the film, is actually the second and twenty-second stanzas (with minor changes) of the poem "Through a Glass, Darkly," written by General George Patton in 1922. The film version was transcribed on a website about reincarnation, accessed September 15, 2016, www.reversespins.com/patton .html. The scene set in the ruins of Carthage that inspires Patton's declamation can be viewed on YouTube, accessed September 15, 2016, https://www.youtube.com/watch ?v=XRoMjoxK5v4. The original version of the poem can be found here: George S. Patton, The Poems of General George S. Patton, Jr.: Lines of Fire, ed. Carmine A. Prioli (Lewiston, NY: Edwin Mellen, 1991), 118–22.

15 François Hartog, Regimes of Historicity: Presentism and Experiences of Time, trans. Saskia Brown (New York: Columbia University Press, 2015), 34, commenting on Marshall Sahlins, Islands of History (Chicago: University of Chicago Press, 1985).

16 Hartog, *Regimes of Historicity*, 34, 35, 37.

17 Hartog, *Regimes of Historicity*, 33, 34, 34–35.

18 Author interview with Jean-Baptiste Mulikihaamea, Wallis, June 28, 2014.

CHAPTER 29. DOCTOR DISASTER

1 Alexandre Poncet, *Histoire de l'île Wallis: Le Protectorat français* (Paris: Société des océanistes, 1972), 118.

2 Poncet, *Histoire de l'île Wallis*, 118.

3 Poncet, *Histoire de l'île Wallis*, 141.

4 Mikaele Tui, "La chefferie," in *Uvea*, ed. Elise Huffer and Mikaele Tui (Suva, Fiji: Institute of Pacific Studies, University of the South Pacific, Service des Affaires Culturelles de Wallis, 2004), 12.

5 Virginie Tafilagi, "Le discours sur *l'aga'i fenua* ou la coutume à Uvea," in *Uvea*, ed. E. Huffer and M. Tui (Suva, Fiji: Institute of Pacific Studies, University of the South Pacific, Service des Affaires Culturelles de Wallis, 2004), 28–39 (28).

6 Jean-François Bayart, "Hégémonie et coercition en Afrique subsaharienne: La 'Politique de la chicotte,'"*Politique africaine* 110, no. 2 (2008): 123–52.

7 Societe d'Etudes Historiques de Nouvelle Caledonie (SEHNC), Archives Jean-Claude Roux, David folder, J. J. David, "12.22. Rapport trimestriel au gouverneur de Nouvelle-Calédonie, 11 mai 1936" (1936).

8 Archives de la mission de Lano, DVIIId, Poncet notebooks, Alexandre Poncet, "Cahier 1936–1937" (1937).

9 Archives of the Marist Fathers, Rome, OW 208, Father Marquet, "Lettre à la Maison générale des maristes, 1 mai 1937" (1937).

10 Marquet, "Lettre à la Maison générale des maristes, 7 octobre 1934" (1934).

11 Poncet, "Cahier 1936–1937."

12 Archives de la Mission de Lano, DVIIID, Poncet notebooks, Alexandre Poncet, "Notes sur la conversation avec le gouverneur Siadous, 25 avril 1936 à Nouméa" (1936).

13 Poncet, "Cahier 1936–1937."

14 Poncet, "Notes sur la conversation avec le gouverneur Siadous, 25 avril 1936 à Nouméa" (April 8, 1937).

15 Archives of the Marist Fathers, Rome, OW 208, Father Marquet, "Lettre à la Maison générale des maristes, 20 janvier 1938" (1938).

16 Archives de la mission de Lano, DVIIc, Correspondances avec les gouverneurs de Nouvelle-Calédonie, Alexandre Poncet, "Rapport présenté respectueusement par Mgr Poncet, vicaire apostolique des îles Wallis et Futuna, à Son Excellence le Gouverneur de Nouvelle-Calédonie" (1939).

17 Poncet, "Rapport présenté respectueusement par Mgr Poncet, 9.

18 Poncet, "Rapport présenté respectueusement par Mgr Poncet," 1.

19 Poncet, "Rapport présenté respectueusement par Mgr Poncet," 24.

20 Poncet, "Rapport présenté respectueusement par Mgr Poncet," 8.

21 Poncet, "Rapport présenté respectueusement par Mgr Poncet," 3.

22 Poncet, "Rapport présenté respectueusement par Mgr Poncet," 3.

23 Sophie Chave-Dartoen, "Uvéa (Wallis): Une société de Polynésie occidentale; Étude et comparaison" (PhD diss. [social anthropology and ethnology], École des hautes études en sciences sociales, Paris, 2000), 758.

24 SEHNC, Archives Jean-Claude Roux, David folder, Jean Joseph David, "12.16. Rapport trimestriel au commissaire général de la République dans l'océan Pacifique, 3 mai 1935" (1935).

25 Poncet, "Rapport présenté respectueusement par Mgr Poncet," 17.

26 Poncet, "Rapport présenté respectueusement par Mgr Poncet," 17.

27 Poncet, "Rapport présenté respectueusement par Mgr Poncet," 25.

28 Marquet, "Lettre à la Maison générale des maristes, 20 janvier 1938."

29 Author interview with Michel Hoatau, June 30, 2014.

30 François Hartog, "Marshall Sahlins et l'anthropologie de l'histoire," Annales ESC 38, no. 6 (1983): 1259. I would like to thank Alice Fromonteil for providing me with this interpretation of mythical narratives as articulated at a time of crisis, which also marks, according to her informants, a break in oral transmission.

31 Poncet, "Rapport présenté respectueusement par Mgr Poncet," 16.

32 Centre des archives d'outre-mer (CAOM), BIB SOM e643, Dr. David, "L'œuvre du docteur David, 1933–1937, à Wallis et Futuna" (1938), 39.

33 CAOM, David, "L'œuvre du docteur David, 1933–1937, à Wallis et Futuna," 38.

34 Sophie Chave-Dartoen, "Le Paradoxe wallisien: Une royauté dans la République," Ethnologie française 32, no. 4 (2002): 638.

35 Hélène Guiot, "Forêt taboue et représentations de l'environnement à 'Uvea (Wallis): Approche ethno-archéologique," Journal de la Société des océanistes 2, no. 107 (1998): 181.

36 Quoted in Guiot, "Forêt taboue et représentations de l'environnement à 'Uvea (Wallis)," 181.

37 Guiot, "Forêt taboue et représentations de l'environnement à 'Uvea (Wallis)," 192.

38 Poncet, "Cahier 1936–1937," August 3, 1936. Poncet also wrote in 1945 that it had been a "very grave mistake" to burn the vao matua. Archives de la mission de Lano, DVIIId, Poncet notebooks, Alexandre Poncet, "Cahier 1945" (1945).

39 See, for example, in the colonial medical literature, Dr. Lefèvre: "Quelques notes sur la fièvre typhoïde qui sévit chaque année dans la caserne d'infanterie en Nouvelle-Calédonie," Annales d'hygiène et de médecine coloniales 3 (1903): 312–16; Dr. Lefèvre, "Chroniques documentaires: Les maladies transmissibles dans les colonies françaises et territoires sous mandat pendant l'année 1930 (suite); Par M. le Dr Lefèvre; Fièvre typhoïde," Annales d'hygiène et de médecine coloniales 30 (1932): 552–55.

40 Poncet, "Cahier 1936–1937" (August 12, 1936).

41 Poncet, "Cahier 1936–1937" (December 13, 1936).

42 CAOM, Archives Jean-Claude Roux, David, Jean Joseph David folder, "L'œuvre du docteur David, 1933–1937, à Wallis et Futuna," 56.

43 SEHNC, Archives Jean-Claude Roux, David, Jean Joseph David folder, "12.23. Rapport trimestriel au gouverneur de Nouvelle-Calédonie, 9 août 1936."

44 Poncet, "Cahier 1936–1937" (January 21, 1937).

45 Poncet, "Cahier 1936–1937" (January 28, 1937).

46 Poncet, *Histoire de l'île Wallis*, 131.

47 Author interviews with Emeni Simete, June 2014.

48 Poncet, "Cahier 1936–1937" (April 10, 1937).

49 Michel Foucault, "Of Other Spaces: Utopias and Heterotopias," in *Rethinking Architecture: A Reader in Cultural Theory*, ed. Neil Leach (New York: Routledge, 1997), 330–36.

50 Poncet, "Cahier 1936–1937" (April 16, 1937).

51 Marquet, "Lettre à la Maison générale des maristes, 1 mai 1937."

52 Poncet, "Cahier 1936–1937" (April 18, 1937).

53 Poncet, "Cahier 1936–1937" (June 24, 1937).

54 CAOM, David, "L'œuvre du docteur David, 1933–1937, à Wallis et Futuna," 56.

55 Poncet, "Rapport présenté respectueusement par Mgr Poncet," 14.

56 Jean-Claude Roux, "Espaces coloniaux et société polynésienne de Wallis-Futuna (Pacifique central)" (PhD diss., Université de Paris I–Panthéon-Sorbonne, 1991), 552.

57 CAOM, David, "L'œuvre du docteur David, 1933–1937, à Wallis et Futuna," 56.

58 CAOM, David, "L'œuvre du docteur David, 1933–1937, à Wallis et Futuna," 57.

CHAPTER 30. AFELIKA (AFRICA)

1 Author interview with Jean-Baptiste Mulikihaamea, Wallis, June 21, 2014.

2 SEHNC, Archives Jean-Claude Roux, Lamy folder, Dr. Lamy, "13.1. Lettre au gouverneur de Nouvelle-Calédonie, 22 mars 1938" (1938).

3 Alexandre Poncet, *Histoire de l'île Wallis: Le Protectorat français* (Paris: Société des Océanistes, 1972), 114.

4 Archives of the Marist Fathers, Rome, OW 208, Père Marquet, "Lettre à la Maison générale des maristes, 1er mai 1937" (1937).

5 SEHNC, Lamy, "13.1. Lettre au gouverneur de Nouvelle-Calédonie, 22 mars 1938."

6 Archives de la mission de Lano, DVIIc, "Lettre à Mgr Poncet, reçue le 8 février 1940" (1940).

7 Archives de la mission de Lano, DVIIc, "Lettre à Mgr Poncet, 6 janvier 1939" (1939).

8 Personal archives of J.-B. Mulikihaamea, "*Malamanei (Nouméa), no. 17, novembre 1979*," 2–4.

9 Centre des archives d'outre-mer (CAOM), BIB SOM e643, Dr. David, "L'œuvre du docteur David, 1933–1937, à Wallis et Futuna," 1938, 1–2.

10 Dr. Martial, "La protection de l'enfance dans les colonies françaises, rapport présenté par le Dr Martial," *Bulletin de l'Académie de médecine* 118 (1937): 742–54; Médaille d'argent du Service de l'hygiène de l'enfance, "Séance du 13 décembre 1938," *Bulletin de l'Académie nationale de médecine* 120 (1938): 461.

11 "Îles Wallis: Ces îles lointaines connaissent une douce prospérité (extrait de *La Nouvelle Dépêche*)," *La Revue du Pacifique* 15, no. 1 (1936): 244–46; "Protectorat français des îles Wallis et Futuna," *La Revue du Pacifique* 14, no. 7 (1935): 697–98.

12 J. J. David, "L'œuvre française aux îles Wallis et Futuna," *Revue des Troupes coloniales* 33, no. 265 (1939): 701–28.

13 Jean Joseph David, "Une œuvre française aux îles Wallis et Futuna," in *Les Grandes endémies tropicales: Huit conférences faites au grand amphithéâtre de la Faculté de médecine de Paris du 17 avril au 3 mai 1939* (Paris: Vigo Frères, 1939), 72.

14 David, "Une œuvre française aux îles Wallis et Futuna," 91.

15 Quoted in David, "Une œuvre française aux îles Wallis et Futuna," 30.

16 Romain Bertrand, *Le Long Remords de la conquête: Manille-Mexico-Madrid—L'affaire Diego de Ávila (1577-1580)* (Paris: Seuil, 2015).

17 Sahlins's work has given rise to long, sometimes heated, and somewhat fruitless debates as to whether the deification of Captain Cook is, as Sahlins argues, a mythical interpretation of Cook's arrival by the Hawaiians (who "took" him for a god) and thus a "cultural misunderstanding" or, as Sahlins's main critic Obeyesekere argues, entirely understandable in terms of "universal" practical rationality. Gananath Obeyesekere, *The Apotheosis of Captain Cook: European Mythmaking in the Pacific* (Princeton, NJ: Princeton University Press, 1992). In any case, it is clear that Cook "took" himself for someone else, intoxicated by the tributes of the Hawaiians or by his own imperialist dreams. Francis Zimmermann, among others, wrote about this controversy: Zimmermann, "Sahlins, Obeyesekere et la mort du capitaine Cook," *L'Homme* 38, no. 146 (1998): 191-205.

18 Yves Cohen recently studied the creation of leadership figures in the twentieth century. He rightly emphasizes the importance of colonial military cultures (around the figure of Lyautey, for example) but does not explore the interplay of borrowings with (to put it plainly) non-Western constructions and stylizations of authority. Yves Cohen, *Le Siècle des chefs: Une histoire transnationale du commandement et de l'autorité (1891-1940)* (Paris: Éditions Amsterdam, 2013). For discussions on European imperialism as a matrix of subjectivation, of the "stylization" of existence, see Jean-François Bayart, *Le Gouvernement du monde: Une critique politique de la globalisation* (Paris: Fayard, 2004).

19 Carmine A. Prioli, "King Arthur in Khaki: The Medievalism of General George S. Patton, Jr.," *Studies in Popular Culture* 10, no. 1 (1987): 42-50.

20 F. J. Schaffner, *Patton*. Patton's "Poem" in the film *Patton*, accessed September 15, 2016, www.reversespins.com/patton.html.

21 Jean-Claude Roux, "Espaces coloniaux et société polynésienne de Wallis-Futuna (Pacifique central)" (PhD diss., Université de Paris I–Panthéon-Sorbonne, 1991), 825.

22 Marshall Sahlins, "Captain James Cook; or, the Dying God," in *Islands of History* (Chicago: University of Chicago Press, 1985), 134.

23 Birth certificates, Jean Joseph David and Elizabeth de Louvencourt.

24 Maxime Robert Charbonnier, *Chronique d'un séjour mouvementé aux îles Wallis et Futuna dans le Pacifique en guerre: Témoignage d'un résident de France, 1944-46* (Paris: M. R. Charbonnier, 1987), 27. Document accessed at the Bibliothèque Nationale de France (BNF). Other slightly different versions of Dr. Charbonnier's account exist in the Archives of the Marist Fathers in Rome and at the CAOM.

25 On this episode, see Poncet, *Histoire de l'île Wallis*, 162-81. For a literary exploration, see François Robin, *Le Résident d'Uvéa* (Paris: Harmattan, 2012).

26 Archives de la mission de Lano, DVIIId, Poncet notebooks, "Extrait de 'notes on Wallis Island' by Major Soper—Nov. 1943, recopié par Mgr Poncet" (1939).

27 Frédéric Angleviel, "Wallis-et-Futuna (1942-1961), ou comment le fait migratoire transforma le protectorat en TOM," *Journal de la Société des océanistes*, nos. 122-23 (2006): 61.

28 Maxime Robert Charbonnier, *Chronique d'un séjour mouvementé aux îles Wallis et Futuna dans le Pacifique en guerre: Témoignage d'un résident de France, 1944-46* (Rome: Archives of the Marist Fathers, preliminary edition, 1988), 210.

CHAPTER 31. DACHAU, INDOCHINA

1 Jean-Christophe Notin, *Les vaincus seront les vainqueurs: Les Français en Allemagne (1945)* (Paris: Perrin, 2004).

2 Arnulf Moser, *Die andere Mainau 1945: Paradies für befreite KZ-Häftlinge* (Constance, Germany: UVK, 1995).

3 "Les Français de Dachau seront transférés dans une île du lac de Constance," *Le Monde*, May 21, 1945.

4 "Le rapatriement des déportés francaise par la 1re armée," *Revue d'information des troupes françaises d'occupation en Allemagne*, no. 23 (1947): 23–25.

5 Jean-Claude Roux, *Wallis et Futuna: Espaces et temps recomposés; Chroniques d'une micro-insularité* (Talence, France: Centre de Recherche sur les Espaces Tropicaux, 1995), 825.

6 Personal archives of the David family, "Relevé des notes du médecin colonel David," 1953.

7 Maurice Lamy, Michel Lamotte, and Suzanne Lamotte-Barrillon, *La Dénutrition: Clinique—biologie—thérapeutique* (Paris: G. Doin, 1948), n.p.

8 Moser, *Die andere Mainau*, 83.

9 Lamy, Lamotte, and Lamotte-Barrillon, *La Dénutrition*, n.p.

10 The Nationalsozialistische Deutsche Arbeiterpartei.

11 Guillaume Lachenal, "Médecine, comparaisons et échanges inter-impériaux dans le mandat camerounais: Une histoire croisée franco-allemande de la mission Jamot," *Bulletin canadien d'histoire de la médecine* 30, no 2 (2013); on the liberation of Dachau, see Jean-Christophe Notin, *Les vaincus seront les vainqueurs: Les Français en Allemagne (1945)* (Paris: Perrin, 2004), 424.

12 The link between rubber and sleeping sickness has been identified in several regions of Côte d'Ivoire and caused populations to flee. Danielle Domergue-Cloarec, *La Santé en Côte d'Ivoire, 1905-1958* (Toulouse, France: Publications de l'Université de Toulouse-le-Mirail, 1986), 763, 768–69, 773.

13 Nancy Lawler, "Reform and Repression under the Free French: Economic and Political Transformation in the Cote d'Ivoire, 1942-45," *Africa* 60, no. 1 (1990): 88–110.

14 On this subject, see Guillaume Lachenal, *The Lomidine Files: The Untold Story of a Medical Disaster in Colonial Africa* (Baltimore: Johns Hopkins University Press, 2017), 42–56. On Côte d'Ivoire in particular, see Domergue-Cloarec, *La Santé en Côte d'Ivoire*, 855–82.

15 Centre d'Accueil et de Recherche aux Archives Nationales (hereafter cited as CARAN), Paris, AOF Fonds, 200 MI 1891, Médecin colonel David, "Côte d'Ivoire—Direction locale de la santé publique—Rapport annuel 1948" (1950), 6.

16 CARAN, AOF Fonds, David, "Côte d'Ivoire—Direction locale de la santé publique—Rapport annuel 1948" (1950), 27.

17 CARAN, AOF Fonds, 200 MI 3538, Côte d'Ivoire—Santé publique, "Correspondances" (1950).

18 Domergue-Cloarec, *La Santé en Côte d'Ivoire*, 663.

19 CARAN, AOF Fonds, 200 MI 1871, Médecin colonel Urvois, "Côte d'Ivoire—Service de santé—Rapport annuel 1946" (1947), 79.

20 "Rapport annuel du Service de santé de Côte d'Ivoire pour l'année 1943," quoted in Domergue-Cloarec, La Santé en Côte d'Ivoire, 663.

21 Adolphe Sicé, "Rôle social du médecin colonial en Afrique française," Médecine tropicale 4 (1944): 189.

22 CARAN, AOF, 200 MI 1871, Médecin colonel Urvois, "Côte d'Ivoire—Service de santé—Rapport annuel 1946" (1947), 82.

23 For a discussion of the epidemic of unruliness in the colonies, see Lachenal, The Lomidine Files, 51–53.

24 CARAN, AOF Fonds, Urvois, "Côte d'Ivoire—Service de santé—Rapport annuel 1946," 82.

25 CARAN, AOF Fonds, Urvois, "Côte d'Ivoire—Service de santé—Rapport annuel 1946," 78.

26 CARAN, AOF Fonds, Urvois, "Côte d'Ivoire—Service de santé—Rapport annuel 1946," 77.

27 CARAN, AOF Fonds, 200 MI 1880, Médecin colonel David, "Côte d'Ivoire—Direction locale de la santé publique—Rapport annuel 1947" (1948), 66.

28 CARAN, AOF Fonds, David, "Côte d'Ivoire—Direction locale de la santé publique—Rapport annuel 1947," 62.

29 CARAN, AOF Fonds, David, "Côte d'Ivoire—Direction locale de la santé publique—Rapport annuel 1947," 67.

30 CARAN, AOF Fonds, David, "Côte d'Ivoire—Direction locale de la santé publique—Rapport annuel 1948," 62.

31 On colonial repression in Côte d'Ivoire, one can refer to the famous "Rapport" (over one thousand pages) written in 1950 by the deputy Léon Gontran Damas, "No. 11348. Rapport fait au nom de la commission chargée d'enquêter sur les incidents survenus en Côte-d'Ivoire, par M. Damas (1950)," in Assemblée nationale: 1re législature; Impressions, projets de lois, propositions, rapports (Paris: Assemblée nationale, 1951). Colonel David is mentioned on page 247 regarding the inspection of prisoners who staged a hunger strike in Bassam.

32 Service Historique de la Défense, Vincennes (SHDV), GR 2000 Z 205, 01707, "Dossier personnel Colonel David, Joseph Jean" (1966).

33 Journal officiel de la République française (April 25, 1951), 4153.

34 Hélène Carré-Tornézy, Infirmière en Indochine 1950-1952: D'amour et de détresse (Panazol, France: Lavauzelle, 1999), 94.

35 "Relevé des notes du médecin colonel David."

36 "Le Vietminh effectue un coup de main sur la station de repos du Cap-St-Jacques considérée comme centre hospitalier: Vingt et une personnes tuées et vingt-trois bléssées," Le Monde, July 24, 1952, www.lemonde.fr/archives/article/1952/07/24/le-vietminh-effectue-un-coup-de-main-sur-la-station-de-repos-du-cap-saint-jacques-consideree-comme-centre-hospitalier-vingt-et-une-personnes-tuees-et-vingt-trois-blessees_3030693_1819218.html. For a good description of the ambience at Cap Saint Jacques as seen through the eyes of a nurse, see Carré-Tornézy, Infirmière en Indochine, 1950-1952.

1 Édouard Tamba, "Émeutes à Abong-Mbang: Le calvaire des familles et des victimes," *Le Messager*, September 21, 2007; Édouard Tamba, "Le film des émeutes à Abong-Mbang," "Abong-Mbang, au cœur du sinistre," "Les non-dits sur les émeutes d'Abong-Mbang," *Le Messager*, September 25, 2007, blog post, accessed September 12, 2016, http://edouardtamba.centerblog.net/rub-Emeutes-a-Abong-Mbang.html. The "days of anger" have recently become an object of study for historians and politicians. See especially, on the subject of Burkina Faso, Vincent Bonnecase, "Ce que les ruines racontent d'une insurrection," *Sociétés politiques comparées*, no. 38 (2016), http://www.fasopo.org/sites/default/files/varia2_n38.pdf.

2 Edouard Tamba, "Émeutes à Abong-Mbang."

3 Laurent Olivier, *The Dark Abyss of Time: Archaeology and Memory* (Lanham, MD: AltaMira Press, 2011), 105.

4 Paul Veyne, *Writing History: Essay on Epistemology* (Middletown, CT: Wesleyan University Press, 1984), 13.

5 On mutilation as the necessary condition for the existence of the witnesses of the past, see Laurent Olivier's interesting reflection: "The past that emerges for us, because it is preserved, is withdrawn from us at that very same movement. For something tangible to come down to us, everything around it had to have disappeared without leaving any trace; for this something to be preserved, it had to have been physically changed. For us to be able to identify it, it had to have been absorbed into something foreign to it." Olivier, *Dark Abyss of Time*, 181.

6 Ann L. Stoler, "Colonial Archives and the Arts of Governance: On the Content of the Form," in *Refiguring the Archive*, ed. Carolyn Hamilton, Verne Harris, Jane Taylor, Michele Pickover, Graeme Reid, and Razia Saleh (Dordrecht, Netherlands: Kluwer Academic, 2002), 83–102.

7 Luise White, "Hodgepodge Historiography: Documents, Itineraries, and the Absence of Archives," *History in Africa* 42 (2015): 317.

8 James Ferguson, *Expectations of Modernity: Myths and Meanings of Urban Life on the Zambian Copperbelt* (Berkeley: University of California Press, 1999).

9 Achille Mbembe, "Écrire l'Afrique à partir d'une faille," *Politique africaine*, no. 51 (1993): 85.

10 Pierre Nicole and Blaise Pascal, "Trois discours sur la condition des grands," in Nicole and Pascal, *De l'éducation d'un prince: Divisée en trois parties, dont la dernière contient divers traittez utiles à tout le monde* (Paris: Chez la Veuve Charles Savreux [. . .], 1670).

11 Marshall Sahlins, "The Stranger-King, or Dumézil among the Fijians," *Journal of Pacific History* 16, no. 3 (1981): 77.

12 Peter Geschiere, *The Modernity of Witchcraft: Politics and the Occult in Postcolonial Africa*, trans. Janet L. Roitman (Charlottesville: University Press of Virginia, 1997). On the subversive power of witchcraft (*djambe* in Makaa) as a means of reestablishing equality by targeting the elite, see in particular 93–130.

1 "Wallis et Futuna: Le premier cas de Covid-19 entraîne un blocage de l'aéroport par un 'collectif des intérêts du people,'" *Outremer la 1ere*, October 16, 2020, https://la1ere .francetvinfo.fr/wallis-et-futuna-le-premier-cas-de-covid-19-entraine-un-blocage-de -l-aeroport-par-un-collectif-882622.html.

2 For more on Raoult, see Ariane Chemin and Marie-France Etchegoin, *Raoult: Une folie française* (Paris: Gallimard, 2021).

3 Patrick Boucheron, "In media res" (lecture in "La Peste noire," course at Collège de France, January 5, 2021).

4 Marc Bloch, *Strange Defeat: A Statement of Evidence Written in 1940*, trans. Gerard Hopkins (London: Oxford University Press, 1949), 37.

5 Guillaume Lachenal and Gaëtan Thomas, "L'histoire immobile du coronavirus," in *Comment faire?*, ed. Christophe Bonneuil (Paris: Le Seuil, 2020), 62–70; Guillaume Lachenal and Gaëtan Thomas, "Epidemics Have Lost the Plot," *Bulletin of the History of Medicine* 94, no. 4 (2020): 670–89.

6 For more on this story and my critique of viral forecasting as nihilism, see Guillaume Lachenal, "Lessons in Medical Nihilism: Virus Hunters, Neoliberalism and the AIDS crisis in Cameroon," in *Para-States and Medical Science: Making African Global Health*, ed. P. Wenzel Geissler (Durham, NC: Duke University Press, 2015), 103–41.

7 B. H. Hahn, "The Origin of HIV-1: A Puzzle Solved?" (keynote lecture, Conference on Retroviruses and Opportunistic Infections, Chicago, January 31, 1999).

8 Nicholas B. King, "Security, Disease, Commerce: Ideologies of Postcolonial Global Health," *Social Studies of Science* 32, no. 5 (2002): 763–89.

9 David Quammen, *Spillover: Animal Infections and the Next Human Pandemic* (New York: Norton, 2013); Nathan Wolfe, *The Viral Storm: The Dawn of a New Pandemic Age* (New York: Times Books, 2011), Kindle; Dale Peterson, *Eating Apes* (Berkeley: University of California Press, 2003); Ofir Drori and David McDannald, *The Last Great Ape: A Journey through Africa and a Fight for the Heart of a Continent* (New York: Pegasus Books, 2012).

10 Teju Cole, "The White Savior Industrial Complex," *Atlantic*, March 21, 2012, https:// www.theatlantic.com/international/archive/2012/03/the-white-savior-industrial -complex/254843/.

11 Mike McGovern, "Bushmeat and the Politics of Disgust," Fieldsights/Hot Spots, October 7, 2014, https://culanth.org/fieldsights/bushmeat-and-the-politics-of-disgust.

12 Tamara Giles-Vernick, Ch. Didier Gondola, Guillaume Lachenal, and William H. Schneider, "Social History, Biology and the Emergence of HIV in Colonial Africa," *Journal of African History* 54, no. 1 (2013): 11–30; Jacques Pepin, *The Origins of AIDS* (Cambridge: Cambridge University Press, 2011).

13 Wolfe, *Viral Storm*.